BLOOD HIGHWAYS

The True Story Behind

the Ford-Firestone Killing Machine

ADAM L. PENENBERG

WAYZGOOSE PRESS

PRAISE FOR *BLOOD HIGHWAYS*

Publishers Weekly:
In a stinging invective, journalist Penenberg outlines the ethical failures and calculated improprieties of two principal automotive-industry companies, along with the struggle of attorney Tab Turner to hold them accountable. Already an established consumer-rights lawyer, Turner began to focus on Ford Explorers equipped with Firestone Wilderness tires in the mid to late 1990s, when the number of cases in which the tread separated from a tire and resulted in an often fatal rollover accident began to become significant. . . . Penenberg . . . offers extensive endnotes from an array of sources to back up his claims . . . . It's a comprehensive and disturbing book . . . .

Booklist
Following closely on Keith Bradsher's *High and Mighty*, this latest indictment of sport utility vehicle (SUV) safety may portend the start of a new movement against these popular vehicles based on the threat they pose to the safety of all motorists. Business journalist Penenberg's work focuses on the Ford/Firestone tire debacle, which was a major news story, and the work of an attorney who repeatedly took on two of the most powerful corporations in the world. The book offers a comprehensive look at a notorious corporate scandal and a courtroom drama and investigation that ends in triumph for the many victims.

Boston Globe
Corporate greed is the target of [*Blood Highways*], a dramatic account of problems with Ford's popular Bronco and Explorer sport utility vehicles and the Firestone Wilderness AT and ATX tires. Penenberg's book argues persuasively—and sadly—that in this country, corporate accord and profit seem far more important than safety and conscience.

USA Today
. . . Adam Penenberg, an investigative reporter who exposed a fabricated *New Republic* story by journalist Stephen Glass in 1998, has clearly done his own exhaustive reporting. He even boasts at the start: 'All the characters and events depicted in these pages are real.' So are the truths revealed in these pages. At times, you wish they weren't. Penenberg meticulously marches the reader through a human and journalistic drama punctuated by deadly engineering flaws and corporate arrogance that resulted in lives being lost and ruined in the insatiable quest for profits. This is a book about one lawyer's battle and one woman's struggle for survival and justice as billed. But it is far deeper. These two

stories intertwine to lead us through the blinding maze of suits and countersuits, whistle-blowers, politicians, consumer advocates, journalists, engineers and corporate executives. The only way out: Build safer cars. Penenberg invites you to feel the sweat, the exhaustion, the fear, the frustration and the pain of all concerned. That's good storytelling, and Penenberg lands the details gracefully.

San Francisco Chronicle

In a swift, dramatic account, Penenberg unspins the convoluted political and legal history of the dangerous automotive pairing. Around Bailey's 10-month odyssey—from the accident on March 10, 2000, to her $27 million settlements with Firestone and Ford in January 2001—he weaves the broader, disastrous stories of both car and tire, and of the various struggles to remove them from American roads. Penenberg tracks Ford's Explorer stability problems back to a May 1987 engineers' report; he digs back to the 1988 Bridgestone-Firestone merger—and a subsequent aggressive cost-cutting spree that reduced the amount of rubber in each tire—to find the root of the ATX and Wilderness tires' fatal flaws. (Along the way, he accumulates an exhaustive, 29-page endnote section.) Penenberg fills the narrative with rich, detailed characters: safety advocates and car investigators, victims and executives, lawyers and journalists. . . . [H]owever, the real hero in Penenberg's tale is not Bailey, the bed-bound victim whose case cracked the industry, but Turner, who comes off as a prince among sharp-toothed plaintiffs' attorneys.

New York Law Journal

[*Blood Highways* is] a gripping story, and Penenberg tells it well, deftly weaving together the narratives of victims, lawyers and corporate officers alike . . . [His] comprehensive investigation into the SUV industry unearths problems that go beyond the Firestone debacle. It shows how institutions put in place to protect consumers have been co-opted by the industries they were created to watch . . . SUVs are still not subject to substantial safety regulations, and Americans continue to buy SUVs under the false impression that they are safer than ordinary cars. Penenberg's book begs the question, just who is watching out for our safety?

(These reviews refer to an earlier edition of this book, published as *Tragic Indifference* by HarperCollins, 2003.)

ALSO BY ADAM L. PENENBERG:

NON-FICTION

Viral Loop
From Facebook to Twitter, How Today's Smartest Businesses
Grow Themselves

Spooked
(with Marc Barry)
Espionage in Corporate America

FICTION

Virtually True
A dystopian techno-thriller

Trial & Terror
A fast-paced legal thriller

For the Penengirls,
Charlotte, Lila, & Sophie

Table of Contents

AUTHOR'S NOTES

This is a work of nonfiction. All the characters and events depicted in these pages are real. It is composed from hundreds of hours of interviews with more than 60 subjects over the course of two years, as well as thousands of pages of internal documents from Ford and Firestone, court transcripts, depositions, trial motions, congressional hearing testimony, crash test results, and media coverage. Dialogue comes from the best recollections of one or more of the participants, or via legal transcripts or news stories.

There are no anonymous sources.

BEHIND THE TRUE STORY

- 1 in 2,700 Ford Explorers built between 1990 and 2001 suffered a fatal rollover.
- 1 in 500 Ford Bronco IIs—the Explorer's predecessor—tipped over and killed someone in the car.
- The company manufactured vehicles that were dangerously unstable, trading consumer lives for gigantic profit.
- Ford convinced Firestone to manufacture a lightweight passenger tire for a two-ton truck marketed to families.
- Between 1994 and 2001, Firestone cut corners and hid safety defects in tires offered as standard equipment on the nation's most popular SUV.
- Ford recalled Firestone tires in a dozen countries months before it recalled them in its biggest market: the United States.
- More than 300 people died and hundreds more were critically injured when Firestone tires unraveled on Ford Explorers. Thousands more died in Explorer and Bronco II rollover accidents.
- Seven out of 10 Explorer accidents don't involve Firestone tires.
- There are millions of Explorers still on the road today.

PROLOGUE

SEPTEMBER. 8, 2000

ON THE FRINGES OF CAPITOL HILL, a few long blocks northeast of the Capitol and a block from the United States Supreme Court, the Hart Senate Building seems like a mammoth, million-square-foot afterthought. Unlike the neoclassical grace of nearby houses of government, the Hart building is decidedly contemporary in design, even as it shares the same white marble skin. Across the mall, the cramped Capitol, with its famous dome and history, may have been the site for formal meetings of the House and Senate, but the real business of government, the nitty-gritty of legislation, deal making, back slapping and back stabbing happened here and in the adjoining Dirksen Senate Office Building.

Constructed in the late 1970s and occupied since November 1982, the Hart was named for the late Senator Philip Hart, a Michigan Democrat who served from 1959 to 1976, and who had a reputation for placing principle before political expediency. An infantryman wounded on D-day, Hart was an antitrust enforcer, consumer advocate, environmental crusader, and a leader in the fight for the 1965 Voting Rights Act. Above the building's main entrance, an inscription described him as "A man of incorruptible integrity and personal courage strengthened by inner grace and outer gentleness. He advanced the cause of human justice, promoted the welfare of the common man and improved the quality of life. His humility and ethics earned him his place as the conscience of the Senate."

Tab Turner didn't even see this dedication as he strode into the building with a law clerk in tow. He barely noticed the gargantuan sculpture Mountains and Clouds, with its 39-ton stationary black mountains sculpted from sheet metal and two-ton orbiting clouds made of aerospace aluminum. His mind was on other things.

Turner had been invited to sort through material on behalf of the Senate committee investigating Ford and Firestone after a rash of tragic crashes involving the Explorer, Ford's flagship sport-utility vehicle, and standard-issue Firestone tires. As lives on four continents were shattered in violent squalls of rubber, asphalt, metal, and glass, the companies bickered publicly over responsibility. Ford blamed the tire. Firestone blamed the Explorer. And Turner blamed them both. His mantra, customized for this age of sound bites: "It's a bad tire on a bad car."

Forty-one, bespectacled, and built like the former college All-American football player he was, Turner was dressed in litigation chic: a sports jacket layered over dark slacks and shoes, his hair short and to the point. Often he referred to himself simply as "a car attorney from Little Rock, Arkansas," but in reality there was almost nothing "aw, shucks" about him. He was fast becoming one of the richest trial lawyers in America and a billion-dollar legal empire in his own right.

Over the course of a decade, Turner had filed hundreds of lawsuits against automakers over faulty ignition switches, defective safety latches and seat belts, "sudden acceleration," poorly designed transmissions, exploding gas tanks, and rollovers. He had faced off against just about every car company—Ford, General Motors, Chrysler, Isuzu, Toyota, Nissan, KIA, Hyundai—and a host of tire makers. But it was the SUV that made up the vast majority of his practice, and Ford his greatest adversary.

In the absence of effective government oversight, Turner had become a self-appointed national auto safety magistrate. Although lawyers are often justly lampooned for bringing frivolous suits against corporations, litigation has become far more effective in shaping responsible business practices than government. When juries speak, Corporate America listens. It's why trucks have alarms that sound when they back up and farm machinery comes equipped with safety guards. It's a reason cancer-causing asbestos no longer poisons homes, schools, and workplaces, and why fast-food restaurants, aware of their potential super-sized liability, have forced meat packagers to clean up processing plants. And one day, Turner hoped, it would convince SUV makers like Ford to build vehicles that would be less prone to roll over and kill people.

Turner made his way upstairs in the elevator and down a long hall-way to join one of Senator John McCain's aides, who led him to a modest conference room. Inside, by Turner's count, were some 40 boxes of Ford material to which Firestone had added 15 more, all of it piled high against a wall and clearly labeled, covering everything from vehicle stability and suspension to tire testing. Arriving at 9 a.m., he figured he would need the entire day to comb through everything, especially the document dump Ford flew in especially for the occasion.

He had first met with congressional researchers in late August and found they shared a mutual respect for documents. Unlike depositions, which relied on witnesses' memory and were colored by bias, the written word would help them re-create events to determine what executives and engineers were thinking at a particular time. More to the point for Turner, they played well with juries, who were more likely to believe an internal memo than a paid expert witness. But with time running out, the researchers needed a guide familiar with the terrain, someone who knew what needles to look for in this haystack of paper.

They showed Turner a document index from Firestone and another from Ford. "This, this," Turner told them, quickly marking the relevant entries, "these are the key things you need to look for. The rest is junk." He also handed them a package of the top 20 critical documents he had unearthed over the years and a detailed chronology he compiled listing key internal memos, failed stability tests, engineers' notes, correspondence between Ford and Firestone and lawsuits.

A few days later he found himself taking stock of the material inside the Hart Building. Just as he thought, about half of the boxes Ford had shipped pertained to its F-Series pickup truck and not the Explorer; Ford's way of burying the committee in paper. But Turner couldn't chance missing anything, so he carefully reviewed each document one at a time—in case someone at the automaker had misfiled something, either by mistake or on purpose. (It had happened before.) He plucked out what he thought was relevant and piled it on the table. At one point McCain's aide poked his head in and told Turner that Ford representatives were on their way up. "OK," Turner mumbled, and continued on his paper chase. Although the aide didn't say it, Turner knew he was to stay behind the closed door until they left.

Turner already possessed most of the juicy documents, but it didn't take him long to find material he had never seen before, evidence that would only serve to strengthen his case against the two companies. Stuck in the middle of one of the boxes labeled "tire testing" was a brand-new affidavit by James Avouris, a Ford engineer, who stated he had tested Firestone tires on an Explorer when Turner knew his studies had been performed on a Ford F-150 pickup truck, which didn't handle at all like a fully loaded SUV. Turner had been at it barely an hour and already caught Ford in a lie. There were also quite a few recent documents pertaining to the Middle East, correspondence between the two companies that illustrated the automaker's concern over tire quality. Turner put brackets around the pertinent sections.

One dated Feb. 25, 1999, from John C. Garthwaite, the national service manager of Al Jazirah Vehicle Agencies Inc., a Saudi Ford dealership, noted that tread separations were "beginning to become an epidemic." Firestone was "clearly trying to distance" itself from a potentially serious problem and had "done nothing to re-assure me that there may not exist a defect in a particular batch" of tires. Another from Glenn R. Drake, Ford dealer operations manager in Dubai, questioned whether Firestone was "not telling us the whole story to protect them from a recall or lawsuit." A third cited Firestone's qualms about alerting consumers about free replacements because "the U.S. [Department of Transportation] will have to be notified . . . since the same product is sold in the U.S."

Firestone also provided good reading. Turner knew the company had conducted more than 1,000 tests on the AT tire, but in the course of litigation he had only come across about 400 of them. He also knew he couldn't study all of them in the conference room. Besides, he wanted the complete boxed set. So Turner had his law clerk call some friends to help out. When they arrived Turner began passing them boxes, which they carried down the hall and into the elevator, out the front entrance, and to a waiting car, which the clerk drove to a local Kinko's.

Turner had requested that congressional staffers photocopy the material and send it to Little Rock, Arkansas, when he agreed to work for the committee, but they had told him it was against policy, which was how he ended up in the nation's capital. No one, however, said anything about the human train he set up. He knew they knew what he was doing, and Turner believed it was better to apologize after the fact than ask permission first.

At the end of the day, Turner handed the material he had pulled to McCain's aide. He got the distinct impression from his archival search that Ford and Firestone had rushed to make the deadline and included documents they either hadn't read through or fully comprehended.

He was sure the committee would find them useful.

IT WAS THE BIGGEST AUTO SAFETY SCANDAL IN HISTORY, affecting more than four million sport-utility vehicles. Treads were peeling off tires on the nation's number-one-selling SUV, leaving a trail of death and misery in their wake, and no one seemed to know why. Two corporate icons whose brand names were eponymous with the products they sold were at each other's throats, quarreling over seemingly minute engineering differences. A trial lawyer armed with a treasure trove of internal documents had made it his mission to shine a light on their darkest secrets just when the companies were at their most vulnerable. A rollover victim who survived against all odds refused to settle for anything less than the one thing she craved above all else: justice. The media, sensing a cover-up, saturated the airwaves and monopolized the front pages of newspapers for months, unheard of for a consumer story. The result was a massive recall, consumer panic, governmental hearings, and the culmination of a lawsuit that would become a watershed for all future auto safety lawsuits—and shake the foundations of both companies.

The feud between Ford and Firestone meant the end to an almost century-long alliance that had once captured the public's imagination, a partnership that had survived an economic depression, two world wars, the deaths of their respective founders, creeping globalization, the sale of Firestone Tire & Rubber Co. to Japanese rubber giant Bridgestone, and countless changes to the U.S. car market. For the two blue-chip manufacturers, which shared bloodlines and a common history, it wasn't just business, it was personal. Chairman William ("Bill") Clay Ford, Jr., was great-grandson to both company founders. His father married Martha Parke Firestone, granddaughter of Harvey Samuel Firestone, in 1948 in an imposing display of extravagance, and the public embraced the two families as American royalty. He called the fallout between the companies "a horrendous period" for him.

The Fords and Firestones maintained a famously cordial and profitable relationship since before the days of Woodrow Wilson and the League of Nations. Henry Ford, Sr., and Harvey S. Firestone were friends and fishing buddies long before most people had heard of their companies. They first met in the 1890s when Firestone worked as a salesman for the Columbus Buggy Company and Ford, an employee of Edison Illuminating Co. in Detroit, was experimenting with the newfangled automobile. Thirty years and 15 million Model Ts later, both men were rich beyond their wildest imaginings.

As their success grew, so did their friendship. Clad in starched-collar shirts and three-piece suits, Henry Ford and Harvey Firestone car-camped with luminaries like Thomas Edison and President Warren Harding in a "chuck wagon," an early SUV-like vehicle Ford adapted from a roadster he designed. They traveled around the country, sleeping in tents with their wives, hairdressers, and butlers. Newspaper editors ordered reporters and photographers into trees to document these trips for articles like "Millions of Dollars Worth of Brains Off on a Vacation" and "Genius to Sleep Under the Stars."

Their close relationship helped them weather the first threat to their partnership, and it too involved tread failures. In 1932 Ford introduced a V-8 engine so powerful that quick starts turned the tires to scrap, leaving "snakes" of rubber on the road. Harvey Firestone gave his engineers 48 hours to come up with a solution, then kept his factory open 24-7 to produce enough tires to fulfill its contract—and ensure that Ford wouldn't have to pay a nickel more than the agreed-upon price. When asked to describe his business friendship with Harvey Firestone, Henry Ford once said, "During all those years in business, I knew I could trust his word all the way. And I think he felt he could trust mine."

But in the year 2000, as the death toll rose and public confidence in the two manufacturers plummeted, trust would be in short supply. The companies' survival depended on convincing consumers and government investigators that the other was at fault for crashes that claimed almost 300 lives and crippled hundreds more.

Only one of them could win back the public; otherwise they both could lose.

INTRODUCTION

THIS BOOK IS ABOUT ONE LAWYER'S BATTLE against two mighty corporations that knowingly traded human lives for profits. While carving out a niche in his father's chosen profession, Clyde "Tab" Turner was thrust into a case bigger than anything he ever imagined. He had amassed the evidence to beat his enemies in court, the guile to outflank their legions of lawyers and publicists, and the means to threaten their very existence.

It recounts the heroic struggles of Donna Bailey, who fought back from the brink of death to take on those she believed responsible for crippling her. An outdoor enthusiast, Bailey loved camping, hiking, kayaking, running, and rock climbing. She was 20 credits short of a degree in kinesiology—the study of how the body moves—and worked as a volunteer at Youth Odyssey in Corpus Christi where she led troubled teens on backpacking trips. All that came to an end on a lonesome stretch of highway outside of San Antonio, where she was paralyzed in a violent rollover. Her case paved the way for hundreds of others to follow.

It relates the contributions of individual heroes—auto researchers, consumer advocates, crash test drivers, journalists, whistle-blowers—who filled in key parts of the puzzle at key junctures, and details the messy divorce between Ford Motor Co. and Bridgestone/Firestone, Inc. Most of all, it is about one lawyer's belief that in this age of deregulation and voluntary compliance, the only way to force companies to act responsibly is to make it too expensive for them to conduct business as usual.

Of course, it's hard to think of a trial attorney as a courageous foot soldier in the war against corporate malfeasance. After all, lawyers' reputations precede them. They are viewed as "conniving," "dishonest," "greedy," "heartless" "hypocrites"; "ambulance chasers" who "manipulate the media" and are not only "a drain on the economy" but perhaps "a threat to national security." Dressed in $3,000 suits, they jet around in private planes, a hundred times richer than any judge, a thousand times more arrogant. The public is convinced they cry crocodile tears for their crippled clients while gnawing on 40 percent of the take (plus expenses).

In 2001, an e-mail forward made the rounds over the Internet announcing the first ever "Stella Awards," named after Stella Liebeck, the little old lady famous for suing McDonald's after spilling hot coffee on herself at a drive-through in February 1992. The award listed six nominees, including Kathleen Robertson of Austin, Texas, who received $780,000 after breaking her ankle in a furniture store after tripping over a toddler: her son. Carl Truman of Los Angeles won $74,000 and medical expenses when he sued his neighbor for running over his hand with a Honda Accord while the 19-year-old Truman tried to steal his hubcaps. Terrence Dickson of Bristol, Pennsylvania, was held prisoner in the garage of a house he had just finished robbing. Since the family was on vacation, Dickson was locked inside for eight days, forced to subsist on Pepsi and dry dog food. He sued, claiming undue mental anguish, and a jury awarded him half a million.

These cases pointed out how absurd the situation has become. They made a mockery of Americans' sense of justice and fair play. And with the exception of Liebeck's, they were completely fictitious. The awards were a hoax, an "e-rumor" as real as *The Onion*'s January 2003 faux headline: "Hershey's Ordered to Pay Obese Americans $135 Billion." There was no Kathleen Robertson, no toddler, no Carl Truman or Terrence Dickson, no hubcaps, no dog-food-eating burglar. Yet few questioned it (and many posted the awards on their Web sites) because they seemed to confirm what most people already believed about the legal system.

So which is it? Are trial lawyers money-grubbing leeches reaping excessive jury awards at the expense of innocent companies? Or are they the last line of defense against greedy corporations unwilling to take responsibility for dangerously defective products? As with Liebeck's case, the truth lay somewhere in between.

Seventy-nine-year-old Stella Liebeck of Albuquerque was in the passenger seat of her grandson's car when she ordered coffee at a McDonald's drive-through window. The grandson pulled ahead and stopped so Liebeck could add cream and sugar. She placed the cup between her knees, but when she removed the lid from the Styrofoam cup the coffee spilled into her lap. Her sweatpants absorbed the spillage and kept it in contact with her skin. Liebeck suffered third-degree burns over 6 percent of her body and was hospitalized for eight days, during which she underwent extensive skin grafting. She ended up with permanent scarring over 15 percent of her body.

Liebeck asked McDonald's to pay her medical expenses, about $11,000. A $20-billion company, McDonald's countered with an offer for $800. A mediator recommended a $250,000 settlement, which the fast food company rejected. During discovery, Liebeck's lawyers dug up more than 700 consumer complaints McDonald's had received regarding too hot coffee, some involving third-degree burns similar to Liebeck's. Corporate officers testified that, based on the advice of a consultant, franchises served coffee at between 180 and 190 degrees to maintain optimum taste, but the company never evaluated the safety ramifications, even though competitors sold coffee at substantially lower temperatures.

At the trial, a quality assurance manager testified a burn hazard existed with any food served at 140 degrees or above, and admitted McDonald's coffee was not fit for consumption at the point of sale because it would burn the mouth and throat. McDonald's asserted its customers liked their coffee hot and intended to drink it at home or work, even though its own research contradicted this, showing that customers generally consumed coffee while driving.

The jury sided with Liebeck, awarding her $200,000 in compensatory damages, which was reduced to $160,000 because jurors found Liebeck 20 percent at fault. They also slapped McDonald's with $2.7 million in punitive damages, which they calculated as two days' worth of coffee sales. The court subsequently cut the punitive award to $480,000—three times compensatory damages—even though the judge called McDonald's conduct reckless, callous and willful.

Tort reformers point to Liebeck's case as a prime example of a legal system out of control. Her suit became synonymous with frivolous lawsuits and the butt of jokes. Talk show comedians questioned how any octogenarian's thighs could be worth $2.7 million. Puffy-faced cable TV pundits debated the legal significance. The United States has become lawsuit crazy, they argued. Lawyers were ruining the country. What about personal responsibility? What about all those frivolous actions clogging up judges' dockets, which only help attorneys to get fat and bankrupt American Industry? Patriotic-sounding organizations like American Tort Reform Association, Civil Justice Reform Group and Americans for Lawsuit Reform pressed for change. State politicians pushed through bills to limit how much a victim—or a victim's survivors—could recover if injured or killed due to a company's negligence, easing financial burdens on corporations, who also happened to be their most generous constituents.

In reality, "tort reform" is a term corporations have co-opted to persuade Americans of the need for a cap on personal injury cases. Tort reformers point to a few oddball lawsuits that are more often than not tossed out by the first judge to see them to indict the entire system. But their idea of reform isn't to make the system fair. It is to blunt the impact of damage awards on companies' bottom lines.

And what of those high-minded civic organizations pushing for change to the legal system, the ones with "Reform" and "Civil" and "America" in their names? Often they are corporate lobbying groups. "Civil Justice Reform Group" is just another name for Aetna, Exxon, Ford, GM and Metropolitan Life. Membership in the "Tort Reform Association" is by no means limited to Dow Chemical, Eli Lilly, Monsanto, Philip Morris, and Union Carbide. "Americans for Lawsuit Reform" receives its funding from Allstate, Chevron, Eli Lilly, General Dynamics, New York Life and R.J. Reynolds.

Justice is illusory. Verdicts that go against Big Business usually result in some bad PR and a few weeks of unflattering corporate headlines in the business trades, but have only a negligible affect on the bottom line. Almost immediately trial judges reduce punitive damages. What remains rarely holds up on appeal. Corporations can lock up cases for a decade, ultimately paying a fraction of any verdict. Meanwhile, trial attorneys like Turner don't get paid unless they win or settle, which means they have little incentive to take on "frivolous" cases.

Facing a logjam of litigation, companies like Ford and Firestone are paying the price for years of treating safety and quality control as pieces of data in their cost-benefit analyses. They have used their political connections to emasculate the very agency in charge of regulating them, leaving victims—who face astronomical medical costs and a permanent loss of income—little choice but to sue. SUVs are almost three times more likely to tip over than passenger cars, even during simple defensive driving maneuvers, and five times more likely to kill when they do. More people (10,000 every year) die in single-vehicle rollovers, which comprise almost a quarter of all vehicle deaths in the United States, than in any other type of accident. The rollover fatality rate in single-vehicle crashes among SUVs is two-and-a-half times greater than that of passenger cars and nearly one-and-a-half times higher than that of pickup trucks. Build them with flimsy roofs and outfit them with tires that can unravel without warning at highway speed, and the result is often tragic.

Ford in particular has a troubling history of recognizing safety defects in its SUVs and then leaving no stone unturned in its efforts to deny design problems, hide pertinent data, and cover up the truth. Between

1990 and 2000, Ford sold about 4 million Explorers, with 1,461 of them rolling over and killing someone. That means roughly 1 in 2,700 Explorers that emerged from factories ended up in a deadly rollover. And it's even worse for the Bronco II—the Explorer's predecessor: 1 in every 500 Broncos that came off assembly lines has been involved in a fatal rollover crash.

If 1 in 500 cans of Coca-Cola made you sick, the government would declare a public health emergency. If 1 of 500 TV sets blew up when you plugged it in, you'd have a consumer-led revolt. But if you are Ford Motor Company and 1 in every 500 Bronco IIs you manufactured rolled over and killed someone, you quietly settle lawsuits and continue to profit.

Although Ford claims Turner is "one of those sharks out there who think they've found the keys to the ATM," it only has itself to blame for his success.

Because there is one sure way for Ford to put lawyers like him out of business: Build safer cars.

1 Blood Highway

TARA COX AND DONNA BAILEY were driving through central Texas in a blue two-door Ford Explorer. It was late afternoon on March 10, 2000, T-shirt and shorts weather, and the two friends were on their way to Enchanted Rock, a popular climbing and hiking destination north of Austin. There they planned to pitch camp before dusk and spend Saturday and Sunday rock climbing. In the backseat was Kevin McCord, a 25-year-old classmate of Bailey's at Texas A&M, where she studied kinesiology (the study of how the body moves) and he, architecture. Their gear—tents, backpacks, climbing ropes, pitons, and cook stove—was crammed in the back of the cabin. Hanging from the rearview mirror was a stethoscope that Tara, a trained paramedic, never left home without.

A billion years old, Enchanted Rock is one of the oldest exposed rocks in North America and the geologic center of Texas. After a vertiginous climb of several hundred feet, the gargantuan granite dome offers breath-taking views of the surrounding hill country. Donna and Tara had climbed it a dozen times together. This was the best time of year to go, before it got too hot. Although vultures floated above in lazy circles, the only hazard they expected once they got there, besides gravity, was rattlesnakes. These they figured they could handle.

Tara, five feet two inches, a well-knit redhead in her early 30s, and Donna, 10 years older, blond and seven inches taller, had gone on numerous hiking and climbing trips together, as well as canoeing, kayaking, and (on girls' night out) dancing. Life was a triathlon. It was as if they couldn't stop moving. Even their conversation was nonstop, usually slipping into their favorite topic, what they liked to call "smut talk"—an unvarnished discussion of sex.

They were as different as they were similar. Donna was a divorced mother of two living on food stamps who recently moved in with her mother. Despite this, she had never been happier. She married young and was now just coming into her own. She had gone back to school and was working toward her degree. A people-person who spoke her mind, she had little trouble attracting men. She took great pride in her appearance and always brought makeup and a blow dryer on camping trips, playfully boasting she could find an outlet anywhere.

Tara, who was more self-contained, bordering on shy, also had two kids. A former high school athletic star, she lived in jeans and T-shirts and was more comfortable around animals, symbolized by tattoos of a raven on her shoulder, partially obscured by her long red hair, and a horse inked to her ankle. Theirs was a friendship cemented by a love of sports and the outdoors. They both worked at Youth Odyssey, a Corpus Christi nonprofit organization founded by Kim Cox, Tara's husband, that took troubled teens on hiking and climbing trips to teach them that the pressures that defined their lives (money, clothes, status and ethnicity) counted for very little in nature.

Kim Cox had purchased the 1997 Explorer used at the Ford dealership in Corpus Christi. It came equipped with Firestone AT Wilderness tires, which Tara got checked at Jiffy Lube whenever they planned a long trip. The Coxes had put 50,000 miles on the car in the year and a half they owned it. Unlike 89 percent of SUV owners who never venture from pavement, Tara took the Explorer off road on several occasions, often with Donna.

The sun beat down on the Explorer as Corpus Christi suburbs gave way to wide-open Texas desert. The tires hummed against the pavement. Inside the vehicle, Donna, Tara, and Kevin traveled in cushy comfort. Tara set the cruise control to 70 mph as they headed north on Route 181, past dusty towns like Paplote, Beeville, Tuleta, and Hobson. While Donna and Tara were strapped in the front, Kevin sat in the back without a seatbelt, nudging forward to participate in the conversation, which, punctuated with squeals of laughter, had turned bawdy. The three of them were having so much fun they didn't even bother turning on the radio.

They were on the road about two hours when the trouble started. Although they couldn't have known it, the 15-inch right rear Firestone tire had begun to peel apart. A separation developed around the tire's shoulder. Every minute the SUV was in motion, the two layers of rubber rubbed together. In some areas the rubber was completely worn through. Twenty miles outside of San Antonio, Donna and her friends had just passed a sign warning of a bridge coming up when the tread snapped away from the tire.

Suddenly an explosion from outside the cabin seemed to rock the Explorer. The car jerked hard to the right. Tara struggled to stay on the road by turning the wheel left and hitting the brakes, but the Explorer had plans of its own. Tires screeching, the back end fishtailed, skidding out of control. Tara spun the wheel the other way, and the rear responded by coming around as they continued to skid in a 180-degree turn. But she was still unable to regain control.

The Explorer slid into the left lane and its rear end went off the shoulder and into a ditch. "Hold on!" Tara called out as the car flipped into the air, cartwheeling end over end. The Explorer twisted upside down in midair and 3,000 pounds of SUV pounded down on the ground, crushing in the passenger's side roof. Because of the 10 inches of slack in her safety belt, Donna's head was pushed against the top of the car. The force snapped her neck and she was blinded by white light as a sharp pain jolted through her spine. The Explorer spun sideways, rolled over one-and-a-half more times, and careened into a chain-link fence, propped up on its side, the driver's side door mirror dug into the dirt.

The fury of the crash was followed by eerie calm. A breeze flowed through the wreck, then died down. Tara came to her senses while swaying upside down in her safety belt, the ceiling now the floor and the floor the ceiling. Her first thought was, *Kim is gonna be pissed!* She asked if everybody was OK. Kevin responded. Donna didn't.

Tara turned her head, but all she could see was Donna's arm hanging limp. Tara's neck hurt and part of the shattered door was digging into her ribs. She smelled gas and began to panic. She desperately sought a way out. The driver's side door had been partially ripped off its hinges and the side view mirror was holding the car up. There was just enough room for her to squeeze through the window and out onto the dirt, where she crawled to safety.

Kevin had avoided serious injury by balling himself up like a caterpillar and bouncing around the cabin, a technique he'd learned in the Coast Guard. He escaped the Explorer by climbing through the broken passenger-side window, which was now facing skyward. In the process he suffered various cuts and scratches to his arm and side. Once on top of the vehicle, he jumped down.

When Cox and McCord peered through the crackled windshield, they saw Donna upside down, strapped in her safety belt, hanging in the air, turning blue, blood trickling from her mouth. Her eyes were wide open and glazed. She looked at them and tried to say something, her mouth opening and shutting noiselessly.

Tara screamed, "Get her out!"

Kevin peeled back the windshield but couldn't reach her.

"Kevin, she's going to die!" Tara reentered the Explorer the same way she had gotten out and edged her way up toward Donna. Both she and Kevin had emergency medical training and knew it was important to keep Donna's neck immobile. Cradling her friend's head, Tara unhooked the safety belt but couldn't pull her out. She looked down and saw that Donna's legs were wedged in the crumpled dashboard. With time running out, Kevin took hold of Donna while Tara worked to free her legs. Finally she was able to yank them out and pass Donna through the windshield to Kevin, who dragged her from the wreck to a patch of grass by the side of the road.

They crouched by her, shouting her name, asking what was wrong, trying to wake her. Silently praying the car wouldn't blow up, Tara ordered Kevin back to the Explorer to retrieve her stethoscope. She tried to give Donna mouth-to-mouth resuscitation but was having difficulty keeping Donna's airway open. There was a lot of blood in her mouth. Tara thought Donna's tongue might be stuck in her throat. Her two front teeth had been knocked loose. When Kevin returned with the stethoscope, Tara listened to Donna's lungs. At least she was getting a little oxygen. She was still blue, but less so now. Maybe a punctured lung, Tara thought. She didn't know what else was wrong except Donna's neck had probably been broken. Her limbs were flaccid, a strong indication of paralysis.

An ambulance pulled up. A volunteer fireman living around the bend had heard the crash. He produced an oxygen tank and advised Tara to perform CPR. "You can't do CPR on a person whose heart is beating," Tara replied, "otherwise, you'll kill them." The man passed her an oxygen bag, which he had just put on that morning. Tara had to tell him not to squeeze the bag so hard, "you'll blow her up." She didn't want to yell at him. He was a fireman, not a paramedic. Both of them were nervous. Tara kept a hold of Donna's wrist, silently promising to never let go. She believed as long as she held on, Bailey would stay alive. But Donna turned blue again. For a few seconds she faded away, like Tara had seen animals die, their eyes open but pupils drained of life. Miraculously she came back.

Sgt. Ray Gutierrez of the Poth police department had been on patrol when Wilson County dispatch advised there had been a major traffic accident on Route 181 South, over the bridge. It was beyond his jurisdiction, but since he was the closest unit available he flipped on his siren and floored it, arriving within 45 seconds of receiving the call. He surveyed the situation. The injured woman's friends appeared to know more about emergency medical procedures than he did, so he stood watch until another ambulance arrived five minutes later. It parked between the police car and the crashed Explorer, blocking the view of the onboard video camera.

While paramedics administered to the crash victim, Gutierrez set up flares and directed traffic, shooing away rubberneckers. He took statements from Tara and Kevin, both of whom were "visibly shaken." Tara told the police sergeant she was upset she hadn't been able to take control of the situation. She stayed nearby, never venturing far from her friend. Kevin paced back and forth between Donna and the smashed Explorer. With the help of some bystanders, he rounded up their gear, most of which had fallen out along the roadside.

Kevin couldn't believe what had happened. A simple blowout shouldn't cause a car to jackknife off the road. Kevin decided to document things, just in case. He located his pack and dug for his camera. The Explorer had been demolished—the roof, the sides, the front grille. When he took a closer look at the right rear Firestone tire, he realized it was still partly inflated, with a section of the tread hanging off like a tongue. He snapped pictures from various angles of the car, tire, and skid marks on the road. Then he searched around and retrieved another piece of tread that had broken off. When he studied it, he noticed a tear between the two layers of ply. He slipped the rubber into his pocket.

Day seeped into dusk, and another ambulance arrived. EMS loaded Donna into one while Tara, Kevin, and their gear rode in another to nearby Floresville hospital. When they arrived, Donna was wheeled into the ER and Tara and Kevin were shepherded into a waiting room.

After Tara changed out of her bloody clothes she called her husband Kim, who was in Colorado on business. She wanted him to hold her, to promise he'd hop on the next plane to San Antonio. Instead he asked about the car. When he found out it had been totaled, he complained he still owed $11,000 on it. He voiced concern for Donna but neglected to ask how his wife was. Before hanging up, Kim informed her he'd be home in a few days.

Tara steeled herself for her next call—to Donna's boyfriend, Amiel Garcia, whom she worked with on the ropes course at Youth Odyssey. When Tara told him what happened, he immediately began heaping blame on her. The trip to Enchanted Rock had been her idea, hadn't it? She was the one driving. He accused her of being jealous. "That's why you hurt Donna!" he cried. The more he talked the madder he got. He was screaming by the time the line went dead.

Consumed by guilt, she joined Kevin in the waiting room. Why did it have to be Donna? Why not her? Why not Kevin? Tara thought of her two young sons. She had dropped them off at her ex-husband Mike's parents' place for the weekend before picking up Donna and Kevin. It could just as easily have been them injured in the accident. She called her children's grandparents to tell them what had happened but begged them not to tell the kids. Tara didn't want to frighten them. They had been through enough. Before their father—her first husband—had gotten sick, Mike Simmons had been a loving husband and doting father. After he was diagnosed with a brain tumor, he turned into a raging psychopath who didn't recognize his own wife and children. In the end he deteriorated into a bedbound vegetable on life support.

The doctor came to see them and reported that Donna Bailey was in critical condition. She had fractured her C2 (second cervical vertebrae) and would most likely never walk again. He commended Tara and Kevin for their heroic rescue. The doctor said if it weren't for them, Donna would be dead. As it was she was in grave condition. He expected major complications. The strain on her organs was enormous. He was especially concerned about her heart and kidneys and was on the alert for opportunistic infections. Her heart had stopped, but they had been able to shock her back. They weren't equipped to handle this type of thing in Floresville, so Donna would be flown by helicopter to San Antonio.

Tara spotted Donna down the hall, strapped to a gurney near the elevator, and ran to her. Donna's head was held in place by a halo— medical scaffolding designed to keep her neck still so the bones could knit. A tube was planted down her throat so she could breathe. She was plugged in to a variety of life-saving devices and monitors. The former triathlete, beauty queen, and mother of two couldn't move.

Donna stared up at her friend and smiled dreamily.

Tara didn't know what to say. She knew the accident had been all her fault. All she could do was stay with Donna until she was rolled away to a waiting helicopter.

2 Bronco Buster

Tab turner's phone rang in his office in North Little Rock. For a man on track to settle almost a billion dollars in cases over the last decade, it was decidedly modest digs. On the wall was his University of Arkansas law school diploma and on his desk, a PC, keyboard, and two toy SUVs he used for demonstration purposes. Littering his office were some delaminated Firestone tires and boxes of legal files.

When Turner picked up, Paul LaValle, an attorney from Texas, asked if he was interested in a rollover case. A woman had been critically injured just outside of San Antonio.

"What kind of car?" Turner asked. He had worked with LaValle on two previous rollover cases, both of which resulted in hefty settlements.

"An Explorer," LaValle said.

"Tread separation?"

LaValle didn't know. He'd just found out about it and was trying to lay his hands on the accident report. The lady was still in the ICU. It didn't look good.

Turner suggested LaValle find out how the accident happened and secure the vehicle. "If it was a 'tread sep' make sure you get the tire, too," he added. Turner couldn't count the number of times a referring attorney had botched this, ruining the chain of custody. One had actually lost the vehicle to scrap because he was too cheap to pay for hauling it away. Turner told LaValle to take pictures of the crash scene and vehicle.

Then Turner got back to what he was doing. The day after Donna Bailey had been crippled, he was working on dozens of similar cases: a Nissan Pathfinder, an Isuzu, negotiating with GM over 15 to 20 Chevy Blazer crashes at any given time. But recently it was the Ford Explorer equipped with Firestone tires that was causing his caseload to grow exponentially—from a few in 1994 to a dozen in 1997 to more than 40 in

1999. This year he estimated he would have more than 100. He thought he was as busy as any man could possibly be.

Over the years he had settled hundreds of SUV rollover cases involving exquisitely branded consumer products: Broncos and Explorers, Rodeos and Troopers, Pathfinders and Samurais, Blazers and 4Runners. When companies wouldn't meet his terms they risked facing him in court, where he almost always came out on top, and in the process revealed some of their darkest secrets in their own words from their own documents.

Working out of an office in a low-slung building bordering a Comfort Inn, Outback steakhouse, and Circuit City, Turner kept his game plan simple, usually taking on only slam dunks—no alcohol or drugs or mitigating circumstances like poor road conditions, another vehicle, or inclement weather; the client had to have been wearing a seatbelt at the time of the accident; and it had to be a single-vehicle rollover. Armed with a laptop, cell phone, private jet, and an encyclopedic knowledge of SUVs, Turner had become a highly mobile litigation machine, and companies like Ford, even with their battalions of attorneys, couldn't keep up with him.

His plane was less a spiffy corporate jet than a Pontiac with wings—narrow and weepy-looking on the outside, its steel skin dulled by endless air miles. Somehow its designers had figured out a way to cram a dozen seats onboard. Owning his own jet, which he had bought used a few years earlier, ended up being only a little more expensive than flying commercial airlines and infinitely more convenient. Turner got it because he was tired of calling home in the middle of the night to tell his wife he was stuck in a hub like Chicago or Dallas, waiting for the next available flight home. They were raising three daughters and Turner made it a point of pride that he took them to church, piano lessons, dance class, soccer practice, and after-school activities, even if it meant leaving the office early. The plane allowed him to save half days every other day, and he probably did twice as much work now than before.

Turner spent much of his time in the air answering e-mail, which he would transmit after arriving at his destination, reading through depositions and background material, and downing diet soft drinks. Some days he would fly to three or four different cities, visiting clients, plotting strategy with other attorneys, talking to witnesses. Since most of these Firestone-Explorer accidents happened in hot, southern states it cut down on his travel time. Settlement negotiations had to be conducted in person, as were depositions, but he tried to return home for dinner whenever possible.

When Turner left his office and told his secretary he'd be back later, that could mean later that day, that week, or that month. No one, not even Turner, knew for sure. His pilot regularly ripped up flight plans; sometimes his office changed his hotel reservations three times in a day. As the old saying goes, Time is nature's way of making sure everything doesn't happen all at once. Which was too bad, Turner thought, since it cut down on what he could accomplish. With so many clients and trials, settlement negotiations and court hearings, phone calls and e-mails to return, depositions to take, expert witnesses to hire and press conferences to attend, Turner was notorious for missing appointments. Unless it made it onto his daily "To Do" list, it didn't get done; and even that didn't offer any guarantees.

Buddy Sutton, Turner's boss at his first law job out of school, dressed down Turner's secretary when he couldn't keep track of his peripatetic young charge. CBS reporter Sharyl Attkisson routinely read him the riot act over his voice mail when she couldn't locate him to corroborate a fact for broadcast. Consumer safety activist Ralph Hoar would often swear to never to talk to him again when he disappeared for days on end. Once Turner had come to town and offered to take Hoar and some associates to dinner at his hotel. While they waited for him, they shared a pricey bottle of wine, and then another. They ordered a nice meal and more wine. Four hours later, when the check came and there was still no sign of Turner, Hoar charged it to his friend's room and sent a note to his office. "Thanks for the dinner," it said. "Sorry you couldn't be there."

Those who knew Turner thought him "brilliant," "driven," fiercely independent, "a lone wolf," "a pit bull," a "great lawyer" who "immediately hit the ground running" and "won a lot of cases." Paul Byrd, a fellow Arkansas trial attorney, recalled bumping into Turner after they took the bar exam, and was "stunned" by his classmate's responses on the essay part of the test, which "showed a unique mind, someone who wasn't afraid to tackle a problem from a different angle." Turner ended up receiving the highest score in the state.

He was not worldly and couldn't care less about social standing, preferring tangy barbecue to French foie gras, sports jackets to business suits. A millionaire many times over, he drove a beat-up Chevy Suburban, which he bragged you couldn't flip over with a forklift. In the back were a suit rack, shoes, and half a dozen garbage bags stuffed with clothes in need of dry cleaning. At his firm, every day was considered "casual Friday." On days he conducted business at the office his preferred style of dress was more Southern Bubba than button-down attorney: shorts, a T-shirt, sneakers, and a baseball cap.

Turner didn't like to delegate, preferring to handle his own business. "He was the first lawyer I knew who prepped his own pleadings," said a former secretary, Lee Jones. He was "likeable" and "easy to please" in part because "he was never there." Once Turner and some staff were stranded in a rural Mississippi backwater where he was trying a tread separation case. They stayed at a ramshackle motel and grilled steaks at night in the parking lot, making a party of it.

The friends he made were the ones he kept. His two closest growing up in rural Arkansas were Ronald and Donald Harris, African-American brothers who forged a bond with Turner that would last their lives. In the 1960s and early 1970s, Turner's hometown maintained separate schools for blacks and whites. When integration hit and the schools were combined, the state was overwhelmed with racial problems. Yet the three friends, who lived within a mile of each other, were together constantly, and were often referred to as "Thunder, Lightning, and Rain."

Loyalty didn't just extend to his friends. The people who worked for him also tended to stick around. His secretary, Brenda Gwim, has been with Turner for longer than he has been in solo practice. His pilot has been with him for 12 years. His investigator, William Miller, was a tailback on Turner's college team.

No matter where he traveled, Turner was accompanied by a rural Arkansas twang—all throat and flatted diphthongs. It led him to pronounce two core terms of his profession as "*in*-surance" and "*ve*-hicle." He grew up in a southern plantation house with white columns and a screen porch, a giant oak tree in the front yard. His father had been born in that house and would die there.

Clyde Talbot ("Tab") Turner was the younger of two sons of Otis Hawes Turner, a small-town country lawyer, president of the local chamber of commerce, and pillar of the community. The Turners lived in Arkadelphia (pop. 10,000), 54 miles from Little Rock, and the elder Turner handled a dash of everything in his practice: fender benders, divorces, property disputes. When his father was made a judge on the circuit, traveling around three Arkansas counties (Nashville, Texarkana, Arkadelphia) to adjudicate disputes, Turner and his brother Neal, who was two years older, would sometimes accompany him, getting into the paper clips and Coca-Cola machine.

Otis Hawes Turner was a larger-than-life figure to his sons: six and a half feet tall, stoic, the John Wayne type who because of a hip injury walked with a gait and answered to the nickname "Duke." A pillar of the community, he was "so honest" you could "play poker with him over the telephone." But theirs was a traditional "yes, sir," "no, sir" father-son relationship. His father was strict and hard to please.

It wasn't until the latter years of his father's life that Turner was able to penetrate this shield. By then they had become best friends, golfing buddies, confidants. Turner was even able to hire his father for a case. An artist at heart who doodled in church, his father designed the logo that Turner used on his stationery and even on his Cessna Citation: two highly ornate Ts flanked by scales of justice. Every time Turner saw it he thought of him, as if his father were never far away, watching over him.

By the time Otis Turner passed away, his son's legal career had equaled (if not eclipsed) his own. Carrying on the nickname of a favorite uncle Talbot, "Tab" Turner came to believe there were three fundamental truths to life: faith, family, and football—not always in that order. A Baptist who thought it wrong to sip a beer in front of his daughters, he claimed everything he knew in life he learned from sports. To this day he can reel off his college football coach's home phone number. Sports taught Turner about discipline and teamwork, giving 100 percent effort, taking each game as it came; lessons that were reinforced by his father. He would remember this and other well-trod sports clichés when he worked late into the night preparing a case for trial. Sleep deprivation, hostile defense attorneys, demanding judges, needy clients, a media microscope—he took on each challenge as it was presented.

Although football was his first love, it was baseball that offered his first life lesson. When Turner was 13, he was named starting catcher on his summer baseball league team. He was also the youngest. His father took him aside and gave him a lecture he never forgot. His father told him that few people in life rise to the occasion. His teammates, friends, and opponents all expected him to fail. They assumed the older boys would be too much for him. But here was a rare opportunity to meet a challenge head on. His father asked, "Will you fail or will you succeed?" Energized by his father's challenge, Turner had a strong season and was named to the All-Star team.

He also excelled on the gridiron. When he assumed the captaincy of the Arkadelphia High School football team in his senior year, it had been a decade since it had been competitive. In the early 1970s there were race riots after Arkadelphia merged the county's segregated white school with the black school. But it never affected Turner's relationship with his two best friends, whose house he stayed in overnight countless times. In his last year of high school, Turner was part of a core group of talented teammates that turned around the team's losing ways. They went undefeated that season and invigorated the community over high school football. This was Turner's first opportunity to lead a group to victory. It also gave him a taste of winning.

Heavily recruited by colleges, Turner and the Harris brothers made a pact that where one of them went to school, they would all go. The three friends settled on Ouachita Baptist College, which was not only nearby but also offered the three of them full football scholarships and the chance to play as freshmen in a solid Division III conference. In addition, Turner's brother, Neal, was on the team. The coach, Buddy Benson, was in the Woody Hayes–"Bear" Bryant mold, one of the winningest coaches in Division III history.

A stern taskmaster, Benson ran his program like Marine boot camp. He taught Turner and his teammates about hard work, self-discipline and meeting adversity head-on. A man who could always be found in crisp white pants and black shoes, Benson pushed his players beyond their limits of endurance. He told them the way to handle any challenge was to pour on the steam. He preached the Book of Self-discipline and Sacrifice. He told each of them to look in the mirror every morning and ask, *Do you want to win or do you want to lose? If you want to win, are you ready to do what it takes to succeed?* The confidence he gained in sports enabled Turner, years later, to take over a courtroom and command center stage at a televised press conference.

When he was a sophomore, Turner switched to offensive guard and became a starter. In his day, linemen weighed about 240 pounds. At 220, Turner was never the biggest or the strongest, but he had good footwork and was quick and smart. His brother Neal was the quarterback, a tremendous athlete who set state collegiate passing records. While Turner's friends the Harris twins played on defense, he and Neal starred on offense. Turner and his brother were kin in body but not in spirit. They didn't run around together, and associated with different friends. Theirs was a surprisingly distant relationship although they got along, especially on the football field, where their contrasting natures complemented each other—the fiery older brother at QB, the more cerebral, steady younger brother protecting him from would-be tacklers.

Benson ran spirited practices, and at times players hit harder there than they did during games. Once Turner's brother wore a "sissy shirt," which meant the defense wasn't supposed to hit the quarterback, but a defensive end barreled through and plastered him anyway. While his teammates snickered and the defensive player was 15 yards away, his back turned, Neal whipped the ball at his head, practically knocking him out. It took half the team to stop the inevitable fight.

Unlike his brother, Turner took pride in keeping his emotions in check and bottling up his intensity, tapping into it only when he needed it. Undersized for a lineman, Turner relied on guile to beat the guy across the ball from him. In a game against Southeastern Oklahoma University, he faced an All-American tackle bigger, stronger, and faster than Turner. After studying game film, Turner figured out a way to exploit his opponent's tendencies. The guy was quick off the ball, the type of pass rusher who sought any edge to hit the quarterback—an estimable trait, which Turner used against him. Turner deduced that the defensive end had been basing his actions on the knuckles of the offensive player. It was an old football trick. When the offensive lineman's knuckles were white, that hinted a running play was coming, since that meant he was leaning forward and putting pressure on his hands to get a stronger push off the line of scrimmage. When they weren't, that indicated the player was back on his heels to prepare to block for a pass play.

During the game, Turner, in his three-point stance, would lean forward for a passing play and rock back on his heels before charging upfield to run block. He would lean left and then fire off the other way, or lean right and then go left. Sometimes he went where he should, other times he didn't. By switching it up Turner psyched out the other team's star defensive player, and Ouachita controlled the line of scrimmage and won the game handily.

Turner played his final football game in 1976 and graduated in 1977. He had been an excellent student, graduating near the top of his class. But he learned more about life from his college football coach than from almost anyone else except his parents.

It was also during college that Turner encountered his first defective Firestone tire. During summers, Turner worked at Rental's Aluminum driving a forklift during the graveyard shift. He was driving home early one morning when one of his Firestone 500 tires disintegrated on the freeway. He had received a recall notice, but when he went to the dealership they didn't have replacement tires in stock. Driving to and from the plant, he had three tires come unglued in a month. Because Impalas were built close to the road, he had little trouble keeping the car under control. But the blowouts exasperated him. Finally Turner just replaced the tires himself—and at his own cost—with Goodyears.

The following football season Turner worked for Benson as an assistant coach and was in the ROTC. He also married his college sweetheart, Mary J. Gosser ("Jenny"), the oldest of five kids and whose father was a pediatrician, and started a family. Since Turner had earned a full scholarship to college, his father agreed to pay for law school, where Turner thrived, completing his coursework in two-and-a-half years and graduating in 1985 near the top of his class.

After law school Turner assumed he would return to Arkadelphia to work for his father, but Friday, Eldredge & Clark, one of Little Rock's most prestigious firms, offered him a position. His father advised him to take it. "You can always go back to Arkadelphia," he told his son, "but opportunities like this don't come around very often."

From the beginning Turner displayed an uncanny ability to win. Since the firm had more work than it could handle, Turner, just 25 years old, jumped headfirst into litigation. His first trial involved a man who had been found burned to death in his car. Even though the man had taken out a $100,000 life insurance policy, Travelers Insurance Company refused to pay, claiming the deceased had committed suicide. After Turner pointed out the unlikelihood of a man killing himself in such a painful manner—without leaving a suicide note—the jury awarded his clients $200,000 plus attorney's fees.

By the late 1980s Turner had developed into a legal special ops guy. If something came into the firm that was different, litigation-wise, the file usually ended up on his desk. Some lawyers specialized in tax work or insurance, medical malpractice, or bankruptcy, but Turner, like his father, thrived on litigating a variety of cases—medical malpractice to car accidents to commercial disputes. He greeted every case, every trial, as a personal challenge.

That began to change after he stumbled on his first Bronco II case when a former Friday, Eldredge & Clark secretary contacted the firm about her brother, Kelly Klemetsrud of Memphis, Tennessee, who had been brain damaged in a rollover while on his way to a karate tournament. The file—including the accident report and photos—wound around the firm until it got to Turner. It sat on his desk until June 1989 when *Consumer Reports* published an article titled, "How Safe Is the Bronco II?", rating the Bronco's handling as "poor" in a test that simulated rapid lane changes—much like the evasive maneuver Klemetsrud's driver undertook. The magazine told readers to steer clear of the Bronco. Days later Turner filed suit.

Turner had done car wreck cases but never before tackled a design or manufacture issue. In discovery, Ford produced 40 boxes of documents, which Turner spent 10 hours a day combing through, in addition to handling his other cases. While in Dearborn, Michigan, taking depositions from Ford engineers, Turner met with an in-house attorney, who glared across the table and said the automaker would pay $100,000 and not a dime more. When Turner turned it down, the man told the 30-year-old lawyer from Little Rock that Ford would bury him.

The Friday before trial, Turner was in court setting up his exhibits—crash scene pictures, engineer reports, the *Consumer Reports* article—when Ford attorneys announced they had additional discovery, some 20 boxes of internal documents the automaker had neglected to provide earlier, which led Turner to file a flurry of heated objections. After quickly reviewing the documents, he concluded these were the very documents he needed to prove his case. No one had seen them because no one had taken Ford to trial before.

Turner figured Ford kept two sets of discovery: The first 40 boxes for settlement purposes, the other 20 to be released only when it absolutely had to, or face jail. But Turner only had the weekend to digest thousands of pages of new information, much of it in dense engineer-speak, and prepare his opening statement. Ford was angling for a continuance, which would have delayed the trial a year, but the judge, sympathetic to Turner's plight, gave him until Sunday to consider his options. By the time he returned to his hotel room he had made up his mind, although to keep Ford in the dark he didn't call the judge until the last minute. Turner stayed up 48 straight hours reading through the documents, mapping out detailed chronologies that showed what Ford knew about its stability problems with the Ford Bronco and when it knew them.

Monday morning, as prospective jurors milled outside the court, a Ford attorney made his way to the judge's chambers. *What the hell is he doing?* Turner wondered.

After some hush-hush whispers, the judge asked Turner if he objected to his talking with Ford's attorneys privately in his chambers. Turner told him he had no objection as long as they didn't discuss specifics of the case without him present. A few minutes later, the Ford attorney emerged and, refusing eye contact with Turner, returned to his seat. The judge poked his head out and asked Turner to come inside. He told Turner that Ford wanted to settle the case but didn't want to talk directly to him. They wanted to negotiate through the judge.

"I don't mind if you don't mind," Turner said.

Even though it was 9 a.m., the judge sent prospective jurors to lunch and Ford began conveying settlement offers through the judge. Turner and Ford's attorneys spent hours crisscrossing into judge's chambers. Ford started a little above its initial offer and progressively worked its way up. Turner kept telling the judge he really liked his case. "I'm not just gonna give it away," he said. In the end he squeezed Ford for every dollar he could.

Just because he settled the case, however, didn't mean he was going to let the automaker off the hook. Turner had the documents, and the documents didn't lie.

3 PAPER CHASER

ONCE THE KLEMETSRUD CASE SETTLED, Turner decided to take a closer look at the last-minute discovery Ford had thrown at him. The first thing he did was put the documents in chronological order, then key in on the 15 or so memos relevant to rollovers. His goal was to piece together what happened between those pieces of paper. When Turner cross-referenced the documents, he realized he couldn't find certain tests and events referred to in the minutes of corporate meetings. This led him to file various motions for discovery that listed the AWOL documents and provided him the names of Ford management to depose, who under oath helped Turner fill in the gaps. What he found—or more accurately didn't find—led him to ask for sanctions against Ford.

The evidence showed that Ford had embarked on an unprecedented project of listing, collecting, reviewing, sanitizing, and ultimately discarding Bronco II documents, all of which was done in anticipation of litigation and was closely monitored by company attorneys. Prior to the Bronco coming off assembly lines, the automaker's Office of General Counsel (OGC) had ordered engineer Fred Parrill to collect all documents that related to vehicle "handling." In an inter-office memo dated July 27, 1982, Parrill relayed OGC's request to 12 department heads within the Ford organization.

"Comprehensive identification of documentation of matters pertaining to Bronco II handling has been requested by OGC," Parrill wrote. "In order to establish what documentation is present in the files, please establish a list of documents which may have any bearing on Bronco II handling, including discussion of track width and vehicle height. This will facilitate review by OGC of selected material."

Incensed, Turner charged "obstruction of justice." A judge in Indianapolis, David L. Rimstidt, would use harsher language. He found clear and convincing evidence that the document collection scheme that Turner uncovered amounted to "outright fraud."

On Aug. 13, 1982, a test driver put a Bronco II through its paces on a football-field-sized circular track in Dearborn. Watching were Ford's top corporate lawyer, Henry R. Nolte, Jr., safety director Roger Maugh, and his boss, Herbert Misch, vice president in charge of environmental and safety engineering. The company was deeply concerned about the vehicle's stability. With Broncos scheduled to emerge from factories in less than six months, Ford management knew it was in trouble if a prototype flunked another test.

When the first SUV, the Jeep CJ-5, hit American Motor Corporation dealerships in 1976, it was a humbling time for the American automobile industry. The muscle-chic Camaro, Corvette, and Mustang, cars that defined one generation and defied another, were outgunned by higher gas prices and stricter pollution laws. Japanese imports were not only better quality but cheaper. The only car made in America that could compete was the minivan. By the early 1980s, Jeep commanded its own category. Realizing it was losing out on a promising market, Ford planned its own SUV called the "Bronco II," which the *Wall Street Journal* would label a Jeep "knockoff." The company approved the first detailed design of Bronco II on Jan. 5, 1981, with work on the first mechanical prototype beginning five days later.

Loopholes in the Clean Air Act of 1970 exempting "light trucks" from regulation provided automakers a key incentive to manufacture sport-utility vehicles. In 1973, the American Motors Corporation didn't have the resources or expertise to create an engine that could meet more stringent pollution standards. Afraid the cash-challenged automaker would go bankrupt, the Environmental Protection Agency categorized the Jeep as a light truck instead of a passenger car. Officials at the EPA didn't want the Clean Air Act and other pro-green legislation blamed for putting America's fourth largest automobile company out of business. After the 1973 OPEC oil boycotts, Congress required carmakers to double fuel economy (to 27.5 mpg by 1985), but in a sop to industry, allowed that light trucks were in a category beyond regulation. Automakers lobbied furiously for this, pointing to farmers, ranchers and construction workers—always a sympathetic constituency—who needed big, powerful pickup trucks for hauling heavy loads.

Just because the government offered entry into a largely deregulated market didn't mean consumers would play along. At first, Ford held modest hopes for the SUV. The first indication it was on to something came when the company conducted pre-launch test marketing. Surveys showed potential buyers wanted four-wheel drive even though they had no need for it. These urban cowboys, mountain men, hunters, fishermen, surfers, and kayakers may have traded in their fantasies for a charter membership to Reality U.S.A. (kids, careers, mortgages, and debt) but that didn't mean they couldn't pretend.

The Bronco II's popularity would catch Detroit by surprise. Auto executives didn't think there would be a market for a vehicle that let luxury-minded suburbanites crash through forests and up vertigo-inducing trails in their off hours. At the same time, Ford discovered the Bronco also appealed to women, who often exerted a strong influence over the family vehicle. They too pined for an alternative to the traditional family station wagon and ho-hum minivan, a phenomenon Ford fully exploited.

A 1986 Ford TV advertisement illustrates the company's ham-handed efforts to lure women drivers. A handyman was putting up a sign in a suburban office complex parking lot when two men in suits approached. Looking at the sign, the first man said, "Uh-oh, our new boss is here." The camera pulled back to reveal a Bronco II Eddie Bauer model. They agreed the new executive must "like to be on top of all situations—like ice or snow with four-wheel drive," a "rugged outdoor type," who's one powerful boss. "The baby's got a V6," and definitely appreciates luxury. ("Look at that interior!") A woman in a suit and floppy bow tie walked up behind them. She had on tortoiseshell glasses and her long hair was in a bun. "Excuse me gentlemen," she said.

"*He* is a *she* . . ." Man Number One said.

"Definitely," agreed Man Number Two.

What the advertisement didn't mention was that the characteristics that made the Bronco II attractive—the commanding view of the road, roomy cabin with space for three kids and all their gear, the ability to go off road—also made it more dangerous. "The irony is that people are buying SUVs because they think they're safer vehicles," says Brian O'Neil of the Insurance Institute for Highway Safety. "The reality is, because of the rollover risk, they rarely are safer vehicles than larger passenger cars."

It boiled down to simple physics, as inevitable as the fall of Isaac Newton's apple. Just working out the dimensions on the truck yielded a formula for disaster. Too narrow times too high multiplied by the force of a sharp turn on too rigid a suspension system equaled big trouble.

These weren't natural laws by which Ford alone had to abide. Two months after the Bronco II had been approved for development, the CBS news program *60 Minutes* took a good hard look at the Jeep CJ-5, the main inspiration for the Bronco II. With cameras rolling the Jeep, controlled by a computer, flipped over at 32 mph. In other tests, it keeled over at speeds as low as 22 mph.

AMC tried to cast doubt on the validity of the study. In a letter it sent before broadcast, the number-four automaker claimed the test was rigged and dismissed the crash test dummies falling out of the Jeeps as "pure theatrics." The company sent *60 Minutes* a tape of tests it had conducted and bragged that the Jeep performed J-turns at 32 mph with a live driver, 10 mph faster than the ones the Institute shot. But when Brian O'Neil of the Insurance Institute slowed the film down on an editing machine, he showed that the Jeep's right side wheels had lifted off the ground.

With that grim image etched in their minds, Ford executives and engineers held a meeting the very next morning. Lifetime car guys, they were well versed in the Jeep's stability issues. "There wasn't anybody building a utility vehicle in 1980 who wasn't aware of the *60 Minutes* and CJ controversy," said Warren Platt, a Phoenix lawyer who represented Ford in Bronco II litigation. A little due diligence would have turned up a Department of Transportation decree that Army jeeps were not to be sold to the public because of the danger they posed. The military had mandated special training for drivers of Jeeps, especially on taking tight turns. A narrator on a training video on the do's and don'ts of driving a Jeep cautioned drivers about swerving sharply.

Ford executives decided to test the Bronco to see how it would do in the same type of maneuvers, equipping it with outriggers, roll bars, and roll cages to duplicate what *60 Minutes* and the Insurance Institute had done with the Jeep. The Bronco II failed at speeds as low as 30 mph.

When David Bickerstaff, an engineer from England who worked in the light truck engineering department of Ford Motor Company, first received the design on paper of the Bronco II, he became concerned. The Bronco II as proposed had the worst stability index of any car Ford had ever made.

Stability index was simply a formula: divide the vehicle's center of gravity by two times the truck width. The higher the number, the better the stability. Engineers were shooting for an index of 2.25, but early designs Bickerstaff reviewed yielded a figure of only 1.85. Bickerstaff, who was primarily in charge of the testing and handling work on the Bronco II, filed a memo in early February 1981, in which he warned of "a dangerous propensity of the vehicle to roll over in foreseeable highway maneuvers."

He and his colleagues were well aware that putting a stout SUV cabin atop a slender frame made the Bronco II top-heavy. Bickerstaff submitted five proposals to make the Bronco II less tipsy. Three of them addressed widening the vehicle's track and lowering its center of gravity, which would have required scrapping the Ranger chassis, costing hundreds of millions of dollars and delaying "Job One"—the day vehicles would roll off assembly lines. But this would squelch management's plan to launch the Bronco II within months of the new GM Blazer, risking that ever-important market share.

Ford engineers would get only so many cracks at solving the problem, and only within the parameters management allowed. That meant no serious design changes to the "package." They were stuck with the dimensions of the Ranger pickup truck, which ensured the Bronco could be manufactured with the same robots in the same factories and rely on the same Twin I-Beam suspension system. In fact, the two vehicles would be identical from the driver's seat forward.

This made the Bronco II cost-effective to design and manufacture, its development costs a fraction of the $7 billion Ford squandered on the forgettable Contour, which it created from scratch. But reliance on the Twin I-Beam suspension was controversial at Ford. Tom Feaheny, a former Ford vice president of vehicle research, said a number of engineers he worked with believed it contributed to rollovers. As the steel suspension arms crisscrossed under the engine, the engine and transmission had to be raised vertically two to three inches, also raising the vehicle's center of gravity. The front seat had to be even higher to achieve visibility over the hood. The suspension system's rigidity also led to "jacking," when the vehicle could suddenly lift up during an emergency maneuver or a skid. Jacking could cause a rollover in circumstances where other suspensions would permit a driver to maintain control.

Bickerstaff and his team made do with the Ranger chassis, stretching the frame and axles as wide as they could go. Still, at Ford's Arizona Proving Grounds in April 1982, a Bronco II on 15-inch wheels tipped up at 35 mph. Desperate to lower the center of gravity, Ford outfitted a test model with smaller tires wrapped around 14-inch wheels, which helped realize modest improvements in performance. Now the Bronco II could handle a J-turn at 55 mph. But Ford's marketing department vetoed the smaller wheels. Customers told them they wanted a tougher look, four-wheel drive, and higher clearance for off-road driving. After a Bronco II broke an outrigger before rolling over on a J-turn test in May, Ford halted stability tests out of fear for the test drivers' safety.

If the Bronco blew this August test, Ford would be forced to take drastic action. The company had a number of undesirable (read: expensive) options. It could delay the unveiling of the Bronco II until its engineers could figure out a way to keep its wheels on the ground during sharp turns. It could scrap the Twin I-Beam suspension system and Ranger chassis and specifically design a wider chassis for the SUV. It could redesign the car from the ground up. Or it could manufacture the vehicle anyway, knowing it was tipsy, and batten down the hatches for a torrent of rollover lawsuits after the Bronco II hit highways.

Ford chose the latter.

In mid-August Bickerstaff fired off a memo and Ford immediately halted all testing on the Bronco II. Ford president Harold Polling called Bickerstaff into his office. Within a month Bickerstaff, whose father had been killed in a rollover of a Ford van in 1979, left Ford, claiming he wanted to make more money. By the late 1980s, plaintiffs' attorneys identified Bickerstaff as a key witness, and in depositions he voiced doubts about the Bronco II's design. But he began to sing a different tune after meeting with Ford lawyers in a Dearborn hotel room in June 1990, when he agreed to become a full-time defense witness for Ford.

Through the company's internal correspondence, Turner discovered that warning signs persisted after the first Bronco II emerged from factories on Jan. 10, 1983. A computer simulated the Bronco II in a March slalom test. During an emergency swerve at 32 mph, the simulated Bronco raised two wheels off the ground. A month later, a Ford driver leaving the Dearborn test track in a Bronco II rolled over while doing a U-turn at less than 20 mph. Ford blamed low tire pressure and a crack in the road.

In the fall, GM introduced the S-10 Blazer, which had a stability rating of 2.20, better than Ford expected and significantly higher than the Bronco II's best: 2.03. The relative ratings worried executives, who discussed, among other things, product-liability problems the comparison might cause. Ford's in-house lawyers asked that the vehicle's stability index be a minimum of 2.1. At the very least, "Ford understood that irrespective of how the vehicle actually performed, no matter what its rollover rates were, there would be an allegation that the vehicle was not suitable unless the stability index was as high as you can make it," Platt, the Phoenix-based Ford defense attorney, told the *Wall Street Journal*.

The automaker exhibited remarkable forward planning for a car that hadn't even been manufactured. "What they were getting ready to do, they were canning their defense to the Bronco II," Tab Turner would tell a jury 13 years later. "They were canning it so they could play it over and over again every time somebody is killed, every time somebody is crippled. . . . They were getting ready for the lawsuit."

Parrill admitted he knew he was collecting evidence for future lawsuits, and that the collection process was to be carried out in relative secrecy. There was an "understanding" there would be no written documentation or records kept of the project, referred to internally as "closing the loop." Ford lawyers even created a methodology to categorize the various documents, with a special emphasis given to those that discussed "track width and vehicle height."

Although Ford originally objected to producing the lists of documents accumulated in 1982, claiming they were "prepared in anticipation of litigation" and therefore protected by the "work product" doctrine, at least one court overruled the objection. Out of legal options, Ford finally complied with the order and produced the lists.

Somehow along the way, Ford personnel destroyed 50 documents, including some that pertained to vehicle stability and others containing results of various tests—this despite the fact that the entire process was initiated in "anticipation of litigation"; the involvement of attorneys who knew the importance of retaining and preserving evidence; the company's own knowledge that "handling" documents were directly relevant to the litigation concern that formed the basis for its evidence-sanitizing actions in the first place; and the clear and admitted knowledge that these documents would be needed and requested in the very litigation the corporation anticipated.

"Ford," Turner charged, had "carefully covered its tracks." The law didn't permit Ford to gather documents in anticipation of litigation and rid itself of the ones it didn't like. In its defense, Ford claimed its mishandling of the documents was inadvertent and was done pursuant to a Corporate Records Retention Manual. One problem: Ford also destroyed the alleged manual.

In June 1988, NHTSA (National Highway Traffic Safety Administration) informed Ford about an investigation into the Suzuki Samurai the agency was conducting on single-vehicle rollovers—a category the Bronco II led with 42 fatal rollovers in 1987. A 1988 Ford internal analysis of federal accident statistics projected 141 "first event" rollover deaths a year for every 1 million Bronco IIs—a rate higher than the Jeep CJ and almost three times that of the S-10 Blazer. The following February, NHTSA initiated a recall investigation of the Bronco II but ultimately decided against taking action because it could point to no "component failure or malfunction." Nonetheless, in its June 1989 issue, *Consumer Reports* told readers, "We think it's wise to avoid the Bronco II."

The Insurance Institute for Highway Safety concluded in a 1992 report that the fatality rate in accidents involving the rear-wheel-drive version of the Bronco II was the highest of any compact SUV studied—three times the Suzuki Samurai, which had also been the target of a devastating exposé in *Consumer Reports*. That same year Texas State District Judge Ann Cochran ruled that sealing Ford documents regarding the Bronco's stability against rollovers could "have a probable adverse effect upon the general public health and/or safety."

Stung by the criticism—and more to the point, the bad PR it spawned—Ford had already discontinued the Bronco II in 1989, after manufacturing more than 800,000 of them. But there remained hundreds of thousands of them still on the road, and many of them were rolling over.

4 $25 Million Verdict

ON MAY 14, 1992, JENNIFER CAMMACK, 21, was crammed into the back of a Ford Bronco II with six classmates from Texas A&M, on their way from College Station to the Shiner Brewery. It was around noon and the friends had stopped at a Dairy Queen in Schulenberg for lunch. As they headed west on U.S. 90, eating their burgers and shakes, the tread completely tore off the right rear tire and the driver lost control. The Bronco fell into a sideways skid at 50 mph, tripped, and rolled over on its side. Cammack and three others were ejected through the side windows.

The Highway Patrol arrived within minutes, but only the driver and front seat passenger had been wearing seatbelts. The rest, except for one, had been thrown from the vehicle. The driver ended up with a bump on his head and the woman next to him a badly lacerated leg. Another friend had ridden out the storm inside the cabin and merely chipped a tooth. The others weren't so fortunate. Jennifer's unconscious boyfriend had received a serious head injury and was flown in a chopper to Houston. Another passenger was flown by helicopter to Austin. But they lived, unlike Jennifer Cammack, who suffered severe internal injuries when she hit the pavement, her last 45 minutes on earth spent in agony. She was crying and fell in and out of consciousness while a passerby held her head. When the paramedics loaded her into the ambulance, she passed out for good. Minutes later she died, after drowning in her own blood.

Her father, Robert Cammack, an engineer at Texas Utilities, had just returned from lunch when two colleagues came by his office and told him to call home. Cammack could tell something was wrong from the way they were acting. After Glenda, his wife, told him, his friends took Cammack straight home. He was in shock. He had talked to his daughter on the phone just a few days earlier. Everything was fine. She had decided to hang around campus after finals to be with friends before coming home for the summer. They had always been a close-knit family. They had traveled around the country in an RV. Camping was a popular family pastime, as was boating. Jennifer was a particularly good water-skier. Now she was dead. It occurred to Cammack the dead suffer less than the living. He didn't think he would recover.

Cammack phoned his other daughter, Shannon, four years older than her sister, who took it so hard his wife had to call her daughter's fiancé to ask him to go comfort her. Jennifer was buried a few days later, her family and friends standing in witness. Within the flood of tearful condolences, Cammack heard of a similar accident that had injured the son of a local attorney, who ended up settling with Ford. On his computer, Cammack checked *Consumer Reports* and read an article about the Bronco II. The magazine claimed the vehicle was so unstable it was unsafe to drive. This made Cammack angry. As an engineer, he never built anything that couldn't stay up if put under stress. How could Ford let this happen?

He considered suing, but his wife was ambivalent. She knew it would be a long, bitter fight, and it wouldn't bring their daughter back. But they put off any decision until after they got back from vacation. After visiting some cave dwellings near Silver City, New Mexico, they saw a college student buying a soft drink at a roadside stand. He was driving a Ford Bronco II, a University of Texas sticker on the back. The Cammacks looked at each other. Then and there they decided to do something. Their daughter Shannon was thrilled when she heard. She wanted to destroy Ford.

But the company wouldn't even talk to the first attorney Cammack hired. Meanwhile, his late daughter's boyfriend, Kyle Kepple, who had also been seriously injured in the crash, reached a settlement. After the accident Kepple was in a coma for three months and sustained nerve damage to his neck. But his lawyer pushed ahead and negotiated agreements with both General Tire and Ford in late 1994. Cammack had no idea how much Kepple got. That was a secret. But it was enough for Kepple to live on for the rest of his life.

Cammack looked elsewhere for legal representation, retaining Michael Kerensky, a lawyer who worked with John O'Quinn, the hard-living Houston attorney who had helped negotiate a $15.3 billion settlement agreement between the state of Texas and the tobacco industry to recover the medical costs associated with treating smokers. O'Quinn in turn brought in Tab Turner, who advised settling with General Tire first, then going all out against Ford. Except they ran into trouble right out of the gate. Turner had a conflict of interest. His law firm, Friday, Eldredge

& Clark of Little Rock, did tax work for General Tire. This meant Turner would have to bow out, although this didn't stop him from offering behind-the-scenes advice and strategy. Kerensky went after General Tire and reached a settlement in January of 1995. Now that General Tire was out, Turner was back in.

Three months later, Cammack had a heart attack and quadruple by-pass. Kerensky called him at the hospital and told him Ford wanted to settle. Since Cammack couldn't go to them, the lawyers came to him. Ford offered $200,000—about what the lawyers had amassed in expenses—and Cammack and Kerensky's counter was $500,000. Ford's representatives were "take it or leave it" types. They reminded Cammack that Ford had never lost a rollover case. When they wouldn't increase their offer, a bedbound Cammack promised them he would see them at the courthouse.

By the time jury selection began in June 1995, Ford's Bronco lawyers had only one blemish in court: A federal jury in Binghamton, New York, in November 1992 awarded a woman $1.2 million for injuries she sustained when her Bronco rolled as she swerved to avoid a deer. The jury found Ford negligent in how it designed, tested, and marketed the Bronco but determined that the negligence was not the "proximate cause" of the accident. The jury found no negligence in the company's safety warnings to buyers and found no "defect" in the vehicle. Nonetheless, the jury did find that Ford had breached an implied warranty that the product was fit for ordinary use, thus making the company at least partly responsible for the accident. In its $3 million award, the jury found the plaintiff, Nancy Denny, 60 percent at fault and Ford 40 percent at fault. That exposed the company to a total damage award of $1.2 million, which Ford appealed.

In Cammack, Ford pursued the same defense strategy it had used in more than 100 other product liability suits involving Bronco: blame the person at the wheel. Ford lawyers argued the driver lost control because the vehicle was overloaded and the tire blew out. They also claimed that Jennifer Cammack shared responsibility for not wearing one of four safety belts provided.

Turner countered by eliciting testimony and entering documents into evidence that told of a tendency for the Bronco II to lift its wheels on low-speed turns, and described stability problems with the vehicle's Twin I-Beam suspension. He grilled a smug, graying Ford publicist, who testified he had shared a ride from the airport in a Bronco II with three engineers and a driver. That meant five people had ridden in a vehicle with only four seat belts. Up to this point Ford's position had been, What three idiots would sit in the back of a Bronco II with only two seatbelts? Turner was able to identify three for the jury: all engineers from Ford's automotive safety department.

Next Turner eviscerated the credibility of Ford's chief expert witness, David Bickerstaff. In earlier testimony, Bickerstaff admitted that both track width and the height of the center of gravity were important to the stability of a vehicle. He also reported that the wheels of the Bronco had come off the ground during internal rollover tests. But in subsequent depositions Bickerstaff claimed the opposite. "We never had a concern about this vehicle," he would say. "It was one of the safest vehicles we ever marketed. We would have never sold it if we had safety concerns."

Bickerstaff was a good witness, confident, personable, hard to cross-examine. He'd effectively explain the contradictions away by obfuscating. Tall, with a soothing British accent, Bickerstaff was the kind of gentleman at a cocktail party who could hold court with his stories. He was bright, knew his stuff, and connected with juries. In other words, he was a problem for the plaintiffs.

After Ford's lawyers used Bickerstaff on direct examination to set up the automaker's defense, Turner got a crack at him. In Texas, you don't have to stand up to ask questions, so Turner remained in his chair, legs crossed, and started off without notes, as if he didn't have a care in the world.

"Now, Mr. Bickerstaff . . . at some point in 1990 you bargained with Ford Motor Company to provide favorable testimony in Bronco II cases, did you not?" Turner asked.

Bickerstaff seemed offended. "I didn't bargain on providing favorable testimony. No."

"Well, did you ever tell them that if they would pay you what you demanded, $4,000 per day, you would testify and permit them to help you testify in Ford's favor?"

"I told them that I would testify and this is what my rates would be," Bickerstaff said, challenging Turner with a look of contempt.

Turner uncrossed his legs, looked at the floor then looked up at the witness. "Now, Mr. Bickerstaff, are you telling us that you never told them that if they would pay what you demanded, you would testify in Ford's favor?"

"I told them that I would testify," Bickerstaff insisted. "I'd tell the truth and nothing but the truth."

The trap sprung, Turner asked the judge to approach the witness. When his request was granted, he produced a letter dated June 20, 1990, that Bickerstaff had written to the Ford lawyers trying this case. Turner had received it a week before trial, tucked inside an envelope with no return address. It put in writing Bickerstaff's offer to testify "in Ford's favor" in exchange for $4,000 a day. Turner didn't know who had sent the letter, although he had heard that Bickerstaff was embroiled in a quarrelsome divorce.

Turner blew up the letter to the size of a door and placed it on an easel, under a cloth. He handed Bickerstaff a paper copy, which he marked as evidence, then made Bickerstaff read the letter to the jury. Further dripping Tabasco into the wound, he ordered the witness out of his chair to underscore "in Ford's favor" with a yellow highlighter.

After that, Bickerstaff was a most cooperative witness. He testified he had been concerned all along that the design of the Ford Bronco had rendered it unstable. He admitted that track width was important, center of gravity affected rollover propensity, and that in development, the Bronco's wheels had come off of the ground in stability tests. When Turner was finished and Bickerstaff was allowed off the witness stand, Ford lawyers turned their backs and refused to speak with him.

While the jury deliberated, Ford tried desperately to settle. Since it was pre-cellular times, the attorney had to rush out to a hallway pay phone to run Turner's counter-offers by upper management. Eventually Ford upped its offer to $2 million but insisted the family concede it was a seatbelt issue. But Shannon wouldn't let her father settle. "We didn't come down here for that," she told him. For the entire trial, Cammack divided his time between the courtroom and his hotel. While his wife, daughter, and son-in-law went out at night, he ordered room service on account of his heart condition. Just as the Ford attorney was about to unveil the carmaker's final offer, the bailiff rapped his knuckles on the judge's bench and announced that the jury had reached a verdict.

"Too late," Turner said.

He was right. The jury awarded the Cammacks $25 million, marking the first time a jury found a sport-utility vehicle defective. Of that, $22.5 million was punitive, the rest to compensate the parents of the victim and her estate. The jury agreed that Ford was grossly negligent for safety flaws and design defects that made the Bronco II unstable in its handling. Despite the tire failure, it found Ford 100 percent responsible for the accident and Jennifer Cammack's death. Because the jury concluded that Ford did not intentionally harm its customers, however, the damage awards were capped at no more than four times actual damages. Under Texas law, punitive-damage caps could only be overcome by a jury finding the defendant acted with malice. On that count the jury sided with Ford.

Afterward, Robert Cammack told reporters he hoped Ford would "be more conscious of what this vehicle does." His wife, Glenda, advised the *Houston Chronicle* that Bronco owners should "get rid of it before the same tragedy happens to someone else." When Shannon was asked by a TV news reporter what people should do if they owned a Ford Bronco, she echoed her mother: "Get rid of it!" After the verdict the Cammacks drove the 275 miles to Richardson laughing and crying, recounting the highs and lows of the trial and telling stories about Jennifer, who they knew would have approved. A week later Robert Cammack returned to work.

Far from the prying eyes of the media, the courts began to whittle down the amount. Two months after the verdict, the judge, acting under Texas tort reform laws, cut the award to $5.8 million. He lowered actual damages against Ford from $2.5 million to $1.8 million, and punitive damages from $22.5 million to $4 million. Even though Ford had spent about that much on its defense, the carmaker filed an appeal based on a technicality. Robert Cammack had never probated his young daughter's estate. Since she wasn't technically a minor when she died, Ford claimed he had no legal standing to sue on her behalf.

The appeal stagnated in the courts until early 1999, when Ford made a move to settle. Cammack had re-sued Ford over the estate probation issue, and the automaker offered to up its offer if he dropped his latest suit. By then, Cammack just wanted to get it over with. All along he felt the important thing was showing people that Ford had put a dangerous vehicle on the road. With the money he received Cammack was able to retire. Sadly, his wife never got to experience closure nor share in their newfound wealth. While the suit wound its way through the courts, Glenda Cammack was diagnosed with breast cancer and died two weeks before Ford got around to cutting them a check.

That was the thing with Ford, Turner thought. Even when you won you lost. Corporations neglect to mention cases like the Cammacks' when they complain about runaway juries and outrageous damage awards. Ultimately, a lawsuit came down to people like Robert and Glenda Cammack, grieving over the loss of someone they loved.

Although a pyrrhic victory for the Cammack family, it was a career high point for Turner. The resulting media attention caused his phones to ring off the hook. The trial in Binghamton had been the first crack in Ford's façade. Now Turner's victory had shattered the automaker's air of invincibility in court.

Four months later, a state court jury in Indianapolis needed only two-and-a-half hours of deliberations (after a three-week trial) to award $62.4 million in damages against Ford for injuries to two teenagers in a Bronco

II rollover accident. The jury heeded the advice of trial lawyer Randy Barnhart, who urged them to calculate punitive damages by multiplying $58—the amount he calculated it would have cost Ford to fix the stability problem—by the number of Bronco IIs sold. The resulting amount was equal to the revenue Barnhart estimated Ford generated by not making safety changes.

The automaker appealed. "Ford . . . should not be punished for the driver's reckless judgment," said company spokesman John Harmon.

5 THE EXPLORER CLUB

THE RISE OF THE SUV OCCURRED in an era of endless possibilities. The Cold War ended, the Berlin Wall tumbled, Communism collapsed, American-style Democracy triumphed, consumerism thrived. There was rampant optimism, talk of a "peace dividend," an influential essay on "the end of history," a dynamic economy floating skyward on a speculative bubble. Stories abounded of geek billionaires who launched entire industries from their parents' garages, and wondrous new gadgets and services that would revolutionize our lives. Nike's "Just do it" campaign became the clarion call for a generation, and the Internet the place they chatted about it. People were as much judged for what they did for play as what they did for work.

Versatility became a selling point. Consumers swiped (ATM) cards to buy (all-terrain) vehicles and (hybrid) bicycles while wearing (unisex) clothing like (expandable) cargo pants, (cross) trainers, (reversible) jackets and (deep-sea-diving) watches. They lugged around (portable) laptop computers, (electronic) personal organizers, and (multi-use) Swiss Army knives. They made calls on their (mobile) phones and sent instant messages over their (wireless) pagers. The vehicles they chose had to express this cultural aesthetic. "SUVs are simply the latest example of America's gear fetish," asserted Paul Roberts in *Harper's*. "[It] says, 'I am a man of action, a woman with purpose. I go places. I have real, important things to do. . . . '"

For the SUV, however, there was an engineering trade-off to this versatility: The ability to go off road meant the vehicle required a high clearance, which gave it a narrow margin of error in the event of a sharp turn or tire failure at highway speeds.

Along with the boom in SUVs came a boom in lawsuits. As a result
of his victory in the Cammack trial—and the resulting publicity—Turner
became the nation's preeminent rollover lawyer.

Within a month of the verdict in June 1995, he had 25 new Bronco II
rollover cases. He leveraged his success by filing a motion for summary
judgment claiming that since the Bronco II had been found to be defective by design in Texas, Ford could no longer say it wasn't. When a judge
granted it, Ford quickly settled the case—and every other Bronco case
Turner has had ever since. By January 1999, Ford had settled 679
rollover claims, more than 200 of them Turner clients.

Cammack wasn't just a watershed for Turner—the first time a jury
laid complete blame on Ford for a design flaw—it also introduced a
profound change to his career. The conflict of interest his firm had with
General Tire confirmed something Turner already knew. It was time for
him to strike out on his own. It wasn't the first time he had run up
against the firm's conflict of interest statutes. Friday, Eldredge & Clark
was a corporate defense firm. That's where the safe $400-dollar-an-hour
money was. But Turner wanted to run his own show. He informed
Buddy Sutton, one of the firm's partners, of his intention to start his own
practice, offering to leave the firm his entire client list—40 rollover
victims. Sutton appreciated the offer and kept a quarter of them. A month
later he returned the cases to Turner. No one at the firm knew what to do
with them. Sutton asked for out-of-pocket expenses. Turner gave him that
plus part of the fee.

While his new offices were being renovated, Turner founded Turner
& Associates in 1996 on a card table in his den in a suburban niche of
Little Rock and burned through his savings. At the same time he noticed
a profound change in his caseload. As the number of Bronco IIs on the
road decreased, so did the percentage of his cases that dealt with them.
There was a new rollover king on the highway: The Ford Explorer.
Dubbed "the four-door Bronco" during development, the Explorer was a
bigger version of the Bronco. Longer and wider than its predecessor, the
Explorer would be marketed at older buyers, which Ford assured would
yield a "less aggressive driver profile and fewer accidents." Just in case, it
changed the car's name as scrutiny intensified over mounting deaths from
Bronco rollover crashes.

Turner immersed himself in Ford's internal communications and was
amazed to discover that the automaker hadn't learned anything from its
experiences with the Bronco. The documents told an unsettling story, a
repeat of the litany of mistakes Ford had made with its predecessor.
Management decreed that the Explorer use the same Twin I-Beam

suspension system and be built in the same Ranger factories on the same assembly lines with the same robots. Prototypes consistently failed internal stability tests, both real-world and computer-simulated. The only difference Turner could see was that Ford hadn't tried to cover it up this time.

Through the documents Turner was able to pinpoint when the Explorer first exhibited stability problems: May 1987, three years before it hit America's roads. Engineers in Ford's light truck department reported that the Explorer's stability factor was worse than the Bronco II's. As Bickerstaff had done when he received the first drawings, the engineers advised that Ford increase the vehicle's track width, lower the height of the vehicle's vertical center of gravity, and use smaller tires. Management never acted on its engineers' recommendations.

While undergoing handling maneuvers in 1989, an Explorer prototype exhibited a greater tendency to raise its wheels than a Bronco II. The report noted that the Explorer had to be "at least equivalent to the Bronco II in these maneuvers to be considered acceptable for production." After *Consumer Reports* panned the Bronco II in June 1989, Ford engineers acknowledged that passing the Consumers Union test had become an implicit requirement for Explorer due to the potential for adverse publicity, even though they knew there was a risk that testing would indicate that the Explorer prototype was similar to the Bronco II.

As the Explorer progressed through its development cycle, computer simulations continued to underscore its tendency to lift two wheels off the pavement in typical emergency maneuvers. Ford engineers noted that "the relatively high engine position of the Explorer, unchanged from the Bronco II, prevents significant improvement in Stability Index without extensive suspension, frame and sheet metal revisions." With the Explorer's 1990 production date approaching, they listed four ways to improve stability: Widen the chassis by two inches, lower the engine, or stiffen the springs and decrease tire pressure—something it had rejected for the Bronco as early as 1982.

Before deciding anything, Ford management authorized a test on an Explorer, a Bronco II, and a Chevy S-10 Blazer at its Arizona Proving Grounds in June 1989. The Blazer won hands down. The Explorer prototype lifted two wheels off the ground "with a number of tire, tire pressure, suspension configurations." Engineers who prepared the 1990 Explorer Handling Stability memorandum report believed they knew why: "The Chevy T-Blazer passes J-turn requirements with an apparent large margin of reserve. The difference in reserve between the Explorer and T-Blazer in the J-turn Test has been traced to the differences in front suspension roll center," which "dynamically raises" the vehicle's center of gravity. "No reduction in roll center is possible without major revision to the front suspension and steering systems."

Engineers again promoted four basic design changes to achieve performance on par with the Blazer. Management chose the one that wouldn't delay production: let air out of the tires, setting the inflation level at 26 psi. To help quell concerns, the executives agreed to consider the rest of the design proposals as "running changes" in subsequent model years.

It rejected Ford engineer Roger Stornant's suggestion to go with a smaller tire, even though Stornant had "a high confidence of passing" the *Consumer Reports* test "with [Firestone's] P225 tires and less confidence on the [Firestone] P235." Management went with the bigger P235—to give the vehicle a sportier look. Ford "management is aware of the potential risk with P235 tires and has accepted [that] risk," Stornant wrote.

To extend the Explorer image, Firestone named the P235 the ATX, then later the Wilderness AT. In 1990, the Explorer went on sale with Firestone tires as standard equipment. By 1991, the Explorer was the country's best-selling sport-utility vehicle, a title it would hold for a decade, and contributed $559 million to the company's coffers that year, with a profit margin of 38.8 percent.

But Ford quickly realized its decision to lower tire pressure had unintended consequences. The mushier tires held the road better but worsened gas mileage. Immediately after "Job One," Ford management began raising concerns about the poor "rolling resistance," or higher friction, provided by the ATX tire and the effect on fuel economy. The vehicle was 7 percent worse than its competition from a miles-per-gallon standpoint.

The company ordered Ford employee James Burdette to address the problem. He had three options: Modify the rubber compounds by using low rolling resistance compounds, increase air pressure, or reduce the tire's weight. Reformulating the tire to include low rolling resistance compounds altered the traction characteristics of the tires; the wheels of the Explorer wouldn't stay on the road in test maneuvers. After learning this, Burdette requested that engineers raise tire inflation pressure from 26 to 30 psi. This too caused the wheels of the Explorer to lift up during turning tests.

This left Ford with one last possibility: reducing the tires' weight. This accomplished two objectives. It would lessen the Explorer's tendency to roll over, and it would save money. This fell in with Ford's prevailing corporate ethos. The company's rising star was Australian-born Jac

Nasser, known as "Jac the Black" for the color of ink that ran from his spreadsheets. In public, the automaker declared, "Quality is Job One"; while in private Ford pursued an almost manic drive to cut costs and better the bottom line.

In the mid-1990s, Ford management came to the conclusion that it could get away with squeezing its suppliers. A 1995 Ford Dealers Report claimed the cost of a tire wasn't what it cost to make it; it was whatever Ford was willing to pay. The automaker offered Firestone less to design and produce a tire that was a pound-and-a-half lighter. Firestone didn't make money from supplying original equipment for the Explorer; it made it on replacement tires. But Firestone didn't dare to say no. The automaker made up almost a third of Firestone's total business and was its oldest and most important customer. Firestone couldn't afford to jeopardize the Explorer contract.

Since tires consist mainly of two things, Firestone cut the only elements possible: rubber and steel. This way it successfully lowered the tire's weight by 10 percent—and in the process lowered its material costs, helping the tire maker close in on the break-even point. But lighter meant less durable. The tire wasn't designed for heavy-duty use, even though Firestone would proudly stamp "Wilderness" on the sidewall. To accommodate Ford's request for a truck-looking tire that performed like a passenger car tire, the ATX was equipped with a more aggressive-looking tread pattern. But it was a car tire that only *looked* like it could handle the rigors of transporting 3,000 pounds of truck, cargo and passengers over searing hot roads of the South and Southwest, day in and day out, for tens of thousands of miles. The Wilderness was assigned a "C" rating for temperature/heat resistance, the lowest allowed under NHTSA's Uniform Tire Quality Grading System.

While *Ad Age* reported that Ford had begun a new marketing campaign seeking to redefine its "Quality is Job One" theme, complaints of tread separations began to trickle in after the redesigned Explorer hit showrooms in 1995. In addition to lightening the tire, Ford had replaced the Twin I-Beam with a short- and long-arm suspension, but didn't lower the engine or widen the chassis. Since the new suspension weighed less than the Twin I-Beam, the change actually raised the Explorer's center of gravity. What was even more indefensible, Ford engineers, in an attempt to make the car lighter, reduced the strength of the metal reinforcing the roof, which was already vulnerable to crush.

Lawsuits were sporadic until the tire weight design change was implemented and the new suspension system put in. Then rollover crashes mushroomed.

6 KHOU-TV

SIX MONTHS BEFORE DONNA BAILEY'S ACCIDENT, Anna Werner was trawling for ideas. An on-air reporter for KHOU-TV in Houston, Werner and the station's investigative news team known as "The Defenders" often juggled three stories at once. They had recently broadcast a segment on a local New Age doctor who sexually assaulted his patients while claiming to heal their chakras, and were now investigating possible police links to Mexican organized crime. Since Werner was a known TV news personality, she knew to stay away from the undercover portion of the operation, which required the use of a hidden camera in a raunchy bar. This meant she had time to chat up sources.

Werner decided to check in with Lance Olinde, a local attorney. From experience, Werner knew trial lawyers were a good source for stories with sweeps-week oomph. They represented disaffected clientele right out of the pages of the tabloids—of the hot-coffee-blanched-my-thighs, fast-food-made-me-fat, a-power-station-gave-me-cancer, I-found-a-syringe-in-my-soda-can variety. Werner had met Olinde while looking into a local dental clinic, a jack-in-the-box for dentists that offered low-cost care. The clinic was staffed by salespeople who pressured patients into having unnecessary work done (phantom root canals, orthodontia) while, worse, others were misdiagnosed and mistreated. Werner interviewed one of Olinde's clients on the air, who'd had six teeth pulled when a periodontal cleaning would have cured her gingivitis.

"Working on anything interesting?" Werner asked.

"I have this case about something called 'tread separation,' " replied Olinde. Werner didn't know what it was, so Olinde explained, "It's when the tread peels off your tire." He told Werner about Kelli Gilmore, who was driving her two boys in an Explorer on a highway leading to Lubbock, Texas, when the tread skimmed off the tire at 60 mph. Panicking, she stomped on the brakes and the Explorer shot right. The nose of the car slid off the road. The car tipped end over end and the roof caved in. On the first or second roll, the nose of the Explorer slammed into the ground. Gilmore's seat was wrenched from the Explorer's frame and her seatbelt snapped. She flew 20 feet out of the car before colliding with a tree. The police found four-year-old Shawn Gilmore shaking his dead mother, crying, "My mom's asleep, I can't wake her up," while his brother lay unconscious in the mutilated vehicle.

Olinde hired an expert to do an accident reconstruction, who told him he had been encountering a growing number of cases involving Firestone tread separations on Ford Explorers. The expert postulated there might be an epoxy issue with the tire, which could be exacerbated by heat. How else to explain all these Ford Explorer tread separations clustered in hot-weather states?

Werner was intrigued. After she got off the phone she pitched the story to her producer, David Raziq, formerly of ABC's 20/20. She didn't have to venture far to find him. The office they shared was barely big enough to hold their desks. Greeting the idea with healthy skepticism, Raziq asked, "Do you really think there could be something catastrophically wrong with these tires?"

Werner didn't know but thought it was worth checking into.

Raziq wasn't so sure. Hadn't the competition already beaten them to it? He recalled a KPRC story from 1996 about a Firestone tread separation, when local TV newsman Stephen Gauvain had died in an Explorer rollover. Werner said her source thought there might be more cases out there. Raziq considered this. From the way Werner described it, the accident was reminiscent of Gauvain's. The tread had wrapped around the axle and the car came to a screeching halt. Gauvain hadn't been wearing a safety belt and was launched from the car when it rolled over. Raziq told her if she wanted to proceed she would have to locate many more examples.

Werner agreed, but when she followed up with Olinde, he apologized for not being able to offer further assistance. A rival firm from Florida had snatched the case out from under him. That was the trouble with his business. No one was safe from sharks. Olinde referred Werner to two other local attorneys with Explorer rollover clients. The first told Werner about a client, Cynthia Jackson, who had lost her husband and legs in an Explorer rollover outside Houston. The second represented the parents of 14-year-old Jessica LeAnn Taylor, a junior high school cheerleader from Mexia, Texas, who died on her way to a homecoming football game. As the tread on the left-rear Firestone ATX tire came off the Explorer she was riding in, the SUV tumbled over.

"That's amazing," Raziq said when Werner told him, "but let's not overly localize. We need to look beyond Texas."

"I'm way ahead of you," Werner replied. Cynthia Jackson's attorney had referred her to his tire expert, Rex Grogan, who claimed he'd had nine new cases since the beginning of the year and five of them involved the ATX tire and Explorer. Keep going, Raziq advised.

She did. Werner prided herself on her persistence. In her mid-30s and TV pretty, Werner was a tenacious investigator. She had been at KHOU for a year and a half after kicking around TV stations in the Midwest for a decade. Illinois born, bred, and educated, she majored in journalism at Northern Illinois University and paid her dues in radio before moving to TV. The salary at her first job in Rockford, Illinois, barely edged her over the poverty line. In 1987 she took a position as a general assignment reporter in Peoria, where for seven years she covered city hall and churned out two-minute hard news pieces. Eventually she worked her way up to station anchor for both the 5 and 10 o'clock news. It was a plum position, but she knew she didn't just want to read the news; she wanted to uncover it.

Around the time she married in 1995, she landed a reporting job at a 24-hour news outfit. But while she was in Chicago her husband, a computer technician, lived in Indianapolis. Werner cried for days when they returned home to separate cities after their honeymoon. She liked her job, but wasn't willing to ruin her marriage over it. This prompted her to seek work at WISH-TV, a CBS affiliate in Indianapolis, where her boss told her she could do investigative pieces as long as she anchored the Early Show, which meant starting her day at 4 a.m.

At WISH Werner hit her stride as an investigative journalist. She was honored with an Edward R. Murrow award for her series on abuse at a state center for the mentally ill, in which she used a hidden camera to capture violent and abusive behavior on the part of caretakers. The distressing story prompted the governor to fly in a helicopter to the facility and hold a dramatic press conference. The state shut down the facility and two workers were charged.

A year later Werner and her husband relocated to Houston, where she joined an investigative news team KHOU was developing. "The Defenders" was popular among viewers and heavily promoted by the station.

As Werner became immersed in research, she began to believe the American legal system was designed in part to help corporations conceal malfeasance. Citing the need to protect trade secrets, judges allowed companies to keep incriminating documents under court seal and settlement amounts quiet. But was it a proprietary secret that customer warranty claims for Explorer-mounted tires were skyrocketing, as Firestone claimed in one lawsuit?

This passive conspiracy between judges and corporations did not just afflict Ford and Firestone litigation. Asbestos, car-door latches, medical devices, tobacco, and overly abrasive toothbrushes: name the lawsuit-prone product and some corporate litigator somewhere was petitioning the court to keep a lid on it. It let companies limit bad publicity, victims get larger settlements, and courts clear crowded dockets. The only way for the families to gain access to the documents to prove their case was to agree to protective orders.

The legal system also allowed corporations with defective products to deal with their mistakes one victim at a time. With each settlement the companies made one irrevocable demand: secrecy. In exchange, the victim, often in dire financial straits because of the accident, would receive hundreds of thousands—if not millions—of dollars in compensation. No lawyer who in good conscience was looking out for his client's best interests could turn that down, even if it meant signing a nondisclosure agreement. Better to grab guaranteed money than take your chances at trial, because as a plaintiff only three things could happen then, two of them bad. It put the lawyer in a difficult position. He had to balance moral responsibility to the public with fiduciary duty to the family. In the end he was bound by law to do what was best for his client.

Unfortunately it strengthened Ford and Firestone's hand. The protective orders, combined with confidentiality agreements in settlements, allowed the companies to state publicly that there were no known problems with the tires, even as they continued to settle cases around the country.

Werner wondered what the National Highway Traffic Safety Administration had on Ford and Firestone. She visited the NHTSA Web site to access its database. She typed in "Bridgestone"; nothing. Then "Firestone." Again nothing. The tires were original equipment on Ford Explorers, so she ventured over to "Trucks" and plugged in "Ford Explorer." Digging deeper she located a subset labeled "Tire Complaints." There, Werner discovered two-dozen complaints that had been assigned numbers by the agency's Office of Defect Investigations (ODI).

In one letter dated Nov. 30, 1998, a Ford Explorer owner claimed his Firestone tire tread "peeled off like an orange . . . Imagine my shock when the mechanics looked at my tire and told me I was lucky to be alive." He added that his mechanics informed him that Firestone tires on Explorers "are known to lose tread and contribute to or cause Ford

Explorers to flip." An irate Texas motorist wrote NHTSA to say she lost control of her 1992 Explorer when her rear passenger side tire fell apart: "I hit an 18-wheeler and bounced off his truck—twice. I then crossed the median of Highway 288 toward oncoming traffic. I have and will continue to tell everyone that these tires are a hazard and should be recalled."

After printing out summaries of the complaints Werner contacted NHTSA and inquired about the two-dozen deaths being blamed on the Explorer and Firestone tire.

"What are you talking about?" responded an NHTSA publicist. Every year NHTSA investigators sifted through 50,000 complaints from consumers and lawyers on everything from brakes to child seats to tires and vehicle safety. The agency launched preliminary investigations after receiving as few as five complaints. "Where did you get this information?"

Werner told her.

When an NHTSA researcher failed to locate the complaints on the agency's Web site, the publicist asked Werner to fax the agency a list of all the cases, which she did, along with their corresponding ODI numbers. Later NHTSA would blame a cataloging glitch as the reason it didn't respond sooner to the crisis. Firestone complaints had been filed under the Ford Explorer, since the tires were considered original equipment.

Over the next few weeks Werner amassed a pile of court documents—civil complaints, depositions, engineer's reports, expert testimony, motions, countermotions, and trial transcripts. All told she identified 20 rollover cases in Texas, Florida, and New Mexico, involving 30 deaths in which the victims blamed Ford and Firestone. She was struck by how similar they were: tread comes off, driver loses control, SUV rolls over, passengers killed or critically injured. It was like seeing the same horror movie over and over with different actors.

Raziq suggested Werner contact Joan Claybrook, president of Public Citizen in Washington, D.C., the consumer advocacy organization founded by Ralph Nader. A former head of the National Highway Traffic Safety Administration, Claybrook was the first to use the word "recall" in connection with the Firestone ATX Wilderness tire and Ford Explorer. "If you have that many (cases)," Claybrook told Werner, "the actual number is twenty times higher."

When Raziq heard this, his jaw dropped. Up to then he hadn't fully comprehended the scope of the problem. He scheduled the piece for the February 2000 sweeps, less than a month away. Raziq advised Werner to schedule on-camera interviews and, to make the story airtight, track down a Firestone worker who could talk about what went on inside the plant.

A few days later, Werner and KHOU cameraman Chris Henao pulled up outside the home of Cynthia Jackson in a Ford Explorer. The station maintained a fleet of them, all equipped with Firestone AT tires. Before leaving the station Henao and Werner counted almost a dozen Explorers in the parking lot, and a few of the even bigger Excursions, which she thought looked like Explorers on steroids.

Werner asked Henao if they should ditch the car down the street and carry their gear inside. "I wonder if we're rubbing salt in her wound," she said.

"I don't know," Henao replied, "but I'm going to think about it every time I get in and out of the freakin' car," he said, getting out of the car.

Werner laughed. What was even funnier was the irrational invincibility she felt riding in the Explorer, as if catastrophes only happened to other people. She wondered if the Explorer, parked on its Wilderness tires, really was unsafe. It sure didn't feel that way when they rode around in it. But that could be because she had been brainwashed by the TV commercials. Branded into her mind was the image of an Explorer transporting a family in comfort to the hinterlands. Or maybe it was the vehicle's macho exterior. Perhaps it was the commanding view of surrounding traffic. Most likely it was a defense mechanism, a way for her to get her job done: blasé courage in the face of unknowable danger.

Jackson greeted them in a wheelchair, a blanket modestly covering her lap. After Henao perched his Sony video camera on a tripod and set up the lights, Jackson recounted the June 1997 accident that changed her life.

While her husband CJ napped beside her, Jackson was driving to Houston in their 1994 Explorer after visiting Galveston. "As I went to change lanes, I heard a *pop*," Jackson said. She yelled at her husband, "Hey, baby! Wake up! The truck is shaking!" The next thing she knew she woke up in the hospital. That was when she found out her legs had been amputated and her husband was dead and buried.

The interview with Cathy and Jim Taylor, the parents of 14-year-old Jessica LeAnn Taylor, was even more heart wrenching. Jessica's death left an unscalable void in her parents' lives. The mother collapsed into tears before Werner could pose her first question. "She was my little girl, she was my little girl," Jim Taylor murmured over and over, shaking his head in disbelief more than a year after the accident, as if it had happened yesterday. A seasoned professional, Werner had interviewed her share of victims—women who had been raped, parents whose child had been kidnapped, families who lost everything when their homes burned down. She had learned to focus on the job and not get emotionally tangled. But even she choked up. She could just feel their grief. She dared anyone to sit there and not tear up. For a minute, Werner felt guilty about capturing the Taylors' tragedy on video and despised what she did for a living. Then she remembered she was in a position to make a difference.

A few days later Werner and Henao flew to San Diego to interview tire expert Grogan, who told them that tread separations often made it impossible to control the vehicle. "The driver is panicking and doesn't know what to do, in fact, there is very little that he can do," Grogan said. In Washington, Joan Claybrook was astonished by the number of accidents that Werner had found. She blamed both companies: "These are original equipment tires," Claybrook said. "Ford ordered these tires put on their vehicles."

Keeping her promise to Raziq, Werner continued her search for a source inside Firestone. She finally found one in a deposition for *Van Etten v. Bridgestone/Firestone*, a tread separation suit. Alan Hogan, a former Firestone tire builder from Wilson, North Carolina, testified for the plaintiffs that the company sometimes used old rubber stock in its tires and that quality took a back seat to productivity. Immediately Werner got on the phone to Georgia attorney Rowe Brogdon, who put her in touch with his witness.

At first Hogan would not consent to the interview, but he changed his mind when Werner reminded him it would only be shown in Houston. "No one in North Carolina will see it," she promised. The next day she and Henao met Hogan at a Hilton hotel in Raleigh. "I didn't like building bad tires; I didn't like it, didn't like it at all," Hogan told them. A mechanic and former tire builder whose father was a "gung-ho, gum-dipped Firestone man if there ever was one," Hogan divulged that workers were under constant pressure to make quotas and sometimes "cut corners" if they fell behind.

Now that the research was complete, it was time to talk to the companies. Werner contacted Firestone company spokesperson Christine Karbowiak, who accused Werner of conspiring with plaintiff attorneys and demanded to know whom Werner had consulted. When Werner refused to reveal her sources, Karbowiak shunted her aside to an in-house lawyer, who asked Werner to read off the names on each lawsuit. Three days before the segment was scheduled to air, the company sent KHOU a letter. In it Firestone claimed the accidents were caused by poor tire care. "Out of respect for the persons involved," the letter read, "Firestone took no steps to publicize the results of its investigation of the incidents."

Ford also turned down the chance to appear on-camera but in a statement said tread separation accidents were "isolated events." When they did occur, they were the driver's fault.

7 BROADCAST NEWS

ON FEB. 7, 2000, THE DAY KHOU aired Werner's story, the Nasdaq index, riding a wave of technological exuberance, shot up 9.2 percent in its biggest weekly percentage gain in 26 years, ending at a record high: 4,244. At the same time, smokestack industrial giant Goodyear's stock was falling as the company, which controlled 20 percent of the global market for tires, suffered serious operational difficulties. It was presidential primary season, as Gov. George W. Bush, Jr., and Sen. John McCain sniped at each other in South Carolina while New York mayor Rudolph Giuliani, running for the Senate, criticized Hillary Rodham Clinton because a soundman played Billy Joel's "Captain Jack" to warm up the crowd at a campaign event. Giuliani claimed the song glorified drug use.

At 10 p.m., KHOU viewers in Houston saw the usual splashy swirl of News at 10 graphics in shades of electric blue, dissolving to a man and woman behind a desk.

"Good evening, I'm Greg Hurst."

"And I'm Lisa Forondo. Thanks for joining us."

"They are among the most popular vehicles in Texas," Hurst said. "Ford Explorers: But if you're driving one you could be in danger."

Forondo continued, "Tonight, we have an 11 news investigation revolving around tire trouble. Investigative Reporter Anna Werner is here with exclusive information that could be vital for your family's safety . . . Anna?"

Werner read from the teleprompter. "For much of the time they've been on the market, Ford Explorers have been equipped with these tires: the Firestone Radial ATX. And they're still being sold and used on some Explorers. But experts are now starting to notice what they say is a string of accidents with Explorers—and those tires—a combination they say could be dangerous."

The story she had worked on for five months began right after the "Defenders Investigates" logo faded from the screen. Werner watched the feed on the monitor, feeling helpless like she always did when her stories played out on TV.

The piece began with a wedding video: Cynthia and CJ Jackson dancing.

Instead of leading with the accident like Werner had done in her initial draft, Raziq chose to start with Cynthia Jackson's wedding. He remembered what it was like when he found out that Steve Gauvain, a colleague and friend of his, had died. Raziq wanted the audience to feel how devastating these accidents were, not just to the victims but to the people in their lives.

"We were just two middle-aged people trying to start over and to have fun," Cynthia Jackson said.

Werner narrated: *One June day in 1997 Jackson and her husband packed up her Ford Explorer and took off for Galveston. But as Jackson drove back to Houston something went horribly wrong.*

"As I went to change lanes I heard a pop," Jackson said.

What she heard was the tread coming off a back tire. A Firestone Radial ATX that came with the car.

Jackson: "I yelled at my husband, hey baby, wake up! The truck is shaking!"

Then the car began to roll.

"Next thing I remember is waking up in the hospital," Jackson said.

And she was facing bad news. Both of her legs would have to be amputated below the knee. Henao had patched together a series of powerful images: A photo of Jackson in a wheelchair, one on her metal legs, on crutches in physical therapy, shots of her artificial foot and ankle. *But worst of all, her husband of a year and a half was dead, leaving her with one haunting memory.*

A photo of Cynthia and CJ kissing at their wedding.

"So the last time you remember seeing CJ was when he looked up?" asked Werner the day she and Henao visited her.

Jackson, overcome by tears, could only nod.

"Do you find yourself thinking about that?"

"Yes," Jackson whispered.

Now, she does the best she can with a life that's very different than the one she had planned.

They cut to video of Jackson at her church in a wheelchair, playing the piano and singing with the choir.

"Even after three years, it's still pretty hard," Jackson said.

But Cynthia Jackson wasn't alone.

Werner let Cathy Taylor introduce the next victim: "Jessica LeAnn Taylor . . ."

Cathy and Jim Taylor's daughter loved being a cheerleader. One afternoon in October she was heading to a homecoming pep rally.

"She had a big smile on her face," Cathy Taylor remembered. "She said, 'Mom, I love you and I'll see you tomorrow.' "

But there was no tomorrow for Jessica. A few minutes later, a terrifying crash. Police say that the tires, Firestone ATX, came apart at highway speed. The force caused the Explorer to flip three times, and Jessica was killed.

"She was prepared for her trip to homecoming," said Taylor, crying by her daughter's grave, which was decorated with homecoming ribbons. "We just didn't know it was the final homecoming."

The scene dissolved to a "stand in," a visual insert Werner and Henao filmed the day before. Henao had been grouchy because it was raining, which ruined his light. Werner suggested her garage. Her husband was a neat freak, every tool in its place, the floor spic and span. She often teased him about how it looked like a Hollywood set. Werner and Henao drove over and parked inside. With the company Explorer in the background, Werner propped up a shredded Firestone tire on her husband's bicycle stand and draped the tread over it.

While it poured outside, Henao filmed her walking around the car toward the tire stand. *But as it turns out, those are just two of many similar cases the Defenders found all over Texas, as many as a dozen over the past few years,* a pre-taped Werner said. *And all of them have a familiar combination: a Ford Explorer and a Firestone ATX tire with what's called "tread separation," where the tread literally peels off the tire.* To better illustrate, Werner lifted the tread off the tire like it were a toupee. *Experts say that with some vehicles, it can mean a devastating rollover crash.*

They transitioned to Joan Claybrook in her office at Public Citizen. "I think it calls for an explanation and to me there is very, very strong evidence for a recall," she said. "I am sure that this number is not all of them. . . . I'm totally shocked that leading up to the year 2000, we manufacture and have this problem."

Rex Grogan, whom Werner identified as the "dean of tire analysts," chimed in, "I am seeing a lot of these, and they're coming thicker and faster now." The reason they are so dangerous is because "the driver is panic-stricken, doesn't know what to do. In fact, there's very little he can do."

The manufacturers say otherwise. For example, take this video produced by Ford. It supposedly shows that when the tread comes off a tire the driver can easily remain in control of the vehicle.

"The driver is an experienced driver; he is expecting something to happen," Grogan pointed out. "This isn't the same as Joe Public who's driving along, not anticipating danger."

Why are the tires coming apart?

"I didn't like building bad tires," said Alan Hogan, strolling on camera with Werner. "But within the walls of the plant it's acceptable."

Hogan used to work at a Firestone plant in North Carolina, where workers were under constant pressure to make their quotas.

"When you come up short and you've only got a couple hours left in the day, me as well as other people, might have to cut corners," Hogan said.

One of the things done was to use old rubber stock, or what tire builders call "dry."

"When you would encounter dry stock, what would happen to that stock?" Werner asked him that day in Raleigh.

"I would reject it," Hogan said. "But if that's all they had, that's what you're gonna use."

In fact, the Defenders obtained this court deposition of one of Firestone's plant supervisors, said Werner, as the camera panned to a legal-looking document, the deposition of David Eugene Kalamajka. *In it, he confirms that workers were sometimes told to use old rubber stock to make tires. And what does Firestone say? The company would not answer our questions about the use of older rubber stock . . . and declined an on-camera interview. But officials gave this statement, saying the company has "full confidence in the performance of Firestone Radial ATX tires." And company officials point out that although 12 million have been manufactured that "no court or jury has ever found any deficiency in these tires."*

Alan Hogan didn't think that mattered. "Somebody from Firestone needs to tell them that they're sorry." *Especially, Hogan says, in the case of Daniel Van Etten. He was a 22-year-old from Florida with hopes of a pro-football career, whose family claimed he died after the tread separated from a Firestone ATX tire. It's the case in which Hogan testified . . .*

"So what do you think you would say to the Van Ettens if you met them now?" Werner asked.

"I'm sorry you lost your son," Hogan said. "Sorry people like me were building rags your son was driving on."

And what about Ford Motor company, who for six years issued the Firestone ATX tires with its new Explorers? Ford also turned down an on-camera interview but sent us this statement. In it, the company declined to answer questions about tires but said tread separation accidents were the driver's fault—that they quote,

*"clearly resulted from driver error." Ford called the 20 to 30 accidents we docu-
mented "isolated" incidents.*

Something Rex Grogan takes issue with.

"What you're saying is, it's all right to kill a few people so long as
you don't kill too many," Grogan said. "Is that moral?"

When Werner asked Joan Claybrook whether she believed that Ford
and Firestone were responsible, Claybrook responded, "Absolutely. No
question about it, because these are original equipment tires, Ford
ordered these tires to put on these vehicles."

The story came full circle, back to Cynthia Jackson, who was in
church, singing and playing the piano.

*Meanwhile, crash victims like Cynthia Jackson struggle to put their lives back
together again, Werner narrated. She says it is only now, after three long years,
that she can finally sing a favorite song of hope.*

Jackson, a capella: "And it goes, 'you don't have to worry, and don't
you be afraid. Joy comes in the morning, trouble it don't last always.' "

They displayed the toll-free number for the Defenders Investigative
hotline and National Highway Traffic Safety Administration. When it
was over, co-anchor Lisa Forondo remarked, "A lot of people looking for
some answers."

As if by cue Channel 11's switchboards jammed up immediately.

THE CALLS AND E-MAILS CAME IN SO FURIOUSLY the station couldn't
keep up. The news desk was inundated. Werner and Raziq's voicemails
overflowed. When Werner reviewed them the next morning, she was
struck by the dozens of viewers who called to say they too had experienced problems with the tread coming off Firestone Radial ATX tires
mounted on Ford Explorers. "The same thing happened to me." "I
thought I was the only one." "I didn't know other people were having
problems." There were sad stories from people who had lost friends and
family.

The next morning Raziq swung by a local Firestone dealership on his
way to work and saw a long line of Explorer owners out front. KHOU
station management ordered a week's worth of follow-ups.

It didn't take long for the companies to respond. In a statement, Ford
pointed out that "no government agency, court of law or jury has ever
found a stability issue with the Ford Explorer," and said that the Explorer met or exceeded government safety regulations. Karbowiak of Firestone dispatched a threatening letter to the station's general manager and
parent company in Dallas. In it she claimed the story contained "false-

hoods and misrepresentations that improperly disparage Firestone and its product, the Radial ATX model tire," and gave "the unfortunate appearance that KHOU is more concerned with sensationalism and ratings during the February sweeps period than its commitment to the presentation of truthful and objective reporting. [You] should be concerned with the obvious fact that your reporter, Anna Werner, and/or her producers have been co-opted by plaintiffs' personal injury lawyers and their purported 'expert' witnesses to present a one-sided view of Firestone's product."

The Firestone spokeswoman didn't have kind words for Alan Hogan either. She claimed he never built an ATX tire for Firestone, and that he left the company after brief employment, "disgruntled and unhappy."

Nevertheless, after complaints began rolling in to the National Highway Traffic Safety Administration in response to KHOU's story, the agency announced it was opening an "initial evaluation."

8 SPEED BUMP

TAB TURNER DIDN'T WATCH THE KHOU REPORT, but he certainly heard about it. The attorney for Jessica LeAnn Taylor's parents had asked Turner to help develop the case for trial, which propelled him into a major donnybrook with Firestone over discovery. The company's attorneys had been papering the judge with motions, contesting witnesses and evidence, denying depositions. They fought especially hard to keep consumer-complaints data and lawsuits under seal. Firestone claimed it was aware of only one accident similar to Taylor's, as if Jessica LeAnn Taylor were a statistical anomaly—just one of two people to die from tread separation–induced rollovers out of the millions of American drivers who jammed the nation's highways. This, Turner knew, was pure fantasy on Firestone's part. He himself represented half-a-dozen ATX tread separation victims.

In November 1999, Texas state judge Sam Bournias directed Firestone to turn over all complaints concerning its ATX, ATX II, and Wilderness tires nationwide, plus any lawsuits and employee depositions taken in these legal actions. Court order in hand, Taylor's attorney dug through a Firestone database of complaints in and outside the United States. When KHOU's story aired, he and Turner had tallied some 1,100 similar accidents, the vast majority involving Ford Explorers and Firestone tires. By their count, 88 people had been killed and 250 injured, three times the number KHOU reported. Moreover, 57 tread separation lawsuits had been filed against Firestone. And those were just the incidents in Firestone's database. Turner believed there were more out there.

Problem was, Turner couldn't talk about them. Not with other lawyers, not with the government, certainly not with the press. Firestone had cloaked the data under judge's seal, claiming it was proprietary information, a designation the two fought tooth and nail, until they convinced another judge to free the data, which helped punctuate the veil of secrecy surrounding Firestone.

Turner was lukewarm to the idea of passing these findings on to NHTSA. To him, the agency was just one more pothole on the road to a settlement or verdict. Turner figured government regulators would respond to the information he had dug up the way it always did: with a coat of whitewash. The agency would launch a slipshod investigation it would eventually drop, and then the tire maker could claim NHTSA had investigated and found that the company had complied with the letter of the law. Firestone would then use the government's findings against his clients in court.

Once an avid enforcer of auto safety, NHTSA since 1981 has been under the purview of House Energy & Commerce Committee chairman, Rep. John Dingell (D-Mich.), whose suburban Detroit district encompassed Ford Motor Co. headquarters and tens of thousands of autoworkers. Chairman for more than two decades, Dingell bragged there wasn't an industry in the entire country untouched by his committee. It controlled in whole or in part half the legislation that wound through House committees and subcommittees. Its somewhat conflicting mission was to oversee autos, railroads, nuclear power and the environment, oil and gas and telecommunications, securities and health care, all of which combined to form 75 percent of this nation's gross domestic product.

Known by friends and foes alike as "Big John," the 6-foot-3-inch, 200-pound Dingell was 100 percent gruff-talking, God-fearing, assembly line American. While heading a committee that through its actions and policies had national and international ramifications, Dingell proudly lived by the axiom, "All politics is local."

"I was sent [to Washington] to serve and protect the best interests of the 500,000-plus people in my district," Dingell declared. "I'm going to do that to my level best, and I won't apologize to anyone." On his congressional Web site he promised to respond "to every constituent request as expeditiously as possible." And he was not above using bare-knuckle tactics to protect his home turf: When Sen. Richard H. Bryan (D-Nev.) sponsored legislation to require carmakers to increase fuel economy 40 percent, Dingell, in a nasty tit-for-tat, pushed for a nuclear-waste dump in Nevada. *Business Week* labeled the hardball tactics "vintage Dingell."

"There has been a symbiotic relationship between John Dingell and the auto industry," Joan Claybrook charged. This was borne out by his campaign finance records, which read like a *Who's Who* of the auto industry. His biggest campaign donor: Ford. When it came to regulating gas guzzlers, Dingell was a cash nuzzler; he protected his contributors' interests. That meant the 70-something Dingell didn't much like the notion of mass transit or a gasoline tax or anything else that could discourage Americans from driving. He didn't care for proposals to mandate higher fuel standards, legislate better pollution controls, create a rollover standard, or strengthen the roofs on SUVs.

At the same time, Dingell wished to be viewed as a public servant who used his prodigious political powers to protect factory workers, consumers, the weak and downtrodden. In the late 1980s, when American automakers were under siege by Japanese car companies, Dingell took the term "Buy American" to a new realm by insisting only U.S.-made parts be used in his hip replacement operation. He once refused to apologize for referring to Honda Motor Co. executives as "the little yellow people," explaining, "I've heard them called worse." He trumpeted investigations that uncovered bribery in the approval of generic drugs and over-billing of the government on university research contracts. He investigated pharmaceutical companies, banks, and universities.

But never the automobile industry. That was strictly off limits.

NHTSA was an agency whose decisions could cost or save auto companies hundreds of millions of dollars. It set vehicle safety and fuel economy regulations and ordered the recall of defective products. Consequently, carmakers made it their mission to hamstring the agency's ability to regulate. Their front man: John Dingell. Not only did the Michigan lawmaker repeatedly badger agency heads to cut back on enforcement, he held up political appointments until he ended up with someone palatable to the automobile industry. Year after year he scuttled long-term reauthorization of NHTSA, which meant the agency was forced to survive on a series of stopgap funding measures. He pushed for a tangle of bureaucracy so investigations could take 18 months to conclude regardless of how deadly the defect. He stifled debate over auto safety standards and frustrated attempts to force Detroit to build cars with better crash protection. He blocked revision of the Clean Air Act for a decade, as well as curbing measures to mandate air bags and improve gas mileage.

But Dingell wasn't the only one riding shotgun for car companies in Congress. Between 1990 and 2002, the auto industry donated some $77 million to federal candidates and the political parties, $12.5 million alone during the 2002 election cycle, and about $37 million on lobbying in 2000. As Arianna Huffington put it, "you can bet that money wasn't spent trying to convince Congress to designate a 'Windshield Wiper Appreciation Week.' "

The last time had NHTSA flexed any muscle, Jimmy Carter was president, Turner was a star high school football player, and Joan Claybrook was at the agency's helm. After the 1978 Pinto and Firestone 500 recalls, Claybrook proposed tough safety standards for tires and light trucks that would have affected all future SUVs. But Ronald Reagan rescinded several of them—including a tire-inflation warning light located on the dashboard—and NHTSA never recovered. Now it was just another underfunded, over-bureaucratized government entity with scant power to police or punish corporate malfeasance. It hasn't done much regulating since 1981, when President Ronald Reagan gutted the agency as part of his campaign to shrink government.

Turner disliked NHTSA for a whole bunch of reasons. It had not revised its standard for fuel tank safety in 25 years, despite the agency's findings that thousands of deaths and injuries occur every year in fire-related crashes. It failed to upgrade a 30-year-old standard concerning head restraints, despite hundreds of thousands of injuries annually and billions of dollars in whiplash payments. It declined to set a minimum strength requirement for latches on rear lift gates of minivans, acting only after reports of 37 deaths of people ejected from the rear of the vans. Even though SUVs have a well-documented tendency to roll over—necessitating a warning sticker affixed to every driver's side visor—roof-crush standards have not been strengthened since 1973 and the agency never bothered to formulate a rollover standard. More specifically, it never recalled the Jeep CJ, Suzuki Samurai, or Bronco II even when they were proven to tip over at speeds as low as 28 mph.

At one time the agency concluded that to reduce the rollover rate would mean getting rid of every Ford Explorer, as well as other midsized SUVs, but that would require "drastic design changes for a vehicle type sought after by consumers." In essence, a governmental safety agency was claiming it didn't have the authority to remove an unsafe vehicle from the roads.

While auto safety was a major public health issue and the leading killer of Americans ages 1 to 34, the National Institute for Dental Research received more money than NHTSA. The automakers made sure the agency's budget in 2000 was a third less than it had been in 1980, the result of three terms of pro-business Republican presidents and eight years of a business-friendly Democratic administration. Government allowed the auto industry to regulate itself, which was like allowing drivers to decide which traffic laws to obey.

Ford has played a leading role in weakening NHTSA. A Ford "policy and strategy" memo from January 1986 shows the company led the effort to kill auto safety measures being debated in Congress, including provisions covering improved vehicle crashworthiness and protection, stronger side impact requirements, and criminal penalties against corporate officers who willfully conceal defects. "Through the efforts of a broad-based coalition led by Ford, we were able to keep the mandatory air bag bill from moving forward, delete the criminal penalty provisions, modify the vehicle side impact requirements, and limit the vehicle crashworthiness proposal to a [Department of Transportation]-coordinated research project. If a bill emerges from the Congress in 1986, we expect it to be in a form that we would find acceptable."

NHTSA also became an incubator for car industry witnesses. Since Dingell assumed the position of Commerce chairman in 1981, there has been a revolving door between the agency and the industry it monitored. Former agency heads—with all the prestige their titles could buy—paraded before juries as consultants for automobile companies. They could then (truthfully) testify that the vehicle in question met or exceeded federal safety requirements with regards to roof crush or rollover propensity—standards they had scuttled as NHTSA administrators.

Others became heavyweight lobbyists. Andrew Card, former secretary of transportation, under which NHTSA operates, became president of the Automobile Manufacturers Association for six years before assuming the role of chief of staff for President George W. Bush, Jr. Diane Steed, who ran NHTSA from 1983 to 1989, accepted a job with a consulting firm for auto industry front groups. Jeffrey Miller, a former number-two man at the agency, morphed into a consultant for vehicle manufacturers and their suppliers. Former U.S. Army Maj. Gen. Jerry Curry, NHTSA chief from 1989 to 1993, became a well-compensated witness for automobile companies, as did William Boehly, an ex-top enforcement official for the agency.

As a practical matter, this meant Turner had to confront well-versed adversaries on the witness stand who cloaked themselves in the perceived impartiality and credibility of public service. Actually, he didn't mind. In fact, he enjoyed it. It offered the opportunity to discredit NHTSA by humbling one of its leaders. In Turner's experience, an expert witness never won you a case but sure could lose it for you. It all came down to credibility, which was something you couldn't buy.

In 1996 Turner faced Curry in a "sudden acceleration" case he brought against Ford, in which a malfunction in the electronic control system of the engine caused a late model Grand Marquis to speed off for no apparent reason. Two sisters, 75-year-old Jasmine Stell and 79-year-old Cecil Pugh, got into Stell's Grand Marquis at a shopping mall in

Little Rock. When Stell turned the ignition key, the car shot across the parking lot so fast one shopper had to leap onto the hood of his car to escape. In seconds the Marquis collided with a concrete planter and was completely totaled. Just before Stell died she told a medic she kept pumping the brake but the car kept going faster. The nimble shopper said he heard the sound of pumping brakes as the car sped by. But when the brakes were tested, they worked fine.

Because of a 1989 NHTSA study that concluded no sudden acceleration defect pattern existed—the agency blamed "driver error"—no lawyer had ever beaten Ford in any of these cases. The automaker's core witness was Curry, who supported the agency's position under oath.

At NHTSA Curry was, next to Dingell, the automobile industry's staunchest ally. Ignoring legal restrictions on lobbying by federal agencies, Curry created a slick crash-test film (complete with a voiceover) that warned of the dangers of tighter fuel standards. To ensure he got the results he wanted, Curry carefully chose the test vehicles: the Crown Victoria, one of the heaviest cars on the road; and two of the lightest— the Subaru Justy and Suzuki Swift, both Japanese imports. The resulting auto carnage package was leaked to the Coalition for Vehicle Choice, which used it in an ad campaign that equated better fuel economy with more traffic deaths. Nobody mentioned that the crash dummies in the small cars emerged from the experience intact; their crumple zones had worked as designed, forming a protective bubble around the passengers and dampening the impact.

On the witness stand facing Tab Turner, Curry offered an explanation for the women's accident. "If they do what the normal people do when that has been documented by the government, they put their foot on the wrong pedal." The federal government, he assured, would never permit dangerous vehicles to be sold. The crash, although tragic, was surely the driver's fault.

In court, Turner's currency were the facts and his ability to state his case. Reality was whatever he, the Ford lawyers, the judge, evidence, and all the witnesses cobbled together said it was. With that in mind he proceeded to eviscerate the general's credibility. He got Curry to acknowledge that after leaving the government's employ he went to work for the automobile industry as a $340-an-hour witness. Then Turner asked Curry how he could say the federal government wouldn't allow a dangerous vehicle to be sold. "What about the Pinto?" he asked.

This was a sensitive subject for Ford. The frightening image of a subcompact fireball was so indelibly etched in Americans' minds that *Saturday Night Live* created a macabre spoof: a Pinto lighter. But Curry couldn't just sit there in the witness box and bash his employer in front of a judge and jury—not for what he was being paid. "The Pinto got a very bad rap," Curry responded, his credibility up in smoke.

While preparing for the trial, Turner learned that Ford had collected owner complaints. Six months of discovery later, he'd located 1,000 of them—10 boxes worth. After digesting the information, Turner jetted around the nation to take depositions from a dozen upstanding citizens with exemplary driving records. He spoke to Virginia state trooper Ronald Campbell, who said when he turned the ignition to his wife's Grand Marquis to move it from in front of the house to the driveway it raced across the yard, and no matter how hard he pressed the brake, it kept accelerating until he shut off the ignition, stopping inches from a propane tank. He consulted with three Secret Service agents, including one who protected former vice president Dan Quayle, and each described a frightening instance when a Ford leapt forward from park and kept going, even though the drivers hit the brake. He interviewed David McEachen, a California Superior Court judge, who claimed his Ford Crown Victoria shot forward and banged into his garage.

But the testimony that killed Ford came from Joseph Gorman, a driver for William Clay Ford and his wife, Martha Firestone Ford. One day, after Mrs. Ford got into the car to spend the day seeing the sights in New Orleans, Gorman prepared to pull out from in front of the hotel and shifted from park to drive, keeping his foot on the brake. "There was a sudden surge," he recalled. "I immediately hit the brake, but the car did not stop. We hit the front of the building, the pillars . . . and I think we hit one or two automobiles that were parked along the front of the building and then we came to a stop." In seconds the car had gone 60 feet. "I just couldn't get the car to stop, and I was scared for my life and scared for Mrs. Ford." Gorman said Ford engineers didn't believe his story. "One of the engineers indicated to me that he thought that it was human error," he testified.

"Was it?" Turner asked.

"I told the gentleman that I didn't think so."

The jury didn't either. In a seemingly unwinnable case, Turner won a $311,000 verdict against Ford. (The automaker settled on appeal.)

Turner received another transmission case via referral from Texas litigator John O'Quinn, who told Turner his firm had a Ford case scheduled to go to trial in Oklahoma in a week. Although a law firm he hired in Tulsa had spent a lot of money, he couldn't get a good feel as to how the lawyers were doing. He asked Turner to check it out.

After Turner flew to Tulsa to read the file, he reported back to O'Quinn that the case was "a lost cause." Nevertheless, since he had dealt with Ford a number of times before, Turner told O'Quinn he would try to recoup his expenses for him. The case involved a high school student, Craig Simon, who was days away from graduation when he stopped for gas. While he served himself, another customer pulled up in a 1976 Ford Galaxy, put it in "park" and left it idling while he ran in for a cup of coffee. Without warning the "rooster tail" transmission—so-called because of the way the gear cog was shaped—jumped into reverse. The Galaxy backed into Simon, pinning him between the two cars and severing his leg at the knee.

Turner brought home half a box of Ford discovery documents to study and found that Ford had received numerous complaints about the C5 transmission before. All it took was a certain vibration and the car could skip from "park" to "reverse," prompting Ford to recall the "vibration damper" in its C5 transmission in 1985.

But when he approached Ford about a settlement, Ford's lead counsel Bob Grant laughed him off. Turner knew his case was weak, and the more he researched it the worse it got. The driver had installed the car's transmission himself and the car had lurched from park to reverse on several other occasions. The vehicle should never have been on the road.

In the end, however, not only did Turner win, he convinced the judge to levy sanctions against the automaker. Just before trial, Ford claimed it did not possess an index of all its documents, which Turner knew was untrue since he had already snagged it in another case against Ford. He had a paralegal drive the document from his office in Little Rock to Tulsa. The judge fined the automaker a couple of hundred thousand dollars and ordered one of its lawyers to teach a seminar on ethics for the local Bar Association. (Ford appealed, ultimately settling.)

It turned out the problem wasn't confined to the Marquis and Galaxy.

There were stuck-throttle complaints for virtually every Ford product line—the Explorer, F-series pickup trucks, Crown Victoria, Lincoln Continental, Mercury Marquis, Taurus. But when customers confronted Ford, the company invariably blamed the driver, claiming a) he must have confused the accelerator with the brake, or b) a frayed floor mat had pinned the gas pedal to the floor. When victims requested that NHTSA investigate, the agency based its findings on Ford's statistics and a priori accepted the carmaker's contention there couldn't be a design defect.

Although it might seem farfetched that a car on its own could suddenly act as if taken over by a poltergeist, there was a logical explanation.

For 20 years Ford offered the option of "cruise control," but had never gotten all the bugs out. In depositions, Ford engineers admitted the system could fail in a variety of ways: It could misinterpret electronic signals and without notice skip into highway speed; react to radio transmissions and suddenly race out of control; and fail to shut off when the brakes were engaged.

In 1999, Ford recalled 31,000 Ford Focus compacts due to a defect with the speed control cable, which "could develop and cause intermittent speed control operation or prevent the throttle from returning to idle. A throttle that does not return to idle could result in unexpected acceleration, increasing the risk of a crash." It also had to recall 279,000 Lincoln Town Cars, Mercury Grand Marquis and Ford Crown Victoria sedans from 1992 and 1993, equipped with factory-installed cruise control. Ford admitted "a potentially defective cruise control deactivation switch could short-circuit, which in turn could overheat and catch fire. A short also could disable the cruise control system and blow the brake light fuse." The company reported 47 incidents involving fires that might have been caused by this defect. A spring 2000 documentary entitled "Runaway Cars" that aired on Channel 4 TV in the United Kingdom cited several examples of Explorers that had taken their owners for a ride.

Poor quality is endemic throughout the industry. Every year automakers conduct dozens of recalls covering millions of cars for potentially dangerous defects, leading to lawsuits and calls for greater governmental involvement. In fact, it was the infamous Corvair, which Ralph Nader contended was dangerous even when parked in his landmark book *Unsafe at any Speed,* which led to the creation of the National Highway Traffic Safety Administration in the first place. Throughout the 1990s Renault/Chrysler, Volkswagen, Isuzu, and BMW conducted 14 separate recalls covering millions of cars involving the same heater core defect, which led to hundreds of drivers splattered with boiling fluid. Chrysler took back 4.1 million unsafe minivans that resulted in more than 37 deaths and 76 injuries—half younger than 12, three-quarters younger than 18—the result of door latches failing to hold even in moderate crashes, tossing unbelted passengers out the rear. The death toll was probably higher, but NHTSA stopped counting in 1995 even though its engineers determined it was a safety "defect that involves children."

General Motors has initiated several recalls in recent years. Due to a suspension part failure, GM issued a plea to owners of the 2002 Chevrolet Trailblazer, GMC Envoy, and Oldsmobile Bravada to stop driving immediately, and ordered dealers to pick up the vehicles and provide alternate transportation. "If the component failed, it could cause some concerns with vehicle control," GM spokesman Mike Morrissey explained. The company also announced a problem with power sliding doors on 314,000 minivans that could open while the vehicle was moving, the second such recall for these cars.

During one six-month period in 2001, automakers recalled 4 million cars, covering 1 in every 55 cars on American roads. There was Nissan, which called in 130,000 Sentras for a steering problem. DaimlerChrysler took back 701,000 Dodge Ram pickups because of a spring problem with a latch that could cause the hood to open unexpectedly, and 515,000 Dodge and Plymouth Neons for faulty brakes. Suzuki summoned 59,888 Grand Vitara SUVs for a fuel malfunctioning pressure regulator that could potentially lead to a fire. Audi recalled 41,980 vehicles for potential rust problems in the rear suspension.

But no company has recalled more cars more often than Ford. During that same six-month period Ford took back 1.1 million Windstar minivans, Mercury Cougar coupes, and Contour and Mystique small sedans because of fire hazards; 159,645 vans with fuel tanks that could potentially crack and leak fuel; 12,669 2002-model Explorer and Mercury Mountaineer sport-utility vehicles, to fix a defect that could cause the glass in the rear liftgate to detach or shatter; and 108,000 additional Ford Contour and Mercury Mystiques for front coil springs that could corrode, fracture, and possibly puncture a tire.

Since 1997, Ford has issued more than 250 safety bulletins to its dealers. One addressed Ford Taurus and Sable "because of potential for depressing both accelerator and brake." Another covered a fix to fuel tanks on the Crown Victoria, because "some high-speed rear-impact crashes have resulted in fuel tank puncture and fires." On the Ford Crown Victoria, Lincoln Town Car and Mercury Grand Marquis, "the speed control deactivation switch can develop a resistive short in the electrical circuit that could potentially result in an underhood fire." The company published an alert for the Windstar because of a potential for brake line corrosion, ultimately "increasing the risk of a crash," while another concerned "an 'O-ring' seal in the fuel injection system [that] could be damaged, allowing fuel leakage. In the presence of an ignition source, fuel leakage can result in a fire."

Ford released advisories covering defects with airbags, fuel lines, headlights, seat belts, sunroofs, throttles, transmissions, and, most infamously, Firestone tires. All this prompted J.D. Power to rank Ford dead last in initial quality in 2001.

Concern over the company's problems has filtered down to Ford's rank and file. In an internal e-mail, Norm Lewicki, a quality control engineer, wrote: "The drive for quality has to start at the beginning of the process," but "what I see in a significant number of programs is alarming. . . . The program chugs on in relentless pursuit of [Job One]. If there is significant deviation from performance criteria, the deviation is rationalized, criteria modified to suit the situation, and more coal is fed into the train to make it go faster. The result is a massive amount of partially done work that is pushed into the manufacturing arena with the hope of fixing it as we go. (And if we don't fix it at Job 1, that's ok, we will just add another Job 1). We in effect drive through our own red lights, right from the start. . . . As an old time superintendent from Kentucky told me once, 'You can't pour s**t into a funnel and get ice cream out the end.' "

It was bad enough a 4,000-pound vehicle could leave the factory with bad brakes, bad tires, bad windshield wipers, operate simultaneously in drive and park and blow up in a minor fender bender. What Turner found indefensible was that Ford was never required to issue a recall for perhaps its most serious and widespread safety defect—5 million unstable SUVs still on the road.

The fact that every sports utility vehicle came with a warning on the driver's side visor alerting the owner to an increased risk of rollover and to avoid any sharp turns proved the automaker was aware of the problem: rollovers were clearly a foreseeable event. Yet Ford refused to strengthen the roof, which was so weak that if you took an Explorer, lifted it off the ground, flipped it upside down, lowered the vehicle to the ground, and knocked out the front windshield, which typically happens in a rollover, it would collapse under its own weight.

As a direct result of the company's crisis in quality and safety, more than two-thirds of Turner's caseload involved Explorer rollovers that didn't even involve tire failure. As was true with the Bronco, most of his clients were injured simply because they made what Ford called "unnecessary sharp turns."

Turner had yet to figure out what an unnecessary sharp turn was. Jana Fuqua was on her way to a St. Louis Cardinals game when she was cut off by a sports car. Forced left, then right to miss the guardrail, then left again to straighten out the car, the back end slid around and the Explorer pirouetted over the centerline. Fuqua made for a particularly gruesome sight when paramedics found her. She'd been partially ejected through the sunroof still in her seat belt, the crushed roof circling her waist, a brain-damaged quadriplegic.

Evelyn Joyner, a real estate saleswoman in Jackson, Mississippi, was crushed to death on her way home in a two-door 1995 Explorer. Like Fuqua, she was cut off by another car. Gordan Sudduth, a Texas preacher, lost his 16-year-old daughter when she swerved to avoid a cow that wandered into her path. She steered left, right, then left and was killed when the Explorer overturned.

Contrast the Explorer's record with what many consider the worst auto crash fire defect in history: GM's side-saddle fuel tanks on 10 million recalled pickup trucks made between 1973 and 1987. More than 1,800 people died, with about 1 in 7,500 GM pickups ending up a fireball. The Explorer had a fatality rate three times that—while the Bronco was 15 times more likely to kill.

Turner believed there were only two ways to force Ford to manufacture an SUV that wouldn't keel over at highway speed: money and jail time. Ford executives who overrode engineers' recommendations to improve stability should be sent to prison and the vehicle recalled. Then there wouldn't be any more rollover victims and Turner wouldn't have any clients. Turner could retire and play golf all day, spend time with his family and friends instead of waking up in exotic locales like Corpus Christi, Tupelo, and McAllen.

Since jail time for Ford executives was out of the question, Turner went after the company in the only way he knew how. He vowed to make litigation so expensive Ford would have no choice but to improve stability—and in the process take care of its many victims. Turner didn't work for the money anymore. Already he had more than he could spend in five lifetimes. His mission was to make Ford a responsible corporate citizen.

Only then would he rest.

To do that what he needed was a case like Cammack for the Explorer. This time a victim who had survived a rollover, someone who could put a human face on the tragedy that ensued when an automaker put money ahead of safety.

9 CHAIN OF CUSTODY

DONNA BAILEY'S BROTHER, RICK BURCHFIELD, arrived at the University of Texas Science Center in San Antonio at the same time his father did. Owner of a small technology company that provided wireless solutions to businesses, Rick was 42 years old, 6 feet 2 inches, and about 240 pounds, good-natured and fun loving unless he was angry—and then he could be mean, very mean. He left Houston at 5:30 a.m., as soon as he heard the news. All he knew was what Kevin McCord told his father: Donna had been severely injured and probably paralyzed in an Explorer rollover.

In the waiting area he came upon Donna's children—who, because they were minors, had not been allowed in the intensive care unit to see her. Cassondra, a senior in high school, had turned 17 the day of the accident, and Jeremiah was 14. Rick's heart ached just looking at them. He was glad Amiel was there to fill him in on the situation. Then, since only two visitors at a time were allowed in, Rick and his father went inside.

Nothing he had experienced in his life could have prepared him for what he encountered in the ICU. His sister was alive only because machines breathed for her, provided nourishment, and mimicked organ function. Bruised, broken, and unconscious, Donna looked like a casualty of war. Tears streamed down Rick's face.

A neurologist took him and his father aside to inform them Donna was in a coma. She had suffered a catastrophic injury and would probably not survive. The doctor suggested the best course of action might be to let her die and delicately broached the issue of whether Donna could donate some of her organs. Rick looked at his father and could tell what he was thinking because he was thinking the same thing. Even if Donna survived, she wouldn't have any quality of life. He couldn't imagine what it would be like for her. Christ, he couldn't believe this was happening.

Before his father could answer, Rick said, "We have to let Donna make that decision." The way he said it left no room for debate. That was the way it was going to be.

He went to stand by Donna's bedside. All around him people were dying. Gunshot victims, stab wounds, cardiac arrests, grief stricken families and friends. It was a busy day in the ICU.

The minute Rick heard Donna had been injured in a Ford Explorer rollover, he was pretty sure he knew what had happened. His father said it was a blowout, but Rick figured it was a tread separation. In 1996, he had bought a Ford Explorer, which came equipped with Firestone Wilderness tires. But he didn't like the way the car handled with them, so he went back to the dealer and switched to a new set. After driving his Explorer 250 miles a day, 50,000 miles a year, in all sorts of weather and conditions, he understood the vehicle's shortcomings. The visor came with a rollover warning on it, and more than once he had swerved to avoid a road hazard and felt the car lurch.

Rick peered down at Donna and listened to the machines' whirs and beeps. If it hadn't been for a news report on local KHOU-TV in Houston a month earlier, he might be the one who was a prisoner of his body. The day after it aired he charged down to his local Firestone dealer and demanded different tires. When they refused to pay for them he switched to a different brand at his own expense.

He wished whoever owned the Explorer Donna had been riding in had done the same thing.

HOURS LATER RICK BURCHFIELD WAS IN HIS EXPLORER, sitting in the parking lot in front of his hotel in San Antonio. His stomach was all tied in knots. He couldn't remember the last time he'd slept. Adding to his stress, his cell phone would not stop ringing. Either a relative expressing condolences or wanting more information, an employee from work with a question or issue that needed his attention, even a grifting attorney who tried to solicit business. The pressure was building so high he was tempted to chuck the phone out of the window.

After spending the better part of a day at the ICU, Rick had divvied up tasks so each member of the family could share the burden of calling relatives in case there was a funeral, although Rick took on more than his fair share. In many instances he left a message, brief and to the point. *Donna . . . car accident . . . paralyzed . . . call me.* He said it so many times it had begun to lose meaning, like when you look at a word you know and it just doesn't look right anymore. While he gathered up Donna's purse and cancelled all her credit cards and cell phone accounts, Michael Bailey, Donna's ex-husband, hit him with the information that Donna had no medical insurance. She had allowed it to lapse a few months earlier because she couldn't afford the monthly premiums. Even with insurance, proper medical care would be astronomical. Without it, the cost could reach hundreds of thousands of dollars, if not millions.

In the rearview mirror he spotted a white police car pull into the parking lot. Upon closer inspection he realized it wasn't a policeman at all, just some guy who drove a refurbished cop car, a Ford Crown Victoria with tinted windows. Later in the ICU waiting room that same man approached Rick and handed him a business card. His name was Paul LaValle, an attorney who lived in the same town as Rick, a good ol' boy in a suit and shiny cowboy boots, with a chunky ring and Rolex watch. He claimed that Bubba Bean, Rick's uncle by marriage, had referred him. There were also three other lawyers hanging around, offering their services. Rick couldn't believe how fast news of the accident traveled. They practically beat Donna to the hospital. But Rick remembered LaValle's name because Bean had told him he knew a lawyer working on his aunt's lawsuit. She had suffered a stroke and heart attack and retained LaValle to sue the makers of the diet supplement Fen-Phen, a case that was still pending.

LaValle found out about Donna when Bean returned Rick's call from his law offices, which Paul LaValle shared with his father Peter LaValle. As soon as the younger LaValle heard the words "Explorer," "rollover," "ICU" and "San Antonio," he grabbed his coat and made for the door. After LaValle discovered where Donna's family was staying, he checked into the very same hotel then drove to the hospital. He told Rick it was imperative he retain an attorney as soon as possible, because evidence trails quickly grew cold, and bragged he had the guy for vehicular rollovers, this contact in Little Rock, Arkansas, who would scare the bejesus out of Ford. When Rick warned that any attorney Donna's family hired would have to agree in writing to underwrite her medical expenses, LaValle didn't even blink. Not a problem, he said. He asked Rick to sign a contract there and then.

Rick didn't like that LaValle was soliciting. He decided to put LaValle off by telling him they were going to take it slow and planned to interview a number of law firms. After visiting a few in the area, however, he found no one else willing to underwrite Donna's medical expenses. Rick called his uncle, who described LaValle as "bright and energetic." So he invited LaValle to give a presentation at their hotel.

Before the meeting, Rick gathered with his brother Tim, sister Sherry and Donna's kids to pray together and ask the Lord's guidance. Then they made their way to LaValle's room, where he greeted them, all smiles and glad-handing. He had a laptop, a printer and a gun, which, along with a deputy badge, he carried at all times.

After handing out glossy folders that held a history of the Ford Explorer and Firestone tire he offered a PowerPoint demonstration, complete with laser pointer. He talked about other cases he had settled and warned they had a limited time to get moving or evidence would evaporate. He ticked off a list: Take pictures of the crash site, find the tread, gain control of the vehicle and tire, otherwise they could lose the chain of custody and fatally botch their case. "Even if you don't hire me you should do this," he said, reiterating his promise to pay all legal, medical and, if necessary, funeral bills. He summed up by suggesting they sign a contract so he could start working on the case. But Rick was adamant that the final decision lay with Donna—and she was still unconscious.

When LaValle finished and they were walking out of his room, 14-yearold Jeremiah piped up, "Nice presentation, and if it were up to me I'd hire you, but your fly is open."

Sure enough, LaValle's pants had been unzipped the entire presentation. They all fell down laughing. After 48 hours of unrelenting stress, it felt good to break the tension. LaValle handed the boy his laser pointer and said, "Next time you can point it out to me."

The adults regrouped in Rick's room to drink beer and reminisce about Donna, and LaValle joined them, trying to insinuate himself into their lives. This was practically the first time they had been together since their parents' divorce 25 years earlier. Their emotions were rubbed raw. Forces pull families apart and forces bring them together. If the force of attraction is stronger, they get back together. They had always thought of themselves as a normal, lower-middle-class family striving to be middle class, but as they got older they realized their upbringing had been anything but normal.

If it were possible to be four opposites, the Burchfields would have been it. Donna, the oldest, had, like her mother, married and bore children at a young age. Tim, the next in line, left home for the merchant marines at 17 before becoming an actor, finding bit parts in shows like Dallas, and playing Shoeless Joe Jackson in a New York Off-Broadway production. Rick was the alpha-male, the hard-nosed businessman, while Sherry, the baby, became a special needs schoolteacher. They all discovered ways to fix themselves. They had to.

Their mother started having children when she was 16 and their father worked 70 hours a week at Woolworth's to pay the bills. They grew up miles from nowhere in rural Texas, where their mother's compulsive behavior dominated their lives. Raised by nuns in a convent, she had developed a serious passion for cleanliness and discipline. She would go into her children's rooms, take out their drawers and dump the contents on the floor, and then have a tirade until they folded everything neatly and put it away.

Donna had often received the brunt of these outbursts. She was awkward and had a learning disability, and her mother was always on her about her grades. Always vocal and demanding, Donna required more attention than the others. When they would go Easter egg hunting in the grass, she would get sticker burrs in her bare feet and stand there crying until someone took care of her. She bit into some dry cleaning plastic when she was six and pulled out her two front baby teeth, which hung there by a thread. It had been a severe blow to her vanity, even then.

After their parents' divorce, any pretense of middle-class living came crashing down. Their mother made do by working menial jobs and making $300 a week. As they sprouted toward adulthood, the kids went their own ways, using separation as a survival mechanism.

Donna wasn't popular in school. She got in with the wrong crowd, smoking and drinking as a teenager, and married when she was very young. She divorced, then wedded Michael Bailey, who came from a fundamentalist Christian family, and had Cassie and Jeremiah. As her children grew, Donna became restless. Tired of being a dowdy housewife, she wanted to go to college, but her husband resisted. She took a part-time job at a brokerage company to earn tuition, filling in whenever the secretary wasn't in.

First she got her high school equivalency and then was accepted to Texas A&M. After earning a scholarship, she received a student of the year award and made the dean's list with a 3.75 grade point average. She started working out and developed biceps, alternating five-mile runs every other day with aerobics, and got into rock climbing and kayaking. Sometimes she went on weeklong expeditions, hiking through wilderness, camping by moonlight, scaling peaks. The little girl who couldn't climb trees or throw a ball turned out to be the most athletic of all. She divorced Michael because she realized there was a whole world out there waiting to be conquered. Just when it seemed she was blossoming, she had her accident.

LaValle drank with the family, laughing and chatting. While Rick, a salesman, appreciated LaValle's tactics, aware that any attorney who represented Donna's case would have to be unusually assertive, Tim resented them. He was feeling glum. Although he and Donna had not been close growing up, over the years they had achieved a connection, despite his living 2,000 miles away. When Kevin McCord called about the accident, Tim turned completely numb. His wife had to call the travel agent to book tickets to Texas for him. He wasn't surprised after he arrived that Rick took care of the hotel for the family—he was the only one with money and wasn't shy about spending it. Tim remembered he even dry-cleaned his socks. So Tim grabbed a notepad and began acting as his brother's secretary. It was funny, Tim thought, how easy it was for them to fall into old roles.

The next day Rick tracked down the police report and talked to Kevin McCord, who told him he had a piece of tread that had torn off and would drop it off in Houston. Then he and Tim drove to the crash site, about 10 miles from San Antonio. LaValle had urged them to hurry. He claimed that Ford's modus operandi was to buy damaged vehicles from the insurance company and destroy them. As per LaValle's instructions, Tim snapped pictures of the black skid marks on the pavement and the grass tamped down near the shoulder where the Explorer had lain. Alongside the road, they picked up bits of tread and plastic, part of the car's red turning signal. Tim squeezed the plastic in his hands and wished he could time travel. That way he could warn Donna.

With the sun beginning to set, they went to find the car. By the time they pulled up to Strozier's Wrecker Yard it was closed, but they could see the Explorer through the chain-link fence. They could scarcely comprehend the damage. The roof on the front seat passenger's side was crushed in so far it was touching the back of the seat. The de-treaded tire looked as if someone had taken a machete to it. The car's side panels were wavy; the taillights obliterated, electrical wiring spilling out; the windshield was shattered, which left gaping holes. The side view mirrors were bent. It was a miracle Donna was alive. Quiet as church, Tim hopped the fence and shot more pictures.

Emotionally spent, they returned to the hotel, where they met up with Sherry, who was livid. She told them she didn't want Paul LaValle handling the case or coming anywhere near Donna. Earlier she had run into him in the elevator and LaValle pulled out a contract and asked her to sign. He said he couldn't operate as their attorney without it. When Sherry said she didn't have the authority, LaValle winked and told her to sign it anyway and he'd take care of the rest. It would be their little secret.

10 Angels In The ICU

DONNA WOKE UP WITH HER FAMILY GATHERED around her bed, holding hands and singing softly: "We come before You, Father, with thanksgiving and praise for you are a Great and Mighty God, through which all things are possible . . ."

She watched and listened, groggy from the cocktail of morphine and steroids in her system. Her mother and father, Rick, Tim, and Sherry, her ex-husband, all of them praying for her. Somehow she knew she was in a hospital. The last thing she remembered was the car spinning out of control, Tara fighting the wheel, a devastating shock to her spine, then being caught upside down unable to breathe, Kevin trying to rip the front windshield off to get to her.

It must be pretty bad for all of them to be here. Donna couldn't remember the last time they had all been in the same room. She wondered how long she had been unconscious. But when she tried to speak, nothing came out. She tried to turn her head, lift an arm, signal to them that she was awake. But she couldn't. Worse, no one noticed.

They continued to chant, "Jesus already paid the price, dear God, through His pain and suffering, and we receive your healing for Donna, and not just a temporary fix, Lord, no." A sense of peace washed over her. Donna lay there smiling. It was out of her hands now. She wanted to tell them to stop now. They were concentrating too much on her and not enough on connecting with God. If she could have, she would have said, "If you are not really worshipping, God can't hear you."

As if by cue they stopped when they saw her eyes on them. Donna tried to tell them what she had been thinking, but all she could do was move her lips. They tried to guess—with little success. Her mother leaned over, studying her daughter's mouth. As a result of encroaching deafness, she had taught herself to read lips. It took a while but she finally figured out what Donna was trying to say.

"Pray harder."

After the accident the days bled one into another for Donna. She was hallucinating from the morphine, slipping in and out of consciousness, barely aware of her brother Tim singing to her: "Oh, Donna, Oh, Donna Oh, Donna, Oh, Donna I had a girl, Donna was her name. Since she left me I've never been the same."

She experienced tremendous pain, which she took as a positive sign. It would be worse if she didn't feel anything, because that would mean she was paralyzed—and she couldn't imagine how terrible that would be. Her skin felt as if someone had poured acid on it, and her neck was almost unbearably sore. Donna was frustrated at not being able to speak. One of the nurses explained that she was on a ventilator, which Donna believed would be temporary.

There was death all around her in the ICU. A 17-year-old boy, his head split open, had been brought in after a bloody accident. His family held a vigil nearby and every time his alarm would go off they would scream and cry until doctors were able to get a pulse. He died a few days later. Donna wanted desperately to see her children, but they weren't allowed into the ICU. One of the nurses cruelly ignored Donna when her morphine wore off. It wasn't like she could push a button for help, so she would try to transmit messages with her brain. Eventually she became strong enough to gurgle noises through her ventilator. But the nurse still refused to ease her pain.

Donna wanted to tell her family about this. She asked her ex-husband for a pad and pencil. If she couldn't speak, at least she could write down what she needed. Michael looked surprised. But even when she couldn't communicate verbally, Donna had a powerful presence, piercing blue eyes like an Akita's. He did as he was told, returning a few minutes later. Donna thought she was scrawling notes. When he still didn't understand what she wanted, she assumed he couldn't read her handwriting.

She discovered she was paralyzed three days into her stay when a doctor examined her and found "no evidence of voluntary motion in lowers or uppers." He wrote in his notes that Donna could not perceive "touch in the lowers" and had "no ability to localize stimulus." The news left her reeling. She withdrew into herself, unable to stop crying, and became anxious and found it hard to breathe.

A week after the accident she had a heart attack. Her blood pressure dropped and her pulse stopped. By the time the ICU doctor got to her she was in full cardiac arrest, had stopped breathing, and according to doctors' notes was "critically ill and unstable." Her ventilator had clogged with her secretions and the alarm had not gone off. Donna was treated with atropine and bagged with oxygen until her pulse returned. The staff checked the ventilator and it appeared "to be working properly." An hour later Donna flatlined again. Her "eyes rolled back" in her head, her skin was "pale" and she was completely "non-responsive." Again her ventilator had filled with mucus. After that Donna didn't trust it. She lived with the constant fear it would stop working and she would suffocate.

Doctors performed a tracheotomy so her ventilator could be reattached through her throat. The first time Donna tried to drink water she heard wet, gurgling sounds come from her neck. She was fearful something terrible was happening to her and became agitated. The nurse tried to calm her, showing her how the new ventilator attached to her throat, how it would enable her to speak when she was ready. But Donna wasn't convinced she could talk and breathe at the same time.

They also extracted her two front teeth, which were almost ripped out in the accident, because they were a choking hazard. Donna refused to eat, afraid food would clog her ventilator. She suffered from a bladder infection, and when she wasn't in tremendous pain, she was having violent, uncontrollable spasms, which left her exhausted and curled up in a fetal position for hours on end. The nurses found her a difficult subject. She refused medications and wouldn't allow them to bathe her, demanding the curtains always be drawn. Hospital staff didn't turn her enough, which resulted in the onset of a bed sore on her back. Within a week, it had grown to a stage three "sacral decubitus" with a "greenish foul-smelling discharge."

The nurses convinced Donna to try a "speaking valve." She tolerated it for an hour, although she found she couldn't breathe as deeply with it. One of the first things she said was that she wanted to go home. While being put back on her ventilator she became anxious. Her heart rate dipped, she stopped breathing, and her pulse ceased. Once again the ICU doctors initiated CPR and chest compressions to save her life. A cardiologist was brought in and he recommended a pacemaker.

During the operation, while Donna was unconscious, she dreamed of four angels with wings. They spoke, telling her to stay alive because she had a message. Then they floated away to heaven, four stars glinting and then fading away, leaving Donna behind. When she awoke from her temporary death, her family was gathered around her.

Donna couldn't speak but her mother read her lips, channeling her daughter's words through her. "Did you see the angels?" she asked. Donna wasn't afraid to die anymore. The angels made her feel warm and safe.

While Donna straddled the line between life and death, Rick tried to locate the resources to pay for her care. The hospital inquired how he planned to pay for her treatment, and Rick said he had not been able to secure any funds yet. After consulting a lawyer who was a friend of the family, Rick realized the first thing he had to do was appoint someone to be Donna's legal guardian. At first Rick thought Sherry would be best, but she didn't want to do it. Sherry was afraid Donna was going to die and didn't think she could handle the responsibility. When Rick reminded her this was about Donna and not her, she threw a piece of pizza at him.

Rick didn't want to do it either. There were already mumblings of resentment that he was taking over. The more he thought about it, the more he realized that the best guardian Donna could have would be her daughter Cassondra. Not only was she bright and compassionate, it would also help him to keep things within the family. There was another bonus: Since Cassie was a minor, any contractual arrangement she entered into for Donna would offer special protection—the most important being that it would limit how much a law firm could charge to represent their case in the state of Texas.

LaValle wasn't pleased when he heard this, but nevertheless accompanied Rick and Cassie to a judge's office, where Cassie was officially appointed Donna's guardian by the court. Now that this was handled, Rick could start hammering out a contract with LaValle, capping his fees at 33 percent.

They needed to get this lawsuit started as soon as possible. It would be the only way that Donna would be able to receive the medical care she would need if she were going to survive.

11 SLOW LEAK

SEVEN WEEKS AFTER DONNA BAILEY'S CRASH the front page of the Sunday *Chicago Sun-Times* carried a headline that read like a health warning: "Faulty Tires Carry Fatal Consequences." By investigative reporter Mark Skertic, it described the misery of Jeanne Zolo, who lost her husband and mother when the family minivan tossed them out of the window after one of the Uniroyal tires unraveled. Skertic's investigation revealed that tire companies had been amassing reports of tread belt separations for years but never informed federal authorities.

After combing through three decades worth of government recall records, court documents and online databases, locating experts and victims (persuading some to cooperate despite court-ordered gags), Skertic discovered that tread separations were not as rare as tire makers would have people think. He tracked down evidence of 48 serious crashes and 43 deaths related to them between 1990 and 2000; although Skertic figured the number of deaths was much higher, but no government entity had checked. The accidents involved a variety of tire brands and models and cars, but by far the most deadly were tire failures involving sport-utility vehicles and vans, which were significantly more likely to tip over after a tire mishap.

The story had an immediate impact. The day after it appeared, NHTSA sent letters to all tire manufacturers seeking more information, and ordered them to explain why they haven't been reporting safety concerns. On May 2, 2000, the agency opened a preliminary probe of Firestone ATX, ATX II, and Wilderness tires, and six days later, spurred by complaints following KHOU's broadcast and the *Sun-Times* story, NHTSA issued a request to Firestone to hand over any and all relevant information regarding the tires and their use on Ford's product lines. Two days later it asked the same of Ford.

As Ford's internal correspondence shows, there existed a well-documented trail of engineers' concern over the Explorer's stability—from its initial design and first prototype to Job One and beyond. The tire's performance, engineers believed, would be key. Even before the first Explorer came off the assembly line, Ford asked Firestone to issue a dealer bulletin emphasizing the importance of air pressure, warning that failure to properly inflate tires could affect stability.

Yet after the Explorer hit America's highways no one at Ford bothered to keep track of rollover accidents, just in case. The Fatal Accident Reporting System (FARS), a federal database, contained detailed information on traffic accidents. If the company had analyzed data from 1995 to 1998, it would have learned the Explorer crashed significantly more often than its competitors, with fatalities almost three times as likely to be tire-related as those with other SUVs.

But one thing Ford management did notice when its new SUV emerged from factories was that the new inflation, 10 psi lower than on previous models, meant the Explorer got terrible gas mileage, as poor as 12 miles per gallon in stop-and-go traffic, 7 percent worse than the competition. The SUV was already an environmentalist's worst nightmare, a road hog with an insatiable thirst for gasoline that belched 30 percent more carbon monoxide and hydrocarbons and 75 percent more nitrogen oxides into the air than passenger cars did. Many types of vehicles had fan clubs, but only the SUV spawned hate groups, with activists going to mall parking lots and planting stickers on fenders. Since it produced the nation's top-selling SUV, Ford wanted to deflect the inevitable criticism.

Planning ahead for 1995—the beginning of a new five-year production cycle for the Explorer—the company decided to introduce a new tire with the same traction, better rolling resistance and improved wear properties, which engineers believed would improve fuel economy. Despite the Explorer being categorized a "light truck" under applicable federal laws, Ford did not request (nor did Firestone provide) a light truck tire. In step with many of its competitors, Ford ordered Firestone to create a "P-Metric" tire—by definition designed for lighter "passenger" cars.

While in public and over the airwaves the automaker declared, "Quality is Job One," internally it pursued a ruthless drive to shave expenses, ordering suppliers to decrease expenses by 8 percent. Firestone met Ford's cost target by putting its second-generation AT tire on a diet, whittling down the gauge of various components, modifying the sub tread compound, implementing a lightweight belt package, and altering the sidewall.

The tire maker was a willing partner. It had adopted a cost-cutting program of its own, to help pay off a $2 billion debt Firestone had accumulated. Saving a pound-and-a-half per tire would translate into almost 72 million fewer pounds of material over the course of the AT, ATX, and Wilderness' manufacturing run. Indeed, internal records show that thickness reductions were the "most significant" components of the program, even though it created the risk of missing or partially missing layers and that "countermeasures" could not completely eliminate the "problem." But Firestone never questioned the wisdom of manufacturing a lightweight passenger car tire that would be called on to convey a two-ton truck and an additional 1,000 pounds of people and gear over (at times) irritable terrain and often through interminable heat.

In addition to its lighter weight, the tire maker drained nine pounds of air pressure out of an already flimsy tire. Its engineers intermittently recommended raising the inflation rate in response to criticisms about rolling resistance, but in the end Firestone agreed to Ford's insistence on 26 psi.

Tire makers knew about the evils of underinflation. Most manufacturers even molded a safety warning on the sidewall to point out that serious injury could result from tire failure due to underinflation or overloading. The Tire & Rim Association recommended against operating light truck tires in excess of 65 mph—highway speed in this country—unless the operator lessened the load and *increased* tire pressure from 50 to 80 psi, three times Ford's. Less air meant greater deflection of the tire surface on the pavement, which caused greater friction, generating excessive heat and leading to rubber fatigue.

In particular, low inflation made the belt edges of the ATX vulnerable to heat buildup. The recommended inflation rate also contributed to an additional problem. Every month the average tire leaked a pound of air. Twenty-six psi quickly became 23, 21, 19. A March 2000 Firestone survey of 243 tires on 63 vehicles showed that 31 percent of 15-inch tires were underinflated, as were 51 percent of 16-inch tires. Nine had less than 20 psi.

Ford Ranger pickup trucks equipped with the same tires—on the same suspension system operated on the same roads in similar climates—suffered a fraction of the tread failures as Explorers. The major differences were the Ranger's recommended inflation, 10 psi higher than the Explorer's, and its weight: on average 350 pounds lighter. Ford's two biggest SUV competitors, Jeep Cherokee and Chevy Blazer, also set 35 psi for their tires, and touted significantly lower rollover rates.

But the decision that sealed the Explorer's fate was Ford's choosing a dangerously lower rating for heat resistance than tires designed for rivals' SUVs. NHTSA assigned the Wilderness AT tire a "C" rating for temperature/heat resistance, the lowest possible allowed under the agency's passenger car Uniform Tire Quality Grading System. A "C" rating meant a properly inflated tire could be run in a lab at 50 mph for two hours, then half an hour each at speeds of 75 mph, 80 mph and 85 mph without disintegrating due to increased heat buildup, a test that had little in common with real driving conditions. Temperatures in some places Ford Explorers were sold—parts of the United States, the Middle East, Latin America—topped 100 degrees for weeks on end.

Although Ford was satisfied with a "C"-rated tire even on vehicles marketed in scalding climates, the vast majority of its competitors outfitted their SUVs with "B"-rated ones, designed to resist heat buildup and handle higher speeds over longer distances. GM's Chevrolet Blazer and GMC Jimmy were equipped with Uniroyal Laredo, Goodyear Wrangler, and Goodrich Longtrail tires, all of which had "B" temperature ratings. The Dodge Durango, Jeep Cherokee and Grand Cherokee rode on Goodyear Wrangler and Michelin LTXs, also rated a "B."

As the lower-cost, lighter-weight tires were placed on Explorers and "monitored," Firestone quickly realized the very risks it assumed were materializing. In early 1995, Firestone studied the field performance of 1993–1995 tires and noted problems with belt edge separations, belt-leaving-belt separations, and rapid wear of the tires. The 15-inch ATX tire was the worst of all: 70 percent of the tires showed belt edge separations, which Firestone viewed as "noteworthy conditions."

Predictably, the frequency of tire-related rollover lawsuits increased after Ford switched to the lighter, more "aggressive looking" Wilderness tire in 1995. *Blackballer v. Ford* claimed two injuries and two deaths; *Rogers v. Ford*: one injury, one death; *Welch v. Ford*: three injuries.

Tread separation complaints crossed over to other product lines. Arizona Deputy Yuma County Attorney John K. White penned an August 1996 memo to warn about Firestone Firehawk ATX tires, which were used on emergency vehicles. "Some tires of this model have had their tread separate from the body of the tire," he wrote. "Firestone is aware of the problem and will be replacing tires when needed. . . . It is strongly recommended that you do not drive vehicles equipped with these tires at 'freeway speeds' (or at all, if possible) until you have them . . . evaluated." Ten days later Arizona's State Procurement Office asked Firestone to replace all Firehawk ATX tires bought under state contracts. The following month, the family of KPRC reporter Stephen Gauvain filed suit against Bridgestone/Firestone, alleging his death was caused by a defective ATX tire.

The defect became so apparent that in 1996 a Firestone engineer, citing the large number of customers suffering separations, "strongly recommended" the company investigate the lack of thickness of the rubber between the steel belts. Within weeks, other Firestone engineers joined in, pointing out "increasing belt edge separations" and "belt leaving belt separations," with a "high ratio" of these types of separations occurring in the "south region" of the country.

By early 1997, the number of customer complaints was so high that David Laubie, executive director of Firestone's sales engineering, brought it to the attention of Robert Martin, vice president of quality assurance. In February 1998, Martin issued a memo directing that belt edge separations had to be reduced by 50 percent immediately. The following day, a memo instructed Firestone plants to change the wedge component of the belt edge to a larger light truck size.

While Firestone scrambled to fix the defect, the legal department had a discussion with Martin about the increasing numbers of failures resulting in accidents, deaths, and lawsuits on the Explorer. Meanwhile Firestone engineers were asking, "How much drop in [tire] performance can we tolerate?"

Then State Farm Associate Research Administrator Samuel Boyden e-mailed NHTSA in July 1998 to advise the agency of 21 Firestone ATX P235/75R15 tire failures causing injuries, 14 of them on Explorers model years 1991 to 1995. By late 1998, Firestone's tire monitoring program was showing that 80 percent of the warranty claims were belt edge failure-related, and Firestone's chief executive officer, Masatoshi Ono, was "concerned."

Meanwhile, the parent company, Bridgestone, was beginning to cut and run. On Oct. 15, 1998, Osamu Nishiyama authored a memo recommending that the Japanese "avoid getting involved in the GCC [Saudi Arabia] situation" for "liability reasons." In April 1999, Ford's lawyers were openly discussing the threat Firestone tread separations posed, stating in a memo that the company would "address the issues related to [Firestone] rollovers on a case by case basis." By 2000, tread separations had become epidemic.

Twelve years earlier, firestone had been in such bad shape it considered getting out of the tire business altogether. Even though at the time it controlled almost 22 percent of the American market in sales to carmakers and 9 percent of sales to consumers—second only to Goodyear in each category—it was weighed down by debt, hobbled by inefficient factories, its stock spiraling downward. One reason was that the Firestone 500 recall a decade before had devastated its reputation and bottom line.

Another was the emergence of more durable, fuel-efficient radial tires. Introduced in France in 1954, they became standard equipment on French cars within four years and were soon adopted across Europe. It took longer for them to catch on in the United States, whose tire manufacturers had substantial investments in traditional "bias ply" tires. In 1975, 60 percent of tires in the United States were bias ply, while 40 percent were radials. By 1980, virtually all tires sold in America were radials.

To compete, Firestone would have had to plow a quarter of a billion dollars into updating its manufacturing facilities at a time the replacement market was drying up, since radials lasted 50 percent longer. As a result, then-president John J. Nevin was forced to shut some inefficient plants (seven alone in 1980) while selling others, slashing 50,000 jobs in the process. At the same time he placed a new emphasis on auto repair, retail sales, car rental, and even roofing supplies.

After completing his restructuring program in late 1987, Nevin established three subsidiaries: tire, non-tire, and retail businesses, all under one holding company. Wall Street viewed the move as a ploy to sell its tire business. From then on, Firestone was fair game among other tire makers looking to expand into North America.

Like other companies, Bridgestone wanted Firestone's tire business. Because of the strong yen, which made Japanese exports more expensive, it needed to base more manufacturing in the United States to compete in the American market, and found Firestone's ties to Ford and GM especially attractive. If Bridgestone tried to build all those factories itself, it could take 15 years.

More importantly it would be a necessary step in Bridgestone's efforts to globalize. The industry had already evolved into a high-stakes game of musical chairs with Continental (Europe's No. 2 tire maker) buying General (America's No. 4), and Sumitomo Rubber's taking over Dunlop two years before. If Bridgestone, the third largest tire maker in the world after Goodyear and Michelin, lost out on Firestone, the chance to develop into a global concern would most certainly pass it by. Company president Akira Yeiri rushed to Akron to personally handle negotiations with Nevin.

Yeiri was that rare breed in Japan who personified the globalization that Kanichiro Ishibashi, Bridgestone's chairman, wished to promote. A graduate of Tokyo University, Yeiri had earned money for tuition by playing jazz at American Army dance halls, and was fluent in five languages—English, French, German, Chinese, and Thai. Ishibashi realized that Yeiri was a strong manager, very international, and could speak to Americans in their own language. But he was a controversial choice within the company, which was, at its heart, a family-run dynasty. Yeiri's wife was German and he had spent significant time abroad. The Ishibashi family didn't trust Yeiri, but they couldn't do anything about it because Kanichiro, the son of the company's founder, had personally picked him. Yeiri was particularly adept at corporate politics. He had been with the venture that made the steel for Bridgestone's steel-belted tires, and was part of the overseas group, considered a source of excellence within the company and a proving ground for upper management.

Bridgestone had gotten its start in the early part of the 20th century as Nihon Tabi K.K., a company that found success crafting *zika tabis*—traditional rubber-soled footwear. Although advisors and family members were dead set against entering the tire business, which was controlled by American and British interests, Senior Vice President Shojiro Ishibashi secretly imported machinery from the United States in 1929. But the machines were only for forming and vulcanizing; the bulk of the work had to be done by hand, and the only technical advisor he had was a 10-page instruction booklet shipped with the equipment. Nonetheless, four months later 20 workers he chose personally from various divisions created their first four-ply tire.

Given that virtually all the passenger cars on Japanese roads at the time were imported and rode on foreign-made tires, Ishibashi decided to adopt an English name for his. Following the lead of J. B. Dunlop, Harvey Firestone, B. F. Goodrich, and Charles Goodyear, he wanted to stamp his own name on the sidewall, which, translated into English, was "stone bridge." But no one in the company liked the sound of that, so Ishibashi flipped the syllables around, ending up with Bridgestone, a name everyone could agree on—except, ironically, Firestone, which filed suit in Japan, alleging trademark infringement. Eventually the court ruled for Bridgestone since it was a translation of the owner's name, albeit backwards.

Yeiri's relationship with Nevin dated back to 1980, when Sony chairman Akio Morita brought their two companies together when he told Bridgestone's then-chairman Kanichiro Ishibashi that "Firestone is selling its factories. Why don't you buy one?" Yeiri handled the negotiations, which took more than two years, with Bridgestone purchasing Firestone's Nashville truck-radial plant for $52 million in 1983. After taking over, Bridgestone invested $81 million into new equipment and a new warehouse, and an additional $70 million to expand facilities to produce auto tires. Productivity soared and Bridgestone ultimately offered jobs to all the workers Firestone had let go.

In February 1988, Nevin greeted Yeiri in Akron, and soon after Bridgestone announced a tentative deal to purchase 75 percent of Firestone's manufacturing operations for $750 million, which would have rendered the company largely an auto repairer and seller of tires made by others. According to *Zaikai*, a Japanese business magazine, Bridgestone didn't try to buy all of Firestone's tire business because it thought a complete takeover could trigger anti-Japanese sentiment. But that didn't mean Nevin wouldn't scuttle Bridgestone's offer if a better deal came along, which he did three weeks later when Italian tire maker Pirelli, backed by Michelin, offered to buy the entire company outright for $1.93 billion, two-and-a-half times Bridgestone's bid. Yeiri was shocked that the almost-done agreement unraveled at the last minute. He had blundered when he announced the takeover while it was still only a verbal promise.

Bridgestone had been victimized, in part, by its entrenched insularity. It had no relationship with an American investment banker, since full authority for the negotiations had been given to the company's management planning team under the direct control of Yeiri. The Japanese tire maker only learned of Pirelli's bid when it was reported in the media. But Yeiri refused to give up. Because Bridgestone had reorganized the factory it bought a few years earlier, Yeiri believed that Firestone saw the Japanese tire maker as the best partner, since Pirelli's plan was to sell Firestone in pieces, which Bridgestone learned from documents Pirelli submitted under the Italian Securities and Exchange Law.

It also added urgency to his mission. If Pirelli succeeded, it planned to award Firestone's factory in Brazil and distribution network in the United States to Michelin for $650 million, and Michelin would have the right to sell half of Firestone's synthetic rubber production businesses for $150 million. Yeiri believed the stronger Michelin became, the worse off Bridgestone would be, since he viewed the French tire maker as the most serious threat to Bridgestone's global aspirations. Michelin's presence behind Pirelli's takeover bid made him determined to win at any cost.

Learning from its mistakes, Bridgestone retained an M & A specialist, Lazard Freres, who informed Yeiri that Bridgestone had only 20 days from the time of Pirelli's announcement to make a counter-offer. One reason Bridgestone bid $80 a share for a total of $2.6 billion, a sum Wall Street deemed "crazy," was because Yeiri heard a rumor that Pirelli might substantially up its price from $58 a share. He realized $60 wouldn't cinch the deal. Yeiri decided to settle things once and for all.

Until then, Bridgestone had the reputation as a careful, conservative company. The Japanese proverb "hitting a stone bridge (ishibashi) while you cross it" implied a deliberate attitude, making sure it was stable before trusting it, while Bridgestone was said to be a company that "wouldn't cross a stone bridge even after hitting it." Usually the company conducted painstaking research before acting, as it had in purchasing Firestone's truck factory in 1983, deliberating ad nauseam until a broad-based consensus could be reached.

The tire maker's bold purchase of Firestone surprised industry watchers in Japan and was viewed in the press as Bridgestone's "second birth." (The first was from *tabi* maker to tire manufacturer.) At the time it was the largest foreign investment ever by a Japanese company, more than half a billion more than Sony's $2 billion purchase of CBS Records a year earlier. As the Japanese magazine *Keizaikai* put it: It was "like a medium-sized whale swallowed a huge whale."

After Bridgestone's board approved the merger on March 14, 1988, the company discovered that Firestone had serious problems: unpaid taxes in Argentina, environmental pollution suits, decrepit production facilities, and a demoralized workforce. When engineers from Japan inspected Firestone's factories, they were appalled by the conditions. Firestone hadn't invested in its manufacturing plants in a decade of rapid technological advancement. Now Yeiri knew why Nevin had been in such a rush to sell.

The merger also brought up a host of other issues. The two companies didn't even use the same units of measure, since Japan was on the metric system. The purchase created something like 40 millionaires at Firestone, longtime employees who had accumulated shares at $8 and sold them for 10 times that. A whole slew of them made more money than Yeiri did, and Bridgestone management was stunned by the existence of Firestone's corporate jets. There weren't enough Japanese managers who could speak English available to institute changes on the ground. Fax machines would whir all day at Firestone HQ in Akron, with the day's instructions in Japanese, sent to Japanese staff, which alienated American management who were kept out of the loop.

Once the Japanese took stock, they realized they had paid way too much. Some Bridgestone executives wanted to immediately resell the company. They grumbled that Bridgestone had been robbed. Then General Motors, advocating a "Buy American" policy, announced it would no longer do business with Firestone, which supplied 20 percent of GM's passenger-car tires in North America. Now one of the major reasons for the purchase had evaporated.

Bridgestone didn't panic. It opted to spend money to bring Firestone up to speed, investing an additional $1.5 billion to modernize its factories in 20 countries around the world, driving the total cost of the deal to a staggering $4.1 billion. Part of the deal required Nevin to stay on to help oversee the transition. The Japanese needed Nevin because he knew so much about Firestone's problems, and he functioned less as CEO than a consultant. He was so wealthy now that he had nothing to lose by being brutally honest. Nevertheless, in 1991, Firestone lost $350 million, nearly canceling out a record year for Bridgestone, which netted $382 million.

In an attempt to staunch the flow of red ink, Bridgestone asked Yoichiro Kaizaki to take over for Yeiri at Firestone. Like Yeiri, the 58-yearold Kaizaki wasn't a typical Japanese salaryman, a role where conformity was usually valued over leadership (although he did profess a love of golf and mahjong). Unlike Yeiri, he was far from global in outlook and experience; and instead of looking at the big picture he was more interested in the pixels. He was a blunt, strong-willed cost-cutter who didn't care a whit what colleagues thought of him, and had made a reputation for himself by turning around Bridgestone ventures as diverse as conveyor belts and golf balls. When first asked to take over Firestone, he declined. Not only did he know nothing about tires, he didn't speak one verb of English. But chairman Ishibashi overrode him, saying, "This is the order of the company. Take care of it."

Kaizaki wasted little time laying off workers and slashing costs. When told a building had to be expanded to hold manufacturing equipment, Kaizaki asked for a tape measure so he could see for himself, proving his underlings wrong and saving the company millions of dollars. He reorganized the company into 21 divisions and melded Bridgestone and Firestone tire sellers under a unified marketing approach. Instead of encouraging competition between the brands, he gave each a distinct niche: Bridgestone would sell high-end tires; Firestone would be its mass-market brand, and Dayton would fill the need for low-cost tires. Bridgestone moved its corporate headquarters from Akron to Nashville in 1992 to consolidate the two companies into one and get out from under the shadow of Goodyear.

In 1993, the newly forged Bridgestone/Firestone unit turned a $6 million profit. Kaizaki handed over the keys to the company to Masatoshi Ono while he returned home to Japan to collect his reward: the presidency of the parent company, which he inherited from Yeiri.

Although Kaizaki was an ocean and half a continent away, his eye never strayed far from Firestone. With the company $2 billion in debt, Kaizaki instituted an even more aggressive cost-cutting strategy, affecting everything from employee salaries and work rules to materials costs, which was, according to internal documents, the "most significant" part to the plan. Since Firestone spent $5 more manufacturing each tire than its competitors did, Kaizaki ordered a reduction in the amount of rubber in each tire, even though company engineers recognized this could cause a safety "problem."

The second part of Kaizaki's cost-cutting plan dealt with worker productivity by addressing the company's labor contract with the United Rubber Workers union. Kaizaki had been amazed by the complexity of Firestone's labor pact. He complained that "work that should be done in five hours, they schedule for eight," something he intended "to fix." Looking to ape the success the company was having in Japan, Kaizaki wanted to move Bridgestone/Firestone's factories in America to continuous operation, which would require workers to perform four 12-hour shifts per week.

But Kaizaki's relentless drive to wring productivity concessions from workers may have made their jobs more dangerous. In October 1993 a worker at a factory in Oklahoma City was killed when his head was crushed in a tire-making machine. This and another accident prompted U.S. Labor Secretary Robert Reich to appear at the plant with a police escort to personally levy a $7.5 million fine for alleged safety violations. The following July, the tire maker's contract with the union expired, and 4,200 URW members at five plants went on strike when the company insisted on work rule changes and offered them less than Goodyear was paying.

Things got ugly fast. Picketers carried signs that said "Nuke 'Em" and "WWII Part II: Japan's Bridgestone Attack on American Economy." With the company losing $10 million a month, Kaizaki ratcheted up the pressure by threatening to permanently replace strikers, a warning condemned by President Clinton, who accused Bridgestone of "flagrantly turning its back on our tradition of peaceful collective bargaining." Kaizaki brushed off the criticism: "Even if 80 percent of people resist me, I don't care," he said. "I'm not a politician, so I don't need to be elected based on popularity."

The workers stayed off the job 10 months, returning in May 1995. Firestone rode out the strike by relying on existing inventory and replacement workers, ramping up production from non-striking plants, and cutting the cost of materials. In 1994, the company's net profit was $29 million. It shot up to $130 million in 1995, and the following year reached $285 million on sales of $7.4 billion, with Firestone accounting for more than 43 percent of its parent's consolidated sales and nearly a third of its operating profits.

While the tire maker thrived in America, it was facing the worst recession to hit Japan since the 1970s oil crisis. Kaizaki turned his attention to the home front, cutting a third of Bridgestone Corp.'s workforce from 1993 levels, and pressuring older employees into early retirement. One longtime manager, Masaharu Nonaka, confronted the CEO in his office, demanding a change in Bridgestone's harsh employment tactics. When Kaizaki refused, Nonaka stabbed himself in the stomach with a dagger. The Japanese media labeled his 1999 death "restructuring seppuku" after the traditional samurai form of ritual suicide, and blamed Kaizaki's coldhearted cost-cutting. When Kaizaki responded—four months later—he pointed to Bridgestone's record profits, which were $799 million in 1998, at a time many Japanese companies were experiencing steep losses.

But everything Kaizaki, now 67, had accomplished was in jeopardy after KHOU and the *Chicago Sun-Times* reported that Firestone AT tires were detreading at an alarming rate.

12 Faith

Rick stood over Donna and gently rubbed her forehead. "Are you awake?"

"Yes," Donna said softly, almost mournfully. When she was asleep she was whole. Only when she was awake did the nightmare of her new life return.

Her family was sitting in a semicircle around her bed—her parents, kids, siblings; everyone but Tim, who couldn't afford to make the trip from New York. They were all there to find out what Donna's next step would be. Joining them was Dr. Douglas Barber, a pale, lightly balding man in a lab coat; a nurse; a hospital administrator; and Donna's physical therapists.

Dr. Barber got started. He explained that the neurosurgeons had basically signed off on the case. They took the halo off a few weeks ago and her spine was stable. Donna had been stricken with numerous panic attacks, usually revolving about the fear of not being able to breathe. It had taken her a while to get used to a ventilator that afforded her the ability of speech. At first she didn't want it. She imagined she couldn't breathe with it—which was almost funny to her family, since there wasn't a time in Donna's life she didn't want to talk about something. Then she had to learn how to speak all over again.

"She's medically stable," Dr. Barber continued. But he warned that her muscles were withering away from lack of use. For the moment the biggest concern was a pressure sore in her back that was so deep it went straight to her tailbone. Every day a nurse had to vacuum away the pus. His best guess was that it wouldn't heal on its own and hoped that a plastic surgeon would operate soon.

"They said next week," Donna offered.

"What stage is it?" Rick asked.

"I would call it a four," the doctor answered.

"What's the worst stage?"

"Four." Dr. Barber explained that the surgeon should be able to cover it with a flap of skin. If it were to heal on its own, it would leave a bigger round scar where the hole was and that would be at risk for recurring infection.

He went on to discuss other potential problems that could crop up at any time—blood clots, gallstones, urinary tract infections, pneumonia. Since Donna had no feeling, these could easily go undetected if they weren't vigilant. She was also having bouts of spasticity that were so bad she couldn't eat. Sometimes her foot started shaking uncontrollably, or she'd get board-stiff and no one could bend her to sit up. The reason for all this was that the spinal cord was still trying to figure out what happened to itself.

"That's where she's at medically," the doctor summed up. He handed out a piece of paper that explained what it meant to have a level C1–C3 spinal injury. He asked for someone to hold it up to Donna so she could see it. "I want you to know this," he said. "Given her neurological level, if there's no improvement—and my personal opinion . . . [is] this is the way things are gonna be—she's gonna be on a ventilator the rest of her life. She will require 'total assistance.' " He ticked off the categories. "Respiratory: ventilator dependent. Bowel: total assistance. Bladder care: total assistance. All the way down at the bottom: 24-hour attendant care." He said Donna would have to direct her own care. She would have to understand what needed to be done and how.

Dr. Barber continued. "At some point in time she will be medically ready to be discharged from this place. The question is where will she be discharged to?" Medicaid would only pay for a nurse once a week. There would be a lot of time where she would need people to support her. He warned that 24-hour care was exactly what it sounded like. The person watching her had to be there all the time without fail. He couldn't take 10 minutes to drive to a convenience store for a gallon of milk, because what would happen if the ventilator stopped working? "If it malfunctioned, the alarm goes off and the person would have to call 911," then squeeze an oxygen bag 20 times a minute until the ambulance arrived. He suggested that if the family couldn't provide 24-hour care, the next best option would be a skilled nursing facility.

Rick asked, "How do you find places that will assist you with Medicaid, that take ventilator patients, that's not a nursing home?"

"It's either going to be to your house or to a nursing home," Dr. Barber responded. "I think there is no other option."

"Are there different levels of nursing homes? Where there's assisted care but just not so she'll have to be around a whole bunch of old people?"

"There are very few nursing facilities that will take ventilator dependent patients anyway. In San Antonio I think there's a couple—two or three tops—and there are more than a million people in the greater San Antonio area."

Jeremiah asked about weaning Donna off the ventilator, but the doctor said there was no indication this would be possible.

"How long will the pressure sore take to heal?" Rick asked.

Six weeks, where Donna would have to remain immobile in a specially designed bed.

Rick wanted to know how the bedsore came up so fast.

"She can't feel her bottom," the doctor replied. "Most of us don't have much between our skin and tailbone. Those of us who feel our bodies [get messages] from our bodies to move." The standard order was for the nurses to move the patient's position every two hours.

"Is that not the protocol in the ICU?" Rick asked. That was where Donna first developed it.

Dr. Barber sidestepped the question. "Well, I don't work there. I can't say what happened there. It doesn't take long for the skin to break down."

Rick asked if there were any resources to help families find funding. He had sent numerous letters to the Texas Rehabilitation Commission asking for help so Donna could transfer to a cutting edge research facility like the Texas Institute for Rehabilitation and Research (TIRR) in Houston, which specialized in spinal cord injuries. But there was a long waiting list of people like Donna without medical insurance who were in similar straits. Donna could go to TIRR anytime, provided she had the money: about $40,000 a month. "We all want Donna to come home," Rick said. "We're all willing to sacrifice. But we don't want to lose her because we want her home so bad."

Dr. Barber pointed out that after Donna had plastic surgery, she would have six weeks of bed rest for sure in San Antonio. "After that six weeks that's when we'll have to start questioning what happens next. Is the Texas Rehabilitation Commission money going to kick in so she gets rehab and can go to TIRR? If it doesn't, what are we going to do? That's what I'll be asking y'all. If we don't get the funding, what are we going to do?"

Six weeks. That was it. After that they would either have to find a nursing home or find a way to keep Donna alive at home. Neither was a pleasant prospect.

"Donna, do you have anything you want to say?" Rick asked.

"You covered everything," she said quietly.

"You know we love you a lot and care about you a lot and that's why we're all here," Rick said. "We are trying to help you along the way, understanding the limits that we have. The most important thing for me personally is to honor what you want."

Sherry chimed in: "This is such a huge life change. Whatever you need to do, get angry with us, we can separate your anger from how you feel about us."

"I have a lot of questions," Donna's mother said, "but they are locked up inside of me, because Donna's coming home with me."

"It's gonna be awhile before we probably head back home to Portland," Rick warned. "But Houston, TIRR has been the plan all along. I hope that's what you want because it's going to be very costly, and if you go there you're gonna have to get something out of it. It's $2,000 a day."

"What happens if you can't?" Donna asked.

"We will," Rick responded. "We've been operating on faith this whole time. There's no reason to change now. It'll happen."

"I miss being home," Donna said, her voice trembling. She had missed her daughter's graduation and prom, and her son was quietly becoming a man. She didn't want to go to a nursing home. Although she didn't want to be a burden, she wanted to be with her family, even if it meant she could die.

"We miss having you," Rick said.

He looked to the doctor and hospital staff and said, "She would probably never have believed it six months ago this many family members would rally behind her."

13 TIRE SLEUTH

FORD AND FIRESTONE RESPONDED TO NHTSA'S May 2000 request for more information by stalling. They claimed they would need until October to pull together all the necessary documentation. The longer they could drag things out, the better their chances the investigation would peter out. As spring gave way to summer, the story became stagnant: with nothing new to report, the media stayed away. This, auto researcher Sean Kane realized, meant that Ford and Firestone stood a good chance of getting off the hook—something he was desperate to prevent.

Kane had been chasing Firestone for two years. Co-founder of Strategic Safety, a firm that conducted investigations and analysis of potentially defective products, Kane was working for a powerful trio of trial lawyers with a growing cache of Firestone ATX cases—Tab Turner; Roger Braugh, a litigator with Watts & Heard of Corpus Christi; and Bruce Kaster of Ocala, Florida.

It was an ideal assignment for the 33-year-old Kane, a self-professed "car nut" who bought his first automobile before he could legally drive. Out of college he took a job with a small New England tire distributor, where he learned the business from the dealer on down. At the Center of Auto Safety (CAS), the Ralph Nader–derived consumer rights organization in Washington, D.C., Kane's work prompted several safety probes and the recall of 2 million vehicles, including Nissan's repurchase of 33,000 minivans for irreparable design defects, the first time an auto manufacturer had to repurchase an entire model line. He left CAS to work for Ralph Hoar, another consumer rights maverick, before heading out on his own in 1997.

Turner and company had retained Strategic Safety to find out why their caseloads were growing so rapidly. From his home in rural Massachusetts, Kane worked the phones and canvassed other plaintiffs' attorneys, interviewed crash victims, and mined NHTSA's database for tire complaints. He scanned newspapers for accidents and trolled the Internet for tire data, consulted vehicle dynamics experts and chemists, and tapped into his network of tire dealers. Pooling Kane's data with their own, the lawyers counted almost 100 deaths from ATX tire failures. They also spotted the telltale signs of a corporate cover-up.

Kane learned that shortly after KHOU's broadcast, Firestone dealers in Houston began quietly replacing ATX and Wilderness tires free for anyone who asked. Following another critical TV report on KNBC, Firestone offered the same deal in San Diego and Los Angeles, awarding local dealers a $7.50 commission per tire plus $1.00 scrap fee for drilling holes and disposing of them as scrap. An internal memo showed the company emphasized that even if the tires appeared acceptable, the dealer should replace them upon request and charge the customer based on the percentage of tread worn.

There had to be a compelling reason Firestone was willing to take back product. Kane's time in the industry had taught him the extent tire makers went to avoid refunds. In most companies, salespeople were responsible for what was known in the trade as "adjustments," the amount of credit customers received when returning tires to dealers. Tire makers relied on the aggregate number to track quality, but the stats were skewed by design. Sales personnel weren't trained to spot defects; they were trained to sell tires and fill healthy quotas. A dealer would commiserate with the customer, eyeball the tire in question, maybe run his fingers over the tread and along the sidewall, *tsk tsk*-ing the entire time, then state unequivocally it had suffered an impact injury. Or had been improperly patched. Or was worn out. The one thing he never did was utter the word "defect." If he ran across a spate of bad tires he was to simply offer a "goodwill adjustment" toward customers' next set, because every effort was made to keep the numbers in the database as low as possible.

When Kane tried pitching what he knew to ABC's *20/20* and NBC's *Dateline*, news producers told him to phone back when he found a "smoking gun" document or the government demanded a recall. Kane contacted a source in NHTSA's Office of Defects Investigation, who delivered a similar message. All the agency had was a series of paper cut charges against Firestone, a hundred lives against 15 million ATX tires over billions of miles. Without additional proof the investigation was in danger of fizzling.

Kane was pretty sure Firestone was concealing a defect. The question was how to prove it. He assumed a company Firestone's size was bound to leave tracks somewhere. You could hide only so many crashes before customers and dealers began whispering beyond the confidentiality agreements. He decided to expand his research, knowing there were bound to be ATX tires wherever Ford Explorers were sold. If there were problems with the ATX, he swore he would find them.

As a kid, Kane dreamed of working for a car company known for its quality. When Saab wasn't hiring, Kane took a drastic pay cut from his job in the tire business to work at the Center for Auto Safety for $18,000 a year. Friends thought he was crazy. He had recently married and had been earning four times that. Nevertheless Kane moved to D.C. and six months later his wife joined him.

When he arrived, CAS was in organizational chaos. He met the center's director, Clarence Ditlow, who showed Kane his office, told him to handle European and Japanese cars, and promptly left for three months. Kane knew neither goals nor duties. In true Ralph Nader nonprofit style there was no training, no supervision, no explanation of the job.

Kane first learned of problems with heater cores in certain foreign car models from a mechanic who told him what a pain they were to replace, requiring removal of the entire dashboard assembly. Located at the foot of the driver, a heater core was a small plastic radiator that warmed the car's interior. Following up on the mechanic's tip, Kane tracked down 60 reports where the component cracked, sending pressurized steam through the air vents and into the passenger compartment, fogging windows and splattering the driver from ankle to thigh with boiling engine fluid. A number of people suffered third-degree burns. The one death occurred when a woman in a Renault Alliance crashed into a building as her car filled with steam.

After learning the plastic component that was failing had been installed in several foreign brands and across model platforms, Kane petitioned the federal government to recall a million Volkswagen Golfs and Jettas, AMC/Renault Alliances and Encores, BMW Three-series and Isuzu Troopers—the automakers that received the lion's share of complaints. In addition he requested NHTSA survey other carmakers for their use of plastic in heater components. The agency didn't respond to the center's call for a survey but did grant Kane's petition, leading to 14 recalls since 1992.

While at CAS, Kane uncovered another major safety defect that plagued the Toyota Camry. An electrical malfunction caused the car's power doors and windows to jam shut and smoke to pour inside. Some people had been trapped for an hour or more. Kane informed Toyota of the problem to give the company a chance to fix it. When nothing

happened, he told NHTSA and *Consumers Reports*, which published a well-publicized story. CAS put out a press release advising motorists to carry hammers with them to bash out the windows just in case. After a public flogging, Toyota capitulated
and recalled the cars.

A year and a half at CAS was enough for Kane. He had gained keen insight into the world of Ralph Nader. From the outside, his organizations appeared to work ceaselessly on behalf of the consumer. On the inside, turnover was high, politics endemic, resources limited, morale low, learning curves ridiculously steep. The term "not-for-profit," he and his colleagues joked, referred to their salaries. Frustrated by the lack of career advancement opportunities, Kane left to join Ralph Hoar & Associates, where he brought with him an investigation he'd begun at CAS into Nissan minivans that were catching fire.

Taken by surprise by the emergence of the American Soccer Mom in the late '80s, Nissan decided to market an economical stopgap until it could build a van from scratch. The company took a Japanese delivery truck designed for Tokyo's serpentine back streets, relocated the steering column, doubled the size of the motor and shipped them to the United States. The sticker price was significantly less than for a Chrysler, which practically defined the category. Nissan sold 36,000 minivans between 1987 and 1990, mostly to families on a tight budget who needed the space and utility of a minivan but couldn't afford more than $10,000.

But there was a flaw with the vehicle's architecture. Nissan had incorporated a mid-engine design, with the motor located under the driver and front passenger seat where it received insufficient ventilation. Nissan issued three separate recalls covering rubber components that melted from the intense heat (a valve cover, hose and belt) but refused to address the core problem: the engine's location.

After wading through a deluge of complaints Kane came in contact with Lori Kelly, a housewife and mother of five kids in Florida, who knew a number of women who'd had fires in their Nissan minivans. In turn, each of them had friends who'd suffered similar travails. The dealers were no help. They denied there was even a problem. Pretty soon Kelly had organized an extensive network of angry housewives across Florida, Texas, California, and Arizona, all of whom felt burnt by Nissan. They volunteered to monitor local dealerships with video cameras they'd bought to film their children, contacted victims whenever there was a van fire story in the local paper or on TV news, and took out *Penny Saver* ads.

Eventually Kane's network put the pieces together. Nissan was secretly buying back burnt-out vans, offering a fraction of the retail price: Sometimes $500, up to $1,000, toward the owner's next car, for a vehicle that originally cost $10,000. Then a corporate representative would accompany the car to a scrap yard, where it was smashed. They didn't have hard proof though until Lori Kelly phoned Kane one day to tell him a friend of hers had suffered a fire in her Nissan minivan and the dealer was coming over to buy it back.

"Can you follow it?" Kane asked.

She had her five-year-old with her, but Kelly didn't say no. A half hour later she reported, "They're putting it on a flatbed truck." Tailing the truck to a salvage yard she parked outside the fence, recording the action with her camcorder. When she told Kane she saw a man in a suit surveying the situation, Kane advised her to film him and scan the cars in the parking lot with the camera. Later they traced one of the license numbers to a Nissan executive with manufacturer plates on his car.

After providing NHTSA the videotape evidence, internal documents and a sheath of complaints, he petitioned the federal government to impel Nissan to repurchase the vans, which it had never done before. Nissan denied it was buying back vans to destroy them, saying it had salvaged the vehicles for inspection to look into what caused the fires. The company admitted extreme engine compartment heat was a problem and countered with an offer for a fourth recall, proposing to implement a complex engineering scheme that included a cooling system (new radiator, fans, belts, a water pump) at a cost of more than $3,000 per vehicle.

Kane thought that was preposterous. If Nissan were looking to check into the problem, it wouldn't purchase vans from a wrecking yard, it would get them firsthand from the owners who suffered fires. Questioning the feasibility of Nissan's fix, Kane predicted a lot of shoddy work. Dealers wouldn't want to touch the vehicles. They would be called on to undertake a complex and time-consuming overhaul for the recall rate, a fraction of the retail amount.

But administrators at NHTSA figured, Who were they to tell Nissan it couldn't spend $10 million to recall and fix the remaining 33,000 vans on the road? Within months, complaints began rolling in about recalled vans that caught fire after having undergone the fix, and Nissan agreed to repurchase the rest for blue book value.

It should have been a shining moment for Kane. But he discovered there was a world of difference between Ralphs. Being on the payroll of Ralph Hoar was a far cry from working for Ralph Nader. As long as

Kane received his paycheck from the Center for Auto Safety, he had instant credibility as someone working tirelessly on behalf of consumers and whose opinions could not be bought. That perception changed when he jumped to the private sector intent on increasing his $18,000 annual salary. When Kane called ABC about the Nissan van recall, he heard Peter Jennings in the background scream, "Who the hell is Ralph Hoar?" That had never happened at CAS.

When Kane started work at Ralph Hoar & Associates, Hoar wore baggy pants and dressed like a hippie. By the time Kane left, Hoar employed a personal shopper at Nordstrom's and had moved from a two-bedroom condo to a Washington, D.C., townhouse to his own house in Arlington, Virginia. They had a combined Rolodex of hundreds of paying clients and thousands of names.

Like many business relationships, theirs fell apart over money. For two years Kane had been asking for a percentage of the company. But with Hoar away so much of the time pursuing interests like New Age mysticism and Kane tethered to his desk managing day-to-day operations, they lost track of each other. When Hoar indicated he wanted to spend less time with the company, Kane offered to buy him out. They met up in Massachusetts and Kane laid out his plan. He wanted to take over control of the company, change its name, and keep Hoar on as a writer at large. Hoar refused and Kane left in September 1997, taking key staff with him to form Strategic Safety. Hoar never forgave him for this.

It took a couple of months for Kane to get his business off the ground. But eventually Kane was earning far more than he ever did with Hoar.

Kane's instincts told him Firestone was concealing a defect. He decided to expand his search to foreign markets, reasoning ATX tires would be found anywhere the Explorer was sold. He sent e-mail to an eclectic list of sources from around the world, people who followed industry scuttlebutt—Asian parts dealers, Canadian junkyard operators, European tire and seat suppliers, Latin American auto industry consultants. He tailored the message to each one, but the essence of the query was the same: "Have you seen any Explorer tire problems?"

A South American contact e-mailed back, telling Kane he thought something was happening in Venezuela. Since Kane got a lot of leads, most of which didn't pan out, he wasn't too excited. A few days later, after clearing off another week's worth of work from his plate, he surfed the Net from home after dinner. He found his way to *El Nacional*, a Venezuelan newspaper, where he read a short article in the back of the business section on Ford and Firestone. It was in Spanish but Kane got the gist. What he read stunned him. He sent the story to a couple of friends fluent in Spanish, who told him what he now knew for sure: Ford was replacing ATX tires on Explorers in Venezuela.

Jumping up from his computer to pace the house, Kane pondered the implications. If Ford was willing to take on the expense of a recall in Venezuela, the automaker must have concluded the tires were defective. If so, it was only a matter of time before Ford and Firestone would be forced to recall the tires in the United States. The fact that Firestone hadn't been included in the Venezuela ATX recall indicated the tire maker was going to pursue its usual head-in-the-dirt strategy and claim there was nothing wrong with the tire.

Kane got back on the Internet and followed research links to Automotriz.net, a Latin American automotive site, where he located two relevant articles. One from May 17, 2000, reported a rash of Explorer tire problems, many of them serious, with Ford claiming the problem was due to mileage, excessive speed, and presence of alcohol—although Kane couldn't figure out how drinking could destroy a tire. Ford offered a special deal for Explorer owners. Turn in your five and receive a whole new set for a marginal fee, plus get new shock absorbers. By June, Ford was offering to replace the tires free with Goodyears. The article also noted NHTSA was investigating the tire in the United States.

The next morning Kane phoned his NHTSA contact. "You won't believe this," Kane said. "Ford has recalled the tires overseas." There was a long silence followed by an expletive. The agency had been investigating the tire since May, and neither Ford nor Firestone had mentioned anything about recalling ATX tires overseas.

"It's in Venezuela," Kane added, "and other countries may be involved." He suggested NHTSA ask Ford for a list of markets where it has replaced ATX tires with other brands. A couple of hours later his source called back. The automaker admitted it had recalled tires in Malaysia, Thailand, Kuwait, Oman, Saudi Arabia, Venezuela, and other Latin American markets.

Kane passed the information to KHOU producer David Raziq, who asked "Defenders" cameraman Chris Henao, who was fluent in Spanish, to contact INDECU (Venezuela's consumer safety agency) for comment. That night, KHOU became the first news organization to report that while the U.S. government was investigating the ATX, Ford was recalling the same tires in almost a dozen countries around the world.

Responding to a flurry of media inquiries about the replacement programs, NHTSA announced that a three-month investigation had turned up 193 complaints and 21 deaths related to sudden failure of Firestone

ATX and Wilderness AT tires, with most accidents occurring at between 50 and 75 mph. In two cases the tread wrapped around the rear axle, sending the car reeling. But since there was no law that required the companies to contact the Department of Transportation in the event of a recall abroad, they had done nothing illegal. Still, it prompted the *Wall Street Journal* to suggest, "this case is a costly and tragic illustration of how, in the information age, crucial information can be lost, buried or overlooked amid the tides of data that slosh in to huge global corporations every day."

But Sean Kane knew better. Ford and Firestone didn't just lose, bury or overlook crucial information. They had simply chosen to ignore it.

14 THE WAR ROOM

FROM AFAR, FORD'S INTERNATIONAL HEADQUARTERS in Dearborn seemed more glass than structure, a glistening 14-story steel-latticed box with about 3,000 windows. On the 11th floor, executives manned telephones in the company's "war room," fielding questions from frantic consumers and journalists on deadline. Ford President and CEO Jacques Nasser ordered its creation in late July 2000 at about the time Sean Kane broke the news that Ford had recalled Firestone tires in Venezuela, the Middle East, and Southeast Asia. Starting out in a 20-foot-by-20-foot conference room accessible to Nasser via a private staircase from his office, it quickly became the daily meeting place for a task force of engineering, finance, legal, manufacturing, purchasing and public-affairs officials. As the crisis deepened it became an "amoeba," as Jason Vines, Ford's vice president of corporate communications and Nasser's right-hand man, put it, taking over several additional conference spaces and spreading to other floors.

Although he hadn't been at Ford long, Vines was the ideal choice to orchestrate the company's media strategy. Once a true believer at Nissan, and before that Chrysler, Vines was now Ford tried and true. Hired six months earlier to serve Nasser, Vines brought with him a strong rapport with reporters and a reputation as a consummate professional. At the first hint of trouble, he whipped his 250-member public relations team into a streamlined organization with a well-honed message.

While Firestone, overwhelmed and understaffed, sometimes took days to get back to reporters on deadline, Vines made sure journalists were given prompt and thorough attention. Under his direction, Ford PR supplied its staff a list of potential questions and company-approved answers governing its actions abroad, and distributed stacks of charts and graphs and data to back up the automaker's claims. He dispatched Ken Zino, a testy corporate spokesman with an engineering background, and safety communications manager Sara Tatchio to Nashville to baby-sit Firestone PR and keep Ford's interests in their face. They quickly achieved such control that reporters who dialed into telephone conferences at Firestone were often directed to Ford publicists.

Vines created a list of four "principles" that top management agreed would guide the company's actions through the crisis, handwritten on a sign outside the war room and printed on index cards to "remind everyone why we were doing this." "Safety" was the No. 1 priority, and a promise to work around the clock to find solutions the second. Third was "Be open and candid with all of our communications," and the fourth: "Protect Firestone."

Well, Vines wasn't so sure about that last one. Although no one at Ford wanted to be responsible for driving a vendor out of business, Vines was feeling complete contempt for his counterparts at Firestone. Dealing with them had led him to conclude the two companies didn't need a marriage counselor. They required a divorce lawyer.

Vines thought Firestone's handling of the situation from the top down had been inept from the start. The conflict between the two companies began in 1998, when Hector Rodriguez, a Ford purchasing manager in Caracas, Venezuela, noted a pattern of tread separations on Firestone tires on Explorers and other light trucks. When some of the tires were sent to Firestone for analysis, the tire maker blamed "over-inflation, underinflation, and badly repaired punctures." Firestone refused to pay for replacements because it believed it would give the "subliminal message" that the tires were defective.

Afraid it hadn't requested a tire robust enough for Venezuela's harsh driving conditions, where, as one Ford internal memo put it, there were "virtually no traffic rules, no speed limits [not enforced], drive as fast as you can," and temperatures routinely hit 105 degrees, the automaker asked Firestone to submit a design with a nylon cap ply to make the tires more durable. Ford approved the new specs in June 1999 and Firestone immediately put the tires into production.

But tread separations continued to escalate. After 47 deaths in Venezuela were linked to Firestone tires on Explorers, Ford calculated a defect rate for the Wilderness tire 1,000 times greater there than in the States. It initiated its own investigation and found that half of the tires involved in accidents not only lacked the nylon layer it had asked for, they also had a lower speed rating than it had specified.

Relations between the companies turned frosty after Ford, afraid of consumer backlash, informed Firestone in a May 2000 meeting that it was going to replace Wilderness tires in Venezuela. Firestone, citing a

Ford Venezuela engineers' report that attributed the problem to the Explorer's suspension system, responded that replacing the tires without correcting the Explorer's suspension system "would put in jeopardy the Bridgestone brand in Venezuela," and pointed out that Grand Blazers and Toyota Autanas equipped with Wilderness tires did not roll over even in cases of tire failure. The engineers blamed shock absorbers that were too soft for Venezuela's roads and the Explorer's center of gravity "being taller and less [wide] than other trucks," which made it "more [sensitive] to rollover during hard shift. The report had prompted Ford in Caracas to initiate a program to change the Explorer's suspension system for free, offering a combo package that included switching 15- and 16-inch Firestone tires to Goodyears and installing a bar to hold the new shock absorbers in place—a service that normally cost 273,000 bolivares, or roughly $500.

In a meeting between the two companies, Ford Venezuela President Emmanuel Cassingena became "very aggressive" and "rude," and demanded that Firestone pay for replacing its tires with Goodyears on more than 30,000 Explorers in Venezuela, Colombia, and Ecuador. He rejected Firestone's proposal that the two companies share blame and "under no circumstance" would he accept a statement that the "Explorer has suspension problems." Dismissing the findings of his own engineers, he claimed the suspension system was being changed only because of "customer preferences and driving conditions" in Venezuela. A stiffer suspension was purely to provide a smoother ride.

Firestone finally agreed to recall the tires in Venezuela, but abruptly changed course a few days later after Bridgestone management in Japan weighed in. Vines got the news when Nasser called him into his office as he put Bridgestone/Firestone's chairman, Masatoshi Ono, on speakerphone. Ono's voice trembled as he read from a prepared script. "We cannot recall these tires," Ono said in fidgety English. "There is no need to recall."

Nasser's last words before hanging up were, "Listen, either you're going to do it with us or we're going to do it without you." A few days later Ford made good on Nasser's pledge.

At roughly the time Ford and Firestone were fighting over Venezuela, they were also going toe-to-toe in "Gulf Coast Countries" in the Middle East, a place where blowouts were common, as the scraps of rubber littering the sides of highways attested, especially in summer when temperatures topped 120 degrees.

The first complaints arose in Saudi Arabia, where John Garthwaite, national service manager of the Saudi Ford dealership Al Jazirah Vehicle

Agencies Inc., reported several customers complaining of faulty Firestone tires on their Explorers. But the tires were in pieces, which made it impossible to know whether a puncture or road hazard was to blame. He shipped them to Firestone anyway, which chalked up the failures to improper tire storage, punctures, and underinflation. The tire maker's solution was that Ford dealers should avoid "flat spots" by re-parking cars in showrooms every two weeks.

Meanwhile, Glenn Drake, a Ford executive in the United Arab Emirates, also detected problems. "If this was a single case, I would accept Firestone's response as they are the experts in the tire business, case closed," he wrote. "However, we have three cases and it is possible that Firestone is not telling us the whole story to protect them from a recall or lawsuit."

Two weeks later Garthwaite encountered another tire failure—on an Explorer driven by the secretary of Al Jazirah's president, which flipped over after a tread separation. This time he got a good look at the tire, which was fully inflated with the tread sheared off. Garthwaite complained to Keshav Das, a senior engineer for Bridgestone in Dubai, explaining that the tire hadn't lost any pressure since the day he received it. The tread separation could not have been caused by underinflation or a puncture. "It appears to be increasingly obvious that there exists an inherent problem in the bonding of the tread to the casing," he said, and threatened to "hold Firestone Tire Co. wholly responsible. . . ."

With mounting evidence of a problem, Ford suggested the two companies outfit Explorers shipped to the Gulf with more robust tires and offer Explorer owners the option of upgrading their tires. But Firestone balked at this idea because it didn't want the U.S. Department of Transportation to find out, since the same tire was sold in America. Ford didn't want to tip off the DOT either, and wasn't thrilled with the cost of replacement tires.

Firestone did, however, launch a watered down "customer service program" in Saudi Arabia. Whenever an Explorer came in for tire replacement, dealer staff were instructed to inquire about usage. If the customer drove fast, they should recommend Euro "H"-rated tires, designed for high-speed driving. If he went off-road or rode over unimproved road surfaces, they should push special-service "S"-rated tires, which were developed for Australia/New Zealand and offered greater puncture resistance. Those happy with their present tires should replace them with the same model.

But Al Jazirah wasn't satisfied with this approach and convinced Ford to take action. The dealership instituted a "temporary program" in

July 1999 to offer any Ford Explorer customer who came in for servicing a new set of more durable tires at a 75 percent discount—at Ford's expense. The automaker decided against using Firestone tires. Instead customers received Goodyears. In addition service technicians were to lower the Explorer's top speed—without the owners' knowledge—by electronically reprogramming it. Garthwaite hired three people to contact Explorer owners to ask if they would like to bring in the car for a free inspection, but they didn't use the word "recall," nor did they raise safety concerns.

Not all dealers in the region were pleased with the way Ford handled the situation. After his dealership was sued for a rollover, Danny Hinchin, an executive of Haji Hussein Alireza, told Ford the automaker was merely inflaming the problem. "We are at a position now where Ford is rejecting claims from owners, so the dealers themselves are left to face the customer," he wrote. He pointed out that "incidences of tire failure" were clearly "higher" for the Firestone Wilderness AT than with other makes of tire, which suggested "a tire construction/misapplication concern" not restricted to Gulf Coast Countries. It was also happening in the United States. "I have researched this," he said, "the NHTSA Web site has had comments from owners in this regard." He noted in most cases "the tire that failed was . . . nearest to the exhaust, suggesting the heat properties of the tire were close to critical anyway."

In the Sultanate of Oman a few weeks later, an Explorer holding a family of five along with their maid turned over 200 kilometers from Muscat, killing the father and three children, and seriously injuring the wife and maid. "It is very pathetic that our Explorer customers are losing lives because of the Firestone tires," a service manager from Bahrain Automotive Center wrote. He warned Ford that people in the region were "scared to buy Explorers."

Grodent Baptiste, who worked at Ford's Customer Service Division in Dubai, United Arab Emirates, had other concerns about the Oman rollover. After assuring the director of Ford's Customer Service Office, Worldwide Direct Market Operations, that he and his colleagues had "so far been able to control this issue and managed not to have any kind of rumors spread around the region," he advised that Ford should "be very cautious and make sure that we do not alert the suspicion of the police/insurance in Oman that we may have a problem with our tyres. . . ."

In November 1999 Ford asked Bridgestone to conduct a study of Firestone Wilderness tires similar to those replaced in Saudi Arabia. Firestone surveyed 243 tires used in southwestern states. "No tire deficiencies," a memo to Ford claimed. "The tires performed as expected."

Eventually Ford learned the so-called "Southwest Survey" was bogus. Firestone cut open only three tires—the only sure way to tell a tire was defective—offering a cursory visual inspection of the rest.

Months of internecine squabbling in foreign markets culminated with the Ford team huddling in its Dearborn headquarters with experts from Bridgestone on Aug. 5, 2000. The pressure had been building on both companies. NHTSA doubled the number of reported fatalities due to Firestone tread separations on Explorers from 21 to 46, with 80 injuries and 270 complaints, and Sears (the top tire seller in America), Discount Tire, and a number of other tire distributors announced they would no longer carry Firestone tires.

Sean Kane sent a letter to Ford stating that Strategic Safety had confirmed at least 80 injuries and more than 50 deaths resulting from Firestone tire failures, and repeated his demand that Ford recall the Explorer and offer replacement tires. "Can the American public assume that because of the greater economic effect that accompanies a large vehicle population Ford is unwilling to offer replacement tires in the U.S.?," he asked.

At the meeting an argument broke out, with Firestone's representatives alleging that the low 26 psi tire pressure Ford recommended, combined with fast driving in hot weather, was at the root of the problem. But after Ford showed the tire maker its own data that the automaker had fed into an in-house supercomputer, which indicated the failures were concentrated in 15-inch ATX, ATX II, and Wilderness tires manufactured at the Decatur factory, Firestone's representatives "shit their pants," according to Vines.

Of 2,500 complaints involving eight categories of tires, Ford found that 2,030, or 81 percent, involved the 15-inch P235/75R15 models, which included the Firestone ATX and Wilderness tires. Of the almost 1,700 reported complaints of tread separation on 13 different size tires, 84 percent occurred on Ford Explorers, Broncos, and F-150 and Ranger pickup trucks equipped with 15-inch ATX tires. "They basically . . . called a time out," Vines said. "They went outside and huddled, came back in and said 'OK, we'll recall them.' "

But it wasn't until Vines was prepping for the joint recall announcement in Washington that he encountered the tire maker's intransigence firsthand. Christine Karbowiak, the company's vice president of public affairs, advised him that Firestone wouldn't participate in a live press conference. She suggested instead a one-way satellite feed, no graphs, charts or data, no questions from the press corps.

Vines told her she was crazy. "You've got to show people there's some science behind the decisions," he said. Millions of tires were covered by the recall and millions weren't. Even people within Ford found it confusing. How were reporters—let alone consumers—going to make sense out of it?

Eventually Karbowiak gave in on taking questions at the press conference, but refused to budge on providing supporting material. At the 11th hour she re-introduced the issue of low tire pressure, which Firestone insisted on incorporating into the joint announcement.

There was no way Vines could allow Firestone to bring up psi. He argued that the data clearly showed a problem with tires made in Decatur on all vehicles, regardless of air pressure. The American public didn't get nuances, which was why Vines wanted to release as much data as possible as quickly as possible, to assure the people and politicians that the corporations were doing everything in their power to protect and inform their customers. Any dispute could launch both companies into media free fall. For their plan to work, the companies had to be united. If they weren't, it could lead to a serious credibility gap, and open the door to rapacious trial attorneys eager to advance their lawsuits.

Vines and Karbowiak volleyed back and forth until 2 a.m., when Vines finally had enough. He told her flat out that there was no way Ford would allow Firestone to insinuate the automaker was partially at fault for setting air pressure too low. "If you keep putting this in here," Vines threatened, "I'm going to drop the Goodyear blimp on you." The automaker had asked Goodyear Tire & Rubber Co. to analyze its internal data on Goodyear-brand tires on 500,000 Explorers, and Goodyear officials told Ford they found no evidence of tread-separation problems.

That put an end to the discussion for the night, but Vines suspected it wouldn't be the last time Firestone tried to pull Ford down with it. For the time being the companies were united in a common purpose. But just in case Firestone didn't toe the line, Vines began to formulate a strategy.

Only one of them could be seen as being responsible for the accidents in the court of public opinion—and Vines promised himself it wouldn't be Ford.

15 RECALL

AT 11 A.M. ON AUGUST. 9, 2000, EXECUTIVES from Ford and Bridge-stone/Firestone took center stage in a top-floor room at the National Press Club in Washington, D.C. If history were any guide, the companies could count on getting off with little more than the equivalent of a fender bender—a few minutes of hostile questioning, a few weeks of bad press, and some political grandstanding by a handful of members of Congress before things returned to normal. After all, defective product recalls occurred practically every week in the auto industry. There had been 70 of them affecting 7.3 million vehicles in the first seven months of 2000 alone, which consumers greeted with little more than a collective shrug. But when confronted with the standing-room-only crowd of media that had assembled for the press conference, Ford and Firestone officials quickly realized this time would be different.

Handling the announcement for Bridgestone/Firestone was Gary Crigger, a longtime company man and the tire maker's executive vice president. Unused to assuming a public role, Crigger suddenly found himself speaking on camera to tens of millions of people. In the end, instead of mollifying consumers, he would end up enraging them.

He kicked things off by apologizing for "the lack of information over the past few days" and for any confusion it created and explained that Firestone viewed the recall as merely a "precaution to ensure consumer safety and consumer confidence" in the Firestone brand. It covered 6.5 million 15-inch tires still on the road out of the 14.4 million the company had produced at its Decatur, Illinois, plant: 3.8 million Radial ATX and Radial ATX II, and 2.7 million Wilderness AT tires.

Crigger emphasized that accidents were "rare," although admitted the data showed a higher failure rate for the 15-inch Radial AT and ATX tires than with other sizes in this line and that tires manufactured in

Decatur were "over-represented" in claims. Since the company had not been able to pinpoint any defect in the tires and the majority of failures had occurred in the southern-most states of Arizona, California, Florida, and Texas, Crigger suggested that driving in hot temperatures and low tire pressure may have been factors.

He asked customers with tires covered under the recall to call their local Firestone retailer to set up an appointment for an exchange, but warned that "given the limited supply of replacement tires" that Firestone would be undertaking a "three-phase recall." The first part would en-compass Arizona, California, Florida, and Texas, followed by recalls in Alabama, Georgia, Louisiana, Mississippi, Nevada, Oklahoma, and Tennessee. The final phase would cover the remaining states.

Crigger also urged consumers to take additional steps to increase the lifespan and safety of their tires by maintaining proper inflation. "When underinflated, all radial tires generate excessive heat," he said. "Driving on tires in this condition can lead to tread separation. Maintaining the proper inflation level will enhance the performance and lifespan of these tires."

He noted that Ford recommended 26 psi, while Firestone recom-mended 30 psi. "We believe the higher inflation level that we are recom-mending will enhance the performance and lifespan of these tires," Crigger said.

As soon as Crigger finished his opening statement, reporters began firing questions at him. Why hadn't Firestone and Ford begun recalling tires at the first hint of trouble? Certainly two-dozen death claims must have been a tip-off that something was wrong. Why did they recall tires abroad but not in the United States?

While Crigger stonewalled with answers like "We have a continuing effort to review all our incidents involving our tires," Ford vice president Helen Petrauskas jumped in. Forced to deviate from her prepared script, she claimed that driving conditions in the Middle East were different than in the southern United States. In Saudi Arabia, "we were getting . . . anecdotal reports of people taking sport utility vehicles, loading them up very heavily, deflating the tires, and taking them out for riding around in the desert, and then getting back on the highway, and then reporting tread separation," she said. "We also had anecdotal evidence of some maintenance concerns."

She addressed the discrepancy in tire pressure between Ford and Firestone by assuring the public that Ford "evaluated the performance of these tires at 30 psi and has determined that the vehicle maintains good performance characteristics at this higher pressure. Customers with other vehicles should check the door plate on their vehicle for recommended tire pressure and make sure that tire pressure does not fall below the recommended level."

As Vines had predicted, Firestone's handling of the recall announcement led to more questions than answers, panicking the public and touching off a media hullabaloo. He was particularly livid that Firestone brought up the air pressure issue. *They just made a bad situation worse,* he thought. *They have no idea what they're doing. They're in way over their heads.*

Almost immediately after the press conference, Firestone's Web site crashed from a huge spike in traffic. Motorists looking to book appointments for tire replacements jammed the phone lines of its dealers around the country. Mike Barbaro, senior vice president of Town Fair Tire, an East Haven, Connecticut–based chain of 52 stores, told the Associated Press, "When customers hear there's a recall or a death involved, they come in screaming and say, 'Get them off the car.' " He criticized Firestone for not providing adequate information until the day of the recall, leading to a lot of unnecessary confusion and angering his customers. In Southern California, some drivers were being told just an hour after the recall announcement that, because of the heavy demand, it would be more than a month before replacement tires could be fitted to their cars.

New York State Attorney General Eliot Spitzer lambasted the phased-in recall plan, which could take more than a year to carry out: "The premise under Firestone's action is wrong," he said. "It seems inconsistent to recall tires in one region of the country and thereby admitting there's a risk attached to the tires and tell the consumers, 'You take second place.' " He pointed out it was the height of the summer and New Yorkers would be driving to other parts of the country for vacation, "in precise parts of the country where they say because of the heat, the tires are dangerous." He suggested that Firestone provide coupons so that consumers could redeem them for other brands.

Meanwhile Vines recognized opportunity in the ensuing "cluster fuck."

When reporters deluged Ford with calls, he was ready for them. He had printed out graphs and data to explain why Ford urged Firestone to recall the tires from Decatur, and included safety information that cast the automaker in the best (and Firestone in the worst) light. His public relations team papered journalists with material that claimed the Ford Explorer offered better protection to its occupants in multi-vehicle crashes, such as in front- and side-impact collisions (although he neglected to mention it was also 16 times more likely to kill occupants in the other car).

Vines leaked the Goodyear information to the *Wall Street Journal* and released documents that showed that the tire maker first started receiving complaints of injuries and property damage involving ATX tires as far back as 1997, with some models plagued by rates of injury and personal damage claims 100 times greater than non-recalled tires. Lobbyists fanned out over Capitol Hill to present the case that Ford acted responsibly and to subtly blame Firestone. Their ultimate point, which they dispersed via fax, e-mail, and phone conversation, was, If you removed the Firestone tires from the equation there wouldn't be a story.

Ten minutes before a Fortune magazine photographer arrived at the Glass House, Vines eyed the sign posted outside the war room listing the company's goals and ordered a subordinate to remove the last one: "Protect Firestone."

Well, he thought. *I'd warned them.*

THE DAY OF THE RECALL, DONNA BAILEY appeared on television, an interview Tab Turner had set up for her. "It's been tough," she told CBS reporter Byron Pitts. "I am confined. It's like being in jail." She said that she still dreamed of running at night. "That's hard. I miss that."

Afterward she began receiving letters from well-wishers. Actor Christopher Reeve, who became a quadriplegic after falling off a horse, sent her a note, telling her to "be strong during difficult times. I feel stronger each day, and know that, you too, will make great strides during your life. My family and friends rallied around me after my accident. I know that with your loving family and friends surrounding you, you will have all the support you need during your life's journey."

A week after the recall, Donna took a three-and-a-half-hour ambulance ride to the Texas Institute for Rehabilitation and Research in Houston. It was the first time she had been outside the hospital in five months. Although Donna was frightened by the prospect of travel—she wondered what would happen if her ventilator jammed with pus again, or she went into cardiac arrest—the journey to get into TIRR had been even more traumatic.

She was relieved to be getting away from San Antonio, blaming some of the nurses and orderlies there for the gaping sore in her back. When her family complained, hospital staff claimed Donna was "noncompliant." Although Donna admitted she could be testy, she couldn't figure out how a quadriplegic could be uncooperative. It wasn't as if she could prevent them from flipping her on her side as the need arose.

Donna believed the fact that she didn't have medical insurance influenced the care she received and colored their bedside manner. They couldn't wait to get rid of her. In their eyes she was just a drain on hospital resources. At times they withheld pain medication. They didn't wash her hair for weeks. One orderly told her he was going to unplug her ventilator and let her die.

Before she could leave San Antonio, however, she had to have surgery on her bedsore and then lie on a hot silicon sand bed for six weeks. In the meantime, Rick contacted every governmental organization he could think of. He'd almost given up when the Texas Rehabilitation Commission came through with three months' worth of funding.

At TIRR Donna's life improved dramatically. The place was cleaner and the staff experienced in dealing with quadriplegics. Doctors put her on a combination of Paxil and BuSpar, which controlled her anxiety attacks, experimented with drugs to ease her spasms, and put her on a rehab program. As a result Donna was able to arrest her chronic weight loss and muscle atrophy, and begin to take control of her life.

The fact that Ford and Firestone were under attack also energized her. It removed any lingering doubt in her mind that the two companies were behind her life sentence. Because of their greed, she would never be able to lead a normal life. Not only would she not be able to take of her children, she couldn't even take care of herself. What Donna wanted more than anything was for Ford and Firestone to take responsibility for what they had done, and to take care of her medical needs for the rest of her life.

She didn't think that was asking too much.

16 MEDIA MAVEN

TAB TURNER WATCHED THE FORD-FIRESTONE press conference at CBS News in Washington, D.C., with on-air correspondent and part-time anchor Sharyl Attkisson, who sat at her desk typing notes on a PC.

Attkisson's office was like all the others in the bureau, a 10-foot-by-10-foot Rubik's cube decorated journalist style—books, desiccated magazines, curling newspaper cutouts, and dated photocopies semi-organized into files and folders, crammed into drawers, stacked on shelves, and piled floor-to-knee. For art's sake, Attkisson had adorned a file cabinet with photos of her six-year-old daughter, which were on display beside a wall collage of threatening letters from the Food and Drug Administration, a managed care lobbying group, and a pharmaceutical industry flack. Catty-corner was a newspaper article, an almost word-for-word rip-off of an exclusive Attkisson had reported on a fraudulent drug study at Pittsburgh Children's Hospital that resulted in a baby's death.

Attkisson marveled at Turner's ability to multitask. He was able to keep an oblique eye on the press conference, listen to voice mail messages on his cell phone, two-finger type e-mail on his laptop, plan his next trip, take calls from those able to penetrate his caller ID shield, and still patiently field Attkisson's questions without missing a beat.

Still morning, for Turner it had already been a long day. After his plane touched down at midnight, he awoke at 4:30 a.m. to appear on the *Early Show* with Bryant Gumbel, where he debated the scope of the planned recall with Robert Wyant, vice president of quality control at Bridgestone/Firestone. Soon after, Attkisson whisked Turner to the production studios, where they brushed on makeup, jammed a plug into his ear and focused a camera on him for an in-depth interview.

In a feisty question-and-answer session, he and Attkisson discussed the troubled history of the Ford Bronco II and Explorer. Attkisson was impressed with Turner's mastery of the subject. Usually it was difficult to get sources to support their statements with facts. Those that would couldn't in the succinct, easy-to-comprehend phrases necessary for TV. But Turner was plainspoken and could recite Ford documents he had used in court from memory—a memo, company e-mail, engineer's report. Every once in a while a reporter came across a resource like Turner, someone who could help navigate vast amounts of information and corporate history.

Her producers at *CBS Evening News* put her on the story a week before the recall announcement, when *USA Today* ran a front-page feature on NHTSA's Ford-Firestone investigation. In recent years, *CBS Evening News* had been getting most of its material out of the newspaper. The show was steadily losing popularity. The new editorial regime wanted to compete on a breaking story—one of personal importance to millions of Americans in a highly favorable demographic—instead of providing second-day leads and covering press conferences. They needed somebody with investigative experience who wouldn't back down from aggressive corporations with legions of lawyers.

Attkisson had proven her mettle anchoring CBS's millennium coverage. She broke stories on suspected nuclear espionage at the nation's weapons labs and dangerous drugs being approved by the FDA. She reported on John Glenn's return to space. And she was beautiful, which made her ideal for TV.

Soon after she returned to her desk with the assignment, Attkisson received a call from an editor at *60 Minutes II*, who provided background information and a contact list of 30 names on Ford and Firestone. The TV news magazine had been working on a feature, but in a spirit of cooperation rare for shows competing for resources within the same network, agreed to pass on its research to the *Evening News*, which would be providing the day-to-day coverage.

Attkisson wasn't a transportation reporter. She spent the first few days phoning safety experts and plaintiffs attorneys, tire chemists, accident reconstructionists, and lobbyists, trying to get a handle on the issues. Ford assigned a publicist to Attkisson, who told her straight out the automaker wasn't accepting any blame. Firestone was in such disarray Attkisson couldn't even get through. All she got were busy signals. Eventually she was able to leave a voice mail, but no one called back.

She heard about Tab Turner from Ralph Hoar, who hosted Turner's tire page on Safetyforum.com. Attkisson caught up with him at his hotel in Chicago, where he was speaking at the annual American Trial Lawyers Association conference. It was the same speech he had given before, "When Defective Tires Cause Wrecks." Turner covered such topics as how to read a DOT number, where to locate statistics on rollovers, and chain of custody, Turner's big bugaboo.

They chatted a few minutes about Ford and Firestone and then she asked Turner to appear on camera for an interview. He declined. His family was with him in Chicago and he intended to take his wife and three daughters to see the sights.

Attkisson complained about the secrecy agreements she was encountering. They were difficult to penetrate.

Turner told her he could relate. He'd been dealing with them for years. But he'd promised his wife he wouldn't work after his speech.

They hung up, but Attkisson refused to take no for an answer. It was refreshing to run into someone uneager to appear on camera. In some ways it made him more credible. By this point, most plaintiff attorneys would be negotiating camera angles and demanding to talk to the makeup artist. Attkisson phoned Turner back and said that Ford and Firestone were squelching information. Turner was in a unique position to do something about it.

"Nice try," Turner said. He politely hung up.

Attikisson hit redial. When Turner picked up she told him he could do the interview at the local Chicago affiliate, at any time that suited him. Tired of saying no, Turner scheduled a 7 a.m. interview so he could be back at his hotel in time for breakfast with his family. Early the following morning Turner arrived at the studio to discover that Attkisson was caught in D.C. traffic and would be late. Turner was sorry he'd bothered to throw on a suit at the crack of dawn. He killed time talking to the camera crew. The TV station owned Explorers, and some workers wondered what tires they should put on. "Anything but what you have on now," Turner said. He advised them to get rid of the cars, too.

After Attkisson got to the studio and connected with Turner in Chicago via satellite, she told him she wanted to start by tackling the issue of settlements and silence. She was just getting into the story, and Turner gave her an hour and a half.

Two days later Turner was with her at CBS News Central in Washington, D.C., watching Ford and Firestone announce the recall on national TV together. When Gary Crigger brought up the tire pressure issue during his opening remarks, Attkisson laughed out loud. Just that morning she and Turner had been discussing it.

Turner suggested Attkisson confront Ford. He told her the real reason Ford insisted on less air pressure was "to keep the wheels on the ground during J-turn tests," and diagrammed the principle on a napkin. The Explorer's recommended pressure gave the tire and vehicle a narrow margin for error and in the process created a sticky safety dichotomy. Although 26 psi was as high as Ford engineers could go to keep the Explorer's wheels on the ground in sharp turns, it was as low as Firestone could go to ensure the tires could support almost 4,000 pounds of vehicle and an additional 1,000 pounds of people and their belongings, day in and day out, without disintegrating.

Two days later Attkisson reported back to Turner that Ford denied that air pressure had anything to do with stability. It was for "consumer comfort," a "smoother ride," she said.

Turner riffled through his collection of documents for an internal memo that showed Ford decided against recommending a higher tire pressure after computer simulations indicated it increased the risk of rollover. He produced another detailing a crash test driver who rolled over in an Explorer while conducting lane change maneuvers. An e-mail from Ford Venezuela raised questions about the low inflation rate while a Firestone pamphlet urged 32 psi for ATX tires.

In her Aug. 10, 2000, report, Attkisson deemed the recall "a nightmare for Ford and Firestone," and portrayed a catch-22 where worried drivers lined up to get tires taken off their SUVs while Firestone couldn't make tires fast enough to replace the 6 million tires affected. Attkisson said that Firestone recommended tires be inflated to 30 pounds, but "to minimize the risk of rollover Ford has—for years—instructed drivers to keep their tire pressure much lower: 26 pounds," to keep more rubber on the road where it can get a grip. The problem, she pointed out, was it also heated up the tire.

"You're talking about a catastrophic combination," Turner said in the piece.

Attkisson saved her best conundrum for last. Ford and Firestone still hadn't reached an accord on air pressure. "Ford favors lower tire pressure to protect against rollover; Firestone wants it higher so the tires won't peel apart as often."

And what should Explorer owners do? "We talked to independent experts who recommend inflating your Explorer tires to 35 pounds and driving slowly and carefully. Dan?"

As in Rather. As in 6.5 million viewers. For the next few days Turner's office phone rang off the hook as journalists, playing catch-up with CBS, contacted him for a copy of the documents and an interview. The Associated Press, *Los Angeles Times*, *USA Today*, and the *Wall Street Journal* followed with articles of their own based on evidence Turner had given them, which were reprinted in newspapers, posted on Web sites and replayed on TV and radio. Turner realized both he and journalists shared a common need for documentation. It was the only way to pinpoint what Ford and Firestone knew and when they knew it. But Turner didn't just start dumping paper proof on reporters' laps. He came up with a strategy to force Ford into a public debate.

Turner decided he would "raise an issue then watch Ford lie." He wanted Ford to gag on its own words. A lower tire pressure for a smoother ride? All it took was a couple of documents to refute that, and make the automaker squirm in the process. Suddenly it wasn't just one trial attorney versus a corporation, his word against theirs. The debate would be over the evidence.

He shared correspondence with reporters between Ford and Firestone over recalling tires in Kuwait, Oman, and Saudi Arabia. He raised the issue of the Explorer repeatedly failing Ford's own rollover tests. He outlined the automaker's role in developing the fatal Firestone tire. For weeks, Ford's PR staff found itself drawn into a full-scale effort to contain the damage from internal memos, e-mails, meeting minutes, and engineers' reports that were suddenly made public, some of which its own attorneys didn't even know existed.

Turner even had a name for it: Death by Slow Document Leak. And the result was devastating. "Every day Tab would take one of those documents and say, 'Here's a little grenade—let me throw it in there,' " Jason Vines recounted to the *New York Times*.

But Ford wasn't alone in having to answer for past deeds. Firestone also had a lot of explaining to do.

17 THE WHISTLE-BLOWER

THE MERCURY WAS STUCK ON 95 DEGREES before lunch and Alan Hogan sat at his desk in the auto body shop he co-owned, a telephone pinned between his ear and shoulder. August was always dog-breath hot in Wilson, North Carolina, but it wasn't the temperature outside making his blood boil. Hogan had been doing paperwork on the computer—ordering parts, writing and reviewing estimates—when a friend called to tell him to turn on the TV. His old employer, Firestone, was announcing a major tire recall. Hogan was nowhere near a TV, just car parts, tools, grease, and grime, so he had his friend place the phone by the speaker to listen in, which he did for a good quarter hour, getting madder by the minute.

Besides the typical corporate doublespeak, what upset him most about the press conference was that Firestone officials chose to implicate the Decatur factory, which during a mid-1990s strike had brought in replacement workers. They were trying to blame everything on their old, nasty strong-union facility in Decatur, but they weren't saying that Wilson had been producing the same "rag" tires for years.

A former biker who raised Japanese bonsais, the 33-year-old Hogan sometimes had to reject autograph seekers convinced Andre Agassi was wandering the local Wal-Mart (personally the 5-foot-10-inch, buzzed-cut Hogan didn't see the resemblance). He had been a gear head from the time he could stand. Starting as a "wrench runner" for his father, a Firestone engineer who often took his mechanically inclined son to work, Hogan remembered when the Wilson plant was but a concrete slab and some I-beams sticking out of the ground on the outskirts of town. He was four or five years old when his father taught him how to weld heavy tire machinery, and seven when he began exploring the gargantuan 800,000-square-foot tire facility on his own. As a teenager he rebuilt engines and transmissions and restored his first Porsche.

His father got him hired as contract labor at the plant bolting equipment to the floor in 1991. Soon Hogan was in charge of maintaining Wilson's industrial machinery. He realized he had a knack for making things run better. It was the way his mind worked: He could just look at a mechanical device and figure out a way to troubleshoot it. While Bridgestone's Japanese management was enamored of glitzy gadgetry with buttons, lights, bells, and whistles, "the more trick the better," Hogan preferred simple solutions. After workers suffered a rash of injuries on a machine that processed beads, which helped hold the tire to the rim, Hogan retooled it so the operator had to keep his hand on the switch before the cutter could come down. His redesign worked so well he became known as "the bead machine guru," and Firestone dispatched him to Decatur, Cuernavaca, Mexico, and to the Akron technical center to lend his technical expertise. He was working 12 to 16 hours a day doing what he loved, earning more than $40,000 a year, a lot where he was from.

But then Firestone, hobbled by a strike, asked Hogan to become a tire builder and a promised three-month assignment turned into three years. He was disillusioned by what he saw during his tenure slinging 30-pound tires 12 hours a day. There was no way around it. The company his father spent 25 years with, the company Hogan had always dreamed of working for, was cooking up a lot of bad tires.

Hogan knew that to make a steel-belted radial required several steps, incorporating as many as 200 different ingredients: natural and synthetic rubber, polymers, antioxidants, antiozonants, curing agents, elastomers, sulfur reinforcing agents, and processing materials, which were combined in a giant "Banbury Mixer" to obtain a uniformly homogenous mixture. It had to be completely free of impurities, otherwise pockets of air could develop. Suppliers crated brass-coated wire in sealed containers to keep it moisture-free before shipping to ensure it didn't corrode, which would prevent the rubber from adhering to the beads and belts. The components had to be stored in a properly maintained environment, or the tires might not hold together.

But what was the company supposed to do with tons of rejected material? Toss it? Not with management screaming about numbers and production and rating job performance by how many finished tires a builder had on his counter at the end of a shift. A rejected tire just meant a worker had to make another one after churning out 250 of them (one every 90 seconds) in a shift, and few had the temerity to shut down the line. Besides, Wilson foremen didn't seem to care if half a worker's tires were flawed, so long as they looked good enough to sell. That way the factory could report to Japan it was meeting production quotas.

The squeeze for profits meant quality control got short shrift. Hogan once wrote on a load of corroded steel, "If you get this roll of steel, I've rejected it," signed and dated it. The next day it came back to him with a note from another tire builder. "Hey, Alan, I got that message you left on that reject roll of steel." In the stock room it had been re-ticketed as acceptable and entered back into production.

Hogan saw contaminants of all types make it into the rubber—Band-Aids, cigarette butts, finger tape, a glove, scrap metal, nuts, bolts, screws, wood chips, and there were rumors of a condom ending up in the stock, which he assumed came courtesy of the prostitute turning tricks out of a van parked out back. But management discouraged workers from raising concerns. When the operator of a tire uniformity optimizer reported to his superiors that a plant operations manager was peeling "reject" stickers off of tires and replacing them with "approved," the worker was punished and the manager promoted.

The cavernous building—some 80 acres under one roof—was in chronic disrepair. The air conditioner was constantly on the fritz. In some places the roof leaked so badly that when it rained outside it rained inside, prompting workers to pitch tents over machinery entrusted with processing moisture-sensitive materials. At times tire builders were supplied dry rubber stock, which they refreshed by dipping paint brushes into buckets of solvent that sat within arm's length and swabbing each tire by hand. This restorative method was forbidden under Firestone's own policies; policies that were openly ignored.

Disheartened by what he saw, frustrated by the job's repetitive nature, the brutal 12-hour shifts, mandatory overtime, and tired of smelling like a tire all the time, Hogan quit in 1997. He had wanted to return to what he'd been doing before tire making, and that was making machinery better. It saved the company money and made him happy. When his boss refused, Hogan left the factory, and he and a partner founded a new venture in town, Automotive Body Shop.

Business had been good from the get-go, but he sometimes wondered what happened to some of those tires he and his co-workers built. Within a year he found out when he agreed to testify in a case involving a Wilson-made tire, and in the process it changed his life.

A couple days after Firestone's August 2000 recall announcement, Hogan was kicking back with a post-work can of beer at home when the phone rang. "Did you see the press conference?" Sharyl Attkisson asked.

Hogan said he had heard it. Attkisson had tracked him down from his appearance on KHOU six months earlier and had been trying for days to get him to tell his story on CBS, but Hogan kept turning her down. Basically shy, Hogan didn't like the idea of speaking in front of big crowds. Closer to home he was afraid his neighbors would see it. In fact, a lot of people would. You didn't last long in a place like Wilson (pop. 44,000) picking a fight with the county's biggest employer. People became attached to jobs that paid $40,000 without the need of a high school diploma.

"Alan," she said, "it's time for you to talk."

Hogan thought about it. Although he had promised himself he wouldn't get involved, he wasn't about to let Firestone get away with making Decatur a scapegoat for bugs inhabiting the company's entire operation. He saw what his keeping silent meant to Daniel Van Etten, a 19-year-old University of West Virginia football player who was killed returning to school after a tread separation. For all Hogan knew he had built that tire. Even if he hadn't, he could have easily been responsible for others that disintegrated at 60 mph. Production lines changed all the time. One day he could be building tires for the Thunderbird, the next for the Explorer. Hogan agreed to do it.

Attkisson instructed him to drive to an affiliate in Raleigh to do the interview via satellite but Hogan told her he would do her one better. "Get me a plane ticket and I'll do it in person," he said. She called back a few minutes later with his flight number. He grabbed a pair of pants and shirt, threw them into a backpack, and flew out of Raleigh to D.C., where a waiting driver took him to the TV station. When Attkisson met him downstairs in the CBS news bureau lobby, she confessed she had thought Hogan would be older; something about the sound of his voice, the ease of his phone manner. From his end Hogan was starstruck. Attkisson was even prettier in person than she was on television.

They scrambled to get the interview done. No time for makeup and they barely edited it. Nevertheless, Hogan sure felt good sitting in the CBS studio watching the monitors as Dan Rather called him a "whistle-blower" on national TV. He couldn't help but reflect how he'd gotten here and what the folks back home must be thinking.

IT HAD STARTED WITH A PHONE CALL IN SEPTEMBER 1998 from Rowe Brogdon, a duck hunting, quail shooting (albeit "courtly") car crash attorney from Statesboro, Georgia, who told Hogan he had a case that involved a tire made at the Wilson factory. Brogdon wanted to talk with someone familiar with the tire-making process there. Hogan responded that not only had he worked as a tire builder but had also maintained the plant's machinery. He made a general statement about the working conditions and materials, which he characterized as "awful."

That on its own would have been enough for Brogdon to drop everything and hop on an airplane. The more Brogdon questioned Hogan the more impressed he became. An experienced litigator a few years shy of 50, Brogdon viewed former employees as risky witnesses. Often their anger tinged their testimony, and when it didn't, few could articulate the problems in a way a reasonable juror could understand. But Hogan had a gift for explaining highly technical principles, and had a lot to say about quality control.

Brogdon rushed home, pecked his wife Cindy on the cheek and told her, "I might have a good one," packed some clothes, called a cab, flew from Savannah to Raleigh, rented a car, drove the hour to Wilson, and took a room at a Holiday Inn Express, where he prepared for an early morning meeting with Hogan.

Brogdon tried his first tire case in 1995 when he brought suit against Cooper Tire for a weak inner liner that gave way without warning on a 21-year-old driver on his way home from work. In an instant his left front tire went completely flat, a flap of rubber spun off and wrapped around the axle, and he lost control. The vehicle shot off the road and into clear-cut forest, where a six-foot-long tree limb plunged through the windshield and into the man's head, dislocating his eyeball and lodging in his brain. Doctors removed his pituitary gland and treated several severe head injuries. Besides permanent disfigurement, the man lost sight in his left eye and had trouble in his right. Miraculously he survived.

Fifteen months later he and his wife approached Brogdon. They had consulted one lawyer who suggested suing the paramedics. After the couple told him their story and showed him a picture of the wooden javelin surgeons pulled out of the man's head, Brogdon said, "The hell with the paramedics, let me see the tire." They were able to locate it still on the car at a local junkyard. Brogdon flew around the country deposing expert witnesses and questioning Cooper employees. After investing about $160,000 in developing the case, Brogdon settled just before trial.

Shortly after, a lawyer in West Palm, Florida, contacted Brogdon to develop a similar case against Firestone on behalf of the family of Daniel Van Etten, who was driving a 1995 Ford Explorer through Georgia back to West Virginia University after spring break with three other football scholarship players and a girlfriend when the left rear tire separated. The

Explorer tumbled over and ejected Van Etten, who died of massive head trauma.

Brogdon saw his role as a products liability attorney as prosecuting a successful case against a defective product. His first act, as it had been in Cooper, was to track down the tire. At the scene of the crash, a state trooper had noticed it didn't have the tread on it and traced the path of the vehicle by its skid marks, until he retrieved the outer steel belt and tread on the side of the road. The trooper kept the tread, the insurance company the tire carcass. Brogdon made arrangements for the expert he had retained in the Cooper case, Dennis Carlson, to examine the tire and vehicle. Carlson reported back he believed there had been a lack of adhesion between the first and the second belt—the last place you wanted a problem.

In 1998, Brogdon filed a wrongful death suit against Firestone and Ford for $21 million. The first six to eight months involved the usual sparring. Brogdon believed that was when the other side tested your mettle, saw what you knew and how far you were willing to go. Ford provided a CD-ROM of evidence that Brogdon believed was purposely indecipherable, with thousands of pages of documents organized haphazardly, but ended up settling.

Firestone also played hardball, forcing Brogdon to file a motion to compel the tire maker to hand over adjustment data. When he saw that 73 percent of ATX failures were due to tread belt separations—normal is considered in the 40s—Brogdon knew the problem went well beyond one tire.

In autumn 1998, he wrote the eight members of the American Trial Lawyers Association (ATLA) who hailed from Wilson County, North Carolina, and asked if anyone represented any ex-Firestone employees. At trial, the tire maker would have its well-coiffed experts with their advanced university degrees, but if Brogdon could produce a credible witness who had actually seen what happened, he stood a good chance of winning.

A week later one of his ATLA colleagues called Brogdon with the name and number of a client he'd represented in a worker's compensation claim against Firestone, although the lawyer warned there were problems with the man's employment record. Brogdon was thankful for a departure point. The first number was disconnected, and the man, Keith Walston, was living with a relative without a phone. Brogdon called a neighbor to fetch him. It turned out Walston had worked in the storage area and had evidence of poor working conditions, but Brogdon needed information on tires. Walston told Brogdon he knew the perfect guy, but refused to give his name until he had first talked to him. He called Brogdon back later with Alan Hogan's number at the Automotive Body Shop.

The first thing Brogdon did when he met Hogan at the hotel conference room in Wilson was to share the case circumstances. When Brogdon handled a case in which someone had been killed, he didn't call a potential witness out of the blue and say someone died. He did it face-to-face and did it as soon as he met the person to underscore the gravity of the situation.

Brogdon assumed Hogan would be wondering why he'd come all the way from Georgia. Not for whiplash, that's for sure.

When Brogdon told him a young football player named Danny Van Etten had died, Hogan stopped him. "I don't want to know how old he was," he said. "I don't want to know the color of his eyes. I don't want to know anything about him." In his heart, Hogan always knew he and his coworkers had at times built tires destined to peel apart, but until now he hadn't known anyone had died from one. He would help because it was the right thing to do, but he didn't want to become emotionally involved.

It didn't take long for Brogdon to realize his initial assessment was correct: Hogan was the witness of a lifetime. After Brogdon showed him a photo of the tire it took Hogan all of 10 seconds to declare, "I know exactly what went wrong with this tire. Old stock."

He could tell all that from a picture? Brogdon thought. *Either this guy is some kind of tire savant or he's putting me on.* "How do you know?"

Hogan tracked his finger on the photo, outlining the line of separation in the rubber between the two steel belts. "When you put the second belt on the first belt, which is already on the tire, the belt is made out of steel wires with rubber on each side," he explained. "The rubber is there like glue. When you put the second belt there you must have good adhesion. But if the rubber stock is dry, then with time and use the tire is going to come apart."

Brogdon began to take notes.

"I'll bet you this tire was made right after a shutdown," Hogan said. Wilson closed the plant twice a year: around July 4th and at Christmas, to retool and clean. Unused stock sat around for an extra week, drying out. It took a good two to three weeks go through it all. Hogan told Brogdon to check the DOT number on the tire. Brogdon consulted his notes. The tire had been made during the 28th week of 1993; July 11th, to be precise. Hogan smiled, his look saying, *You think that's interesting, wait until you hear what else I have to say.*

While working at the plant, Hogan saw dry tire stock, a combination of steel belts and rubber that should have been thrown out because it was no longer tacky, continually placed in a storage area known as the "bank" and recirculated into production, particularly after scheduled plant shutdowns in July and December. It was no secret when the rubber stock was dry. The plant TV monitors that carried production reports would list the lines of workers that had to swab tires that day. "If you didn't swab you couldn't even build a tire," Hogan said. "Without solvent the second belt just slips to the floor because it won't stick."

Swabbing made old rubber look and act new, but production didn't allow for it to be done properly. The brushes were 4 inches wide, while steel belts were often between 6 inches and 8 inches. A worker had to spin the tire twice to swab the first belt, then twice more for the second. Done correctly, he would miss his quota, "so people just swabbed once," Hogan said.

Brogdon asked what he thought had happened to the Van Etten tire. Hogan said judging from the photo it was a separation between the first and second belts. He could picture a car on the highway, perhaps the tires somewhat underinflated, which meant greater surface area on the pavement, more friction and heat. The steel belts were located right under the tread. If the tire hadn't been fully swabbed, sections of rubber would begin to rub against each other. The rippling pieces would migrate across the tire, until the tread pulled completely away.

When Hogan finished, Brogdon asked if he would appear as a witness in depositions and at trial. He couldn't pay him, couldn't even buy him a Coca-Cola because that could taint his testimony, although he could cover expenses. Hogan said casually, "Sure, fine, I'll do whatever you want. Tell me where you want me to be and I'll be there."

Brogdon flew Hogan to Louisville to meet with Carlson, his tire expert. He wanted to be sure Hogan knew what he was talking about and wasn't embellishing, but mostly he wanted Carlson to hear about Hogan's experiences at the Wilson factory. Up to then Carlson had identified a belt adhesion problem but not why. Later that day Carlson called Brogdon to let him know he had never been around a tire builder like Hogan. Not only had he been privy to everything that went on in that plant, he could talk about it in a way a twelve-year-old could understand.

On the morning of March 31, 1999, Hogan confronted two Firestone lawyers and one from Ford, men in fancy suits with fancy names, at the same Holiday Inn Express he had met Brogdon, a video camera set up on a tripod to catch his every word, tic, movement. After Hogan sat down, his hands folded in front of him on the table, Brogdon noticed his fingers shaking, his knuckles white. Brogdon stacked a couple of legal tomes—a book on evidence and another on pleadings—in front so the other attorneys wouldn't see.

Hogan started badly, his voice quavering. The questions came in a well-rehearsed ticker tape, his answers in mumbles. *Where do you work? Where do you live? What do you do? What do you say? What do you recollect? Have you ever testified in a deposition before? Were you served a subpoena? Do you have any Firestone documents in your possession? Do you possess any travel documents from your trip to Louisville?*

Several times Hogan found himself tongue-tied. "I might have [an airline boarding pass] at home but that's, ticket stub or something like that, but you . . ."

"We'll come back to that," interrupted the Firestone lawyer.

"Okay. If I thought it was necessary," Hogan said.

"I understand."

"I would have . . ."

"I don't think literally I asked you for that," the attorney said coldly.

"Okay," Hogan said.

Brogdon was concerned. Hogan was rattled. Most anyone would be. A good inquisitor could make even the most hardened witness squirm. Perhaps Firestone had hired detectives to canvass people who knew Hogan over the years. Maybe they'd found someone who'd once had a fight with him, or a girlfriend angry over a broken relationship. Or they had record of something Hogan had done at the factory to undermine his credibility. Brogdon held his breath. He had been at the game long enough to know that all it took was just one well-placed question to destroy a witness.

"What is your home telephone number?" asked one of the Firestone suits.

"No home phone," Hogan said. He carried a cell phone at all times, but after the grilling he was getting he wasn't about to volunteer anything.

The lawyer eyed Hogan suspiciously. "What caused you to stop having one?"

"Because I answer the phone all day long at work," Hogan said.

"Sounds like a good idea for everybody in here," Brogdon chimed in a little too cheerfully.

"When I go home I don't want to answer a phone," Hogan continued.

The lawyers took turns zeroing in on his past. They discussed Hogan's childhood, brought up the three months he'd spent at a halfway house when he was a teenager for possession of a stolen computer, dredged up a 10-year-old DUI, inquired about his ex-wife, his girlfriend, his brother, and nephew, and cast aspersions on Hogan's reasons for leaving the factory. When they got to Hogan's employment record, which neither he nor Brogdon had reviewed because Firestone had sealed it under a protective order, Brogdon called for a break, claiming he had to inquire about some plane reservations.

Instead he took Hogan outside. "Relax," Brogdon said. "Have a cigarette."

He knew Hogan was dealing with nicotine deprivation on top of everything else. While Hogan sucked down four cigarettes in succession, Brogdon offered a pep talk. *Don't let them intimidate you*, he urged. *They're paid to promote propaganda, to cover up the fact that people are dying from bad Firestone tires. But your job is to tell the truth. As long as you do that, everything will be fine.*

"OK," Hogan said, snuffing out his last cigarette, "I'm ready." He marched back inside and for the next five hours completely smoked Firestone's attorneys. Once they got into the technical nitty-gritty, Hogan asserted control over the deposition. He testified the factory had a "chronic problem with tire separations." When Firestone's attorneys asked why he was qualified to speak as an expert, Hogan replied, "I was there, *Bud*."

Hogan said he'd seen "people build 200 bad tires in a row" without realizing it because of bad stock or an incorrectly calibrated machine, and walked lawyers through the steps for refreshing rubber. "You run the one ply on the drum, dip the swab in alcohol, place it on the drum, hold your foot on the pedal, and manually run it around," he said. "If it was a wide tire you might have to run it around twice. . . . Move the swab across, try to get 100 percent of it, then [flip it on automatic and] run the two-ply arm. A lot of times it would get a little bit tricky. While it's running, I'll swab it, you know, while it's running on the drum. It's a little bit faster to do it that way."

He testified he was certain the Van Etten tire "came apart due to dry stock" based on an analysis he conducted in the company of another expert witness, Dennis Carlson. Hogan said he and Carlson had put the tire up on a rack, "put the lights on it . . . looked at it, saw it, how it came apart." The cause? "Separation. Separation between the one and the two ply" where the rubber had been inadequately joined. He couldn't resist adding, "You could clearly see it."

When Hogan said that, Brogdon swore he saw the blood drain from the face of one of the Firestone lawyers. Later that afternoon Brogdon deposed Hogan's former plant supervisor, who confirmed that workers often violated the rules of Firestone's tire-building manual, such as using outdated stock and benzene swabs—although never between the first and second belts. But he changed his testimony when Brogdon pressed him. To swab or not, he subsequently claimed, was a judgment call.

With the trial date approaching, Brogdon invested $25,000 on a juror survey. A research firm collected a hundred participants to read summaries of the evidence and deposition testimony, then fill out a form with a series of questions, answering with options ranging from "least" to "most favorable." When all the data was sifted, crunched and analyzed, Brogdon would know which hot-button issues to expect, which witnesses were viewed as credible, which weren't, which evidence best promoted his case. Almost to a man, participants drawn from a pool of blue-collar peers believed Hogan's testimony. Unlike "gun for hire" witnesses, he had credibility that Ph.D.s with their million-dollar vocabularies and thousand-dollar per diems couldn't touch.

Firestone filed a flurry of motions to suppress evidence and disqualify witnesses, but Brogdon defeated every one of them. And on Sept. 2, 1999, a week before jury selection, Firestone settled.

Eleven months later Hogan was listening to himself over the TV monitors at CBS' Washington, D.C., studios. The thrust of Sharyl Attkisson's report was that while Ford and Firestone poured through plant records in Decatur, consumer groups like Public Citizen, Safetyforum.com, and Strategic Safety were accusing both companies of "trying to isolate the crisis—and the recall—mostly to Decatur tires" when millions more might pose a safety threat.

"You don't believe it's isolated to one plant?" Attkisson asked Hogan, identified as a "former Firestone employee," a description he hoped didn't do him justice.

"No," he heard himself reply, "because I saw it and actually probably built some bad tires in Wilson. I witnessed and practiced assembly of tires with bad materials."

"Tires you think would be dangerous to ride on?" Attkisson asked.

"Yep."

Attkisson called Hogan "a model employee" and pointed to his deposition in which he recalled poor material being used almost daily. "What happens if you make a tire with old rubber?" she asked.

"If not done properly, it'll cause a separation," Hogan replied. "They're not gonna throw away thousands and thousands of dollars worth of rubber; they're gonna figure out a way of keeping it in the tire."

The camera panned to Sharyl Attkisson live in the studio, as she read the standard denials from Ford and Firestone.

After Attkisson signed off, Hogan thought, *This is pretty cool.* His mind mulled the technical reasons behind the tape delay, which caused a split second lag between what happened in the studio and what appeared on the monitor, when suddenly it hit him: *Oh, shit. What have I done?* He knew life back home would never be the same.

The next morning Hogan grabbed coffee on his way back to CBS, where Attkisson and a cameraman took him to meet Ralph Hoar, whose well-wired garage served as Safetyforum.com's offices. Attkisson shot footage of Hogan surveying some shredded tires Hoar had on hand. Hogan looked at one that looked like the rim had cut into it and told Hoar, "It's been run flat. Firestone lawyers will laugh you out of court." He studied others that appeared to have suffered belt separations similar to Van Etten's. Hoar was so impressed he called Tab Turner to ask permission to show Hogan one of the tires involved in an ongoing legal action. Turner told Hoar he could look but not touch.

Hogan studied the tire that had been on the Explorer Donna Bailey was paralyzed from. The first thing he noticed: it was a 16-inch tire made in Wilson, while the recall covered the 15-inch from Decatur. Hogan saw it had come apart just like the Van Etten tire. He could tell where it had been swabbed, and where the builder missed. The worker also neglected to supply a tire builder number, something Hogan used to do when he built a questionable tire. Hogan wondered where he had been the day the Bailey tire was built. It was a Sunday, a shift he always worked, but in 1993 he was still auditing machinery and hadn't built his first tire. He silently prayed none of his "rags" had led to any accidents.

That evening Hogan returned home to Wilson. Other than a few friends who called to say they saw him on television, his appearance seemed to have gone largely unnoticed. He was relieved. There didn't seem to be much fallout. That was until he got to work the next morning to discover a poison fax on his desk.

It was a copy of a letter, anonymously written and without letterhead that had been made into flyers, one of which had been faxed to the Paul Berry Chevrolet dealership, which leased Hogan and his partner the body shop space. It began "Dear Fellow Employees" and asked Firestone workers at the Wilson factory to hold responsible Hogan's body shop and the dealership it leased space from for the "viscous [sic], malicious allegations stated by a disgruntled former employee of Firestone." The letter went on to say the boycott should continue until Paul Berry Chevrolet, the region's largest seller of Chevy and Toyota vehicles, ceased all business with Hogan, including all bodywork he performed for the dealership.

Hogan noticed a number accompanied by Firestone's "accounts payable" department printed on the top of the fax. He asked his friend and business partner, Jerry Dorsey, what they should do. Dorsey, technically the president of Automotive Body Shop, Inc., said, "I think I need to fire you."

"That's kind of extreme," Hogan said. He knew Dorsey didn't want to fire him. He couldn't. They were partners. If he did, the business would go under. They decided just to pretend he quit. Hogan grabbed some personal items, his Rolodex, cell phone, a file with some Firestone material in it, and a copy of the fax. Before he could leave, his partner received a call from John McQuade, the Wilson plant manager. With Hogan eavesdropping over speakerphone, Dorsey told McQuade that Alan Hogan no longer worked at the shop.

"I sure hope he left town," grunted McQuade.

Hogan was probably more scared than mad when he heard that. He imagined an angry mob at his door waving ATX tires. The factory had a payroll in excess of $100 million, and Firestone had been running the hostile flyer on the Wilson factory TV monitors for all its workers to see.

Dorsey, a pillar in the community, on a hospital's board of directors and a trustee for a local college, tried to mollify the irate Firestone manager. He suggested that McQuade was condoning the fury of his own workers, and that was wrong. "We are all in this community together; we have to get along," Dorsey said. He didn't say much more than that. After McQuade was convinced Hogan was gone, the plant manager agreed to remove the flyer from the factory monitors.

Hogan went home and called Rowe Brogdon and Sharyl Attkisson. Both demanded a copy of the flyer. He didn't want to go back to work, so he went to a "pack and send" shop. When the guy working the counter recognized Hogan from the news, he told him he had "big balls" and didn't charge for the fax.

After Brogdon verified the fax's return number as belonging to Firestone, he called Hogan and almost cracked his ear by shouting *Hallelujah!* "I got 'em," Brogdon said. "That's tortious interference with a contract. Probably broke half a dozen civil laws I don't know about."

Ironic, too, he pointed out. At the beginning, Firestone had made a fuss about Hogan being covered by a nondisclosure agreement and accused the lawyer of tortuous interference. The company claimed that Brogdon, by pushing Hogan to testify, was interfering with a preexisting secrecy agreement between employer and employee, and that trumped any right Hogan had to testify against Firestone. Problem was, Hogan was a contract worker for his first four years at the company and never signed a confidentiality agreement. He didn't ink one when he was brought on board full time to build tires in 1994 either. Typical of Firestone, Brogdon thought: dumb and proud of it.

Brogdon told Hogan he was going to flip the law on its head. This time the whistle-blower would be the one to scream "tortious interference." Paul Berry Chevrolet and Hogan had a lease and a lease was a contract, so the authors of the flyer had tried to get Paul Berry to break its contract with Hogan. Brogdon faxed a cease-and-desist letter to Firestone lawyers in Akron, Ohio: "Obviously," he wrote, "you are certainly aware that Firestone has tortiously interfered with Mr. Hogan's contract with the Berry dealership as well as his business relations with all of his clientele." He demanded Firestone stipulate that Hogan's testimony was completely accurate and truthful and apologize.

But it was Sharyl Attkisson who dropped the bomb. Hogan rarely watched the news on TV but did that night. He saw the words "Firestone Whistle-blower Attacked" roll across the screen over footage of Hogan at Ralph Hoar's place. Attkisson didn't waste any time letting Firestone have it. "People worried about driving on Firestone tires that are not part of the giant recall may have good reason for concern: a significant number of complaints involve other tires made by the company, tires that Ford and Firestone still insist are perfectly safe." She said CBS News learned that more than a third of the tires federal safety investigators looked at were not made at Decatur, or were sizes not covered by the recall—like the faulty tire that caused the crash that paralyzed Donna Bailey.

Nervously Hogan watched a calmer version of himself analyze the Bailey tire on TV.

"What are the chances that's just something that happened on the highway that's not related to how the tire was built?" Attkisson asked.

"No way!" Hogan said. What's more, the tire's special tracing identifier was missing. "If you know you built a bad tire you certainly don't put your number in the tire."

Attkisson moved on to the flyer, prominently displayed on screen. "After Hogan appeared on CBS News Monday alleging dangerous practices at Wilson, this memo was allegedly faxed from the plant management's office. It instructs 'Firestone employees, family members and friends' to boycott Hogan, his body repair shop and 'anyone associated with him.' " Then to Attkisson live in the studio. She reported that Firestone management claimed it didn't approve the memo but can't control what its employees do, and added that Hogan had temporarily resigned from the body shop.

Hogan swigged the last of his beer and crunched the can in his hand. He realized the story had just become bigger. The *Chicago Tribune*, other newspaper reporters, a local TV station, all tried to track Hogan down, but he felt for the time being he owed it to Attkisson to grant her exclusive access. Besides, he didn't want to stoke the flames of hometown dissent. By threatening a boycott, Firestone had taken the battle to Hogan's business. While his partner Dorsey privately supported him and publicly urged "community," Bryan Berry, co-owner of the dealership, allied himself with the tire company. His family had sold a lot of cars over the years with locally made Firestone tires. "Those folks at Firestone have a lot of pride in their operation, and they have been put on the defensive," Berry said. "If I were in their position, I could have felt the same way."

Bridgestone/Firestone officials didn't respond to Brogdon's demand for an apology. Instead, Firestone spokesman Ken Fields called Hogan "a disgruntled employee who never had any involvement with the production of radial ATX," which Hogan knew was a lie on two counts. In the course of the Van Etten lawsuit, executives acknowledged that the majority of the tires made at Wilson when Hogan worked there were ATX tires, and workers rarely knew the models of tire they were building, only their dimensions.

Plant manager John McQuade claimed he had no idea who had created and distributed the flyers, attributing them to Wilson workers upset that Hogan criticized their plant on TV. "We're having employee meetings telling folks it's OK for them as individuals to voice their concerns," he said, "but as a company we do not want to be accused of retaliation."

Hogan laid low for a while. He visited friends out of town, took a short fishing trip, and thought about trying the paint distribution business. But he wanted his old life back. He drove back and forth between the body shop and Raleigh getting parts, slowly working his way back to the job full time.

ONE EVENING HOGAN WAS HOME WHEN THE PHONE RANG. "Alan?" asked a woman's voice.

"Yeah?" Hogan figured it was another reporter.

"This is Kim."

"Yeah?"

"Kim Van Etten."

Hogan was speechless. Van Etten had to say, "Hey, are you there?" before Hogan could collect his wits.

Van Etten thanked Hogan for all he had done. She told him he was a hero, and felt bad about the boycott of his business. She began to cry. Her son had been "beautiful," a "big, gentle giant" with green eyes. "Everybody loved Danny."

Over the summer Hogan's mother had died, and he connected with Van Etten's grief. He and Van Etten talked once every few weeks for a few months, until she invited Hogan to meet her at a remote cabin nestled in the mountains near the Tennessee border—the longest six-hour drive of his life. He felt like an American soldier meeting a Vietnamese family. The first thing he did at the cabin was to apologize to Van Etten for building the kind of "rags" that killed her son.

Van Etten hushed him. It wasn't his fault. They hugged surrounded by trees and mountains, the sun peeking through the leaves, until she broke the silence.

"I understand you need a mother," she said, "and I don't have a son."

18 Safety Triumvirate

RALPH HOAR WAS ANNOYED. TAB TURNER had promised him documents he could use in some upcoming recall-related press interviews, but had disappeared and wasn't returning his calls. Turner could be anywhere—taking depositions in Decatur, attending pretrial meetings in Tupelo, advising clients in Houston, attending his daughter's play in Little Rock, or even nearby in Washington, D.C., hobnobbing with members of the congressional committee. That was the thing with Turner. He came and went as he pleased. You never knew where he was. But this was the last straw. As Hoar paced his office he swore he would never talk to Turner again.

Hoar and Turner were unlikely friends. While Turner was a Southern Baptist who believed it immoral to drink a beer or use foul language in front of his daughters, and called settlement negotiations "come to Jesus meetings" because in his eyes that meant automakers had seen the error of their ways, Hoar was a gay man involved with a much younger partner (although he had married at a young age and fathered two children). His name was pronounced "whore," which, he liked to joke, "you learn to work if you don't want to lose your sanity." He enjoyed doing TV interviews in a sport coat, shirt, and boxer shorts but no pants, since the camera never showed anything below the waist.

Unlike the quietly intense Turner, whose work took up almost all of his waking hours, Hoar was loud, gregarious, and pursued interests away from the office. In fact, about the only time he used the word "restraint" was in reference to safety belts. He overindulged in wine and food, was well versed in art and politics, ending almost every discussion in a heated argument, and dabbled in poetry. "Your life is a diamond," he once wrote. "There is not another like it. You, like the diamond cutter, will choose the facets that best share your beauty with the world . . . And when this journey ends, the diamond that was your life will last forever."

Born in 1945 and raised in Williamsburg, Virginia, Hoar attended a small college in North Carolina and served in Vietnam, where he was relieved he never had to shoot at anyone. His job was to organize travel and lodging arrangements for visiting Army brass. When he returned home in 1969, he answered a newspaper ad for a position with the Insurance Institute for Highway Safety, where he worked until the mid-1970s under Dr. William Haddon, Jr., who established many of the protocols used today in vehicle crash testing and was the nation's first traffic safety czar.

In 1977, Hoar became the first registered lobbyist for air bags and organized a coalition of 60 organizations called the National Committee for Automobile Crash Protection. Its primary focus was to make air bags mandatory in all vehicles. He moved to the private sector in the early 1980s to work at a small four-man consulting outfit run by Ben Kelley, an Insurance Institute colleague. Kelley had achieved auto safety fame by co-designing the dramatic Jeep CJ rollover tests shown on *60 Minutes* in December 1980, in which Morley Safer reported that the vehicle was prone to rolling over "even in routine road circumstances at relatively low speeds."

One day Kelley received an anonymous package in the mail containing a detailed study by two NHTSA investigators that analyzed the relationship between stability factor with rollovers and injury propensity by looking at vehicles of various designs. One of the worst-kept secrets in Washington at the time was that the agency was suppressing a report it had commissioned that "had blown up in [its] face." The new study contradicted its official position. But releasing it would have put pressure on NHTSA to take action—something it was reluctant to do.

Kelley showed the analysis to some of his clients, who told him they couldn't use it in litigation unless it was an official government document. When Kelley discussed it with Hoar, they agreed that it would be great if it were in NHTSA's docket. Hoar picked up the report and said, "Well, if they won't put it in . . . we had better put it in." He had spent a lot of time in the document room at NHTSA; that was his territory. This was a time when researchers, auto industry lobbyists, and safety advocates could wander in and out freely and access stacks of paper and books at will.

Hoar stashed the analysis in one of the dockets concerning rollovers and then went off and had lunch. When he returned, Hoar informed a clerk he needed a certified copy of the report, and described where to find it. A couple hours later Hoar got it back, complete with NHTSA's official seal and tied with a blue ribbon. Attached was a cover memo stating that the head of dockets certified it was an authentic document. Hoar paid the nominal fee and drove back to the office with a smile.

In 1988, Hoar left Kelley to start his own firm, where he put his inside knowledge of NHTSA to good use. He hit the agency with several Freedom of Information Act (FOIA) requests that it was loath to fulfill. Hoar would continue to hammer away, leaving more than one red-faced staff member. At one point an NHTSA counsel had to tell frustrated agency officials "there is no Ralph Hoar FOIA exemption" and advised them to supply Hoar with his requests whether they wanted to or not.

It wasn't until the advent of the Internet that Hoar really hit his stride. His dream was to supply fast and accurate information to consumers who often didn't even know certain products had been recalled. The result was Safetyforum.com, which he launched in 1996 and quickly became a clearinghouse of consumer safety information available to visitors at the click of a mouse. He used it to respond to corporate spin and to publish a list indecorously entitled "Hoar's Whores," which identified former government officials who had gone to work for the car industry as consultants, lobbyists, and professional witnesses. In the past he had to wait for the media to call him. By having his own Web site, reporters came to him—and in the process made full use of the resources he provided. Safetyforum.com enabled Hoar to shape and direct public debate and to force recalcitrant manufacturers to come forward with honest information about their products. It helped level the playing field between powerful companies and consumers.

During the Ford-Firestone crisis, when one of the companies issued a press release, Hoar would quickly come out with his own competing release with facts and data to contradict them. When Firestone claimed that no 16-inch AT tires had suffered belt separations and therefore didn't need to be included in any recall, Hoar posted a note on his site asking any visitors who have had problems with 16-inch tires to contact him. Within 24 hours Hoar had 30 names.

He published internal documents from Ford and Firestone, posted news articles about the crisis, wrote scathing columns, and organized protests. During congressional hearings, Hoar managed to get 200 Explorer owners to come to Washington to support legislation to criminalize companies that knowingly market defective products. At the height of the Firestone-Ford frenzy, his Web site received 3 million visitors in one month.

Hoar didn't hate corporations; he too was a capitalist. In fact, one reason he didn't work for the public sector was because it paid so poorly, and he couldn't bear the idea of skimping on his lifestyle. But he genuinely wanted companies to manufacture and market safer products.

Because he was a constant thorn in their side, however, Big Business didn't care much for him. After Hoar passed away due to complications from prostate cancer in September 2001, Jason Vines of Ford muttered: "May he rest in peace with Satan."

WHEN HOAR INTRODUCED JOAN CLAYBROOK to Tab Turner in 1995, Turner was fresh off his $25 million verdict in *Cammack v. Ford*. Hoar phoned Claybrook and said he knew this "really interesting trial lawyer," a "real comer" who had recently formed his own law firm, and asked her to join them for dinner. Hoar and Claybrook had just come off working together on faulty door latches on minivans, something Turner was also deeply involved in, and so the three had a lot to talk about. But Public Citizen's resources were already stretched thin, so Claybrook didn't usually get involved in vehicle defects unless they presented a clear danger to the public. Over the next five years Claybrook and Turner talked sporadically—until the Ford-Firestone story broke.

At the time of the recall, Turner told Hoar, "We ought to have a press conference and really pump this up." While the companies were claiming the bad tires were limited to Decatur, Turner himself had clients who had been injured while driving on ATs made at other plants.

Hoar said, "I think to have credibility, we need to have Joan involved, because you have a self-interest in promoting this while she has a safety interest." He proposed an ersatz safety triumvirate.

Claybrook also had something else: an intimate understanding of the inner workings of government and the auto industry. She was a ferocious lobbyist and wandered the halls of Congress almost daily, buttonholing representatives and their aides, pushing issues she believed were in the public's interest. Although she often came across as "an aging version of the Junior Leaguer" in her sensible shoes and dowdy business suit, white pearls draped around her neck, glasses perched on her nose, she had amassed a lengthy list of powerful enemies, many of them linked to the automobile industry. Behind her back, car lobbyists dubbed her "the Dragon Lady." Hill staffers asked rhetorically where she kept her broom. Rep. John Dingell called her "an evil, small-minded woman," which, noting the source, Claybrook took as a compliment.

She had come to Washington as an American Political Science Association fellow in 1965, the first year women could apply, and worked for Rep. James MacKay, a liberal Democrat from Atlanta. Claybrook had just read *Unsafe at Any Speed*, Ralph Nader's withering attack on the GM Corvair, and when MacKay considered introducing the first regulatory bill on auto safety, he wanted Claybrook to meet Nader. The two of them drafted the bill together.

While the legislation wound through Congress, she watched Nader in action, how he cajoled and carried on, manipulated and shocked people with disclosures of corporate wrongdoing. "It was an incredibly fast education," she remembered. Less than a year after Claybrook began working for MacKay, the bill—which led to the establishment of NHTSA—was enacted into law. At the end of her fellowship, Claybrook moved to the agency she helped create to become an assistant to the director, where she remained until 1970, when, disgusted with the Nixon administration for bombing Cambodia, she left.

Claybrook took a job with Nader at Public Citizen, a nonprofit he had founded with money from a lawsuit against General Motors, which had been engaging in a smear campaign against him. The company had called friends and associates, claiming Nader had applied for a job with the automaker. It hired a prostitute to seduce him outside a Safeway supermarket, but he turned her down. It spread rumors that Nader, the son of Lebanese immigrants, was anti-Semitic and a homosexual.

One day Nader was walking in the Senate office building, and a gum-shoe following him asked where Nader was headed. The guards alerted Sen. Abraham Ribicoff's office, where Nader often went to work. He was about to testify at a hearing on auto safety and it was a criminal act to interfere with a witness. Ribicoff's staff phoned American Motors, Chrysler, Ford and General Motors and asked each one if it was tailing Nader. Three said "no" and General Motors said "no comment." Ribicoff called a hearing and ordered General Motors president James Roche to Washington. After Sen. Robert Kennedy torched him on the stand, Roche publicly apologized.

Then Nader testified, attacking Detroit over safety. He condensed his book down to 20 minutes of what was wrong with General Motors and the auto industry: They didn't spend money on safety, and they manufactured and marketed unsafe cars that were killing people. It was at this hearing that the concept of crash-worthiness had its first public airing, and it struck Capitol Hill like a lightning bolt.

Suddenly everyone knew who this tall, lanky lawyer was and what he was about. The media began paying attention to him. He was on *Meet the Press* and quoted in newspapers and magazines. Riding this wave, he sued General Motors for invasion of privacy. After he settled, he used the money to create the Public Interest Research Group and Public Citizen, and brought Claybrook onboard. In 1973, she founded and directed Congress Watch, Public Citizen's congressional lobbying group, and got her law degree at Georgetown. Four years later President Jimmy Carter asked her to head NHTSA.

Her appointment was by no means unanimous: 33 senators, mostly Republicans, voted against her. She was not only a woman in a man's world, she was also a "Nader Raider" at the helm of a federal agency. Her first days on the job were a blur. Almost immediately she had to testify before the appropriations committee. She already knew many members of Congress, and also made it a point to visit every freshman Democrat who came into office in 1978 to introduce herself and explain the program. Her greatest adversary, it would turn out, was Rep. Dingell, who went out of his way to undermine her agency's authority and tie up its purse strings. She viewed him as "a bully" who took advantage of weakness. Claybrook, however, was anything but weak.

It didn't take long for her agency to enter into its first big fight with the automobile industry—over seat belts and air bags. Automakers didn't want either in cars because they reminded people of the inherent dangers of driving. Seat belts were uncomfortable, and air bag technology was still in its infancy. Henry Ford II's view reflected that of the entire industry: "We have so many men working on safety now that aren't doing the forward development (on vehicles) we should be doing," he said. He was adamantly opposed to any type of federal safety legislation, saying he had "never seen anything go so unanimously in the wrong direction." But Claybrook believed seat belts were clumsy to use because automakers didn't put any effort into their design, and General Motors had installed air bags in certain luxury cars, which proved they were feasible, but discontinued them after oil prices shot up in the early 1970s and consumers stopped buying gas guzzlers.

Legislation proposing mandatory interlocking restraints, which were seat belts that had to be engaged before the key was put in the ignition, was already on the floor of Congress. Unlike today, seat belts were not an accepted part of the driving experience. Only 1 in 10 people used them. The public was in an uproar because they wouldn't be able to start their cars with the family dog sitting on the seat or if they didn't have the belt hooked up properly. Consumers would want to disconnect them, but it would be illegal and dealers wouldn't do it. Claybrook proposed a "performance standard" that mandated that drivers and front seat passengers had to either be protected by air bags or automatic seat belts— just so they didn't have to take action to protect themselves. It had to be approved by Congress, and Claybrook spent almost the entire summer of

1977 on Capitol Hill. Despite heavy lobbying by the automobile industry, the measure passed the Senate with a two-thirds majority.

It turned out to be a bittersweet victory for Claybrook. In the early fall, she visited Europe to see how manufacturers there were handling safety issues, and Ralph Nader attacked her in the pages of the *Washington Post* for caving in to the auto industry by allowing too much lead time for the changes. She knew Nader was just being Nader, but she was so angry they didn't talk for more than a year.

Passage of this performance standard would end up saving hundreds of thousands of lives over the next 25 years. As the seat belt and air bag became standard equipment in cars, the number of traffic fatalities in the United States decreased by 20 percent, from a peak of more than 52,000 a year. Although Claybrook wished that had been her legacy at NHTSA, she was probably better known for leading two famous recalls during her tenure, which also involved Firestone and Ford.

When she took the mantle at NHTSA in April 1977, the agency was in the process of recalling 400,000 Firestone 500 tires for a defect with lamination, which was leading to tread separations. NHTSA approached Firestone after the tires had failed internal tests, and the company said not to worry, blaming the problem on a small batch from one plant: Decatur. Firestone agreed to a limited recall.

Later that summer, the Center for Auto Safety filed a petition for a wider recall, which prompted Claybrook's enforcement staff to look at the performance of the Firestone 500 versus other tires supplied as original equipment. The survey showed the 500 was worse than other brands, but not drastically so. Firestone found out about the existence of the study, but didn't know what it contained. As a precautionary measure, company lawyers went to a local judge in Cleveland and got an injunction against public release of the information.

Meanwhile, the Center for Auto Safety filed a Freedom of Information Act request, and by mistake, clerical staff handed over the report. CAS held a press conference, announcing what the organization had in its possession. *Automotive News* printed the information and Firestone asked that the Secretary of Transportation be held in contempt.

The Justice Department dispatched Claybrook to Cleveland to deal with it, since the Secretary of Transportation claimed a conflict of interest because his father had worked at Firestone for almost 50 years. Firestone lawyers put on a big show against Claybrook and Keith Crain, a reporter at *Automotive News*, but were unsuccessful in getting a contempt citation.

When Claybrook returned to Washington, the Justice Department dusted every document in the agency to see whether her fingerprints appeared on any of them, which she knew they didn't. In the midst of all of this, her secretary was going "completely berserk" because she had overheard a conversation between Claybrook and her mother, in which her mother had innocently asked, "I need to buy some new tires, what should I get?"

"You should get Michelin tires," Claybrook told her.

"Why?"

"We've done surveys and Michelin tires come out best."

Technically the injunction meant she wasn't allowed to talk about the survey. To calm her secretary, who was going to be deposed, Claybrook said, "If they don't ask the question, don't answer it." The lawyers never did and Claybrook was cleared.

Then Firestone's strategy began to backfire. Government regulators became so frustrated with the tire maker's blame-the-consumer tactics and legal delays they invented a word for it, "Firestonewalling." With 34 people dead, a syndicated cartoonist conjured an even grimmer nickname for the company: "Gravestone." Between the company's public quest for a contempt citation, the Center for Auto Safety's press conference, and newspapers across the country writing about it, Congress decided to hold hearings. The House Subcommittee on Oversight commented, "We are aware of only one other vehicle safety [flaw] exceeding 34," and that was "the gas tank in certain Ford Pintos." Toward the end of June, NHTSA found initial determination of a defect covering 20 million Firestone tires.

Claybrook subpoenaed Firestone for records pertaining to the 500, but the tire maker continued to fight the agency in court. A month and a half later it lost, and Firestone had no choice but to comply. The company claimed there were so many documents, however, that it would overload NHTSA's offices, so it rented space in downtown Washington and provided a photocopy machine.

Claybrook dispatched Allen Kam, the lawyer who had been handling the case from the beginning. When he got there he noticed a box labeled, "Already reviewed by NHTSA," and was infuriated. *Who had done that?* he wondered. This was his case, and Kam was protective of his turf. As a result, it was the first box he opened. And to his amazement it contained all the dirty documents that showed that the company's board of directors had known of the problem since 1974 and engaged in a cover-up. He figured the tire maker stashed them there assuming no one from the agency would bother to check.

Firestone continued to delay by spending months negotiating the parameters of the recall. But as sales plummeted from the bad publicity, the company finally agreed to take back the tires and run a national advertising campaign explaining proper tire maintenance. Claybrook wanted to fine Firestone the maximum: $800,000, but couldn't without going back to court. She settled for $500,000.

At the same time Claybrook was battling Firestone, she was also taking on Ford over the Pinto. She had learned of the car's propensity to blow up when struck from behind from an article in *Mother Jones* magazine. Investigative journalist Mark Dowie had gained access to NHTSA's library to comb through boxes of Pinto documents when he unearthed a document that showed that Ford had for seven years sold cars it knew would burn perhaps hundreds of people to death. Entitled "Benefits and Costs Relating to Fuel Leakage Associated with the Static Rollover Test Portion of FMVSS208: Fatalities Associated with Crash-Induced Fuel Leakage and Fires," the internal memorandum calculated 180 burn deaths, 180 serious burn injuries and 2,100 burned vehicles at a cost of $200,000 per death, $67,000 per injury, and $700 per vehicle to the automaker. If Ford were to do nothing and pay off families and victims to settle lawsuits, it would cost the company $49.5 million. If it were to outfit all 11 million Pintos with protective bladders for their fuel tanks for $11 per vehicle, the cost would be almost three times that: $137 million.

Ford stalled, lobbying against a government safety standard that would have forced the company to alter its fuel tank design, even while unsuspecting Pinto drivers and passengers were being killed or horribly disfigured in subcompact infernos.

Lily Gray was incinerated, and Richard Grimshaw was scorched but survived when the fuel tank on his Pinto exploded. Dan Lampe's life almost ended when a drunk driver clipped his 1974 Ford Pinto station wagon. The gas tank ruptured, sparks ignited the fuel, and the car burst into flames. The doors were jammed shut. Lampe was trapped. Ninety seconds passed before a passerby yanked open the driver's door and pulled Lampe from the flames. He suffered serious burns to nearly half his body, particularly his face and hands. Doctors told his family he probably wouldn't survive. In the end Lampe endured more than 200 surgeries.

Judy Ulrich's 1973 Pinto was rear-ended by a van. The Pinto burst into flames, trapping her young daughters inside the inferno. Eight hours later Ulrich also died from the burns that covered 90 percent of her body. Ford was indicted on three felony counts of reckless homicide in the deaths of the Indiana girls—the first time an American corporation had been indicted or prosecuted on criminal homicide charges—but was acquitted after convincing the jury that the Ulrich car was stopped when it had been struck and therefore was not a result of reckless homicide.

Dowie published "Pinto Madness" in the September 1977 issue of *Mother Jones* magazine. On Sept. 9 Ford responded with an eight-page statement, asserting the article included "half-truths and distortions." The Pinto "has been tested and met, or surpassed, the Federal fuel-system-integrity standard applicable to it."

Nevertheless, four days later NHTSA's Joan Claybrook contacted Dowie to ask for his notes (he complied). With the Center for Auto Safety petitioning for a recall, Claybrook wanted to test the vehicle. She tapped a researcher, Lynn Bradford, for the job.

"How do we deal with this?" Claybrook asked him.

"We're just going to crash test it, and see what happens," Bradford replied.

Claybrook told him to test it just below the 30 mph standard, which had taken effect that year. "Test it at twenty-nine or something like that, just to see what happens, then test it at thirty," she suggested.

Bradford purchased some Pintos secondhand from dealers and took them to a test track in the Southwest. Instead of filling them with Stoddard, a fuel substitute commonly used in crash tests, he used real gasoline, and rammed them from behind with a full-sized sedan at 29.7 mph. The Pinto's rear-end buckled, the fuel tank broke, gas leaked out and both cars burst into flames. Claybrook was shocked when she saw the films. "It was scary," she said. "No one could have gotten out of that car, even if you had been in the front seat."

She called Ford to inform the company that NHTSA had made an initial determination of a defect and scheduled a public hearing. When Ford protested, Claybrook released the crash-test films to the media. The automaker conceded, agreeing to recall 2 million Pintos to install a shield to protect the gas tank.

Claybrook said, "Why don't you put your fix in and then bring in the vehicle and we'll test it again."

Ford insisted it run the crash studies. The company didn't want NHTSA to film them and release the footage to the media, in case its solution didn't work.

"If you want to test it, you have to film it," Claybrook said, "and I want engineers and lawyers there watching the whole thing from A to Z."

Ford tested its fix, and it failed. *How could they be so stupid not to put a fix in that worked?* Claybrook thought. *Why didn't they do some mini-test before the grand test?* The company went back to the drawing board, and this time its shield performed as advertised. Discontinued two years later, the Pinto caused 27 known burn deaths and had become so embarrassing that Ford's advertising agency, J. Walter Thompson, felt compelled to drop the ad slogan, "Pinto leaves you with that warm feeling."

What saddened Claybrook was that Detroit was capable of manufacturing safe vehicles but chose not to. Automakers could design a car the size of a Pinto that was inexpensive, lightweight, could travel 400 miles on a tank of gas, meet all emission-control standards, yet could race head-on into a concrete wall at 50 mph and the driver could walk away without a scratch. They could market a vehicle that could absorb a high-speed side collision from a car that weighed twice as much and withstand a rollover at 40 mph. And if the driver had the misfortune of hitting a pedestrian at 25 mph, the front end could become a basket and scoop up the person so that he wouldn't be thrown to the pavement. Not only that, it could be sporty, too. Claybrook knew such a car was possible because she had seen one.

When NHTSA was formed, written into the statute was a requirement that the government design an experimental safety vehicle. The original contractors were airplane manufacturers, but they didn't do much. Then automakers got involved. They came up with 6,000-pound steel behemoths that offered crash protection for six passengers up to 50 mph but only got 12 miles per gallon. Dissatisfied, the agency announced a contest. The ground rules were simple. Design a vehicle that met stringent emission controls, got good gas mileage, and offered protection from roof crush and front-end collisions. Ford, VW, Chrysler, and a tiny company run by a former General Motors engineer called Mini Cars entered the contest. The winner: Mini Cars.

The company's founder, Donald Friedman, analyzed crash data so he could figure out how people were hurt. In 1975, half of all serious accidents involved front-end collisions and 10 percent were rollovers. In addition, 25 percent of people injured in accidents weren't even in the car; they were pedestrians. Friedman, who developed the guidance system for the Sidewinder missile, aimed to create a vehicle that would protect 75 percent of people who were being injured.

He accomplished this by conjuring up a number of innovative approaches and completely rejecting the way Detroit designed vehicles. He started with a Honda Accord motor and employed a mid-engine design, so it was located in the middle of the car, not in the front or rear. His car's bare frame was made out of sheet metal boxes filled with foam. He poured it into the holes and it rose like bread and hardened, a technique now used on the space shuttle. The purpose of the foam—besides its light weight—was to take the sting out of an impact. When his Research Safety Vehicle (RSV) crashed, energy was evenly dispersed, much like hitting a pillow. In lieu of a bumper, Friedman bolted a foam nose that weighed 15 pounds to the front end and coated it with a flexible plastic. That way the other car would simply bounce off, and the RSV would spring back into shape. If the foam nose were ever damaged, the owner could bolt on a new one. In the event of a high-speed collision, the gas tank would never burst and engulf the car in flames because it was made of bendable rubber and protected by the front wheel. Nor was there any chance of having a blowout and losing control on the highway, because Friedman's tires could run flat at 50 mph for 50 miles. He installed special headrests to prevent whiplash and broken necks, and the windows were made to bend so a person's head would actually be cushioned by the glass. Because so few Americans wore seat belts at the time, Friedman relied on air bags, which came out of the steering wheel and dashboard, protecting the occupant's chest and cradling his head.

To Claybrook, the most ingenious aspect of the RSV was that it could protect pedestrians, who made up a quarter of all traffic fatalities. Even if they escaped death, they were vulnerable to serious injury. When a person is hit by a car, the first thing that happens is his kneecap or leg snaps. Then he is either thrown onto the pavement, perhaps in front of an oncoming car, or hits his head on the hood. But with an RSV, the front was a luggage compartment that doubled as a "head catcher," which could literally scoop up people in its path. The lid of the compartment was sloped and cushioned, designed to give way and keep pedestrians conscious and on the hood.

Not only that, but the car, available in silver, was sleek-looking—not unlike a Porsche, Claybrook thought—with an aerodynamic design and doors that lifted like a gull's wings. NHTSA awarded Friedman $6 million to manufacture 14 of them. In 1979, five years after Friedman drafted the initial plans, the RSV was sent to France, Germany, and Japan for independent testing: head-on collisions, side impacts, rollovers, handling. All the reports came back positive except from Porsche, which tested handling, something Friedman hadn't been given money for.

Claybrook took the car on a short media tour, appearing on *The Today Show* and *Good Morning America*. On the *NBC Evening News*, Tom Brokaw couldn't dent it with a baseball bat. Claybrook had to miss a press conference in New York with then-Mayor Edward Koch on the steps of City Hall, since she was scheduled to be on Capitol Hill that day, but was surprised to receive a frantic phone call from an NHTSA publicist on the scene. "Joan, you won't believe what happened," he said. The microphones and cameras had been set up, the press assembled, and the mayor and other speakers ready to go. Just as it was about to start, a woman removed her raincoat and stood stark naked. Then she bolted and the reporters, photographers and cameramen took off in pursuit. Claybrook suspected it was a ploy by one of the automakers to disrupt the press conference.

Encouraged by the positive response, she hired two men and a truck to transport the RSV to 52 cities around the country—to county fairs, auto shows, firefighters' parades, and local news shows. She ordered a short public service announcement for TV narrated by Lorne Green of TV's *Bonanza*, and supplied NHTSA's phone number for those wishing additional information. As a result, the agency received 80,000 calls.

When she accompanied the car to the Experimental Safety Vehicle Conference in Paris, a Saudi sheik approached her and asked the price. "Two hundred and fifty thousand dollars," said Claybrook, about what each of the original 14 vehicles cost to produce from scratch.

"I'd like it," he said.

Claybrook shook her head. "It's not for sale."

When she left the agency in 1981, swept away by Ronald Reagan's landslide, the remaining three RSVs were parked at Department of Transportation headquarters in Washington and forgotten about. In the late 1980s, the Smithsonian Institution expressed interest in them for its permanent collection. By April 1990, the agency transferred them to the University of Virginia's School of Engineering "for educational purposes and to augment NHTSA's ongoing research."

Six months later, after the Department of Transportation announced its opposition to higher fuel standards, NHTSA authorized their destruction. Jerry Curry, the agency's top administrator at the time, said that saving gas was akin to trading "barrels of oil for body bags," and believed the bigger the car, the safer it was. NHTSA Associate Administrator George Parker later testified that the Department of Transportation's inspector general "recommended that we dispose of these vehicles because they could see no use for them." No one ever bothered to inform Friedman.

With Curry's blessing, the RSVs were transported to the agency's Vehicle Research and Test Center in Ohio for destruction. The RSVs didn't go down without a fight, recording some of the best side impact scores ever recorded. The lone remaining RSV, the one that had appeared in Lorne Green's Public Service Announcement, was approved for demolition on June 24, 1991. A week later it was rammed into a concrete barrier at 50 mph in a 50 percent offset, a crash almost three times more severe than the federal standard. Since the purpose was annihilation, the government didn't bother to install crash test dummies and activate the air bags. Remarkably, the vehicle passenger compartment held up anyway.

Friedman believed that Curry demolished the RSVs because "they were a thorn in his side. People would inquire why aren't [today's] cars this safe? By eliminating them he eliminated the accident and not the injury."

Claybrook took it a step further. She likened Curry's destruction of the RSVs to book burning by the Nazis.

ON AUG. 14, 2000, CLAYBROOK, HOAR, AND TURNER gathered at Public Citizen before the media. Joining them were Sean Kane and Geoffrey Coffin, a Connecticut businessman who had been seriously injured five years earlier when a 16-inch Firestone tire not covered in the recall failed on his six-week-old Ford Explorer. Although Hoar was hostile to Kane's inclusion, Turner and Claybrook overrode him, believing it would have greater impact if all the major auto safety players spoke with one voice. (Clarence Ditlow of the Center for Auto Safety had also been invited, but he declined due to a prior engagement.)

"The public can afford no further delay in getting these tires off the highway," Claybrook told the assembled journalists. "There is ample evidence to show that vehicle owners with these other, non-recalled tires may be at substantial risk." She pointed to inconsistencies in the recall, asking why Firestone hadn't recalled other lines of tires manufactured in Decatur, and wanted to know why the automaker replaced 16-inch AT tires in some foreign countries, but not in the United States. She called on NHTSA to use its subpoena power to obtain documents from lawsuits that Ford and Firestone had kept under wraps by insisting on secrecy agreements during court proceedings, and urged Ford and Firestone to abandon any and all claims of confidentiality.

Hoar claimed that Safetyforum.com had received "more than a million hits" in the last two weeks, and discussed the fury that many consumers felt. And Kane questioned why Ford and Firestone had failed to adequately explain why environmental conditions and usage patterns affected one size tire but not others.

When it was Turner's turn, he demanded that Ford and Firestone "stop playing statistical games with peoples lives. They need to tell the American people exactly how many tires have failed and how many deaths and injuries have occurred from Wilderness tires other than those that were recalled," he said. "Then let the American people decide whether they want to take those statistical risks with their lives and the lives of their loved ones." He cited several clients who were in horrific accidents after non-recalled Firestone tires had failed, and showed the audience the remains of the Donna Bailey tire, which had been manufactured in Wilson, North Carolina.

But it was Geoffrey Coffin who brought a human element to the proceedings. While on a business trip on Long Island in June 1995, the rear Firestone ATX tire on his Ford Explorer gave out and the car rolled three times, crossing over the opposite lane and crashing into a tree. It took two and a half hours to pull him from the wreck. After he was transported by helicopter to the hospital, doctors found that his back was broken and his spinal cord was compressed by 30 percent. His skull was fractured, one lung collapsed, the tympanic nerve in one ear damaged, several ribs were broken, and one of his kidneys was so damaged he permanently lost function in it. He spent two weeks in the hospital in a morphine-induced haze.

"With all this," Coffin said, "I now consider myself one of the lucky ones." He got to go home again. He lay immobile in a body cast for eight months and lost 80 pounds, which made it necessary for him to be fitted for a second body cast.

"It has been five years since that accident," he told the journalists. "My back gives me pain every single day. Most days I suffer headaches and often the scar tissue gives me pain in my chest. One day while helping my wife in the garden, the pain from the scar tissue was so severe, my wife rushed me to emergency believing I was having a heart attack. I do everything possible not to give in to the pain. I love to dance at weddings but my feet and legs will tingle because of the damage to my back and spinal cord. I go into work in the morning but can rarely last a full day. A few months ago, I formally turned my business over to my son. I still need pain medication to get me through most days. Most painful of all, prior to my accident I babysat for my newborn granddaughter. Now I cannot watch her by myself since if I lift her too often it is too painful."

As Turner predicted, the press conference ratcheted up the pressure on Ford and Firestone. It received wide media coverage in the *Wall Street Journal*, *Chicago Tribune*, *L.A. Times*, and newspapers around the country picked up an Associated Press story. Turner's secretary fielded dozens of calls every day from people asking what they should do with non-recalled Firestone AT tires. She gave them Turner's usual spiel: If the tires were not covered, replace them at your own expense, store the old ones in your garage, and keep your receipt in the event Firestone ever widened the recall at a future date.

But not everything went smoothly. When the conference was over, Joan Claybrook found out Kane had broken the news embargo by issuing a press release on *PR Newswire*, touting his company's role in the Firestone investigation. Claybrook pulled him aside to chew him out, telling him this was about consumers, not credit. Kane, who could match her barb for barb, claimed it had been an "accident." The argument escalated until Claybrook banished him from any future combined role with Public Citizen or the recall effort.

After Kane left and Claybrook had calmed down, she asked Turner to leave the Donna Bailey tire he had shown reporters. Congress was calling hearings and it would make a great prop. Turner agreed, but told Claybrook, "No one can touch [it] because [it's] evidence." She locked it away.

Claybrook then asked Turner for some of the documents he had mentioned at the press conference.

Turner thought about it. They were his life's work and he had spent the last 15 years gathering them. But he also realized they were the best ammunition they had. He agreed, with one condition: She wouldn't release them to reporters without asking first.

Thereafter, whenever reporters asked for hard proof, Claybrook referred them to Turner. And in the span of a few short weeks he became the veritable head of a consumer movement.

19 CRISIS

DESPITE JASON VINES' EFFORTS, THE WHEELS were beginning to come off Ford. Even as replacement tires flowed to its dealers and Firestone tire outlets, the automaker was being bombarded with questions from journalists, politicians and the public: Why hadn't it acted sooner to identify defects, and when it had, why didn't it begin recalling tires then? If Firestone's quality was so poor that it had manufactured thousands of defective tires, then how had the tire maker received Ford's highest quality rating, Q1? Even if Firestone had made bad tires, why would automakers bother to supply spare tires if drivers weren't expected to maintain control of their vehicles after suffering tread failures? As Vines predicted, the fracas between Ford and Firestone blurred the lines of responsibility, making it difficult for the public to figure out whom to blame.

As the days wore on, veteran Ford watchers wondered who would lead the company out of this consumer safety quagmire: Chairman William Clay Ford, Jr., or CEO and President Jacques Nasser. The two men could scarcely be more different. Nasser, 52, a Lebanese-born Australian from the working class, was a short, powerful, energetic man who slept no more than four hours a night. He has been described as "brusque," "hard-driving," "impatient," "ruthless," a "piranha," "a trampling extrovert" who was "confident to the point of arrogance." Not merely a trimmer of corporate fat, he was "a one-man guillotine" in a splashy Saville Row suit.

Starting at Ford Australia, where he punched holes in paper to add to three-ring binders, he was transferred to the United States in 1973 and spent the next dozen years working around the globe as an international financial analyst. He snatched the top job at Ford in 1998 after he turned around the company's failing Australian and European divisions by slashing tens of thousands of jobs, dumping unprofitable product lines, increasing productivity and lowering the cost of developing new models.

Nasser wanted to completely reinvent the century-old automaker, which had been in business so long its stock symbol was merely an "F." His dream was to create a highly diversified "lifestyle company" with numerous components: car and truck manufacturing, auto customizing, maintenance and recycling shops, Hertz rental cars, all under one roof. He wanted to eventually sell cars directly over the Internet to consumers, cutting out the dealers and their commissions.

With a lifelong passion for automobiles—he proudly called himself a "petrol head"—Nasser knew the nitty-gritty, like how whittling down the choice of cigarette lighters from 14 to 1 would save $1 million a year, and how reducing by 25 percent the number of vehicle platforms while doubling the number of parts they shared would shave expenses, speed up product development, and increase productivity. He preached ambition, drive, and loyalty. Shortly after accepting the CEO job, he told a crew of junior executives that the auto business was brutally competitive, nowhere more so than at Ford. If playing at this level didn't make "the hair stand up on the back of your neck when you talk about it, then go somewhere else," he urged. "Go to our competition. We'd love it."

At the other end of the spectrum, Bill Ford, Jr., 42, was, despite his rich-boy pedigree, hard working, self-effacing, and genuinely a "nice guy with a politician's keen instinct." He was an environmentalist who referred to workers as his "extended family" and believed his company could do best for its shareholders by doing good in the community, which meant taking care of its workers and the environment. When the company was negotiating a new contract with the United Auto Workers, Bill Ford arrived at a board meeting sporting a pro-union button that said, "Bargaining for families," because he said he didn't like to think in terms of "us vs. them."

After an explosion rocked Ford Motor's Rouge plant in February 1999, the newly appointed chairman rushed to the scene, despite the warnings of his lieutenants, who told him that generals don't go to the front. "Really?" he replied. "Well, bust me down to private then, because I'm out of here." He visited the injured and dying (six men were killed) at local area hospitals to comfort their families long into the evening. According to Business 2.0, that was a defining moment for Bill Ford, who "made it perfectly clear that he did not intend to be a buttoned-down, 20th-century executive."

Three months after the Rouge disaster, he ordered a complete make-over of the complex that had been built by Henry Ford, and retained

William McDonough, an architect known for environmentally friendly designs, to lead the project. Later that year he pulled Ford out of the Global Climate Coalition, a lobbying group dedicated to undermining efforts to legislate measures to combat global warming.

Bill Ford had spent 20 years shimmying up the corporate ladder and had the solid backing of his family, which had controlled 40 percent of the voting stock since 1956, when the automaker first went public. While Nasser was in charge of the company's day-to-day operations, Bill Ford handled the 14-member board of directors, in which three family members served, including his father, William Clay Ford, owner of the moribund Detroit Lions football team.

In mid-August 2000, with Congress beginning to rattle its sabers and threaten public hearings, the company knew it couldn't risk putting the scion's scion in a situation that could tarnish his image. "The last thing we wanted was to put Bill Ford, the man whose name was on the building, in front of Congress, when he wasn't the expert in this," Vines said. "Congress would have had great delight in trying to emasculate someone whose name was Ford."

The in-house consensus was that the responsibility should fall on Nasser, who had been running the recall effort since the beginning. Besides, Nasser wanted to leave no doubt as to who was in control, demanding that he be the one to speak for the company. At the same time Bill Ford, who also had designs on the CEO job and had no real love, or even like, of Nasser, wanted no part of it. If Nasser succeeded, he would be able to solidify his hold over the automaker. If Nasser failed, Bill Ford could remain above the fray and, if need be, ride up on his white horse to save the company—and the family's name. The risk would be entirely Nasser's.

One of Nasser's first acts was also one of his most courageous: ordering the temporary shutdown of three Ford factories to free up 70,000 replacement tires for the recall effort, a complex and expensive proposition affecting not just Ford but also its suppliers. It required pulling the plug on production lines, canceling deliveries of fresh parts to factories, mothballing heavy machinery, and protecting partially assembled vehicles even as 6,000 plant workers continued to earn 95 percent of their base pay. This action cost the company $100 million. Then, bowing to consumers angry they might have to wait up to a year for replacements, Nasser decreed that other tire brands could be used at Ford dealerships. He communicated with Bridgestone/Firestone management almost daily and, in the few minutes he had free every day, would even take a seat in the War Room and personally field calls.

But the automaker needed a more public way to trumpet Nasser's emergence as its front man. The media had been beating up on both companies, no matter how hard Vines worked to distance Ford from Firestone. "Ford should heed tire perils in U.S.," advised the *Chicago Sun-Times*. "Massive SUV tire recall likely to hit Ford hardest," Canada's *Globe and Mail* predicted. Searching for a culprit, CBS News headlined a piece "Zeroing in on the Explorer." In "Blowout: How the Tire Problem Turned into a Crisis for Firestone and Ford," the *Wall Street Journal* weighed in with a lengthy analysis that detailed how the automaker and its supplier missed the telltale signs of trouble. The *Baltimore Sun* provided commentary entitled, "Recall: If you hate sport utility vehicles, you must love the flap over the faulty tires."

Meanwhile, frightened consumers made for colorful copy. "Thousands await getting their tires changed after recall," said the Associated Press. *USA Today* chimed in with, "Ford owners demand new tires. Many ignore phased recall, head to dealers who've run out of stock." " 'Get them off the car!' " urged the *Grand Rapids Press*. "Job 1 at Ford: Ease fears about Explorer. Owners are scared, and stakes are huge," reported *Automotive News*. Several news organizations alleged that Ford waited too long to push for a recall and made hay over the discrepancy in recommended air pressure. Others covered the Venezuela debacle, wondering why Ford would recall tires there but not in the United States. The *Toronto Star* turned its sights on the upcoming 2001 Explorer Sport, believing it faced a "bumpy-riding" launch "clouded by tire recall."

The competition among journalists was fierce. It was one of those stories that forced reporters to stay up way past midnight to see what the competition had in online editions, and then wait for their bosses to take them to task for not having it first. Wire services like the Associated Press, Bloomberg, and Reuters were really taxed. One Reuters reporter who had written his second or third Ford-Firestone feature in a day chucked off hisheadset and quit on the spot when his editor tried to squeeze one more out of him. (Not long after, he joined Ford PR to help manage financial public relations.)

USA Today reporter David Kiley was particularly frustrated. On the job two months, Kiley, 37, was not only the paper's Detroit Bureau chief, he was its sole employee, running it out of a spare room in his house in nearby Ann Arbor. He was hopelessly outgunned by the *Wall Street Journal*, *New York Times*, *Washington Post* and *Detroit Free Press*, all of which were devoting significant manpower to the issue. And things were only getting worse. Kiley's assignment editor was on a leave of absence due to a death in the family, and Jim Healey, an experienced auto industry colleague, was about to take off three weeks to move into a new house. Now Kiley was alone on a breaking story that was taking place in large part on his turf.

Although a relative newcomer to *USA Today,* Kiley didn't panic. He was a second-generation journalist whose father, Charles Kiley, had a storied career as a journalist and editor. During World War II, the elder Kiley was on staff at *Stars and Stripes,* the U.S. Army newspaper, and was the only reporter allowed in the room at "the little red school house" in Reims, France—where the Germans capitulated to the Allied command—and who also witnessed the Germans surrender to the Russians. After the war he joined the *New York Herald Tribune,* handling such talents as Jimmy Breslin and Tom Wolfe and counting among his pals the great sports writers Red Smith and Jimmy Cannon.

The son took pride in carrying on his father's work. A self-described "Jersey guy" born in Westfield, New Jersey, David Kiley graduated from Fordham University, where he played football on both sides of the line until he blew out his knee. He worked at *Adweek* for several years, had a short hitch with the *Daily Record,* a New Jersey paper, covered the savings and loan collapse for a small trade publication called the *National Thrift News,* and was employed by Lou Dobbs at CNN. Before taking the job at *USA Today,* Kiley had spent time on the "dark side" at a Madison Avenue advertising agency as a corporate spokesman, a job he hated.

He knew he didn't yet have the sources in the automobile industry to compete with reporters who had been covering the beat for years. And he wasn't comfortable basing articles on leaked documents from plaintiffs' attorneys, which he believed told only a fraction of the story. But Kiley was tired of playing catch-up and had lost more than a few nights of sleep over it. He wasn't the only one running on empty. He would show up at Ford for a briefing and could see the weariness on people's faces. Kiley could relate. He was completely wrung out, stressed from starting a new job and preoccupied with the health of his 86-year-old father, who was in a nursing home convalescing from a fractured hip.

Kiley decided to go for broke: an interview with Jacques Nasser himself. Although Kiley had never met the man, he knew that in the event that Ford granted permission for an interview with its CEO it would come down to a handful of major media outlets, those with large circulations and a national reach. That left out the *Detroit Free Press,* Ford's hometown paper, and the *Washington Post,* which owned the Beltway but didn't resonate with American consumers. Kiley knew Ford wouldn't let Keith Bradsher of the *New York Times* within 1,000 yards of Nasser. Although Bradsher was probably the top automotive reporter in the country writing for one of the most powerful papers in America, he was also a well-known SUV-basher. Kiley assumed it would come down to *USA Today* and the *Wall Street Journal.*

Figuring he had nothing to lose, he picked up the phone and dialed Ford headquarters. When Jason Vines answered, Kiley's exact words were, "Hi. I want Jac. I want him this week. And I want him to myself." Kiley couldn't believe how "cheesy" it all sounded. He had never done anything like it before. When Vines didn't immediately hang up, Kiley flexed *USA Today*'s circulation and reminded Vines that his readers were the ones who bought Ford products and were directly affected by the recall. "This is a customer issue, not a Wall Street issue," Kiley said, "and if you want to talk to your customers, you talk to us."

It didn't take long for Kiley to realize he and Vines were on the same wavelength. With Ford getting pummeled in the press, Vines—like Kiley—was searching for a proactive approach for getting in front of the story, instead of remaining in reactive mode. Kiley could scarcely believe his luck. They quickly closed the deal.

In the late afternoon on Aug. 16, 2000, Vines ushered Kiley into a sterile conference room adjacent to Nasser's office, empty save for a table, chairs and a TV. A few minutes later Jacques Nasser joined him. *Jac looks tired as hell*, Kiley thought, even in his natty gray suit, white shirt and silk tie. Short, built like a fireplug, Nasser wasn't bald but he also didn't have much hair. To Kiley he looked like a man with the weight of the world on his shoulders. Although he had never before met Ford's CEO and president face-to-face, Kiley had seen him at press conferences where the usually high-wattage Nasser basked in his Australian upbringing, bantering with reporters and calling them "mate."

For a journalist, the best part about interviewing Nasser was you could always find something to write about afterward. He began ruling Ford when CEOs were supposed to be more like coaches than kings, and created a system in which he was at the top and had some 16 managers reporting directly to him, as if he were supreme royalty surrounded by dukes. He had a volatile mix of intentions and deep admiration for Jack Welch and what Welch accomplished at General Electric. Indeed, Nasser tried to implement a number of GE-like programs, although he didn't get very far because of Ford's renowned bureaucratic resistance to change.

Kiley was an imposing interviewer, six feet tall and weighing nearly 400 pounds, a sharp goatee framing his chin. Always a big man, the stress of his father's infirmity, the new job, and trouble with Type II diabetes had taken its toll, and he had gained 50 pounds over the course of months. Perspiring in a blue blazer, club tie, and khakis, Kiley removed his jacket to reveal a starched white shirt and braces.

As an icebreaker he told Nasser he wished he had come to talk about the new redesigned Thunderbird, one of Nasser's pet projects, instead of the recall—a pale lie, since Kiley thought the T-bird looked like it had been designed with an orthodontist's mistress in mind.

"You and me both, mate," Nasser replied.

"It's pretty tough trying to unravel all the information we're getting and put in proper context," said Kiley, pulling out a reporter's notebook and setting his tape recorder on the table about four feet away from Nasser, who even late in the day seemed perfectly and permanently pressed.

"Try it from our side sometime," Nasser said. "But we're getting our arms around it."

Kiley started the interview by asking Nasser about Ford documents that demonstrated a clear pattern of concern voiced by engineers about the Explorer's stability. Nasser insisted the Explorer was safe and recommended he "look at the data." Ford was "a data-driven company" and "the data shows our vehicles are safe." There was "absolutely no data or incidents of trends of incidents" that indicated a design problem with the Explorer. No, he wouldn't consider a wider recall because "if you look at statistical data, it's very clear where the problem tires are," and he had no intention of recalling the Explorer because that wasn't "in the data" either.

The data. The data. It's in the data. Nasser must have said it a dozen times. "This is a tire problem, not a vehicle problem," Nasser summed up. And if a flaw were found, "we'd be the first to raise our hand" and confess, a pledge Kiley greeted with skepticism.

Ford and Firestone publicists had informed Kiley only the day before that it would take until at least the spring to replace all 6.5 million tires, but Nasser contradicted them. "Spring was unacceptable," he said. When Nasser first learned of the problem he looked at how Johnson & Johnson had handled the Tylenol case, and although this wasn't a medicine recall where he could just pull product off the shelf—it was not physically possible to manufacture and install millions of new tires in the span of weeks—Nasser realized that Explorer owners would not accept driving on potentially dangerous tires for months on end. "We'll get this done by the end of November," Nasser promised.

Kiley tried not to smile. He had his "lead." Kiley didn't think Ford had set it up for Nasser to come across as a hero. He believed Nasser genuinely felt that spring would not work. But the disconnect between what the two companies were saying and what Nasser just told him was important. Hell, the fact he was talking at all was big news.

While prepping for the interview, Kiley had spoken with a source at Ford's ad agency, J. Walter Thompson, who advised him that Nasser had seen tape of a local news report, an interview with a tearful mother who was scared to death about driving her kids around on Firestone Wilderness tires. The report strengthened Nasser's resolve to move faster, which prompted Kiley to ask, "What do you tell parents with kids and only one vehicle and are driving around on pins and needles because they can't get replacement tires?"

"You tell them to call us and I'll get them tires," Nasser replied.

Kiley couldn't believe that Nasser could be so cavalier. For a second, Kiley felt guilty for backing him into a corner. But no one made him say it, so Kiley kept pressing. He asked whether Ford would be willing to go so far as to pay for rental cars for people in the interim and Nasser said he would look at that as one of the solutions to make people satisfied.

In the hour he had with Nasser, Kiley grilled him on why Ford hadn't spotted the problem earlier ("There was nothing in the data that was outside the norm," Nasser replied); inquired into his relationship with Bill Ford, an issue he sidestepped; and noted that the automaker had taken over "the communication process from Firestone," something Nasser made no apologies for.

Kiley brought up the altered suspension systems in Venezuela and Nasser claimed it was done because of "different usage patterns." When Kiley wondered why the automaker recalled tires in the Middle East and South America but not, until recently, in the United States, Nasser put the onus on Firestone. Almost as an afterthought the journalist asked the CEO whether he would come out and talk to his customers in the form of a news conference or advertising. Nasser admitted he was being lobbied by his people to film an ad but hadn't made up his mind yet.

A few more minutes, a few more questions, a few more answers and the interview was over. By the time Kiley made it to his car parked in the lot outside the Glass House it was almost 5:30. Realizing he didn't have time to get back to his office in Ann Arbor and write the story, he phoned Vines, who sent a junior publicist down to spirit Kiley to Ford's media center, where the company held earnings conferences—a small auditorium with phone and computer hookups and seating for 25 reporters.

The flack flicked on the lights and paced around the room while Kiley frantically transcribed the interview tape and reviewed his notes. Some papers allow reporters on a tight deadline to call in quotes to a rewrite desk, but *USA Today* didn't work that way. Kiley actually had to write the story and include a Q & A to run on the inside. He led with Nasser's pledge to speed up the recall, which he knew would get picked up by TV and the news wires, but needed a "ballsy consumer hook" to guarantee a spot on the front page. Then he remembered Nasser's pledge to pay for rental cars for Explorer owners worried about driving on recalled tires until they could get replacements. He threw in Ford's call center for good measure. Deadline was usually 6:30 p.m., but by the time Kiley overcame a dying cell phone battery, computer hook up problems and editorial feedback, it was closer to 8:00, and his editor was concerned about delaying print runs.

Kiley returned to his car and found that in his haste he had left the front door wide open. Nothing was missing.

Aug. 17, 2000, the day his interview with Nasser appeared, was also Kiley's parents' 56th wedding anniversary. It was the first time his father had ever seen his son's byline on the front page of a national newspaper. Kiley was almost 40 years old but felt like a kid whose dad had just seen him knock in the winning run in a Little League game.

FORD DIDN'T APPRECIATE THAT KILEY HAD INCLUDED its call center number in his article, although the automaker had previously listed it in press releases. For three days Ford's switchboard was swamped with people claiming, "Jac Nasser says he will get me tires," and submitting requests for rental cars. The poor operators were caught completely by surprise.

Even though Kiley's article announced that Ford's CEO had "set aside six weeks of behind-the-scenes damage control and grabbed the issue by the throat," Nasser's problems only deepened. The TV ads he filmed in the lobby and shown on primetime TV backfired. Critics said he appeared stiff on camera and sounded like "Crocodile Dundee." He came across as a CEO trying to deflect blame instead of someone interested in the truth.

When Congress announced hearings and invited both Nasser and Bridgestone/Firestone's chairman Ono to appear, Nasser told his staff he looked forward to the challenge. But Ford's Washington office was dead set against him testifying. Things came to a head during a "passionate argument" in the office of John Rintamaki, Nasser's chief of staff. Jason Vines and Ken Zino believed Nasser had to do it while Janet Mullins Grissom, Ford's vice president of Washington affairs, phoned in to maintain he shouldn't. She claimed she had cut a deal. All Nasser had to do was appear before the committee and say "no" to testifying. They would beat up on him for a couple of hours and move on, promising not to harp on the issue. They just want "him with his hand in the air, taking the oath," Grissom said.

Vines became "very emotional," saying it was imperative that Nasser testify. "He can handle it," Vines said. "There's nobody smarter."

Zino grabbed the phone and told Grissom, "We're not talking about a court of law, we're talking about opinion here."

But Grissom stood firm.

Rintamaki listened to their arguments and sided with the Washington office.

It was left up to Vines to announce that Nasser was too busy to testify, a task he found distasteful. "We need the CEO here to run the [recall] program," Vines said blandly during a telephone news conference from company headquarters. Meanwhile Bridgestone/Firestone declared that its chief executive, Masatoshi Ono, would appear before the House committee to answer any and all questions.

This led to a torrent of criticism from politicians and the media, who accused Nasser of dodging the issue. Ken Johnson, spokesman for "Billy" Tauzin (R-La.), a senior member of the House Commerce Committee and co-chair of the hearings, wondered how Nasser had time to film television ads but couldn't squeeze in a few hours to address Congress. "Could it be the recall isn't going as well as we're told?" Johnson asked. "Preferably, we would like to hear Ford's unscripted version of what went wrong."

After being treated like a piñata for 24 hours, Nasser called another meeting. He was livid because he had advised his staff he had no problem with testifying. Attempting to gauge the temperature, he asked, "What's the view out there?"

Not one to mince words, Vines said, "The view is you're a fucking coward."

Nasser's arms fell to his side. The others in the room just stared in shock. "Jesus, Vines," someone whispered.

"I'm sorry," Vines said. "It's not fair. But that's the view."

"What should we do?" Nasser asked.

"We've got to do it," Vines answered. He suggested putting out an announcement in about an hour. Someone said, "No, we've got to think about it," but Rintamaki overruled him. "No, we're going to do it now," he said. "We've taken enough of a beating."

While Nasser prepared to go to Washington, Ford's reputation continued to sink. A few days after the recall announcement, 70.3 percent of people interested in buying a sport-utility vehicle believed that Ford was handling the recall properly. Three weeks later, the percentage dropped to 17 percent.

20 GAG

THE FORD F-150 XLT PICKUP BOUNDED OUT of the Melbourne, Florida, courthouse parking lot, strewing bits of hay in its wake left over from transporting three-quarter-ton bales of cattle feed in the cargo bed. Behind the seat was a red beer cooler; in the glove compartment, a .357 magnum snub-nosed revolver; between them, at the steering wheel, sat Bruce Kaster, furiously working his cell phone.

A shade past 50, Kaster looked more like a rancher than one of the country's top tire litigators—all craggy and sun-dried, closely cropped gray beard, herbal cigarette dangling from his lips, eyes peering through glasses too big for his face. He talked like a rancher, too, his speech spiked with homespun wisdom and a cowhand's profanity. Since Kaster was partial to overstatement, friends and enemies alike automatically subtracted a third from everything he said. If he claimed he'd shot a 300-pound wild pig, you could be pretty sure it weighed 200. If he bragged about a $5 million settlement it was probably closer to $3.5 million. Although he donned a blue blazer and dress shirt for court, he also wore blue jeans and cowboy boots, which he kept polished despite tramping around The Broken Horn, the cattle ranch he planned to retire to someday.

But—and Kaster would go out of his way to emphasize this—don't call him a "redneck." In his eyes rednecks wore baseball caps, chewed tobacco, and drove beat-up vehicles they abandoned in their backyards where the weeds could grow over them. They could be anywhere in the country but were usually Southern, and didn't necessarily know anything about cowboying.

Kaster preferred "cracker," the term for the cowboys who drove cattle through the swamps and scrub of Florida, cracking bullwhips instead of spinning lariats. So what if Kaster, an "Army brat" whose father had been an artilleryman in the Battle of the Bulge, had been born in Oklahoma and spent the first half of his life in Germany, Maryland, and Vietnam, where he volunteered for a tour of duty.

After graduating college from Virginia Tech and law school from the University of Florida, he settled in sedate Ocala. He accepted his first tire case in 1987, when he settled with Uniroyal for $2 million, and has been suing tire makers ever since.

Kaster had just finished an 8 a.m. pretrial meeting with Firestone attorneys. His client, Medhat Labib, had been traveling on Interstate 95 in a 1996 Ford Explorer after a wedding rehearsal dinner when one of the Firestone ATX tires blew apart. Labib's wife and nine-year-old son were killed in the crash, and he was left paralyzed below the waist. When Kaster checked the tire serial number he found it had been manufactured in Decatur.

As soon as Kaster hit the sun outside the courthouse, he called in to the offices of Green, Kaster & Falvey. One of his partners told him that Firestone had scheduled a hearing for another case of Kaster's in Columbia County, north of Gainesville, practically halfway across the state. Kaster spat insults at Firestone. The tire maker's lawyers probably figured there would be no way he'd make the 300 miles in time. (Well, it was really closer to 200, but Kaster was on a roll.) But they thought wrong. There was no way he was going to attend by conference call. This hearing was much too important.

At stake were depositions Kaster had taken from employees at Firestone's Decatur plant, who told him of disturbing quality-control problems in the mid-1990s. Firestone was moving to seal them, which it had done successfully in an earlier case Kaster was involved in. In fact, a prickly judge in New York had also issued a gag order, preventing him from even breathing a word about Firestone.

So while Kaster could hint to his trial lawyer buddies at the Attorneys Information Exchange Group that he had some real good stuff on Decatur, he couldn't share. When Anna Werner of KHOU contacted him, all he could do was refer her to tire expert Rex Grogan and provide background on the sly. He did the same for Mark Skertic of the *Chicago Sun-Times*. Over the summer, as the Firestone issue exploded in the news, he couldn't say squat. And this made Kaster, a chatty man who could hold a press conference all by himself, miserable. He just had to get the judge to unseal these depositions. The public had a right to know what Firestone workers were saying about the tires they had built.

For Kaster it had been a long road to Decatur. The journey had begun not with Firestone but with another manufacturer, Cooper Tire Company, "the poor man's Firestone." Cooper, the fourth largest tire manufacturer in America, made discount tires sold at stores like Sears and Pep Boys—the kind that went for a hundred bucks for a set of four—and were marketed under 50-some brand names like Atlas, Futura, Patriot, Roadmaster, Sentry, Starfire, Superguard, and Viper. As bad as Firestone was, Cooper, which had a smaller market share, might have a higher defect rate. Two struggling attorneys asked Kaster to assist them with a case in Arkansas involving a Cooper tire that had torn apart and led to a tragic accident, and Kaster, who had grappled with the company several times before, was happy to oblige.

It was a particularly gruesome crash, involving two families who were preparing to celebrate a joyous occasion. On May 15, 1998, Scharlotte Hervey, 37, of Little Rock was driving her husband and three sons to her sister's college commencement. The couple had recently reconciled after a trial separation, and her husband Edward Lee Hervey, 44, sat in the front passenger seat while three of their sons rode in the back of their 1984 Volvo. Two other cars with family members followed, all heading east.

Five miles west of Brinkley, Hervey veered into the left hand lane to pass another vehicle and accelerated to 70 mph. By the time the Herveys were a car length ahead, their tire, which had about 20,000 miles on it, exploded, spinning off pieces of tread. The Volvo fishtailed out of control and the driver in the car behind steered onto the shoulder to avoid hitting it. The Herveys flew backwards and spun several times across the grass median, their momentum eventually pushing the car sideways into oncoming traffic, where a red Dodge Stratus in the westbound lane driven by 23-year-old Lane Whitaker plunged into it at highway speed, T-boning them. Whitaker's car slid down an embankment and caught fire, while the Herveys' Volvo heaved through the air and landed upside down.

Jim Farmer, a trucker trailing behind Whitaker, screeched to a halt and called 911. He ran to the Dodge carrying a fire extinguisher. After Farmer and another trucker extinguished the fire, a paramedic arrived and told Farmer the driver had sustained serious head injuries. Farmer put his ear close to Whitaker's face, and listened, "and he wasn't breathing no more."

Police also found Scharlotte and Edward Hervey dead at the scene. As rescue workers struggled to pull the victims from the wrecks, Scharlotte Hervey's brother came upon the crash scene. He knew it was his sister's car and used his mobile phone to call their mother. "Don't tell me. Don't tell me," she begged. The police stopped traffic on the interstate so that three helicopters could fly the sons to area hospitals.

While Cynthia Miller, Hervey's sister, stood in line to receive her diploma from Phillips Community College in Helena, she wondered where her sister was. A family member told her after the ceremony. A hundred miles away, Lane Whitaker's sister, who was graduating high school, wanted to know the same thing about her brother. She noticed he wasn't with either of her parents. A pastor from the family's church broke the news to them. The next day 15-year-old Onterio Jamar Miller Hervey died. His two younger brothers, Demario Hervey, 13, and Rashod Hervey, 7, were paralyzed. Now Scharlotte Hervey's mother cares for her two wheelchair-bound grandsons at her Helena, Arkansas, home.

The Herveys and Whitakers got together to retain Paul Byrd and Jerry Kelly of Little Rock to sue Cooper. Both were modest, hard-working country lawyers who weren't afraid to get their hands dirty. Byrd was serious and soft-spoken and carried a laptop everywhere he went, even fishing. Kelly was outgoing, an affable rice farmer who could talk to a fence post and get a response. But neither had done a tire case before. They were unprepared for Cooper's cynical manipulation of the legal system, the company's brazen refusal to fulfill the judge's orders, the constant delays and filibustering, its refusal to hand over records, claiming they were trade secrets.

Looking for a defect pattern, the pair filed a discovery motion for similar lawsuits filed against Cooper, but the company would only consent to handing over cases that involved the same sized tire in the same type of accident. Cooper employed its standard blame-the-driver defense, claiming Hervey's driving caused the accident. "99.9-something percent of people confronted with various forms of tire disablement simply pull over and change the tire," testified Christopher Shapley, a tire engineer hired by Cooper, in a deposition. Hervey had panicked when "the requirement is to stay calm." Subsequently Cooper changed its story, asserting the failure was the result of "an unrepaired puncture . . . [caused] by a nail or similar road hazard incurred earlier in the tire's service life."

Even though every Cooper tire had a sticker inside, it took several motions before Byrd and Kelly found out the name of the tire builder and the plant where it had been manufactured: Tupelo, Mississippi. A year after receiving the case they were going broke and getting nowhere fast.

Meanwhile Tab Turner was also fighting Cooper in a tread separation case involving a Ford Bronco II. He had unearthed a former Cooper tire builder from Texarkana, Jimmy Oats, who told Turner and would testify that he had complained about tires being made from old stock, but that management ordered him to build them anyway. Oats said the rubber would dry out from being stored too long, wouldn't hold together properly, and wouldn't "cure out like it should," possibly leading to tire failures. Instead of tossing the bad stock, managers instructed workers to use it anyway, hoping the tires wouldn't fall apart. "Some of them did, and some of them didn't," Oats said.

Byrd and Kelly realized their cases were almost identical, except Turner had a Mississippi case with a tire made in Arkansas while Byrd and Kelly had an Arkansas case with a tire made in Mississippi. Turner was more than happy to share Oats' affidavit. After they read it, they knew they needed to locate someone who had worked at the Tupelo plant who could tell them the same things. They considered hiring an investigator, but Kaster warned them he'd had mixed results with detectives and paralegals because they didn't know what questions to ask. He recommended they do it themselves.

They drove to Tupelo and met with local lawyers, asking whether they had represented any workers with complaints against Cooper. They got more names over the Internet when they discovered workers who had sued the company when Cooper tried to prevent the formation of a union. They went to the courthouse and pulled up a hundred worker's compensation claims against the tire maker, which were public record. Byrd called each complainant, asking whether the person answering was a Cooper employee. If the answer was yes, he hung up; if the worker had moved on, Byrd would talk to him. He and Kelly frequented convenience stores and asked for anyone who used to work at Cooper tire. They went to the local waffle house. They talked to the cleaning ladies at the motel. Since Cooper was a major employer in the area, they had no trouble getting names. The problem was convincing anyone to agree to testify. *No way*, they'd say. *Got a family to support and don't want to take on Cooper and the other employees.*

It took a former marine who had left Cooper in 1998 because he didn't like what he saw to provide Byrd and Kelly with their first affidavit. William Douglas Eaton testified he was "worried about some family getting killed. . . . Tire builders didn't want to stop making tires because it would affect their production bonuses." Once, Eaton said, he even performed a test by slitting a tire to see whether it could get past inspection. "I cut it with a knife . . . but it went through the complete process and ended up in the warehouse." Eaton and his coworkers used to sit around coffee shops and discuss the situation. They were afraid if they didn't stop what they were doing, someone was going to die.

Another important witness was a former foreman of the Tupelo plant's curing department, Martin Mahan, who testified about the pressure to produce tires, which overwhelmed Cooper's quality control system. Company officials even rigged inspections. "I personally have shown . . . the same tire thirty times" to inspectors, Mahan said. Once the company sent him to San Francisco to inspect tires that had been manufactured by Cooper plants in Findlay, Ohio, and Tupelo, then shipped by rail to the West Coast. Of the 800 tires Mahan and another man inspected, 50 had to be discarded for faults like blisters and tread separation. One had a glove cured into the sidewall. Other times he had seen tires molded with time cards, paper clips, watches, wrenches, and even a live shotgun shell inside. Once a tire was made with chicken bones in it, because a coworker stored his lunch in the curing machine to keep it hot without telling anyone.

Byrd and Kelly's biggest score occurred while Byrd was taking an early evening nap and Kelly was working the phones from the motel. He talked with a woman who gave him the number of her mother-in-law, who used to work at Cooper. Kelly dialed Gayla Kirby, who agreed to meet but warned, "My husband is out with his buddies tonight, and if he sees two strangers in my living room when he gets home, he won't like this one bit. So you got to get out here fast."

They wasted no time driving to her home and taking her affidavit. Kirby had been a first-stage tire builder and told the lawyers about the use of solvents to freshen dried out rubber and contamination. As Kirby described production quotas, her 13-year-old daughter, rocking back and forth on her feet, said, "Daddy's home."

Jerry kept posing questions while Byrd nervously packed up his laptop, cell phone, and a new portable printer he had bought at Wal-Mart the night before. He hadn't backed up his files and was afraid of a scene.

In walked Jack Kirby, a powerful man with a gut that hung over the lip of his jeans, a beard, and piercing eyes. Before he could throw them out of his house, his wife explained they were lawyers taking statements about the factory. He just stood there, still as could be, intimidating in size and manner. When he didn't say anything, she whispered, "Honey, people are dying."

Jack Kirby grunted. Finally he said, "That's your business. I want nothin' to do with it." But he didn't try to stop her. Instead he grabbed a chair, turned it backward and straddled it, his massive arms resting on the back of the chair while his wife walked Byrd and Kelly through the tire-building process.

After listening for a while, a scowl etched on his face, he interrupted: "You wanna know about tires? I'll tell you about tires." They ended up talking late into the evening.

Jack Kirby was a repairman who cleaned up minor defects in tires—for instance if the whitewall lettering was bad he could buff it out, or remove small imperfections off the sidewalls. But he didn't just deal with cosmetic problems. He also fixed thumbnail-sized blisters by piercing them with an awl issued by the company. Kirby would locate the blister inside the tire with his hands, insert the awl through the tread, the two belts, and the ply, feeling with his fingers until he penetrated down to the blister without going through the liner. The air would escape, and he would retract the awl, smooth it over with his fingers, and let it go.

"You can do that?" Byrd asked.

"Up to eight times per tire," Jack Kirby replied, "depending on the number of blisters."

"You're telling us that Cooper punctures holes in the tires at the plant?" Byrd asked.

"Yup." Kirby also outlined an elaborate scheme that Cooper used to beat inspections. The factory would spend weeks specially producing near-perfect specimens of stock to use when inspectors showed up. "I've seen it happen time and time again," he said.

Afterward Byrd called Kaster, who at first didn't believe it. "Have you been drinking?" he asked. Kaster had been fighting tire companies for 15 years and this was the first he had heard of a company purposely poking holes in its tires. Awling was dangerous. Holes, even small ones, would allow moisture and air inside the inner layers and weaken a tire, causing the tread belts to separate.

Byrd assured Kaster he was sober.

"Here we have a tire with a puncture" that Cooper claimed was the cause of the Hervey accident "and yet they are puncturing tires up to eight times" at the factory? Kaster asked.

Yes, Byrd said. And Jack Kirby, whom Byrd had taken to calling "Mashed Potato Jack," said management knew all about it, since the practice was performed out in the open.

Kaster figured if the Hervey's tire had run over a nail, as Cooper asserted, it would have embedded and moved around, causing small tears in the rubber. He called his tire expert, Allen Milner, and told him to take a look at the X-rays. Milner reported back that the puncture seemed unusual, as if something had been stuck in and pulled out. Kaster said he had a Cooper worker who swore he used an ice pick to smooth out blisters.

He asked Milner to take an awl to another tire, X-ray it and tell him how it compared to the Hervey tire. Milner called Kaster back and told him the Hervey tire must have been awled. After he got off the phone,

Kaster marveled at the brazenness of Cooper's defense. The company claimed that tread separations were caused by road hazards like nails and glass that create punctures. Now Kaster found out Cooper was the one puncturing the tire in the first place.

He wondered whether other tire makers employed similar practices. He had a case brewing against Firestone involving a tire made in Decatur. At the time there were only a few cases pending against Firestone: Tab Turner had one, Rowe Brogdon another, Kaster a third, perhaps a handful of others elsewhere. Kaster represented the family of John Kreiner, whose Chevy Suburban had suffered a tread separation and crashed into a tree. He was trapped inside as the car burst into flames. "Don't let me burn," he begged rescuers pulling him from the wreckage. At first they thought the 61-year-old Kreiner was wearing black gloves. Then they noticed his hands had been charred by fire. At the hospital doctors amputated both his legs and three fingers, but Kreiner died nine agonizing days after the accident.

Kaster decided he would try to reproduce Byrd and Kelly's success in Tupelo.

A FEW DAYS LATER KASTER WAS IN DECATUR talking to a local lawyer who handled workers compensation. The lawyer referred Kaster to a retired Firestone worker who used to be head of safety for the plant and talked about the lack of quality control, the use of solvent and "red tagged" material—rubber and steel that should have been scrapped. He said that inspections lasted 15 seconds and if a tire failed, it was retested until it passed. Kaster learned of brutal 12-hour shifts, even though a Firestone study showed that quality dropped off substantially after six hours, and about the company's incentive system, which based bonuses on the number of tires produced, regardless of quality.

Wearing jeans, boots, and a flannel shirt, Kaster began frequenting blue-collar haunts near the factory like Cracker Barrel, Denny's, and Roy Rogers. Never shy, he would approach anybody who looked like they worked with their hands and start gabbing about the union. One thing led to another. He'd meet a Decatur worker who would introduce him to his father, or brother, his cousin, or a friend. Pretty soon Kaster was invited back to their homes for tea or out for a few beers. Although Kaster was a great talker, when it came to tires he was also a great listener.

It didn't take long for him to locate former Firestone workers bitter over the company's handling of the strike of 1994, when Firestone broke the union by hiring replacement workers. The strike centered on the company's refusal to sign a contract similar to ones the union reached with other major tire makers, which Firestone viewed as "commercial suicide." Firestone wanted to shift workers to a four-day workweek with 12-hour shifts and introduce a new pay system based on workers' and plants' productivity.

Joe Roundtree, a Decatur worker and former union shop steward, informed Kaster of inspections that lasted only 10 to 20 seconds per tire, but tires moved so fast some tires weren't inspected at all. He believed replacement workers were not given adequate training and as a result had made substandard tires. Lonnie Dart, a Firestone employee for 32 years, claimed "globs of solvent" sometimes stuck to the rubber. Plant veteran Clarence Wood protested that quality was sacrificed for quantity. The lack of air-conditioning meant that steel-belt cords were exposed to humidity to the point that "oftentimes there would be perspiration on the outside of the belt cords in the area where they spliced together."

But what made Kaster's heart pump hardest was when Roundtree told him that Firestone, like Cooper, had also handed out awls to Decatur workers, who would puncture the tire and allow air to be forced from the blister or bulge in an activity that occurred "on an ongoing basis" and was "open and obvious."

Armed with this damning evidence Kaster pressed his case, but ended up battling the judge as much as he did Firestone. The company had produced the 721 tire—the precursor to the ATX and Wilderness that was on Kreiner's Suburban—from 1978 to 1989, although Kreiner bought it in 1995. (Firestone never made an issue of the tire's age.) Kaster dug up 54 personal injury lawsuits against Firestone involving the 721 but hit a wall when he tried to ascertain the total number of warranty claims from customers. Firestone had shredded the data, claiming it was standard procedure for out-of-production tires.

"You should have picked a client that got himself killed closer to the time that the production run ended," federal Judge Alvin Hellerstein remarked dryly.

Then Hellerstein proceeded to gut Kaster's case. He ruled that his expert, Rex Grogan, who wrote *The Tire Investigator's Guide to Tire Failures*, a reference book used by his peers worldwide, could not testify. He also excluded Grogan's review of the Firestone adjustment records that hadn't been shredded, in which he called the 721's safety record "catastrophically bad." Although Kaster laid out the same quality control problems that Firestone would later be forced to acknowledge, the judge threw the evidence out of court, saying, "I suggest to you that all things considered on this particular point of tread belt separations, the proof is not adequate." What's more, not only did Hellerstein seal the depositions Kaster took in Decatur, he issued a gag order, prohibiting him from breathing a word about Firestone until the case was settled or the jury rendered a verdict.

On July 5, 2000, after four years of litigation, Kaster was forced to settle for a measly $375,000. Throughout, Firestone never admitted any liability, insisting Kreiner was killed because he fell asleep at the wheel. The family was furious. Five weeks later Firestone recalled 6.5 million tires, all made at Decatur. Kaster swore that if he ever came upon that judge again, he'd run him over.

ON THE HIGHWAY IN FLORIDA FROM MELBOURNE TO GAINESVILLE, Kaster kept in the fast lane, passing cars that respected the speed limit. While he rocketed across the state, a reporter from *USA Today* called. Kaster had completely forgotten he had scheduled an interview, and told her he had to cancel. After he explained why, she asked if the press could attend. Kaster said he didn't see why not. She said she would dispatch a colleague to cover it and a lawyer to argue the case to unseal these depositions for the public good. A few minutes later Kaster received a call from the Florida state attorney general's office to ask questions about Firestone tires and the recall. After Kaster answered them, the lawyer asked if there were anything he could do for him. Kaster told him to send someone from the attorney general's office to this hearing. A few miles later his phone rang again. It was a producer from a local TV station in Orlando, who had gotten wind of the attempt to quash the Decatur depositions. Kaster told him the wheres and whens. For good measure Kaster tipped off the legal affairs correspondent at Bloomberg news service, who promised to attend by conference call.

By the time Kaster arrived at the courthouse in Lake City, a TV camera crew was waiting, shooting his entry into the courthouse. Kaster joined his law firm partners at the door. They read him the motion to quash as he headed inside, where he encountered two lawyers from the state attorney general's office and one representing Gannet, the publisher of *USA Today*.

He quickly briefed them as he walked down the hall and into Judge Vernon Douglas' courtroom. Kaster was pleased to discover that the Firestone lawyers were attending by telephone from Miami, figuring he would do the same from Ocala. They had surprised Kaster with this motion to quash, yet here he was, ready for battle.

Kaster addressed the judge saying he was talking for lawyers all over America. He said the depositions he had taken in the Kreiner case were not just important for his client, but for consumer safety. Many lives were at stake. Since they were permanently under seal, he planned to take Decatur depositions again on behalf of a pool of trial lawyers, and not only wanted a representative from the Florida attorney general's office there, he wanted them open to the media. After he sat down, Gannet argued for a press pool, and then a lawyer from the attorney general's office told the judge he was there to represent the public's interest, and wanted to attend the depositions as well. Firestone's phoned-in arguments didn't go over well, and the judge agreed to allow the Decatur depositions to be open to the press.

On Aug. 14, 2000, Bruce Kaster and Tab Turner took depositions in Decatur on behalf of 20 other trial attorneys with cases against Firestone. Turner let Kaster do the talking. He figured he'd never get a word in edgewise anyway. Also attending was a large press contingent—from ABC, CNN, the *New York Times*, *USA Today*, the *Wall Street Journal*, the *Washington Post*—piling on the tire maker, adding to its woes.

"The Firestone plant in Illinois that manufactured many of the 6.5 million tires recalled last week was rife with quality-control problems in the mid-1990s, with workers using questionable tactics to speed production and managers giving short shrift to inspections," wrote the *Washington Post*'s James Grimaldi. ABC News reported that "eight former employees of Bridgestone/Firestone have testified or promise to testify that they used out-of-date rubber stock for their tires; that radial coils were exposed to humidity, making them vulnerable to rust; and that final inspections were done too quickly." Following the proceedings, Sen. John McCain called on Firestone to expand its recall, because it was "not enough to protect consumers."

Nine days later Kaster took another round of depositions. This time he concentrated on the long shifts, which the Associated Press reported led workers to suffer under the strain of mandatory 12-hour shifts. "I know I don't want a tire on my vehicle made by any manufacturer with workers who've been [on] their feet for 11 hours," Kaster said in an interview.

He was relieved to have escaped from under that gag order. Although it didn't quite make up for the pasting he'd taken on the Kreiner case, it sure felt good to hold Firestone's feet to the flames.

A few days later, on Sept. 1, 2000, federal investigators in the United States raised the death toll to 88 with more than 250 injuries.

21 DEATH BY A THOUSAND STAB WOUNDS

ON SEPT. 6, 2000, MASATOSHI ONO, the 63-year-old chairman and chief executive officer of Bridgestone/Firestone Inc., and two Firestone vice presidents were under attack by three congressional subcommittees in the nation's Capitol, unable to parry the rapid-fire verbal assaults directed at them by irate lawmakers. Ono didn't help matters when at one point he admitted he was "nervous" because he had "never made a public appearance like this before," and begged for patience until his translator could finish filtering English into Japanese. To Rep. Ed Bryant (R-Tenn.), it was "like watching death by a thousand little stab wounds." The company was so ill-prepared to deal with Congress that until the recall he didn't even know that Bridgestone/Firestone was headquartered in his state.

A man unused to being questioned, let alone criticized, Ono seemed more like a crime suspect undergoing interrogation than the smooth manager credited with having restored the tire maker to its glory of years past.

Ono had spent four decades navigating Bridgestone's bureaucracy, the last seven as top man at Firestone in the United States, which Bridgestone bought in 1988 when the American tire maker was hemorrhaging money. In the early years of the merger, Firestone was losing $1 million a day. By the time Ono took over in 1993, annual profits barely reached $5 million.

Seven years and several bitter labor strikes later, the company netted 60 times that, $285 million in 1998 alone. But the recall and the battle with Ford over who was responsible had not only rained on the company's centennial celebration, sales had plummeted, dealers were under siege, Congress was pondering legislation that could impose criminal penalties, and predictions the company would be forced to declare bankruptcy raced through Capitol Hill like a juicy rumor.

Rep. Billy J. Tauzin, the Chackbay, Louisiana, lawmaker who co-chaired the hearings with Rep. Fred Upton (R-Mich.), promised a rough-and-tumble ride for Ono, Nasser, and NHTSA. A native Cajun on the way to his 11th consecutive term in Congress, Tauzin's district stretched from the mouth of the Mississippi River to the outskirts of New Orleans and Baton Rouge. He was a former Democrat turned pro-business Republican who had rarely been accused of standing up to corporate interests. Over the years he had opposed greater government regulation and supported free markets and voluntary compliance for industry.

But Tauzin wasn't just the chairman of the House telecommunications and consumer affairs subcommittee. He was gunning for chairman of the far more influential Commerce Committee—a position he would attain the following year. Perhaps more importantly, he was also the owner of a 1992 Ford Explorer that sat unused in his garage until he could scare up replacement tires.

In the days leading up to the hearings, Tauzin talked to newspaper and magazine reporters and went on TV. On CNN he said, "What we are interested in is: What went wrong with this recall? Why didn't it happen sooner? We shouldn't be satisfied until we have all the facts." On the CBS *Early Show* he wondered whether the recall "could have been conducted sooner, more expeditiously, to avoid perhaps as many as 65 deaths." The evidence "cries out to us from those graves that something was wrong." In his opinion, the recall process had gone "terribly." In fact, it was two weeks before he found out his tires were covered. Meanwhile, a shortage of replacements meant many of his Louisiana constituents were forced to tempt fate. He told *Time*, "This whole thing stinks. You can't tell me someone at Firestone or Ford didn't know they had serious problems with these tires long before the body count started to rise."

It would be a full day of hearings by two House subcommittees and the Senate subcommittee on transportation, chaired by Sen. Richard Shelby (R-Ala.). There was a long line by the time Tab Turner arrived, so he decided to catch it on closed-circuit TV at CBS studios. Anna Werner of KHOU also got there too late to nab a plum spot. The crush of media and spectators forced her upstairs into an overflow room a couple of floors up, where she was unable to follow the action. While she stood, she overheard three different people talk about some story that had been done in Houston. She went back downstairs and found cameraman Chris

Henao, who said, "Hey, Anna. Guess what? When they started the hearing the first thing they did was play our report."

Werner didn't believe him. Henao did a great deadpan and could convince her of practically anything. "Yeah, right," she said.

Henao tried to convince her, but she would have none of it. He had to grab a reporter and photographer from another news organization to confirm it. The committee broadcast the entire KHOU segment and referred to it throughout the day. Tauzin kicked things off by saying their report was "the catalyst for the recall . . . and for the investigation that continues both at NHTSA and at this committee and on the Senate side." At one point during the day, he remarked, "If there are any heroes in this awful saga, it's the television station in Houston who connected the dots to shape this." Gene Green, a Democratic representative from Houston, Texas, congratulated them "for their investigative efforts into the loss of life" and later Jacques Nasser did them one better by testifying, "They deserve a medal, actually, because they did focus attention on this. Channel 11 started everyone to think, 'Well, wait a minute. Maybe there really is something there. Let's dig deeper. Let's ask different questions. Let's look at this from a different perspective.' So that was the start of a very different investigation. It had an impact on us, so I'm sure it had an impact on [others]."

At the Senate hearing, Joan Claybrook accused Ford and Firestone of covering up safety problems for a decade, citing at least five cases that had been filed by 1993, and many others that followed, almost all of them settled with gag orders. She brought along two shredded tires she got from Turner that sat on the floor in front of the table where she testified. David Pittle, technical director for the Consumers Union, added that since 1992 there had been more than 50 lawsuits—and possibly as many as 100—that related to Firestone tires covered by the recall.

But it was the joint House subcommittee hearings that provided the real fireworks. Members were angry that Transportation Secretary Rodney Slater refused to attend and sent NHTSA administrator Sue Bailey in his stead. They kept her under the klieg lights for two hours, even though she had been on the job less than a month. Lawmakers were alarmed to learn that tire standards hadn't changed since 1968, before steel-belted radials were in wide use and decades before SUVs hogged the nation's roads.

Noting the large number of defective tires originating from Firestone's Decatur factory, Iowa Republican Greg Ganske asked if the agency had dispatched investigators to the plant. When he found out the answer was no, he told Bailey, "I can't believe you haven't thought of that." Bailey for her part said she was "surprised" when just the week before Firestone refused NHTSA's request to expand its recall for 1.4 million tires the agency determined had failure rates "significantly higher, sometimes several times higher, than the tread separation rate of the tires that were already recalled."

Samuel K. Boyden, a researcher for State Farm Insurance, testified that in July 1998 he compiled 21 claims caused by the apparent failure of Firestone ATX tires and notified NHTSA by e-mail, following up with two phone conversations in 1999, but the agency took no action. Lawmakers demanded to know why Boyden's e-mail hadn't triggered an immediate investigation.

Clarence Ditlow, executive director of the Center for Auto Safety, offered some historical perspective. When he testified in hearings on the Ford Pinto in 1978, he told Congress that at the time only the Firestone 500 had a worse safety record: 16 deaths, 15 injuries. For the AT and the ATX tires, there had been more than 80 deaths recorded—and the numbers were climbing. "Unfortunately, the records have continued to be broken over the years," Ditlow said. "The GM sidesaddle gas tank is the record now, at 150." The Ford-Firestone fiasco promised to outpace even that.

But the two witnesses most everyone came to see were Ono and Nasser, who made it a point not to sit anywhere near each other while they waited to testify. Ono went first and was accompanied by two Firestone vice presidents, Gary Crigger and Robert Wyant, who worked in the quality assurance department. They received legal advice from Colin Smith, who was from the Chicago office of the politically well-connected law firm Holland & Knight.

After Ono took "the oath of truthfulness" he read a short written statement in tortured English, mumbling apologies to "the American people . . . , especially to the families who have lost loved ones in these terrible rollover accidents"—a slight dig at Ford—and to "accept full and personal responsibility on behalf of Bridgestone/Firestone for the events that led to this hearing." These were not the kinds of words that typically came out of the mouths of Japanese CEOs, who rarely took personal responsibility for mistakes, only responsibility for their companies. He would have been shamed in his home country, having just committed career harakiri. The fact that he was offering the statement in English and testifying at all was sending ripples through the Nikkei index—6,500 miles and 13 time zones away.

Ono told committee members he could not yet offer a conclusive reason for the tire failures, which were "associated with tread separations and accidents primarily on the Ford Explorer vehicle," but promised to appoint an outside investigator to assist in the analysis and "the rollout of a nationwide consumer education program" that would "provide consumers with information on proper tire maintenance through the use of in-store videos, showroom displays, brochures, windshield tags and tire pressure gauges."

When Ono was finished, Tauzin didn't waste time confronting him over Firestone's refusal to take back the additional 1.4 million tires that NHTSA wanted recalled. He demanded to know why the tire maker had not turned over certain testing documents. "Specifically, we have been requesting information as to whether Firestone ever speed-tested these Firestone tires on a Ford Explorer under conditions of 26 pounds-per-square-inch pressure," Tauzin explained. "Your company, as of last night, informed us that it couldn't tell us what tests were run and what were not run. Is that correct?"

Ono turned to Crigger who turned to Wyant. "I'm not certain I understand your question," Wyant said. After Tauzin repeated it, Wyant replied, "I heard you say on a vehicle, and that's why I asked you to repeat the question. The question, as I understand it, is a request for data on high-speed testing. And certainly we have done high-speed testing. It is my understanding . . ."

"No, no, let me ask again," Tauzin interrupted. He knew when a witness was dodging a question. For more than a week congressional investigators had been asking Firestone for documents identifying what tests were run at high speed. "You have not provided them to us," Tauzin said. "As of last night, we were told you could not provide them to us at this time. Is that correct?"

"My understanding is that we have provided computer printouts of this high-speed testing," Wyant said.

"This committee has the power of subpoena," Tauzin threatened, "and I can put it to a vote if necessary."

"You do not have to subpoena us for any of this information."

"Now, let me ask you, did you, to your knowledge, test Firestone tires under speed conditions at 26 pounds per square inch?"

"I cannot confirm that," Wyant said.

Tauzin moved on to an internal memo from Ford that Tab Turner presented to committee investigators on the replacement of tires in Saudi Arabia and read aloud from a section Turner had bracketed: " 'Firestone Legal has some major reservations about the plan to notify consumers and offer them an option. First they feel that the U.S. [Department of Transportation] will have to be notified of the program since the same product is sold in the United States.' Is that report in this Ford memo accurate?"

Crigger claimed he knew nothing of that meeting but wished to clarify that Ford had taken that action for reasons of "customer satisfaction."

Tauzin tried again, directing the same question to Ono, who parroted Crigger's ignorance. All he knew was what he was told. There had been a recall in Saudi Arabia for "customer satisfaction reasons."

Tauzin hounded them, but the executives continually danced around the question. When Tauzin discovered they had never actually read the memo, he advised, "Why don't you take time and read it, since we're talking about it."

After they'd finished, Crigger said, "The only comment I have is that the action that was taken in Saudi Arabia was a customer satisfaction action. . . ."

"Ex*cuse* me," Tauzin boomed, "there were people dying in accidents, and Ford auto dealers were calling Firestone people, complaining about the safety implications of these tires, and you're saying it's a 'consumer satisfaction issue'?"

Rep. Heather Wilson, a first-term Republican from New Mexico, jumped in. A graduate of the U.S. Air Force Academy in 1982, Wilson was the first woman veteran in American history to serve in Congress. She was a Rhodes Scholar and had both a master's degree and a doctoral degree in international relations from Oxford University in England. This gave her clout well beyond her tenure. She referred to a Firestone document that showed a spike in tire separation claims in 1996. "You say that there was no defect and this is all just consumer problems and underinflation and so on," Wilson said. "Can you tell me why it is that so many more consumers were underinflating their tires in 1996 as opposed to other years earlier?"

"Well, I thank the gentle lady," Tauzin said. "That's where I was going. Let me ask you quickly. Look at those statistics. A huge spike in claims for tire separations. Eighty percent of those are separations of Firestone tires resulting in serious accident injuries, bodily, and property damage. She is asking the question we should all ask. Is that because consumers were changing the inflation on their tires in one year out of all these years?"

"No, obviously not," Crigger said.

"Obviously not," Tauzin repeated. "So why do you keep making that claim? Why do you keep telling the American public it's their fault that they are inflating their tires wrong, when we look at statistics that indicate that something is wrong with these tires?"

"We don't mean to say it's America's fault," Crigger said. "It's not. We are very concerned about all the incidents that have occurred. We regret terribly what's happened. And if we could have prevented it we would have prevented it."

"Mr. Crigger," Tauzin shot back, "maybe if you weren't so interested in keeping the facts from the Department of Transportation, maybe you would have prevented it."

He opened up the questioning to his colleagues, who were happy to pile on. The chair recognized Edward Markey (D-Mass.), who pointed out that most of the accidents in the United States occurred in the southern part of the country where people typically drive great distances at high speeds in sometimes tremendous heat. "By not relating the obvious similarities between Saudi Arabia and the United States, you give our consumers the impression that you don't care about their safety, even though the conditions are very similar to those in Saudi Arabia."

Fred Upton, the hearings co-chairman, cited data that indicated that although the recalled tires amounted to 10 percent of Firestone's total production from 1997 to 1999 they resulted in 50 percent of all claims.

"Shouldn't that have put Firestone on notice that there was some problem with these tires, particularly when 50 percent of those tires were from the Decatur plant?"

North Carolina Republican Richard Burr brought up a letter from a Firestone representative to a dealer in Saudi Arabia who had been persistent about the tread separation problem, which recommended he tell his customer to check his tire pressure every two weeks and before every long distance drive.

"I hope that Firestone understands the frustration that I think all members on this committee share," Burr said, "because we read statements like this that clearly lead us to believe that Firestone was attempting to push aside a potential problem. . . . I mean, I'd like to have you stand up and say, 'You know, what we put in that letter was a bunch of crap. That was not a sufficient response to our dealer, for our customer. We should have been more concerned. We should have had our eyes open.' But that's not the impression that we get when we read document after document after document where we're debating who was supposed to check the tires, how often were they supposed to check them, and whether, in fact, Firestone has any responsibility in it. My hope is that you will find that defect and that you will find it quickly and that we will know the scope of the problem."

Tauzin told Burr if he were looking for a solid case in the documents, he had one from a Firestone customer who had been told by the company that his treads were worn. The customer responded, " 'Well, that's neat, but I didn't send you the treads. They're lying on the highway. I sent you the tire without the treads. How do you know they were worn?' And Firestone paid him. That's an interesting document. Read it."

Returning to the tire pressure issue, Tauzin said, "I don't believe that the [car maintenance] habits of Americans . . . has changed significantly in this decade. And the belief that a reduction in tire pressure has caused this aberration, because everybody's running them at a lower rate, is just not believable. If it was the case . . . there would be more than your tires blowing up on the road. . . . I am even guilty of running my tires at less than the recommended rate, because I don't check them as frequently. And I think I'm no more than average in America."

Rep. Wilson redirected the discussion to an issue affecting her constituents. After an outcry, Firestone scuttled its plans for a phased-in recall that would have taken up to a year. Nevertheless, the company chose to direct greater numbers of tires proportionally to areas with the highest number of incidents. Yet New Mexico wasn't on the list, even though 10 percent of the fatalities occurred there.

"Clearly that was a mistake," Wyant said.

"You're saying here tonight that clearly you've made mistakes—boy, that's real clear now," Wilson said. "But it would have been real nice if you had been willing to acknowledge that in 1997 when you began gathering data that said that over 2,500 tires were separated." She wanted to know what Firestone used its claims data for.

Accounting purposes, Crigger said.

"To determine . . . loss and liability? So you looked at it from a financial point of view, but not a consumer safety point of view?"

"I'm sorry to say that I believe that's the case," Crigger admitted.

Wilson got on her soapbox. "I am a pro-business Republican. I am married to an insurance defense attorney. We talk a lot about liability in our house, about tort reform, and I usually lose a little credibility with every audience that I admit that I am married to a lawyer. Despite that, he's a nice guy. But it seems to me I'm looking at a company that pays attention to claims data as it affects profit and loss and liability. And you have lost your way, and it's about time you fired your lawyers and started listening to your hearts and protecting the people of this country. And when you do that, you will recover your reputation as a great American company."

Tauzin ended Firestone's testimony with a reminder that he expected to receive additional data. He wanted to know whether the company ever tested its tires on Explorers after Ford had informed the tire maker it would require 26 psi in 1989. "And, if not, how is it that you certified these tires to Ford so that they would put them on the Ford Explorer line as it went out to consumers, not only in America but across the world?" he asked. "Those are very important questions, and I can't get answers to them because you have failed over the last week to supply us with test data information."

Then Tauzin dismissed them.

WHEN JACQUES NASSER FILMED TELEVISION COMMERCIALS three weeks earlier to stem the tide of consumer angst, he looked right into the camera and said, "I wanted you to hear directly from me." He got his chance as the House joint hearing passed its seventh hour. Before he took the stage, Nasser told congressional staffers he wanted the oath administered in a back room. He didn't want to repeat the mistakes of tobacco industry executives, who were pilloried for standing before Congress, their right hands raised, swearing they knew of no health risks associated with cigarette smoking. But negotiations failed, and he was forced to take the oath publicly.

Up until the moment Jacques Nasser began his testimony, Bridgestone/Firestone executives continued to cling to the hope it could remain a staunch supplier to Ford and had been careful not to blame the automaker for the problem. What they didn't know was that Nasser had already concluded that consumers would refuse to buy new Explorers if they came with Firestone tires. As a result he had no intention of pussyfooting around the wording of documents or to offer remorse. He was here to eviscerate Firestone.

Nasser and Tauzin had gotten off to a contentious start when the automaker initially refused to allow its chief executive to testify. At the time, a Tauzin spokesman characterized his boss as "very miffed" and offered the possibility of a congressional subpoena until Ford changed course.

Nevertheless, Ford had significant advantages over Firestone on Capitol Hill. It paid for considerable lobbying clout and had John Dingell, the ranking Democrat on the committee, and much of the Michigan delegation on its side and in its political coffers. Dingell had even chastised Tauzin for attacking Nasser over ducking the hearings: "Given the Republicans' tardiness in scheduling the hearing, I am not surprised that Jacques Nasser was unable to accommodate this rushed request." He had far less confidence in Firestone: "Every day there seems to be some new disclosure, fostering apprehension that Firestone may not yet have control of the problem," Dingell noted tartly.

Ford had also bedazzled congressional investigators who called on the two companies in late August. On the 11th floor of the automaker's glass headquarters, the staffers interviewed top members of the "Tire Task Force" and wandered through the din of Ford's War Room, where they noted the immense number of personnel assigned to the recall issue and the jumbo-sized map of the United States, with cities in need of replacement tires clearly marked. They came away less impressed with Firestone after spending the day in Nashville and meeting with safety and engineering staff two days later. Unlike Ford, Firestone hadn't bothered to summon its troops and resources in a comprehensive effort.

But Nasser never did anything halfway. A few days before the hearings he cloistered himself for five hours at Ford's Washington headquarters with image-maker Michael Deaver, vice chairman of Edelman Public Relations Worldwide and the man who 20 years earlier conjured up Ronald Reagan's "Morning in America" campaign commercials. Deaver worked with Nasser to come across at the hearings as "forceful without being rude," yet convey a sense the company was concerned about the problem and sympathetic to customers. The company even held mock hearings. Company lawyers prepared detailed responses to every conceivable question, and briefed Nasser, because even though he would have experts with him at the hearing, he had to seem like he knew all the answers.

Tauzin called the third panel to order, surprised to learn that Nasser would face Congress alone. After Nasser raised his right hand and swore to tell the truth, the whole truth, and nothing but the truth, he recited from a prepared text. True to Nasser's management style he didn't waste much time on pleasantries. After calling Ford an "American icon" he never dared dream he would one day lead, he said, "I'm here tonight because I know that you and the public have questions about the tire recall, and I'm here to answer those questions. And I will remain here until you are satisfied. Now, let's get to the heart of the issue. When did Ford know there was a problem with the Firestone tires? What have we done about it? And what are we going to do about it in the future?"

He proceeded to heap blame on Firestone. "Ford did not know that there was a defect with the recalled tires until we virtually pried the data from Firestone's hands and analyzed it ourselves," he said. "It was only then, a few days before the recall was announced, that Ford engineers discovered the conclusive evidence that the tires were defective. We then demanded, insisted, that Firestone pull the tires from the road."

Nasser walked the committee through the chronology of events as he saw them. The first signs of a problem developed in Saudi Arabia when Ford dealers reported numerous complaints of tread separations. Ford asked Firestone to investigate, and the tire maker blamed improper maintenance and road hazards. Nasser said Ford was "very troubled by that explanation" and requested that Firestone conduct a battery of tests on the tires. After each and every one, Firestone reported no evidence of a defect. Dissatisfied, Ford replaced the Firestone tires with Goodyear "because we had no choice."

At the same time, Ford wondered whether its U.S. customers were having similar problems. The company ordered Firestone to review its data and was assured there was "absolutely no problem in the U.S." Ford's data, which was limited because the automaker didn't provide warranties on tires, as well as government safety data, didn't indicate a problem either. The automaker insisted Firestone institute "a deep-dive, thorough evaluation," particularly in hot states like Texas, Nevada, and Arizona "because that's where a lot of these tires and a lot of volume happened to be." Firestone continued to insist there was no defect.

"My purpose isn't to finger-point," Nasser told the committee, "but simply to tell you that at each and every step, Ford actively, proactively, took the initiative to uncover the tire problem and to try and find a solution. But it was not until Firestone's confidential claims data became available to us that it became clear that something had to be done. Looking back, particularly after listening to the testimony this evening, if I have one single regret, it's that we did not ask Firestone the right questions sooner."

Nasser listed the steps Ford had taken to date: It insisted on a recall and in three weeks Ford and Firestone replaced 1.7 million tires. The automaker was working with Firestone's competitors to increase the availability of tires and had temporarily shut three Ford plants to free up even more. He proposed an "early warning system" to detect the first signs of tire defects on vehicles already on the road. And because Ford existed in a global marketplace, Nasser pledged that the company would advise U.S. safety authorities of safety actions taken overseas. "From now on, when we know it, so will the world," he said.

When Nasser had concluded his comments Tauzin said, "You candidly admitted that you regret not asking Firestone early enough for data. Our evidence is that you, in fact, asked for the claims data after NHTSA began the investigation. Is that right?"

Nasser responded that Ford had requested the data from Firestone on four separate occasions starting on June 6, 2000, then July 11, July 15, July 20, and finally received it on July 28.

"Well, let's look at the data," Tauzin suggested. Of 1,800 claims in which Firestone tires caused accidents, 1,400 involved the Explorer. He cited a summary to an Aug. 19, 1996 complaint to Ford's tech service hotline from a dealer. " 'Tires make a knocking, thumping noise. You can see the tire belt distort if you spin them up. Dealer has sixteen Explorers like this. What can be done? Balancing has no effect. You have to replace the tires.' It's a clear indication from a dealer to your service hotline that there's a problem out there dated 8/19/96." He summed it up for Nasser: "A lot of tires are failing. You're being sued. Firestone's being sued. Dealers are issuing calls to your hotline—sixteen Explorers at one dealer."

"Sixteen Explorers," Nasser said. "We don't want one Explorer that has any problem."

"I understand."

"But if you look at the safety record of Explorer, if you look at the quality level of Explorer . . ."

"Mr. Nasser," Tauzin interrupted, "I'm an Explorer owner. You don't have to sell me. I'm bought already." After the laughter subsided, he continued, "What I'm saying . . ."

"Let me tell you," Nasser blurted out, "I just want to keep going there."

Tauzin cut him off. Maybe in Dearborn, Michigan, Nasser was king, but here Tauzin ruled, and he wasn't about to let Nasser—or anyone else for that matter—forget it. "What I'm trying to ask you that when your dealer calls the hotline and says, 'We have 16 Explorers where the tires can't be balanced because the tire belt distorts when you spin them; you've got to replace these tires,' that seems to tell me, as a motor company, that Firestone is selling me some defective tires. Wouldn't that tell you that in 1996?"

"Well, looking back on it now, it certainly seems like that was the case," Nasser admitted.

Tauzin stuck to his script. "Let's talk about what Ford could have known, had some things happened, and I want to find out if they happened." He asked whether Ford had, in the early stages of producing the Explorer, requested that Firestone do any high-speed testing at 26 psi?

"We did," Nasser said. "We asked Firestone to conduct high-speed tests on those tires at 26 psi." He explained that air pressure was one of the specifications Ford submitted, which Firestone signed off on. "In addition to that, we ran our own tests, tougher tests. And we ran those vehicle tests at 26 psi on those Firestone tires."

"Do you have records of those tests?"

"We will give you the records. And they go back to 1989, and also to 1994. And the tests are 200 miles an hour, at a minimum of 100 miles per hour. We can . . ."

"At 100 miles per hour?" Tauzin asked. "You meant 100 miles per hour, not 200, I hope."

Nasser corrected himself. "Two hundred miles at 100 miles an hour."

"I've got an Explorer," said Tauzin. "It will not go 200, I'm telling you."

More laughter. Tauzin's Web site revealed he was an amateur actor. He was not above playing to an audience.

"We'll put a supercharger on it for you, Mr. Chairman," Nasser replied, trying too hard.

Tauzin inquired if Firestone supplied any test data for tires speed-tested at 26 psi. When Nasser said no, Tauzin issued the same request he had to Firestone, asking Nasser to supply the committee with all documentation related to testing the tires at high speed at the same pressure Ford recommended Explorer owners fill their ATs.

Then he jumped to the Middle East. "You made a great commitment here today, Mr. Nasser, and I think we can all appreciate it. You're going to tell not only our federal agency but other agencies around the world when you discover problems. That is obviously the way it should be. But that wasn't the way it was in 1999 in Saudi Arabia. Why not?"

"We didn't really have any good information," Nasser complained. "We knew there were problems. We didn't know what the problems were."

"But in the Ford memo that we've often quoted where there's a mention of Firestone's legal team being concerned about the DOT, a Ford representative admitted he had concerns 'similar to the Firestone concerns.' "

"That's why we're proposing that in the future we take away those fears for everybody and that it becomes open and transparent," Nasser replied, sidestepping the question.

The Chair recognized John Dingell, who worked to resurrect Ford. He produced a Ford warranty book on the Explorer and read: " 'Authorized Ford Motor Company dealers will repair, replace or adjust all parts on your vehicle except tires that are defective in a factory-supplied material or workmanship for three years or 36,000 miles, whichever occurs first.' " He consulted a Firestone book, which said if he had a tire problem he should see his local Firestone retailer. Dingell said this told him two things. That Ford provided the warranty on all parts of a new car or truck except tires, and that tire warranty on a new car was provided by whatever company made the tires. "If Firestone is having a large number of their tires returned off Ford vehicles, Firestone will be hearing about them from their dealers. Is that right?"

"That's what happens," Nasser said.

"But Ford will not hear about it unless Firestone tells Ford?"

"We sometimes hear about it through a hotline, as the chairman indicated, but I would say the majority of feedback from customers would go through the tire dealer."

Dingell didn't have much time. He moved on to fresh terrain. "When you began your designing of the Explorer, you gave to the tire manufacturers the specifications for that particular vehicle and the specifications for the tire. Those specifications you gave on the tire were essentially performance specifications as opposed to design specifications. Have you ever given, or has anyone in the industry ever given design specifications to a tire manufacturer?"

"I don't believe so," Nasser said. "The tire manufacturers consider that proprietary information. They guard that jealously within each of the brands, and the industry practice is to set a standard in terms of speed, durability, ride and handling, and then on a periodic basis have quality input."

"So Ford leaves to the manufacturer of the tire the design of the tire to meet particular sets of specifications. Is that right?"

"Yes, it does."

"Now, bottom line then, tire manufacturers have complete control and responsibility for design, construction, composition, workmanship and materials used for the tires that are manufactured."

"They're the experts, and so that's right."

"Thank you, Mr. Dingell," Tauzin said. "The Chairman now recognizes the gentleman from Iowa, Dr. Ganske."

There was no Ford plant in Iowa, so Rep. Ganske brought Nasser back to earth. He went to the heart of the dispute between the companies: Were the tires flawed or were they underinflated? "It seems to me that when tires are run at low pressures, it causes excess heat which can damage the tires," he said. "Heavier models such as the sport utility vehicle generally need more pressure than a lighter one. But why don't you tell me why on a vehicle most like the Explorer, the Ford Ranger pickup, built on the same frame using the same tires, Ford recommends a higher pressure?"

"We have different tire pressures for different tire sizes for different vehicles," Nasser responded.

"They're the same tires."

Nasser became defensive. "I've got to say, Congressman, that I think it became pretty clear from the Firestone testimony today that 26 psi is okay," Nasser said. "The more we talk about the tire pressure issue the less time we are going to have on concentrating on what the real issue is for our customers."

"Well, excuse me," Ganske retorted, "but it seems to me there has been ample testimony today that the tire failures have occurred in places where it is hotter." He asked if Nasser disputed the fact that a tire on a lower pressure heats up more than a tire on a higher pressure. Then Ganske brought up a May 12, 1999, notice Ford issued to its dealers in the Middle East, several months before it recalled the tires, that directed them to inspect the tires of all SUVs every time a vehicle was brought in for service. "Was this memo," Ganske asked, "Ford's first official response to the tire problem?"

"Congressman, it was during the period where we were trying to understand exactly what the problem was."

"Why didn't you send out a letter to all SUV owners with those kinds of tires at that time?"

"We were asking Firestone, because in the U.S. Firestone warrants the tires. In the Middle East market, where there really isn't a very good network of customer feedback, we were going to our dealers to get them to help us get Firestone data."

Ganske wouldn't let go. "But you're telling your dealers to look at every one of those tires that comes in." Why not make an effort to notify Explorer owners, since "Ford was instructing its dealers that there is a problem?"

The best Nasser could do was blame Firestone and say that Ford was still trying to "understand exactly what the problem was."

Then it was Rep. Bart Stupak's turn. Although he hailed from Michigan, he was odd man out on the state delegation. He was a liberal whose territory, largely rural and in the north, covered almost half of Michigan, encompassing metropolises like Marquette (pop. 21,765), Sault Ste. Marie (pop. 14,689), and Alpena (pop. 11,304). His questions to Nasser took them to a different part of the globe: Venezuela. He pointed out that in July 1999 Ford switched from Firestone to Goodyear on new vehicles, but waited until May of 2000 to recall those that were already out there. "Venezuela, Saudi Arabia, you replaced both 15- and 16-inch tires," Stupak said. "Then why don't you do the same here in the United States?

You did it in . . . Malaysia, and Venezuela and Saudi Arabia. So why would we do it differently here in the United States?"

"Congressman, because the data doesn't support it," Nasser said. "In . . . those countries we were getting anecdotal data, because there isn't any formal data, that there were issues on the Firestone tires."

"But what is the information, your data, that would make you recall 16-inchers in Venezuela, Saudi Arabia, Taiwan?"

"Customer data that they were unhappy with Firestone tires."

"So if the American public says we are unhappy with the 16-inch Firestone tire on our Explorers . . . you will replace them?"

Nasser was getting prickly. "Congressman, look at the data, because that data represents customer input . . ."

"But the reason why we're here is because of consumer input to the U.S. Congress," Stupak fired back. "And that's why the first day back here we've been at this hearing now pretty close to nine hours; I'm sure we're going to be here 12 hours. So I think it's fair to say that consumers in the United States are not happy and certainly have lost some faith here in both Firestone and Ford in this whole tire thing. And when they see the 16-inch tires being recalled in other countries, they're saying, then why not mine, if they're the same tire with the same specifications."

"I'd say we feel for our customers as much as you do," Nasser said. "And we have despair when we can't really get to the root cause of it. . . . We don't want to replace good tires with good tires. We want to replace bad tires with good tires."

"Would you replace the 16 . . ."

"If the data supports it, we will replace it."

Other congressmen took their shots, but for Nasser the worst was over.

When the committee was done, Tauzin dismissed him. It had been a long day. But there was still one last item on Nasser's list. During Ono's testimony it had bothered him that Rep. Wilson worried aloud about her constituents driving around on recalled tires, so he decided to do something about it. By the time Nasser got to the airport and was in his private plane waiting for takeoff, he could barely keep his eyes open. Yet he still took it upon himself to work the phones to make sure that 20,000 tires were airlifted to New Mexico within the week.

Meanwhile, Tauzin closed out the hearings with a mission and a message. "The next job is to follow up on this hearing, to make sure we have all the facts, that nothing is hidden, that the light shines on what happened yesterday, and then to learn from it and devise a policy to ensure that it doesn't happen tomorrow," he said. "I hope we build a policy built upon preventing products from entering the marketplace that are unsafe, because we've properly tested them in the beginning, rather than depending upon a system . . . to detect the trends of injury and death that tell us the products should have never been there in the first place."

He meant it, too. After all, there was an election coming up in two months.

22 MOSES

FIRESTONE'S DISMAL SHOWING AT THE CONGRESSIONAL HEARINGS threatened to push the company over the edge. When Nasser testified that Ford "did not know that there was a defect with the recalled tires until we virtually pried the data from Firestone's hands and analyzed it ourselves," hundreds of Firestone employees watching on C-Span at corporate headquarters in Nashville groaned and cursed. They found their company's reticence maddening. Morale was at an all-time low. Tire dealers and employees alike wondered when management would display some leadership and strike back.

But since the August recall announcement, Masatoshi Ono had been huddling with a team of Japanese executives from Bridgestone in their own section of the building, separate from American personnel who mocked it by calling it the "J Wing." Ono and his compatriots were in constant communication with Bridgestone management, which was directing crisis response from Tokyo. Unfortunately the Japanese didn't understand American media or government and were loath to chastise an important customer like Ford. According to Rosalyn Millman, deputy administrator of NHTSA, "Bridgestone wanted to apologize and leave it at that. They were reluctant to provide documentation." Although no one wanted to take the fall for a customer, the tire maker believed a public spat with Ford would only benefit plaintiff attorneys. The result: the company was paying a lot of money for advice and then ignoring it.

Firestone's advisors, which included Fleishman-Hillard, the second largest public relations house in America; and law firms Holland & Knight and Baker, Donelson, Bearman & Caldwell, whose Washington office was led by former Senate Majority Leader Howard H. Baker, Jr., proposed a three-part strategy: Publicly apologize for manufacturing defective tires, send Ono to Washington to testify, and attack Ford over the safety of its Explorer. They wanted to raise questions about potential design defects, and advised the company to cooperate with NHTSA and congressional investigators. In addition, Fleishman urged Firestone to adopt a more radical, proactive plan designed to inspire consumer confidence by quickly recalling all suspect tires. Only by coming clean could the tire maker hope to begin to repair the damage to its reputation, because without penitence there could be no resurrection.

But there was no Bridgestone/Firestone executive in Nashville, let alone in Washington, who had the authority to give the go-ahead. All decisions had to be approved by Tokyo, which caused long delays as executives there grappled with achieving consensus. Company lobbyists and publicists in the States were forced to wait days before they could act—a lifetime in a corporate crisis. In the end, after much hand-wringing, Japanese management agreed to dispatch Ono to Washington, but, exercising caution, rejected the rest.

Fleishman was still smarting from having been caught off guard two weeks into the job when Firestone announced it was recalling 6.5 million tires. As the crisis grew, Fleishman was hamstrung by Firestone's reluctance to share vital information, which made it difficult to effectively represent its client. The last straw was when NHTSA issued a consumer advisory covering 1.4 million additional tires the agency proposed be recalled. At first Firestone claimed few of them were still on America's highways, but announced it would provide replacements if owners were concerned about them. The next day Ono abruptly retracted the offer: "If the tires are subject to our Bridgestone/Firestone warranty program, the tires will be adjusted and processed accordingly," he said in a statement. That meant the company wouldn't replace the tires outright. Instead customers would merely receive a discount based on the amount of wear on their tires for their next set—provided they bought Firestone tires and not another brand.

Disillusioned, Fleishman-Hillard resigned the $2 million a month account 24 hours later, on the eve of the Sept. 6 hearings, even though it had been on the job only two months, becoming the second PR firm Firestone lost since the crisis began. (In May, Burson-Marsteller quit because Ford was also a client.) All Fleishman would say of the split was that it resigned of its own accord "because it became evident that we could no longer be of service to Bridgestone/Firestone."

When Fleishman bailed, pundits predicted Firestone's death: Rod Lache, automobile industry analyst at Deutsche Banc Alex. Brown, deemed the tire maker "irreparably damaged." David Aaker, vice chairman of Prophet Brand Strategy and author of several books on marketing, said, "I think there's a good chance that the brand is history. I don't think consumers will forget." Allen Adamson, managing director at the corporate identity firm Landor, told *USA Today* that the recall "has become such an inferno, it's unlikely there will be much left when the flames subside." And Laura Ries, a principal at Ries & Ries, believed "the best thing" the company could do would be "to kill it quickly." More than 63 percent of consumers polled by CNNfn answered "no" when asked if they would ever buy a Firestone product again. Then after the hearings, Baker Donelson also deserted Firestone, claiming a conflict of interest because the firm also did work for Ford, which had given testimony "that was opposite the best interests of Bridgestone."

The tire maker was skidding out of control. Its stock price on the Tokyo Nikkei index dove another 17 percent in reaction to Ono's performance in front of Congress, trading for less than half its May 2000 value and eating up $11.4 billion in market capitalization in the process. Bridgestone management didn't have much time to turn things around. The next hearing was less than 72 hours away in front of the ignitable Sen. John McCain (R-Ariz.) and his Senate Commerce, Science and Transportation Committee. McCain made it no secret that he planned to propose criminal penalties for companies that knowingly fail to recall a defective product.

If Firestone didn't acquit itself better this time, not only could it be forced out of business, some of its executives could find themselves in jail.

MOSES CAME TO FIRESTONE IN THE FORM of a deceptively tall, 53-year-old tire salesman from America's heartland named John Lampe. He was a lifer at Firestone, as earnest and true-blue as they came in an industry rank with the odor of burnt rubber. With closely cropped hair and skin that tanned reluctantly but burned enthusiastically, Lampe had two families: The one he had started with his wife almost three decades earlier, and the one he worked for at Firestone.

Born in Kansas, Lampe earned a bachelor's degree in business administration from Kansas State College and a master's from the American Graduate School of International Management in Glendale, Arizona. He learned the tire business from the ground up, beginning at Firestone in 1974 as a trainee, working in the company store for two years, first changing tires and doing oil changes and then managing it, before bouncing around three continents in a variety of sales and marketing positions—Costa Rica, Brazil, Denmark, and Singapore.

During his time abroad, Lampe did his best to melt into the culture. Although no linguist, he learned Spanish fluently, "until," he says, he "ruined it by learning Portuguese." This exposure to foreign cultures shaped his worldview. He was in Brazil when he found out that Bridgestone had purchased Firestone. Unlike many of his colleagues, who feared working for the Japanese, Lampe thought it was the best thing that could have happened. At the time, Firestone's CEO believed the company should be in the retail business, not a manufacturer. Lampe realized if things continued on that way, Firestone would gradually fade away.

In 1991 he returned to run the corporation's Dayton Tire Operations in Oklahoma City. During the strike, when the company assigned its white-collar personnel to the factory, Lampe drove a forklift 12 hours a day, seven days a week, operated a tire uniformity machine for final inspection, and even tried his hand at building tires "until they got tired of me not being very productive" and sent him back to the warehouse. He made it a point to come in a couple hours before his shift started and stay a couple hours after to keep up with the demands of his real job. Four years later he received his reward when he was promoted to executive vice president and president of Bridgestone/Firestone's sales division and moved to Nashville.

At first Lampe was relegated to a background role in the crisis. He concentrated on what he did best: sales, which had doubled during his tenure; and didn't even become involved in the ATX tire affair until the Sunday before the August recall. He was spending time at a nearby lake with his wife and two grown-up children, who were visiting from out of town, when the phone rang at 3:00 in the afternoon. It was Ono who asked Lampe to come down to the office. When Lampe asked what was going on, Ono told him. Lampe made it to corporate headquarters in 30 minutes flat to join in the discussions. Assigned a bit role in the recall announcement, he didn't even attend the congressional hearings. Instead he spent much of his time calling the heads of other tire makers like Michelin, Goodyear, and Cooper, negotiating for replacements, and keeping in contact with the company's dealers and sales force.

As the company's reputation continued its nosedive, Bridgestone chairman Kaizaki announced his intention to "Bridgestone-ize" Firestone to boost its quality, and dispatched a management team from Tokyo. "We will control all the subsidiaries from the head office from now on," he promised.

Over the course of the summer Kaizaki remained behind the scenes, leading a crisis management team of 20 senior officials that met daily, leaving Ono to carry out their orders. When Ono appeared before

Congress, Kaizaki gathered with his executives at Bridgestone Tokyo headquarters to view the hearings on a large-screen TV from 11 p.m. until noon the next day, fortified only by mineral water, coffee, tea, and crackers. Although Kaizaki couldn't follow everything because his English was so poor, one thing became abundantly clear: The mild-mannered Ono was incapable of getting the company's message across. Kaizaki knew he had to make a change—and fast.

He had brought back Firestone from the brink once before. If he were to do it again, drastic steps were needed. Although a Harris poll commissioned by the *Wall Street Journal* indicated that both Ford and Firestone were suffering, the tire maker was faring much worse. Of 814 people polled, 25 percent said it was extremely or very likely the tire recall would affect their decision to buy a Ford, while 67 percent said it would affect their decision to buy a Firestone product. Six out of 10 people believed the recall wasn't broad enough. On the question of whether the companies acted in a timely and responsible manner in recalling the tires, 26 percent thought Ford acted responsibly, while only 14 percent believed Firestone had.

Kaizaki realized he needed an American to deal with the American government and to reassure consumers, who were deserting Firestone in droves. In a significant change in tack, he ordered Ono to step aside and turned to Lampe.

While the newly anointed face of Firestone boned up on what he needed to know for McCain's subcommittee, Bridgestone retained Ketchum PR to take over for Fleishman-Hilliard the day before the hearings. The joint Bridgestone/Ketchum announcement reflected the tire maker's awareness that its previous strategy had failed. In it, Ono acknowledged that the company had been "slow in responding to public concerns, that we underestimated the intensity of the situation, and that we have been too focused on internal details. As a result, there is a high degree of concern about our motives and behavior. We are determined to change all that." Ono also went on to say that he realized that Firestone would "be judged not by our words but by our actions. . . . We know we must be open, honest and responsive both when there is good news and bad."

Meanwhile Ketchum got to work. It quickly set up an information sharing system to handle the overflow of calls from irate consumers and media. It was a month into the recall, and Firestone was drowning in a sea of inquiry. Both Ford and plaintiffs attorneys were leaking documents—and reporters, eager to track down new angles of the story, were bombarding Firestone with highly technical questions, which Ketchum's newly hired publicists simply couldn't answer. Seemingly every day the *New York Times*, *Wall Street Journal*, or *Washington Post* would call in the late afternoon with a hot tip that had been leaked by Ford, giving Firestone precious little time to respond. Half of Ketchum's job early on entailed acting as internal reporters, trying to find the right person at Firestone who could respond to questions in easy-to-understand English—not always an easy task.

And there were other complications. "Read any crisis publication," advised Julia Sutherland, the point person at Ketchum for Firestone. It will say, "tell everyone the story, get it over with. That's great advice if you know everything. But not all the information was out." Firestone had agreed to a recall "even before they knew what was wrong."

When it was time for the tire maker to appear before the Senate committee on Sept. 12, Ono started by stumbling through a short statement in which he reiterated his "deep regret and sympathy" before announcing he wouldn't be participating, suggesting his lack of English "may have limited our ability to explain important issues to you and the American people." He passed the baton to Lampe, who apologized for Bridgestone/Firestone having been so poorly prepared the previous week, and informed the senators that the company had narrowed down the cause of the defects to two possibilities: either the ATX tire's "unique design," which Firestone created to meet Ford's stringent specifications for a lightweight, rugged-looking tire; or "variations" in the manufacturing process at its Decatur factory. It was the first time anyone from Firestone had acknowledged the possibility of a manufacturing or design defect.

Continuing his testimony, Lampe said the company was prepared to replace the 1.4 million tires covered by the NHTSA's Sept. 1 advisory, and would reimburse customers up to $140 per tire regardless what brand consumer chose. "Obviously, if there is a problem, we'll fix it," Lampe promised.

He took issue with Nasser's accusation that Ford had to practically pry the data from Firestone, claiming the delay was Ford's fault, because the automaker wouldn't guarantee the confidentiality of the information, and also informed the committee that the tire maker had retained Sanjay Govindjee, an associate professor at the University of California, Berkeley, to work as an independent investigator to find out the root cause of the problem. Then, much to the delight of Firestone's faithful, Lampe lambasted Ford.

While admitting Firestone was partially at fault—"We made some bad tires, and we take full responsibility for them," he said—Lampe pointed out "tires will fail, and they do fail for a number of reasons. But in most cases . . . the driver can bring that automobile under safe control."

He explained that Firestone had cataloged an alarming number of serious accidents in SUV rollovers after tire mishaps, and cited federal accident statistics that showed more than 16,000 Ford Explorer rollovers causing 600 deaths. "Tire failure," Lampe noted, was "involved in only a very, very small percentage of these deaths." He raised other questions about Ford's role in the crisis, suggesting the entire issue of tire inflation pressure selected by the vehicle manufacturer had to be addressed. "Does that pressure provide adequate safety margin to guard against damage caused by underinflation and overloading?" he asked.

Jacques Nasser also made good use of his allotted time, using the hearing to portray Ford as just another victim of the tire maker's deceit. "Last week, I listened in disbelief as senior Firestone executives not only acknowledged that Firestone had analyzed its claims data, but also identified significant patterns of tread separations as early as 1998," he said. "Yet they said nothing to anyone, including Ford Motor Co." This wasn't "the candid and frank dialogue that Ford expects" from its suppliers.

Although the committee hoped Ford and Firestone's participation could help shed light on the recall and what could be done to prevent future auto safety crises, it only served to further cloud the issue. Sen. Ernest Hollings (D-S.C.), who co-chaired the hearings, believed it boiled it down to Ford wanting to recall Firestone tires and Firestone wanting to recall the Explorer. He likened their bickering to "tying two cats by the tails and throwing them over the clothesline and letting them claw each other." Sen. Max Cleland (D-Ga.) quipped, "Based on what I've heard about these tires, it's a good thing I don't have them on my wheelchair. Otherwise, I wouldn't be here today." McCain believed there was plenty of blame to go around: "Congress sometimes interferes with government regulators in the prosecution of their duties. Industry can be too focused on profits rather than the safety of the public. And agencies can become bureaucracies more concerned with paperwork than advancing the very causes they were created to serve." Sen. Bill Frist (R-Tenn.) sounded a more somber note. He told colleagues how a friend and fellow heart surgeon, Dr. Gary Haas, had been driving his son to college in Texas six days after the recall when the Firestone tires on his Ford Explorer failed. "If he had been in a different car, with a different tire, he would be alive today," Frist said.

Afterward Lampe met with reporters, but since he had been working from early morning straight through, he told them he was really hungry and asked them to keep it short. Based on his performance at the hearing, the journalists sensed he was a man they could work with, unlike Ono, who had played a game of "Where's Waldo?" with them for months. To keep Lampe in the room and answering questions, they rifled through bags and took out apples and Snickers bars. For the first time, Firestone was building relationships with the media.

Ten days later, Tauzin's House committee held its second round of hearings. Tauzin wanted to focus on whether the companies adequately tested the tires in "real-world situations," and to give lawmakers the opportunity to build support for legislation to boost federal regulators' budgets and sharpen enforcement tools. His spokesman, Ken Johnson, vowed that Congress would produce a law that President Clinton would sign before adjournment and "anybody who gets in the way of this will end up getting steamrolled. Congress is mad, and the American public is demanding action. You don't want to be opposite that tag team."

Direct, often hostile questioning uncovered serious flaws in the testing regime of Firestone, Ford, and NHTSA. The federal standard had been instituted more than three decades earlier, before steel-belted radials were widely available in the United States. Firestone's speed tests on the ATX tire were performed at 32 psi, even though Ford recommended to Explorer owners that the tires be inflated to 26 psi. And Firestone documents showed a 1996 test performed in which 129 Decatur-made tires were spun at high speeds on an indoor testing device. At 112 mph, about a dozen disintegrated, half of them experiencing tread separation. Yet this information had never made its way up the management chain.

Tauzin took Lampe to task: "Anyone who looks at this objectively would conclude you have a terribly flawed production process," he said.

Rep. Edward Markey (D-Mass.) chided Firestone for not subjecting tires already on the road to rigorous testing. "Those are the tires people are riding on, not brand-new tires in a special test for six minutes, but a two-year-old tire on a road going thousands of miles at 75 miles per hour with two kids strapped in the back seat. Now, how can you justify that you have not performed these tests to tell these families who assume that you have done these tests that their families are safe?"

"We all agree . . . that we must work together to develop more accurate, more robust, more real-world-type testing," Lampe responded.

Ford, too, came under attack. After the first hearing it had sent a corporate jet to Washington's Dulles International Airport to drop off a dozen crates of internal documents the automaker claimed would confirm Nasser's contention that Ford tested the ATX and Wilderness tires in real-world conditions on Ford Explorers. Four days of searching, and congressional investigators could not find one single document to back up his claim. What's more, Ford admitted it couldn't locate many of the testing documents.

In an affidavit that Tab Turner had brought to the attention of the Senate committee, which shared information with House investigators, James Avouris, a tire tester for the automaker, asserted the tests were performed on an Explorer. But Helen Petrauskas, Ford's vice president for environmental and safety engineering, retracted that claim. It turned out Ford had tested the tires at 90 mph for 200 miles using a "mule" vehicle, a pickup truck modified to simulate an Explorer. Committee members were troubled that the company didn't use an actual Explorer for the test.

"Mr. Chairman, there's nothing devious here," said Petrauskus, subbing for Nasser, who chose to sit out this hearing.

"I hope not, Ms. Petrauskas, but obviously it looks suspicious," Tauzin volleyed back.

In the end, Tauzin concluded that "No one, not the National Highway Traffic Safety Administration, nor Ford, nor Firestone, ever conducted high-speed testing of Explorers on the field fitted with Firestone tires subject to this recall and filled to 26 pounds per square inch. Not before these tires were put on sale on Ford Explorers."

It was clear to anyone following the story that legislation was inevitable. But with Congress set to adjourn in two weeks so members could begin campaigning for the 2000 elections, there wasn't much time. The main difference between the House and Senate bills had to do with criminal penalties. McCain, supported by consumer groups like Public Citizen, believed them to be necessary to compel companies to obey recall laws. But the auto industry, U.S. Chamber of Commerce and National Association of Manufacturers lobbied hard against them, charging they would turn safety engineers wearing white lab coats into hardened criminals.

On Oct. 5, Tauzin's House panel unanimously backed a bill that would require manufacturers to report within five working days any safety recall or similar campaign in a foreign country on equipment identical or similar to a product offered in the United States, give NHTSA the authority to seek claims data submitted to companies for personal injuries and property damage, and increase the agency's maximum fine from $925,000 to $15 million for recall violations. The legislation threatened jail time of up to 15 years for executives who willfully withheld information on products that cause injury or death, but there was a gaping loophole that allowed for criminal penalties to be waived if the information was reported or corrected "within a reasonable time," which the bill didn't define. Tauzin claimed the clause was designed to protect whistle-blowers rather than shield executives, but his real reasons probably had more to do with pragmatism: "You burden this bill with complex, controversial amendments then I promise you we will have nothing done," he told colleagues. "This thing needs to be completed in a very short time frame and I'm not even sure we can do that." The House passed the Transportation Recall Enhancement, Accountability and Documentation (TREAD) Act on Oct. 10.

Meanwhile, McCain couldn't even get his tougher bill to the Senate floor for a vote. Industry lobbyists weren't thrilled with the House bill, but knew there was little they could do to stop it. They could, however, pressure conservative Republicans to keep it off the Senate floor. McCain was livid over the backroom maneuverings. He accused colleagues of siding with the auto industry, and expressed "deep disappointment that the fix" was in "by the special interests."

In an attempt to bring things to a head, McCain threatened to block a $58 billion transport spending measure, but backed off after realizing that voters wouldn't approve of the Senate blocking legislation designed to save lives, even if it were flawed. When Senate Budget Committee Chairman Pete Domenici (R-N.M.) objected on behalf of a group of unnamed senators to a proposal that time be allocated for debating McCain's bill, it died. The Senate took up the House legislation, passing it with unanimous consent, and President Clinton signed it into law soon after. Passing the TREAD Act was one of the fastest actions Congress had taken in years.

THE SAME DAY THE HOUSE PASSED THE TREAD ACT, John Lampe was in Nashville, about to enter Century City, about a mile from corporate headquarters, where Firestone's tire sales and marketing divisions were housed. Although it had been widely assumed Bridgestone would never entrust its top position to a non-Japanese, Kaizaki, who had been impressed with Lampe's performance before Congress, had just appointed him CEO and Chairman of Bridgestone/Firestone's tire-making operations.

To celebrate, Lampe was spending the day going office to office, visiting with staff to personally inform them of the changes. When he walked in he saw the atrium was packed to the rafters with Firestone employees. They greeted Lampe with thunderous applause. Firestone faithful reached out to him, trying to shake his hand, pat him on the back, hug him. Some even had tears in their eyes. Lampe, who knew most everyone by name, was stunned.

Finally Firestone had a leader.

23 HELP WANTED

FROM THE MOMENT PAUL LAVALLE invited Tab Turner to run the Bailey case, Turner knew he'd need help. He officially petitioned the court for permission to join the lawsuit on July 10, although he'd been advising LaValle all along. As with most other cases, it began with a standard complaint Turner had created long ago, filled in with the particulars of the Bailey accident and served to Firestone, Ford, and Crosstown Ford Sales, Inc., the local dealership that sold the car to Kim Cox.

The complaint called the Ford Explorer "defective and unreasonably dangerous at the time it was designed, manufactured and distributed," including "defects in design; stability; handling; marketing; instructions; warnings; crashworthiness; rollover resistance and controllability." Turner levied specific criticism covering the vehicle's design "package," which included the combination of track width, wheelbase, and vertical center of gravity height, causing an "unreasonable risk of rollover," and surmised that the front suspension system had "a tendency to 'jack' in a cornering maneuver according to Ford's own documents." He claimed Ford was liable, in part, because the vehicle was marketed as a station wagon for use on interstate highways at interstate speeds, even though it couldn't "handle ordinary emergencies as encountered on a day to day basis and will roll over on flat level surfaces due to tire friction forces." He also alleged that the vehicle didn't provide "reasonable and necessary occupant protection" because the roof would cave in during a rollover accident.

Turner then unleashed his pen on Firestone. The "Wilderness AT tire was defective and unreasonably dangerous," and had come apart in operation well within its expected life. He blamed the catastrophic failure on a "manufacturing defect that resulted in a lack of permanent bond in the components," a "defect" that caused an "emergency condition that was uncontrollable given the vehicle involved." He concluded that this combination of defects was "a proximate and producing cause of the crash and resulting injuries and damages." The defendants were therefore "strictly liable for supplying a defective and unreasonably dangerous product that resulted in personal injury and/or property damage."

Since both companies were headquartered outside of Texas, technically there existed "diversity of citizenship"—meaning the parties came from different states—which created federal jurisdiction. Turner, like most trial attorneys, preferred state court over federal court. In Texas state court he'd only need to convince 10 of 12 jurors, while in federal court verdicts had to be unanimous: 12–0. (In Arkansas the odds were even better. He could win with just 9 votes out of 12.)

State court also offered other advantages. There was less formality in terms of rules and filings, more flexibility because federal judges often put limits on the length of trials, and a more focused jury pool. Potential jurors were drawn from one county instead of five or six. Odds were that local attorneys would know most of them, helping Turner avoid selecting any "sinkers." His desire to try the case in state court led him to name the dealership in the suit. In the complaint he blamed Crosstown for selling the defective vehicle and tire, but a more relevant rationale was that even if just one defendant came from the same state as the plaintiff, federal court was not an option.

Initially LaValle filed the complaint in the wrong venue, Wilson County, the place the accident occurred. So Turner had him do it over again in Nueces County, where Bailey lived and Kim Cox had purchased the car. After that he told LaValle not to do anything without first consulting him.

On the docket the case was assigned number 00-02303-A, filed on behalf of Cassondra Michelle Bailey as "guardian of the person and estate of Donna Lynn Bailey, an incapacitated person," and the cause of action: PERSON INJ/DAM INVOLVING MOTOR VEHICLE. It never ceased to amaze Turner how a near tragic accident resulting in life-changing injuries could be rendered in such succinct shorthand, as if Donna Bailey were a library book to be reshelved and not a human being seeking the resources to survive.

Unsurprisingly, Ford and Firestone responded a month later with paper of their own: Ford requested a change of venue, since south Texas was renowned for being very plaintiff friendly, and Firestone asked that it be transferred out of the case altogether. Both were denied. Then Turner fired off a series of notices to depose Wilson Memorial hospital employees, the rescue workers who came to Bailey's aid and drove her in the ambulance, and the Poth police and State Highway Patrol.

Turner also hit the companies with several motions for discovery, demanding that they answer specific questions regarding the tire that bore the DOT number W2HL1PY396. He asked Firestone where and when the ATX Wilderness tire on the vehicle that Donna Bailey was injured in was manufactured; who the builder, inspector, tester, and plant manager were; what the skim compound code consisted of; and how many of these type tires were manufactured. He asked about past and pending lawsuits and complaints the company had received.

In a follow-up, Turner cast an even wider net: He wanted to see any document that related to the alleged defect and any type of communication or correspondence between Firestone and vehicle manufacturers involving the tire; all documentation pertaining to design or manufacturing changes the company made in the tire from 1985 to the present; and all claims and adjustment data.

The interrogatories were almost laughable in their detail and couched to give the company little if any wiggle room, covering just about anything in Firestone files containing the word "tire." More than once in his career Turner had come across key bits of information in the mass of discovery a corporation supplied—a misfiled document, an odd statistic, a verbal slip or jottings in the margin of a memo—that only took on importance later, helping him bag a bigger settlement for his client in the end. The trick was to keep pressing, suck up a crumb of data here or there until he could make sense of it all.

Turner's questions to Ford were equally detailed. In addition to his usual demands for all documentation on the design and manufacturing on the Explorer, including all engineers' correspondence and stability tests, he wanted to gauge the company's relationship to Firestone, who the automaker's liaison with its supplier was, who created the tire's performance specs, who was responsible for testing the tire on the Explorer, and demanding "any complaint, formal or informal, warranty claim, problem or concern in your possession or control that concerns a complaint or claim about an ATX and/or Wilderness AT tire on an Explorer failing due to tread separation, alleged tread separation, a tread problem, an alleged tread problem, or a failure of a tire resulting in loss of control or alleged loss of control for the period 1990 to the present date."

He also levied a series of questions about Ford's insistence on 26 psi versus Firestone's recommendation of 30 psi. "Did Ford, Firestone, or both jointly decide to recommend 26 psi for the Explorer tires?" he asked. Was it the company's contention that the Ford Explorer was "unreasonably dangerous if operated, driven, or used with any tire pressure greater than 26 psi?" Did the vehicle tire create a hazard "if operated, driven, or used with any tire pressure less than 26 psi?" Was a consumer "guilty of misuse, negligence or misconduct" if the driver operated a Ford Explorer whose tire pressure was set above 26 psi, but below 35 psi on one or more tires? Did the Ford Explorer roll over easier if one or more tires were set at 30 psi instead of 26 psi?

As summer seeped into fall, Turner took steps to retain a local attorney in Corpus Christi to help secure and hold a trial date, someone respected by the judges, adept at parrying corporate defense motions with well-penned ones of his own, and who could assist him in the courtroom should they to go to trial. LaValle didn't have much courtroom experience, so his role was mostly to see to the needs of the family while Turner did the intellectual heavy lifting, developing the case for trial and fronting expenses.

Originally Turner sought David L. Perry, a legal legend in south Texas. Almost 20 years earlier, Perry had won a $100 million punitive damage verdict against Ford over its combustible Mustang II fuel tank, which was almost identical in design to the Pinto's. But Perry was on sabbatical, traveling in Europe and not returning phone calls. So Turner turned to Mikal Watts, a 34-year-old protégé of Perry's who had worked for him until heading off on his own a few years earlier.

Tall, gangly, balding with glasses, Watts was so smart he could debate three sides and win four of them. Confident to the point of swagger, he could, when it suited him, career from abject charm to analytic cool, vials of wrath and tearful indignation all in the same breath. Like Turner, he had grown up in a well-connected legal family. His father was attorney/politician Guy Watts, and his mother, Sandra, was a district court judge. He graduated with honors from the University of Texas School of Law at the age of 21 and, after clerking for a Texas State Supreme Court judge, joined David L. Perry & Associates in August 1990. Within a year and a half, he was named partner.

Promising himself he would start his own firm by 30, Watts left Perry in 1997, after securing more than three dozen settlements in excess of $1 million. As an attorney specializing in personal injury cases, he attacked automakers, drug companies, trucking firms, and refineries. In the mid-1990s he was active in litigation against Chrysler over failing latches on minivans, and won an $80 million verdict against the automaker for the estate of a couple burned alive in their 1977 Dodge pickup when its fuel system failed following a collision. He reaped a $120 million decision against Coastal Corp., a Texas gas refinery, and convinced a jury in

Webb County, Texas, to return with a gross negligence verdict for $19 million in actual damages and $1 million in punitive penalties against Burlington Motor Carriers after a man hit an 18-wheeler parked across a Missouri highway and died.

Turner initially phoned Watts from Dearborn, where coincidentally Watts was also on business. They were both taking depositions at Ford for different cases. Turner was working on an Explorer rollover while Watts was there on behalf of a client injured in a "roof crush" incident that involved a Ford pickup truck.

The way they pursued their cases reflected their approaches to the law. The relentlessly logical Turner based his on science, burying juries in data that showed the automaker knew its SUV was unstable but didn't do anything about it in order to save money. The more visceral Watts, who had 30 Explorer cases of his own, preferred to skip all that. Whether or not the car was tipsy didn't matter to him as much as the fact that the tops of the cars were like tin foil and had a propensity for caving in and killing people. They agreed to meet at the airport, where Watts would give Turner "a lift home" so the two could talk while Turner sent his plane ahead, since Little Rock was on the way to Corpus Christi.

After boarding, Turner and Watts got to know each other by comparing jets the way most guys compare cars. Watts had a 10-passenger Westwind Commander, the same model Turner used to own, until he traded it in for a smaller, faster plane that only required one pilot. Then over a few beers Turner filled Watts in on Bailey, which, from a legal standpoint, was a perfect case. The police report showed no driver error, no alcohol, no speeding, no other car involved, and the pavement was bone dry. She was clearly an innocent victim, properly belted at the time of the accident. Not only wasn't she driving, it wasn't even her car. The Wilderness tire in question wasn't covered under the recall. This was important because Ford and Firestone had been claiming these tires were safe, when Turner could prove they weren't. Not only was Bailey's case at stake, but so were many others, which could end up costing the two companies hundreds of millions of dollars. As a result, Turner fully expected that there would be a trial.

Watts didn't need much convincing to sign on. He believed the greatest rewards went to those willing to take the greatest risks. After they worked out a rough fee arrangement, Watts pledged a staff of lawyers and paralegals to the cause and agreed to split expenses. Then Turner told Watts his plan. The most pressing issue was to avoid a "legislative continuance," a legal loophole often employed by corporations. Turner predicted Ford and Firestone would do just about anything to put off any

Donna Bailey trial and fully expected one or both to approach the local state representative to work on their cases, even though most politicians rarely ventured into courtrooms. The reason: If someone were both a legislator and a lawyer, he could present the judge with an injunction and the trial would usually be postponed until after the legislative session. By then Donna Bailey could be dead. So Turner wanted Watts to preempt the companies by hiring the local Nueces County state legislator to work on the case. In essence they would be paying Vilma Luna, a member of the Texas House of Representatives, to not work for the enemy—money well spent, they agreed.

Turner's strategy was predicated on settling with Firestone then going after Ford in court. He had already been in preliminary negotiations with attorney Patrick Zummo, Firestone's point person in Texas, about coming to terms on Bailey. Turner and Zummo went back a long time. They first worked against each other in the mid-1990s, when Turner was representing a young quadriplegic named Kyle Walsh, who was injured in a Bronco II that rolled over after a Firestone tire separated. Turner knew he had a weak case against Firestone. The tire had been inspected right before Walsh's trip and should have been replaced by Discount Tire. Turner suggested he and Zummo work out a deal. Firestone would pay a modest settlement to be let out of the case and then Turner would turn his attention to Discount Tire.

Fast-forward to August 2000. Turner asked Zummo about agreeing to a Walsh-type strategy in Bailey, but this time blindsiding Ford. He reminded Zummo that Ford was killing Firestone in the press, and the tire maker was far behind Turner when it came to understanding the role of the Explorer in these rollover crashes. Not only that but Firestone had little credibility in its charges against Ford. And with the Bailey case looming, there was no way the company could let Turner try it in the midst of this media tornado. Zummo agreed to float the idea at Firestone and get back to him.

After Watts dropped Turner off in Little Rock, they got together a couple weeks later with Zummo and an in-house Firestone attorney in Akron. They met at a restaurant that had once been an old railroad car, the kind of place Turner thought hoboes might go, except the food was good. Zummo told them how dirty Ford had been playing and related a story about a meeting at Firestone when someone came running into the conference room with a newspaper article that quoted Turner blasting the Explorer and how people in the room busted out in cheers. He admitted Firestone made some bad tires but claimed the real problem was the Ford vehicle. Since Turner had been like "John the Baptist in the wilderness," warning of the dangers inherent with the Explorer, Zummo wanted him to take his battle into the courtroom on behalf of Firestone.

Turner said he would be crazy to give up the simplest part of the case to try the hardest since it would be relatively easy to prove the tire was bad. He would consider it only if Firestone were willing to offer Bailey a "special premium," one he knew was unheard of in this type of litigation. He tossed out an outrageous figure, $30 million, just to gauge Zummo's reaction. Turner knew there was no way he'd get that much, but wanted to put the idea of a large settlement in Firestone's head. Although juries sometimes awarded plaintiffs four times that in punitive damages, companies never offered that much in negotiations, knowing that astronomical verdicts had a way of getting shrunk down to size by the appeals process.

As expected, Zummo complained that he couldn't possibly pay that kind of money. But everyone at the table knew that most other attorneys with Explorer cases had their sights on the easy money: attacking Firestone, leaving Ford virtually unscathed. Turner reminded Zummo how dangerous Bailey would be for them if it were the first case to hit a courtroom. He was one of the few lawyers in America who knew the entire story and could help Firestone turn the tide. Turner had beaten the automaker on a tread separation–rollover case once before in Cammack. If he could do it again, it would take some of the heat off Firestone.

Zummo got up to make some calls to corporate headquarters. By the end of the meal nothing had been settled, yet both parties came away believing it might be possible to do business.

It was in the hands of Bridgestone management in Japan. How they would react was anyone's guess.

24 CRASH TEST HUMAN

ALTHOUGH EARLY NOVEMBER, STREAMERS OF HEAT rose from an abandoned runway at Coolidge airport, which lay in desert scrub about 40 miles from Phoenix. Professional crash test driver Mark Arndt, protected by a helmet, racing harness, goggles, gloves, and a neck brace, was idling in a white 1996 four-door Ford Explorer, waiting for the signal to start another run. Arndt, 40, was founder and president of Transportation Safety Technologies Inc. of Mesa, Arizona, and, along with his brother Steve, had grown up in the business. His father founded an auto safety research firm when Arndt was in grammar school, and he got to watch crash tests from the time he was too short to see over the steering wheel. Starting out by mopping floors, testing equipment, assisting engineers, he even helped construct the test facility. When he got old enough he took part in crash tests, and over the last 20 years had performed hundreds of them.

For this one, Arndt and his brother, who also operated an auto research firm, were trying to ascertain what happens to a Ford Explorer following a tire failure. While Ford and Firestone were about to complete their recall of 6.5 million tires eight months ahead of schedule, Turner had hired the Arndts to induce a tread separation by slitting the sidewall with a sharp knife and race the vehicle at 70 mph until heat and friction tore the tire apart. For comparison's sake they took turns taking a Ford Taurus up the tarmac. As they had predicted, after a half dozen runs the tire shredded. The car swiveled slightly, but Arndt was easily able to maintain control until coming to a full stop. Knowing what he did about vehicle dynamics, however, Arndt fully expected the Explorer to be a different story—and this made him nervous.

This wasn't the first time Turner had worked with the Arndt brothers. In the mid-1990s he had paid them to study the effects of tread separations on Ford Bronco IIs. They found that the vehicle pulled in the direction of the disruption in a phenomenon known as "oversteer." So even if the driver didn't touch the steering wheel, it would turn in smaller and smaller circles as it sped up. This pulling occurred in all cars, regardless of make or model, but the effects were much more pronounced in a Bronco.

Turner had been asking them to develop a similar study on the Explorer. They got together to set up test protocols in June 2000, and the Arndts estimated the cost to be about $150,000. With a recall looming, Turner realized there would be great demand for it and decided to ask other trial lawyers to fund additional tests—on a 15-passenger van, a pickup, a Chevy Suburban and a Blazer, a Jeep Cherokee, and several other versions of the Explorer. For $20,000 each participant would receive the entire package, which included the Bronco II testing that Turner and the Arndts had teamed up on in the early 1990s. Eventually Adam Shea, Tad Griffen, Mike Eidson, Mikal Watts, Rob Ammons, and a number of other high-profile attorneys chipped in, too. But not everyone was pleased with the cost.

"Why the hell is this so expensive?" Watts asked Arndt one day.

Arndt told him they had to purchase the Explorer and Taurus, and were going to specially outfit the Explorer with outriggers, which "adds a lot to the cost. We're also having to build a roll cage to protect the driver if it rolls over . . ."

"Hell, Mark," Watts interrupted. "Why do we need both? If you're going to have outriggers, that'll keep it from rolling over. If you don't want outriggers, then you can have yourself a roll cage to keep from getting crushed. So you're good either way."

But Arndt insisted on both. Watts knew Arndt to be scrupulously honest and not one to pad expenses. So he let it go.

Even with this extra protection, Arndt had read too many accident reports on Explorers not to be worried. With outriggers on each side, the one he was strapped into looked like a large white catamaran. The interior around Arndt had been reinforced with steel supports. Video cameras were attached to the right outrigger, focused on the right rear wheel, and inside the cab, behind the driver. Arndt company employees operated additional cameras set up at the end of the track and along the side.

He and his brother designed the test to measure "side slip" angle or lateral acceleration—the extent to which the Explorer would slide sideways in response to a tread separation. Arndt knew it would pull right as soon as the tread gave way; he just didn't know by how much. The protocol he and his brother designed was intended to take the driver out of the equation, because a well-trained professional would correct for the tread separation by turning the wheel in the opposite direction. In this test Arndt would hold the wheel perfectly straight for a full second before gaining control. Then they would calculate how much the Explorer listed to the right.

Arndt got the signal to start and hit the accelerator. He sped up to 70 mph and stayed to the right of a line of orange traffic cones that marked his path. A few hundred yards later he heard the telltale rat-a-tat sound of the right rear tire tearing apart. Arndt steeled his arms to keep the wheel straight but was surprised by how profound the pull was. The vehicle shot sideways so quickly he found himself heading off the highway. Instead of holding the wheel straight for a full second like he'd planned, he began to correct by steering left within half a second. When that didn't work he turned it some more. He knew not to hit the brakes. That would have been the wrong thing to do. He wanted to gain control of the vehicle first then gradually slow down. But the Explorer wouldn't cooperate. The force was so great he couldn't overcome it. Instead he was veering out of control, slipping sideways at highway speed, the tires squealing.

In less than two seconds the Explorer was flying off the pavement. Arndt figured the outriggers would keep him upright. He'd never broken one in all his years of testing. But the outrigger wedged into the dirt and for a brief moment arrested the vehicle's momentum—until it snapped off on the de-treaded tire side. The Explorer pirouetted in the air and then crashed down on its side. Arndt felt like he was on a wild carnival ride as the car rolled over sagebrush, tumbleweeds, and a bramble of mesquite trees. Dirt poured in the driver's side window. The other outrigger splintered. He could hear metal groan, glass shatter.

While upside down, his head was flush against the top of the car as the un-reinforced parts of the roof caved in around him. Afraid he'd crack his spine and end up a quadriplegic, Arndt lifted his hands over his head and pushed as hard as he could, trying desperately to keep his butt pinned to the seat. Even so, his head brushed against the ceiling twice as the Explorer rolled four-and-a-half times in five seconds, eventually resting on its roof.

The tornado was over as quickly as it had started. The camera affixed to the rear tire swung lazily. Arndt got his bearings and found himself heels over head, shoulders straining against his safety belt. On the headset he could hear someone shout over the ringing in his ears. "Call 911. Call 911. Mark? Mark?"

"Nine-one-one, we've got an emergency," someone else said. "A rollover test. Taxi way, south and west of the hangar. Doing this test, and . . ."

"I think I'm OK, I think I'm OK," Arndt replied.

Then he smelled gas. He had investigated rollover crashes where the filler neck had been pulled off the fuel tank and the car exploded. He was afraid he might not get out in time.

Bracing himself, he flicked a lever and landed hard. As Arndt crawled out of the passenger's side window his colleagues arrived. Once outside he surveyed the damage. Aside from carpet burns on his elbow and a badly skinned knee, he was fine. But the car was completely demolished.

Arndt paced up and down the track hissing obscenities. He was mad something like this could ever be described as "driver error"—Ford's standard defense. He had done everything a driver should have done in the circumstances. If it hadn't been for the roll bar, Arndt could be dead.

He wondered how he would explain this to Turner and Watts. They had paid for a scientific test to measure sideslip angle and all he had to show for it was a wrecked Explorer. He figured they'd never pay for another test vehicle. Besides, there was no way he was going to test-drive another Explorer ever again. Arndt was married and had two kids, one 9 years old, the other 11. He wanted to live long enough to see them into college and beyond.

After he'd calmed down, Arndt called Watts in Corpus Christi, who was in a meeting with his partner, Brian Harris. "Mikal, I ruined your test," Arndt said glumly.

"What happened?" Watts asked.

"I rolled over in the Explorer." Arndt explained what happened. He swore he didn't mean to, it just happened.

"So?" Watts said. "What the hell is wrong with that?"

Arndt didn't understand.

"Mark!" Harris shouted, unable to contain his excitement. "I want you to do one thing for me."

"What's that?"

"I want you to save those underpants you've got on, 'cause we're going to admit those shitty britches as plaintiff's exhibit number one."

25 SIP AND PUFF

THE FOLLOWING MORNING, A FEW THURSDAYS before Thanksgiving, Tab Turner was about to fly to Houston to confer with Donna Bailey and her family. Although he had been working on the case for months, and had spoken with her and members of her family on the phone, this would be their first time meeting in person. He didn't even know what Donna did for a living. He thought she might be a teacher. But those types of details would wait for the week before trial. What was important was that Turner knew everything about her case. More significantly, that Ford and Firestone knew he knew.

Turner was not alone on this sojourn. Accompanying him was *New York Times* reporter Michael Winerip, who had spent the last few days shadowing Turner for a cover story in the Sunday magazine. While Turner's Cessna was taxiing for takeoff, Arndt's brother called. "Howdy, Steve," Turner shouted over the engines. "I had a productive trip. Sorry I missed you, but money always comes first." While Winerip strained to eavesdrop, Turner said, "Oh! How did Mark lose control? . . . Wow! And he's OK? . . . Did you get it on video? . . . All right! . . . Let's keep this quiet for now. The last thing we need at this point is one of these media hounds finding out." As the jet climbed toward the clouds, Turner shut off his cell phone and grinned. He told Winerip about the Explorer crash test. "Rolled over," he said. "Can't do better than that." The test had been worth every penny.

Ninety minutes later Turner was still in a good mood when they arrived at TIRR, where Mikal Watts was waiting in the lobby. After brisk greetings Watts took Turner aside to fill him in on the latest developments. Watts told Turner that Rick was spitting mad over medical expenses, and LaValle was unhappy because Turner had retained Watts without consulting him first. Even Donna had ambushed him. When Watts ventured upstairs to introduce himself she asked him if he was

Guy Watts' son. When he said yes Donna fired him on the spot. It turned out Watts' father had judged her son Jeremiah in a school debate a few years earlier, which the boy won. Afterward, Guy Watts told Jeremiah that if he wanted to be successful in life he would have to lose weight. Donna never forgave him for that. Watts had to backpedal as fast as he could. He wasn't even close with his father, who was renowned for his drop-of-the-hat verbosity. Talking 120 miles an hour, he apologized profusely for his father's insensitivity. Eventually Donna relented and let him stay on the team.

Turner chuckled. This was why he let referring attorneys deal with the clients. Then Watts led him and Winerip to the fifth floor. Stepping off the elevator Turner's mood changed. He reflected that the worst thing about his job was meeting "a freshly minted quad" for the first time. He dreaded it. Of course that didn't mean he didn't have a strategy for it. Hell, he had a strategy for everything. After all he was a trial lawyer: *Look her straight in the eye; don't talk down to her. Although her flesh may be weak, her mind is as sharp as it was before the accident.*

He followed Watts down the hall and around a corner. Outside room 519, Turner saw Paul LaValle talking to—or more accurately, being talked at by—someone he assumed was Donna's brother.

Turner knew LaValle and Rick Burchfield had a querulous relationship. What's more, he had no intention of getting involved. LaValle complained that Rick was giving him migraines, barraging him with irate phone calls and indignant e-mails. Rick was a micromanager who constantly scribbled notes on a pad and had put his entire life on hold to take care of his sister. He approached the job with almost religious fervor. Once, twice, three times a day he screamed at LaValle to fix a bureaucratic snafu, solve a medical records or billing dispute, explain why a doctor missed a scheduled appointment, or complain about the nurses. But Turner didn't feel sorry for LaValle. That's what he got paid for.

After handshakes and greetings, Turner told Rick it was good to put a face to the phone voice. He could tell Rick was upset. So was LaValle, who did a better job of masking it. Watts had been upstairs earlier and warned Turner that Rick planned to confront them with a medical bills crisis. LaValle had been talking for a while about fissures in the family, common after catastrophic accidents like Donna's. In Turner's lexicon it was known as "emotional distress." Turner engaged in some light chitchat with Rick and then ordered Winerip to wait outside Donna's room. Before he agreed to cooperate with the *Times* magazine, Turner had told the reporter, "You'll see what you see but there are some things you can't see."

Turner disappeared inside, trailed by Watts, LaValle, and Rick, and encountered Donna Bailey, bed-bound and tipped up at a 30-degree angle, hooked up to life support machines on both sides. Donna's teenaged kids, Cassie, 17, and Jeremiah, 15, kept her company while other family members—her mother and another brother—hovered in the background. Some lounged in chairs, others stood. Turner approached and tapped Donna on the leg. He knew she couldn't feel it but figured she'd appreciate the gesture. It wasn't like there was a protocol for this. He didn't ask how she was doing because he knew the answer. Before the accident she was a newly divorced mother of two who had just moved in with her mother and was living on food stamps. Now she'd give anything to have that life back. That's how she was doing.

"I look horrible," Donna said, her voice muffled by the plastic pipe jammed down her throat. In the eight months since the accident her weight had dropped below 100 pounds. Because of the angle of the bed she had to roll her eyes to the tops of their sockets to see Turner. Donna took a good long look at Turner. She told him she had watched him on TV a bunch of times and claimed she was intimidated to meet such a celebrity.

"Somebody's gotta do it," Turner replied. He found it oddly encouraging that she wore makeup and her hair had been shampooed and styled. His eyes wandered to the monitors that digitized her blood oxygen levels, pulse rate, temperature; the ventilator that breathed for her; the tubes that carried liquid food in and waste out. A man who greeted the day on a treadmill at 6 a.m., Turner couldn't resist stealing a glance at her withered limbs. It got him thinking: How much would it take for him to change places with her? Would $50 million do it? $100 million? Here he was on track to settle a quarter of a *billion* dollars in accident settlements this year alone, and he knew there wasn't enough money in creation for that.

Turner explained the purpose of the meeting was to get Donna up to speed on where they were and where they were headed. Aware that one of the most difficult things to accept as a quadriplegic was the loss of control, Turner spoke directly to her and only her. He knew it was important for Donna to feel in charge. Turner said her case had become a focal point for the entire Ford-Firestone issue. She put a human face on the tragedy that could ensue when companies pursue profits over safety.

He informed her that he and Watts had been in talks with Firestone and believed a settlement was near at hand, which would put maximum pressure on Ford. The biggest fight looming was securing a trial date. Ford desperately wanted to postpone it and Watts' job was to make sure they didn't. What Turner didn't mention was why he suspected Ford was playing the delay game. Every day that passed benefited the automaker. With Donna's medical expenses estimated at $500,000 a year, quadriplegics put a bigger dent in the bottom line than death cases. The longer Ford could put off a trial, the less likely Donna, who had barely survived several close calls, would ever live to see a courtroom.

Turner asked if Donna had any questions.

"No," she said, "let's just do it." She hoped the lawsuit would take care of her and her kids. Although the biggest question in her life was whether she would ever be able to breathe without a ventilator, Donna wanted everyone to know she fully intended to walk again. For now what she really wanted more than anything was to go home.

Turner knew this was as much an expression of frustration as it was concern over who would pay for her medical care. It was adding to considerable friction in the family. Cassie, Jeremiah, and her ex-husband, Michael Bailey, wanted her home, but Rick, believing they underestimated how difficult it would be to care for an invalid, demanded his sister be treated in a hospital. Turner turned to Rick, who was scrawling notes, and said diplomatically, "I hear you have some questions."

Rick put down his notebook and tried to stifle his agitation. He was worn thin by the responsibilities placed on him by his sister's tragedy. Rick reminded Turner that when he retained LaValle to represent the family he insisted in writing that the lawyer cover her medical expenses. In the five months she was in San Antonio, his sister had racked up a $90,000 bill. After launching a letter-writing campaign he had convinced Medicaid to cover three months at TIRR, but tomorrow was it. Unless they came up with $42,000 to pay for another month, Bailey would be sent home.

"I'm tired of having to deal with all this," Rick told Turner, Watts and LaValle. "You guys are her lawyers. You should be handling this."

Turner assured Rick they were working on it. He described myriad calls his office had made to the hospital.

Rick didn't know about these efforts. What's more he didn't care. Every time Rick brought up the issue with LaValle all he did was hem and haw. Rick hadn't trusted LaValle from the minute he showed up in San Antonio waving a contract while Donna fought for her life in intensive care. What's more, LaValle still hadn't reimbursed him for his sister's medical bills from San Antonio. Rick knew firsthand the value of a lawyer's promise. That was why he demanded proof, preferably cash. His sister was about to be kicked out of the hospital tomorrow, and without round-the-clock nursing she could die.

"We're not going to let that happen," Turner promised.

He excused himself to locate someone who could shed some light. When Donna was paralyzed, she was 1 of 39 million Americans without health insurance, and no government agency or health maintenance organization would touch her. Rick was right that Donna should remain in the hospital. Turner needed her strong for the trial. He couldn't wait to see her in front of a jury. Need be he would hire a helicopter and a team of doctors to take her to court. That would be Ford's biggest nightmare.

After tracking down an administrator in TIRR's billing department, Turner concluded there was little chance of getting the issue resolved any time soon. LaValle would have promised to pull Donna in a rickshaw for a year if he thought it would help him land her case. Unfortunately, he didn't have the money to make good on his promise. It was time for Plan B.

When Turner returned, Rick greeted him with a demand. "I know you're lawyers and not bankers but I also know how much money you've got and your going to take care of her. I signed a contract with LaValle that promised he'd pay Donna's medical bills. He brought you in. No one is leaving this room until one of you agrees to cover it."

"OK, we'll take care of it," Turner said.

Rick didn't believe him.

Turner wasn't surprised by his skepticism. He couldn't possibly understand the lengths Turner's staff had gone to in trying to get Donna medical coverage. They had been bounced around from hospital administrators to government agencies to private insurance carriers—yet still weren't able to locate the resources she would need. So Turner looked to Watts, who announced grandly, "I'll pay Donna's medical expenses"— just as he and Turner had discussed. So far Turner had spent almost $300,000 on the case, which covered everything from accident reconstruction to depositions, expert witnesses, tire X-rays and travel (including jet fuel and a pilot). Now it was Watts' turn. Theatrically, Watts flipped open his mobile phone to dial his office and ordered his paralegal to cut a check for $42,000. He assured Rick he could call her whenever he had a question. Overdoing it, he told Donna to imagine the amazing house she would be able to have built overlooking the bay in Corpus Christi when this was all over.

Now that Rick was momentarily salved, Turner went to fetch Winerip. Part of Turner's strategy was to attract as much media attention for Donna as possible—not only to gain public sympathy, but also to keep Ford off his back while he went after company employees in depositions.

In response to Winerip's questions, Donna said she had loved the outdoors and at one time worked as a physical trainer. In fact, she had been on her way to go rock climbing with two friends when the rollover occurred. Being paralyzed made her stir crazy, mad with boredom. She spent her days watching soap operas, praying, and rehabbing her injuries. Now weekends were the highpoint of her life when her ex-husband chaperoned her children the 200 miles from Corpus Christi to Houston. "They pamper me," she told Winerip. "They groom me and feed me."

Winerip stuck around to observe Donna learn to use an electric "sip-and-puff" wheelchair designed for quadriplegics. To move forward, Donna had to puff out hard; to back up, sip forcefully. Inhale softly to go left, exhale softly to go right. It was great in theory, but she was having trouble putting it into practice. She couldn't puff hard enough to make the wheelchair go straight. Instead she kept veering into walls.

Leaning against the doorjamb, Turner watched and wondered. A father with three daughters, he couldn't imagine what it felt like to be unable to hug his children. He thought back to close calls he'd experienced in his life. A man didn't jet around in a Cessna and not run into turbulence, bad weather and the occasional hairy landing. He decided that sometimes it just came down to "ifs and inches." If only Donna Bailey had been a few inches shorter, or her seatbelt had sagged four inches instead of eight during the roll. If she had been sitting elsewhere in the car, or the Explorer hadn't landed on its roof, if her friend had driven a different vehicle with different tires, or Bailey had just stayed home altogether, she wouldn't be paralyzed, sipping life from a ventilator.

Donna Bailey could be any of us.

26 FEE FIGHT

IN THE DAYS FOLLOWING TURNER'S MEETING with Donna, negotiations between Turner and Firestone gathered speed. Although they were far apart on a dollar figure, a plan began to take shape. Assuming they could come to terms on money, the two sides agreed to keep any agreement under wraps until the first day of trial, when they would announce to the judge they had reached a settlement. Then Firestone's lawyers would slam their briefcases shut and walk out, completely taking Ford by surprise.

Once they settled on price, they would move on to strategy. Zummo proposed that Firestone submit an irrevocable settlement offer to Turner, which meant the plaintiffs could accept it any time they chose. In turn, Zummo wanted Turner to proffer an irrevocable settlement demand that Firestone could accept any time it wanted. The offer and demand would be $1 apart. This process gave both sides the security that the case against Firestone could be settled at a moment's notice without further litigation.

In exchange Turner insisted Firestone quit fighting for a continuance. The tire maker's lawyers couldn't control Ford from trying to delay the trial, but they would no longer join in the requests. Firestone would also attend the remaining discovery, but it would not actively participate unless Ford attacked the tire during the deposition. In addition, Firestone agreed to produce Firestone employees Turner wished to depose without any further legal wrangling. After that they would discuss a plan by which Firestone and Turner could settle every AT tire case he had—all 25—without the necessity of more litigation.

Before any of this could happen, however, Turner had to secure a trial date. His whole plan hinged on this. Without the threat of Tab Turner taking on Ford in court, Firestone wouldn't agree to anything. To make it happen, Turner realized he'd have to convince LaValle to waive a portion of his fee—as Turner was amenable to doing—so they could pay Watts to join the case and expend political capital by hanging around the court house in Corpus, getting in the face of Judge Nanette Hasette and begging her for a trial date. Often getting a case to trial depended on a lawyer showing he was ready, willing and able to put on a case, music to a judge's ears. Judge Hasette was more likely to expedite matters for a local boy like Watts than she would for Turner.

But LaValle had no intention of giving up anything. In fact, he wanted an even bigger piece of the action. In a Saturday, Nov. 11, 2000, e-mail to Turner, LaValle wrote: "When we first discussed my bringing you into this case, you assured me that you and you alone could help me finance, negotiate and litigate this case through appeal on a 50/50 attorney's fee split. Now you have hired another law firm without discussing it with me and you and these new attorneys are filing pleadings and trying to negotiate the case without me. You now want me to give away a portion of my fee on a case I have worked on every day for over six months? I think we have differing views on both business and friendship."

Turner had to read it twice to be sure his eyes hadn't deceived him. It took a lot to light a fuse on his temper. Even his office staff commented on his seemingly inexhaustible patience. Turner didn't feel all that calm inside. He just knew how to control his emotions. Save it for the jury or settlement negotiations, he often reminded himself. If Turner got mad at everyone who did something to annoy him, he would float through life on a sea of wrath. Besides, he was too busy.

But LaValle's e-mail was too much. Who was he to tell Tab Turner whom he could and couldn't hire? And where the hell did LaValle get the idea he had half the contingency fees coming to him? The signed contract Turner had in his file said LaValle received one-third and Turner got two-thirds. That was Turner's standard agreement with referring attorneys who didn't pay expenses, didn't work on discovery, and didn't prepare for trial. After all, Turner was the one who had financed every nickel of this case until Watts agreed to underwrite Donna's expenses at TIRR. He was the one whom Firestone wanted to go after Ford and could get Donna Bailey twice as much as any lawyer in America. He was the one who would age 10 years during trial. And what would LaValle do during that time? Pass a tin of mints back and forth?

Turner replied that a settlement with Firestone was contingent on Watts getting a trial date before anyone else's and he didn't need LaValle's or anyone else's permission to hire another attorney. "If you don't like the way I handle cases, this can be the last one you send me," Turner wrote. "What do you think I do for a living, play golf? I'm not asking you to give anymore than I'm giving up." He added that LaValle's role was "to get the case" and Turner's was "to turn it into money for the client. I can do my part . . . but this business about needing your permission to do things won't fly." If LaValle wanted him off the case, that was fine. Turner had dozens of clients who had been maimed in Ford Explorer/Firestone ATX accidents. Firestone would work out a deal with Turner "on another quad case" and LaValle could be the one to explain it to Donna and her family.

LaValle returned fire the next morning, demanding to be advised on significant matters of the case. "You are asking me to share a fee with attorneys, who, as far as I know, have only been involved in the case for a week, and you have yet to tell me what your arrangement with these new attorneys is." He told Turner that he and Watts "made us all look like idiots" because Turner hadn't handled the hospital bill prior to arrival at TIRR. "Since you are not providing any documents, I have no way of knowing that whatever deal you have working with Firestone has not already been cut and this is just some means of diverting a portion of my fees to your buddies in Corpus Christi."

To buttress his argument, LaValle attached a copy of a contract he'd induced Michael Bailey into signing a couple months earlier, which included a clause that stipulated that LaValle and Turner would split all fees. LaValle had told Bailey he needed his signature in order to handle some vague legal matters. In fact, the contract's small print upped the attorneys' fees from 33.3 percent to 40 percent—and a whopping 45 percent if the case went to trial.

Although Turner had assumed LaValle would at some point ask the family for 40 percent, the attached contract was news to Turner. In April, when LaValle faxed Turner's office the original agreement that allowed him to represent the family, LaValle appended a note in which he told Turner he "did not believe they will sign any contract with a 40% fee this early when they have been told by two different state judges that the court(s) will only approve a 1/3 fee." This didn't bother Turner. He had enough money for a hundred lifetimes. The Bailey case was a chance to make legal history and add to his legacy. That was well worth sacrificing 7 percent. He wasn't even aware that LaValle had gotten permission to raise the fees. And how stupid did LaValle think Turner was that he would have agreed to give him half the fees—whether based on 40 percent or 33 percent? The fact that LaValle was confirming every ill thought Turner ever had about a referring attorney irritated him to no end.

If LaValle wanted a negotiation, Turner would give him a one. He left LaValle a curt voicemail, in which he offered LaValle 20 percent of the contingency fees. Take it or leave it.

While this wrangling was going on talks between Zummo and Turner continued. Although they were closing in on a settlement on Bailey, there were still hurdles. Before Firestone would allow itself to be pinned down on price, Zummo wanted assurances that Turner would indeed go after Ford in court. There were many potential pitfalls. The carmaker had moved to consolidate pretrial evidence matters of discovery on Explorer-related lawsuits before a single judge in the region. If this happened, it could take a year or more for any Bailey trial to proceed. There was always the possibility the dealership could be removed from the case as well, which could mean it might end up in federal court, also leading to long delays.

The only way Firestone would agree to a settlement was if Turner could secure a trial date. LaValle was tying Turner's hands.

The following morning he heard back from LaValle in two e-mails spaced a couple of hours apart, demanding that he receive 35 percent of the fees for Firestone and a third of the Ford case. He accused Turner of stealing money from him. "It appears you have not promised Mikal Watts any of your fee, but rather, a substantial portion of mine, which is not yours to give away." This wasn't true because to make things work, Turner had offered to cut his fee in half to give to Watts for the Ford part of the case, which would potentially amount to several million dollars. LaValle proposed that Turner either "immediately wire transfer $7.5 million," pay him half the fees as funds are received, or earmark 40 percent of the Firestone fee and 30 percent of any Ford fee for LaValle's pocketbook.

In the acid reflux game, LaValle was a carrier, Turner thought. He took to his keyboard and dashed off another reply, telling LaValle his proposal was "ridiculous . . . I give up virtually my entire life to help people like Donna Bailey and then get treated like this by you. Am I upset, damn right I am." So much so that he threatened to shut down the entire deal.

LaValle acted like a jilted lover in his next e-mail. "It amazes me that [all of this] has only become an issue since you have associated new counsel without consulting me." He still contended that Turner owed him half of the Bailey booty on Firestone, as laid out in the contract he'd convinced Michael Bailey to sign. But since he was anxious to conclude settlement talks with Firestone, which he said he believed was in the client's best interest, he offered to take 25 percent, even though "we are still talking about me losing and you and Watts gaining."

They continued to volley e-mails and phone messages back and forth for the better part of three days. Turner called LaValle "greedy" and said he didn't care what he got the client to sign. "You must think I'm the dumbest person on earth if you think I would have ever agreed to pay all expenses and pay you" half of the fees. "I would think you would be absolutely thrilled" with a multimillion dollar fee "for what you have done."

LaValle retorted he was convinced the only interest Turner was attempting to serve was his own. Turner told LaValle he could spin the situation any way he wanted, "but the bottom line is that you are holding up my ability to get a firm offer" from Firestone. LaValle threatened that if he and Turner couldn't work things out, he would "disclose all of our communications to the client and we can let them decide what needs to be done."

Go ahead, Turner replied. He'd written them with the full intent of sharing them anyway. "I will have an obligation to pass [Firestone's] offer on so they can decide," Turner wrote. "I should probably call them tomorrow and inform them of the entire situation, but I keep hoping that you will somehow see that this is about helping Donna, not about how much money you make." He complained he was "in no man's land" because he couldn't give Firestone assurances that he would get an expedited trial date. "You continue to insinuate that Watts is excess baggage. Watts is vital to me being able to deliver what needs to be delivered."

Eventually LaValle gave in when Turner promised him to raise his fees from 33 percent to 40 percent on the Ford part of the lawsuit and to go along with his 20 percent interest in Firestone. One condition he had was that Turner wire the money to his Texas City bank account within 48 hours of reaching a settlement with Firestone. Turner was beginning to seriously wonder if LaValle had ever successfully litigated a case before. He pointed out that any settlement with Firestone would not be funded within 48 hours, but promised to send the money within 24 hours of receiving it.

Now that was settled, Turner had to cross his fingers and hope that Watts could nail down a trial date.

27 FORWARD FAST

ON NOVEMBER 16, MIKAL WATTS WALKED into the Nueces County courthouse and submitted a motion to move up the trial date from March 2001 to Jan. 8, 2001. His argument was two-fold. Since half of quadriplegics die from inadequate care after being released from hospitals to private homes, it was imperative Donna Bailey be allowed to have her day in court as soon as possible. The case had been on file for seven months and her Medicaid benefits were maxed out. The Texas Rehabilitation Commission had funded her stay up to this point but had a 90-day cap that was about to end.

He attached "Exhibit A," a letter from registered nurse Donna Smith, who explained that Bailey had been accepted to Lifebridge, a long-term acute care facility that was a cheaper alternative to TIRR. There Donna's family could complete training in caring for a quadriplegic, arrange for skilled home-nursing services, procure a ventilator, power and manual wheelchairs, bathroom equipment, and complete construction of her living quarters—a garage conversion at her mother's home. The cost: $1,400 per day. Although Watts had agreed to finance Donna's transfer to Lifebridge to the tune of $42,000 a month, her medical condition was chronically poor. "Her quality of life," he wrote, "could be greatly improved in the event that she makes a financial recovery from the defendants in this case."

His second point was "because of the unique posture of this case" discovery could easily be completed in time. Turner had been doing Explorer litigation for almost a decade and Watts had recently settled two Firestone ATX cases. There remained only a limited amount of discovery to be completed. To buttress their argument, the plaintiffs took the unusual step of filing a list of experts who were ready to testify.

In a supporting brief, Watts pointed out that due process required notice of a trial setting that was "reasonable under the circumstances," and that a "first trial setting no less than 45 days before the trial" went *beyond* the requirements of due process. "This hearing is being held 53 days in advance of the earliest requested trial setting," he wrote, "providing defendants eight days more notice than is required under the rules." Based on these facts, he asked that the court exercise its discretion to grant his request for an accelerated trial setting. Over Ford's objections, Judge Hasette granted the motion.

But Turner and Watts knew Ford wouldn't give up so easily. They huddled together to figure out ways the company might gin up obstacles. Then it hit them: Ford might sue the driver of the car, Tara Cox, and claim she didn't have legal representation. With Judge Hasette's docket filling up, it could potentially put off a trial for several weeks. As a precaution Turner and Watts contacted lawyers for Cox's insurance provider, Texas State Mutual Insurance Co., and advised them to appoint an attorney, recommending Guy Allison, who had been trolling Texas courthouses for four decades.

Although 68 years old, verging on retirement, flanked by hearing aids on both ears and in the early stages of Parkinson's disease, Allison still had a keen mind. At one time he was one of the most successful lawyers in America—*Forbes* pegged him as one of the top-50 highest paid lawyers in 1988. A man who thrived in the heat of a trial, he had blazed a trail in criminal defense work before taking on personal injury cases where the money proved even sweeter. In the early 1990s, Allison won a $44 million jury award in Brownsville in what was called the "shrimp dip case." Two brothers had been killed in the hold of their boat in July 1988 after adding a preservative, sodium metabisulfite, to their catch. When mixed with ice the chemical produced deadly sulfur dioxide gas, asphyxiating them. Allison zeroed in on the label, which he claimed hadn't warned clearly enough of the dangers.

A legendary womanizer, he liked to joke he had been married almost 40 years—to three different women. In his practice Allison employed a sliding scale for fees, mixing cases he found interesting with those offering the potential for a big payoff. If he had a strategy for life it might be: If you see a skinny pig, help it over the fence. If you see a fat one, eat it. After finding out he'd be working with Turner and Watts, Allison was more than happy to sign on.

Meanwhile Turner and Watts began deposing medical experts— doctors, radiologists, paramedics—anyone who had come in contact with Donna either en route to or at the hospital. The most detailed testimony came from Dr. William Donovan, a specialist in spinal cord injuries and TIRR's medical director. Donovan equated Donna's injuries with those of Christopher Reeve, a quadriplegic who also suffered a crippling injury to his first and second cervical vertebrae and required a ventilator to breathe.

The force of the crash had damaged Donna's spinal cord as well as the arteries that ran from her heart into the vertebrae and up to her skull. The result was that the only place she experienced normal human feeling was behind her ears. Everywhere else she was almost completely paralyzed, save for involuntary reflexes that manifested in spasticity and searing pain in her skin, which he likened to "rather severe sunburn" where "just a light touch can be a painful experience."

Donovan reeled off her medical problems. She had suffered several cardiac attacks and even with a pacemaker installed her heart was weak; she was prone to blood clots, yeast and bladder infections; even a common flu could kill her; she wasn't able to feed herself because she didn't have use of her arms, although if someone put food in her mouth she could chew and swallow; her spasticity was so debilitating that when she first got to TIRR, doctors couldn't even begin rehabilitation. "Her muscles were so tight and stiff that it was impossible to get her into a chair where she could be comfortable," Donovan said. "It was even difficult to get her positioned comfortably in bed." With Donna's consent, doctors tried an experimental trial of a medication called Intrathecal Baclofen, which was injected into the fluid surrounding the spinal cord via an implanted pump. All of this intensive care came at a price: For the first three months Donna was at TIRR, she wracked up a bill of $200,325.08.

Donovan estimated her life expectancy to be 13 years. If she were lucky she might make it to 55, but only if she were afforded 24-hour care. Without it, she might not survive another day.

Watts finished up with a flurry. "Dr. Donovan," he asked. "Will she ever walk?"

"No."

"Will she ever be able to raise a fork and feed herself?"

"No."

"Will she ever be able to conduct her own bowel and bladder program?"

"No."

"Will she ever be able to live without constant assistance and supervision?"

"No."

"Do you have an opinion as to whether the injury that Donna Bailey sustained was a serious, permanent and disabling injury?"

"I have no doubt that it was."

On Dec. 1, Ford lawyers filed a motion for reconsideration of plaintiff's motion to accelerate trial setting. When that was denied, they asked for continuance at a hearing seven days later because the company had just filed paperwork to sue the driver and Tara Cox didn't have a lawyer.

That's when Guy Allison, playing his part perfectly, stood up and said, "I represent Tara Cox and we're ready for trial."

Judge Hasette denied the continuance. Afterward Turner sent a simple three-word e-mail to his office: "Lock and load."

28 Driver Error

TARA COX COULDN'T STOP CRYING. She was sitting at a table in a conference room at the law offices of Barger, Hermansen, McKibben & Villarreal—Firestone's attorneys—dressed in what for her passed for formal wear: a skirt and a sleeveless denim shirt, trying to answer questions about the crash. But she was having trouble concentrating. She felt they were all ganging up on her. Tara had been doing everything in her power to forget what had happened, and now they wanted to dredge it all up again.

After the accident Tara had locked her doors and cried for two solid weeks. She was afraid to drive. She'd lie around on the couch and all of a sudden it would be 3:30 and the kids would be home from school. Kim told her to get hold of herself and "think happy thoughts." But she couldn't. Her sleep was taunted by a recurring nightmare: Donna trapped upside down in the crashed Explorer, a critically injured marionette. A plastic bag stuffed with bloody clothes and one of Donna's shoes lay in the bottom of her closet.

Tara worked up the courage to visit Donna in the hospital once, but it was an uncomfortable meeting. It wasn't as if they could sit there and reminisce over old times—like when they went camping in New Mexico and Tara got food poisoning. Donna practically carried Tara to the hospital so she could be shot up with an IV, and then insisted they go on their 12-mile hike the next morning as planned. Without Donna's support (and ribald humor), Tara knew she would have never made it. But now that Donna needed help Tara couldn't reciprocate. Instead Donna was the one to offer reassurance. At one point Donna had to tell Tara to get a grip. Tara knew she had enough problems without having to worry about her, too.

Vying for normalcy, Tara returned to Youth Odyssey, where she got a cold reception. Amiel Garcia turned on her viciously after Tara asked him how Donna was progressing. One by one her friends abandoned her. Everyone seemed to take sides in this imaginary feud, even her husband Kim, who attended a wedding from which Tara had been disinvited even though she begged him not to.

At work, Kim told Tara he couldn't display any favoritism because he was the boss. But he confided to her that he believed as everyone else did: The accident had been her fault. A tire blowout shouldn't cause an SUV to lose control. He'd had two Firestone Wilderness tires delaminate on the Explorer before the big accident and had no trouble controlling the vehicle. All you had to do was to ease off the accelerator and gently pull off the side of the road. She must have hit the brakes or steered the wheel the wrong direction. The bottom line was that she panicked, and now Donna would never be the same.

Tara exploded. "You were the one who bought the car in the first place!" she screamed. "How come it isn't your fault!?" She didn't care that she was being irrational. She had an overwhelming desire to make him pay for abandoning her. She fell into a frenzy, destroying the apartment, breaking pictures and pots her husband had collected—things she believed he loved more than he loved her. She hurled the microwave on the floor. When Kim tried to stop her, Tara flailed at him wildly. For a moment he was able to restrain her, until Tara broke free and stabbed him in his leg with her car keys.

When she calmed down Kim called a psychologist friend of his.

"What's up with this woman?" he asked. "She beat me up." He soon filed for divorce and a restraining order. After meeting with Tara the therapist diagnosed her with "post-traumatic stress disorder" brought on by the accident.

Desperate to leave her troubles behind, Tara skiped town. She stayed with friends in Tulsa, Oklahoma, for three weeks and then flew to Belize for a semester of medical school, but that didn't work out. She kept having flashbacks to the accident, particularly when she was under stress. She would be taking a test or studying something she didn't completely understand and suddenly imagine she was losing control of the Explorer all over again. Her heart rate would shoot up, she'd get all hot and clammy, her body and mind gripped by fear. When she couldn't change the thought, she'd get physically sick and throw up. In class, when they were discussing spinal cord injuries, Tara could see Donna in the car, gasping for air, turning blue. Eyes stung by tears, she had to leave the room. After four months of that, she returned to Texas and stayed with relatives in San Marcos before moving back to Corpus Christi to work on her father's horse farm.

She didn't talk about the accident for the first six months after it happened. Her parents thought it didn't bother her, but it did the whole time, all the time. She'd wake up from naps with a start, see the car careen out of control and catch the feeling of being trapped inside as it fell into a broadside skid about to flip. It was more than she could bear.

While she was being deposed, a sheriff's deputy entered and shoved some papers at her, but Paul LaValle stepped forward to intercept them.

"Don't worry about that," he told her. Tara didn't trust him. She had retained LaValle to sue Ford and Firestone shortly after the accident, as Kevin McCord had. McCord's case didn't go anywhere, but hers was inching ahead—at least according to LaValle. Shouldn't the companies take some responsibility for what they'd done? Shouldn't they pay for the madness they'd caused her? But she didn't like the way LaValle treated her. Although married, he was the kind of guy who would flirt with a parking meter in the off chance it was female. And as far as his lawyering went, Tara didn't get the feeling he was working very hard for her. Like just about everyone else in Tara's life, he had Donna on his mind.

Tara wondered what was inside that envelope. But the questions were coming in a seemingly never-ending stream of subtle indictments and she didn't have time to dwell. Ford's attorney, Fields Alexander, was asking her about the accident. But she felt numb and was having trouble remembering. She wished he'd go away and leave her alone.

"These aren't trying to be trick questions," Alexander promised, obviously dissatisfied with her answers. "I'm just seeking your best recollection."

Shut up shut up shut up, she thought. "Yeah," she managed.

"On the day of the accident, you were headed to Enchanted Rock?"

"Yes."

"What time had you left?"

"I don't know."

"Roughly?"

"I don't remember."

He tried a different approach. "Okay. About how long before the accident happened had you left?"

"I don't know."

When she couldn't recount the accident step by step, Alexander allowed her to consult a statement she had typed up a few days after the accident. It had been Kim's idea. Now she was glad she'd listened to him.

"Tell me what was the first thing you noticed at the start of this accident," Alexander asked.

"The loud bang, noise," Tara said.

"Tell me what happened with respect to that noise."

"It went bang. I'm sorry. I'm not laughing," but she was. She was afraid she was going to lose it again. "I don't know what to say. That there was a loud noise." Tara consulted the paper. "I heard a loud bang in the rear of the car, the car jerked hard to the right, off the road and onto the shoulder."

"What did you do with the steering wheel once the car started to jerk to the right?"

"It says here, 'I steered in the direction of the jerk and lost control of the car.' "

"Which way did the car end up going off the road, the right or the left?

"At what point?"

Alexander asked if the car went off the road to the right. Tara said "yes" and Alexander wanted to know what happened next. But when Tara thought about it, all she saw was Donna hanging upside down, pleading with her eyes for her life. Tara couldn't stem the tears. "Can we take a break for a second?" she asked.

But the lawyers wanted to get through this. *They probably have afternoon tee times*, she thought. Alexander kept prodding. "Follow with me down on the statement," he said. "You see where it says, 'I heard a loud bang in the rear of the car and the car jerked hard to the right?"

"Yes."

"Do you remember telling me just a second ago that you couldn't remember where you heard the sound from?"

"Yes."

"Having looked at this statement, does that refresh your recollection?"

"I still don't remember it, but I wrote it down, so at the time I wrote it down, I remembered it."

Alexander couldn't argue with that. He moved from the "bang" to the car jerking off the road to the right. How far onto the shoulder, he wanted to know.

"I don't know," Tara said.

"Do you remember whether the right two wheels went off onto the shoulder or all four wheels went onto the shoulder?"

"I don't know."

"But the car veered to the right?"

"Yes."

"What lane were you in?"

"It was a two-lane road, so I was in the right lane."

"Okay, after the car veered to the right, did it at some point start going to the left?"

"At some point, yes." Tara was beginning to feel sick again.

Alexander said, "I want your recollection as we sit here today as to the sequence of events from . . . the bang until the car stopped moving. Do you understand my question?"

"No."

He tried to clarify, explaining that he wanted Tara to give him a sort of play by play as to what happened in as much detail as she could muster. Shaking, she volunteered to read her statement. Alexander told her she could but was also interested in what her recollection was "as we sit here today . . . under oath." He asked if she understood.

"Yes."

Good. Perhaps now they were getting somewhere. "Well . . . what is your recollection of the accident as we sit here today?" he asked.

"I don't know," Tara sobbed. "I need to take a break . . ."

When they returned from recess, Alexander said he understood it must be difficult for Tara to relive the accident in this deposition, but it was important for him, on behalf of his client, to get her testimony under oath. He continued to press. "You testified earlier that when the accident first started, the car jerked to the right and you're not sure how far off the road it may have gone," he recounted. "And your testimony is that you don't remember whether it might have been two wheels that went off onto the shoulder or no wheels that went on the shoulder or four wheels that went on the shoulder when it first went to the right."

"Yes," she said.

"After it veered to the right at the beginning, what happened? Did it begin to come back to the left?"

"I don't remember."

"Do you recall what side of the road the Ford Explorer ended up on at the end of the accident?"

"The opposite side of the road."

"It would have been as you're driving . . . your left side?"

"Yes."

"So your recollection is . . . the Ford Explorer veered to the right, and then at some point, obviously, it came back to the left because you ended up on the left side in the shoulder."

"Yes."

"Do you recall how it was that the Ford began to move to the left after it started moving to the right?"

"No."

"Do you remember what you did with the steering wheel when you first heard the bang and the car started moving to the right?"

"No."

He requested that she review her written statement. "So when you're saying here that you steered in the direction of the jerk, you steered the steering wheel to the right?"

"Yes."

"Is that your recollection today or is that just what you're reading from this exhibit?"

"That is my recollection today."

"Okay. So when the car began to pull to the right, you also steered to the right?"

"Yes."

"Do you know how it was that the Ford Explorer began moving to the left after it started moving to the right?"

"It went into a broadside skid," Tara said, "up the highway."

"When you say, 'it went into a broadside skid,' which direction was the nose of the car pointing?"

"Left."

"Was the rear of the car perpendicular to the road?"

"At what point?"

"During the broadside skid."

"Oh, I don't know."

"Do you remember telling me a minute ago that during the skid, the front of the car, the nose of the car was pointing to the left?"

"No. Did I say that? I'm just getting confused with lefts and rights and . . ."

Alexander asked if it would be easier if they drew a diagram. When he handed her a blank piece of paper she shook her head. "This is not going to help you?" he asked.

"I thought *you* were going to draw a diagram."

Alexander started over. He wasn't leaving until he'd captured her entire testimony. "After you heard the pop or the bang and the car veered to the right . . ."

Three-quarters of an hour into her inquisition and Tara had barely made it out of the parking lot. And it would just get worse, as she was forced to tell her story over and over in fits and starts, sighs and sobs: "Turned in the direction of the fishtails . . . unable to gain control . . . felt as if the back end was coming back around so we would do a 180 . . . eventually we hit the opposite shoulder . . . car began to flip . . . cartwheeling . . . end over end . . . back over front . . . flipped a couple of times . . . rolled over again . . . all kind of a blur . . . landed upside down . . . so I don't—fuck, I don't know. I don't know . . . asked if everybody else was okay . . . Kevin said he was fine . . . Donna didn't . . . got out between the driver's side door and the ground . . . a rearview mirror . . . sticks down, giving enough space to crawl out . . ."

"When you got out of the car and looked back in—I'm going to give you a minute," Alexander said.

"It won't help," Tara replied. "Go ahead."

She continued to relive those terrifying moments immediately after the accident, when all she had to rely on were instinct and training. Donna was "hanging from her seatbelt . . . her, her arms, her hands [were] really, really blue gasping . . . mouth opening and shutting . . . eyes open and glazed . . . but not what I would consider conscious . . . Kevin . . . tried to reach in the window [but] couldn't . . . tried to peel back windshield . . . couldn't . . . I crawled back in through my window . . . unhooked the seat belt . . . [Donna] slid down the seat into my arms . . . brought her down to my arms with her head resting on the inside of my elbows . . . and got her out."

"How is it," Alexander asked, "that you know she was paralyzed immediately after the accident and not after she was taken out of the car?"

So not only does he think I caused the accident, he's implying I paralyzed her by pulling her out of the wreckage? "Because she never achieved any level of muscle tone," Tara said.

"What do you mean by that? I'm not an EMT."

"She . . . she had . . . her muscles were completely flaccid."

"And is that something you have been taught in your EMT training?"

"I don't remember that."

"How was it that you knew that not showing muscle tone indicated to you that she was already paralyzed?

"I don't remember."

Alexander moved on. He asked about her educational background, medical training, how often she brought the car in to be serviced at Jiffy Lube, but the worst was over—until it was Firestone's turn. Attorney Ann Hennis produced the police report, which stated that after the right rear tire blew out the driver "applied brakes and went into a broadside skid crossing both lanes of US 181 . . . then overturned on the west side of the roadway." An accompanying diagram contradicted everything Tara had told Alexander under oath. It showed that the Explorer shot left after the tread separated, slid sideways then did a clockwise 360 before shooting off the road.

"I don't recall applying the brakes," Tara protested. "I don't know if that was their idea or if I said that or whatever. And I don't remember spinning around like they have the drawing done. Who writes these, the police?"

"Typically, the investigating officer does," Hennis answered coldly.

"And the diagram doesn't show how you described that broadside skid. Is that correct?"

"No, it doesn't."

"And how you described it veering to the right, it doesn't have that in there either. Right?"

"No, it doesn't."

"But all the other factual information with regard to your age and all the other information about the occupants, all that is correct?"

Tara thought she detected a note of sarcasm. She hated this woman more than anyone in the world, except for maybe this Ford attorney— and all the other people who believed she had paralyzed Donna. "Yes," she managed.

When Hennis was done, Alexander asked her the name of the psychotherapist she saw in Tulsa, but Tara couldn't remember.

"Was it a male or female?" he asked.

"It was a female."

"Do you remember the name of her office?"

"No," she said, afraid they'd tell her she was crazy. "No."

"And she is the only therapist or counselor or psychologist that you've seen since the accident?"

"I don't remember. I can't remember right now."

"You might have seen another one, but you can't recall?

"Yes. I cannot recall."

Then they let her go, and not a moment too soon.

LATER, LAVALLE TOLD TARA WHAT WAS IN THE ENVELOPE the sheriff 's deputy had tried to give her during the deposition. Ford was suing her, asserting the accident was due to "driver error." He told her not to worry. It was all part of the game, and advised her to talk to Guy Allison, who would be representing her on behalf of her insurance company. LaValle couldn't be her lawyer anymore. Tara asked why and he mumbled something about a conflict of interest. When she protested, LaValle asked her if she wanted Donna to get the most money she could. "Of course," Tara said. Then call Guy Allison, he said, giving her the number.

"I work with topless dancers," Allison bragged the first time he met Tara at his office. He explained that some strippers had retained his firm in a labor dispute. Tara waited for the inevitable pro-bono joke. Allison might have been on this planet for close to seven decades but he hadn't lost his eye for beauty. And Tara knew he didn't really didn't mean anything by it. It was just his way of trying to lighten the situation. But Tara couldn't help but wonder if there were some law she didn't know about that required Texas attorneys to hit on their female clients. When she was divorcing her first husband, she called Kim Cox to handle it, since he had dealt with an estate-related issue for her years earlier. He asked if she had any money and Tara said no. So he said, "Will you go out with me then?" and foolish her, she said yes.

After chatting awhile Allison told Tara she looked depressed and that he had just the thing. He called his doctor on the phone to fill a prescription for an anti-depressant in his wife's name. He told Tara it would perk her right up. Allison drove her to the pharmacy and picked it up. Afterward he called his wife on his cell phone and he told her he was with Tara in the car. His wife asked, "Are you fucking her?" and Allison laughed. "Not yet," he said.

When Tara got home she tossed the drugs in the trash and tried not to think about testifying at the trial. As bad as the deposition was, she knew a courtroom could be far worse.

She wouldn't find out until later that Donna also sued her. Ford alleged driver error, and Donna's lawyers, as a matter of course, were obligated to file a cross claim in the off chance a jury decided she was due compensation. That was why LaValle wouldn't be her lawyer anymore. He represented Donna and couldn't very well represent both the sue-er and the sue-ee.

Now everybody blamed her: Ford, Firestone, Kim, all of Donna's friends, and even Donna. To Tara the cycle of betrayal was complete.

29 'X'

RICK CAME TO SEE DONNA AT TIRR almost every night after work, when he would apprise his sister of the latest developments in her case. As the trial date approached, the lawyers urged him to sell his Explorer, which he did to avoid any potential snickering from the press and public. He prepared Donna for the onslaught of media they expected, and advised her on how to handle herself in the event Ford offered to settle the case: "No matter what they offer turn it down and wait for them to come back with a better offer," he said. "That was just sound business practice." Donna told him what she wanted more than anything went beyond money. She wanted an apology: broadcast on TV and radio, splashed on magazine covers and the front pages of newspapers, and plastered across 80-foot billboards. She was living proof that large corporations like Ford and Firestone took advantage of people, ruining their lives and the lives of their children for a few extra dollars when they knew full well their products were dangerous. Although Donna wouldn't trade an apology for the money she would need to survive this ordeal (she wasn't crazy, after all), just once she wished one of them would stand up and say he was sorry for the harm they had caused.

It had been a rough few weeks for her. She had been in a lot of pain recently. Her skin felt like it was on fire. Medication had kept it under control until she went to her brother's house for Thanksgiving—the only time she'd left the hospital since the accident save for a museum outing— and the ride there had been so bumpy it jangled her nerve endings. Now every time someone touched her was utter agony. She couldn't even stand wearing clothes. It was both painful and humiliating. The doctors upped her dosage and it hurt less now, but the sensation never really went away. They warned she would always have good and bad days.

Nevertheless Donna was in good spirits. Two days earlier she found out she had gotten her legal rights back. She appreciated that her daughter Cassie had assumed responsibility for her when she was in a bad way, but now Donna took solace in the fact that she had control of her life. This meant a lot to her. She might not be able to bathe or feed herself, or even breathe without a machine, but at least in the eyes of the law she was the equal of any man or woman.

It had been the lawyers who suggested it. After the meeting with Turner and Watts a month earlier, the family dynamics had heated up. Everybody seemed to have a different opinion on everything and nobody was shy about expressing it. LaValle told her it would simplify matters and streamline the decision-making process if Donna—who was clearly of sound mind if not body—was put back in charge. Rick immediately agreed. He had been bending over backwards to make sure Donna's wishes were fulfilled. This would be one less burden for him to carry.

After Rick had left for the day, Donna was still awake when Paul LaValle came to visit. If Donna didn't know any better she'd swear LaValle had come by this late to avoid her brother, who made it a habit of leaving Lifebridge by 8:30 p.m. Rick and LaValle were like two tomcats trapped in an alley, always snarling, clawing at each other. She was glad her younger brother stuck up for her, but she believed she could handle LaValle herself.

After a bit of breezy conversation, LaValle told Donna he had a piece of paper that acknowledged the transfer of her rights back to her. He said that to pursue her case he needed her to sign. LaValle had already filled it out for her.

This made sense to Donna, who was thrilled to do something for herself for a change. With her consent, LaValle stuck a pen in her mouth and held the paper up to her face so she could mark it with an "X." When she was done, LaValle left.

What he didn't tell Donna was that nothing on that paper mentioned anything about her rights. She had signed a new contingent fee contract that gave LaValle, Turner, and Watts "40 percent of any gross recovery . . . before the commencement of trial, and 45 percent of any gross recovery after commencement of trial."

The new agreement also contained a number of stipulations not contained in the original contract of employment Rick had negotiated with LaValle eight months earlier. It mandated that Donna couldn't agree to a settlement without LaValle's permission. It reserved the right for LaValle to withdraw from the case if Donna didn't follow his professional advice, and offered him compensation if he did. It awarded him power of attorney.

LaValle had taken away the one thing Donna had left. She would never forgive him for this.

30 Ghosts In The Machines

When a reporter from the *Corpus Christi Caller-Times* called a few days before Christmas, Paul LaValle couldn't help himself. It was about time he'd gotten some attention. Maybe Tab Turner and Mikal Watts had big names with even bigger reputations, but the *Caller* was LaValle's hometown paper. There was a chance that LaValle might enter politics one day. Maybe even run for mayor. He'd be damned if he'd turn down a chance to get his name out there in the community. Besides, a little publicity might help him land more cases.

"We have the full attention of the Ford board of directors and Firestone and all the attorneys [suing the companies]," LaValle bragged. "I get calls every day from attorneys about the trial date, because . . . in essence, we're going to be providing the recipe for other attorneys to follow." Although the accident had taken place near San Antonio, the lawsuit was filed in Corpus Christi because that's where the Explorer Bailey was riding in had been purchased. The plaintiffs sued the dealer too, but LaValle confessed he didn't believe Crosstown acted with malice or independent knowledge that the Explorer was unsafe. "In order to show chain of custody or how the vehicle was put in the stream of commerce, we have to include" Crosstown.

In Texas, Ford and Firestone had a built-in safety net. Legal reforms enacted by then-Gov. George W. Bush limited the size of any damage award. Punitive damages were capped at twice "economic damages" (such as medical bills and lost pay) while damages for pain and suffering were limited to $750,000. But Turner, Watts, and LaValle were able to get around this by estimating the cost of Donna's lifetime medical care in excess of $30 million. In total, Bailey and her family would seek more than $100 million for pain and suffering, mental anguish, disfigurement, loss of ability to earn wages, medical expenses, and other losses. "It sounds like we're talking big dollars," LaValle told the *Caller*, "but how do you put a price on the ability to give your kids a hug at night? I mean, what are your legs worth to you? You use them every day."

Donna Bailey was quoted in the story, too, but it was LaValle's comments that almost made Turner spit up his coffee. He quickly dashed off an e-mail. "You've got to stop this immediately," he ordered. "None of us mind your talking about how sweet Donna is, but do not mention facts, money, settlement, liability, or anything other than Donna. Ford could use your comments about why the dealer is a party to get this case removed to federal court. If that happens everything goes down the shitter. Please, please, keep a lid on it. These chances don't come around very often. . . . The best thing you could do is say nothing to the media and refer them to Mikal Watts. Help us, Paul."

A few days after Christmas, Turner was in Little Rock preparing to move to Corpus Christi for the trial. Sitting around his family's dinner table with his three daughters, Turner held up a picture of Donna Bailey taken before the accident. This was a ritual he went through whenever he left home for long periods of time. He wanted them to understand that he didn't want to go away. He had to. People were counting on him. He knew that from now on, when he called them every night just before bedtime, they would ask about Donna, how she was doing, how her kids were holding up.

"This is who I'm representing," he said. Turner put down the photo of Donna and picked up one of the battered Explorer, which looked like a discarded candy wrapper. "This is the car she was in." He let them study it for a few seconds then showed them another picture of Donna lying on a hospital bed. "This is what she looks like now."

As usual Turner's oldest daughter, 14-year-old Abby, asked the most detailed questions. "What happened in the accident?" "Why isn't Ford taking care of her?" The younger girls were more interested in Donna's kids. They asked what they looked like, what grade they were in. Turner said he thought Cassie was a high school senior and Jeremiah had just begun high school. They all understand the importance of the case because they had seen him on television discussing it. When he had taken Abby to junior high school football games, Turner was surrounded by other parents concerned about their tires and cars. Most of the time they had non-Decatur tires, which meant they weren't covered by the recall. Turner would advise them to switch them anyway. He'd tell them to visit the Exxon station on North Hills Boulevard and McCain St. in North Little Rock, and say Tab Turner sent them. There they would get a discount on a new set of tires and Turner would take the old ones off their hands and have them tested for signs of tread separation.

By the time Turner left for Corpus Christi, negotiations with Firestone were almost complete. Over the past month and a half, Turner, Watts and Zummo had participated in a half-dozen discussions—in Akron, at Zummo's office in Houston, at Watts' firm in Corpus Christi— and were about to meet in Miami. They had come to terms on Bailey when Firestone agreed to pay her $15 million. As per their initial agreement, they kept the settlement secret for the time being, until the trial with Ford could begin.

In a gesture of goodwill CEO John Lampe offered to send Donna a handwritten note to express his sincere condolences: "There is nothing any of us at Firestone can say or do to return to you what you and your family have lost," Lampe wrote. "All we can do is try and help you take care of your needs and those of your family. I am hopeful that with this settlement you can begin to do so. To be sure, this has been a tragedy. Yet your valiant resolve, your spirit and your quiet dignity are an inspiration to us all. Please know that I carry you and your family with me in my thoughts, and that you have my best regards and my respect."

Over New Year's, Turner and Watts met with Zummo to hammer out details to the final part of their plan. Firestone agreed to settle every single ATX case Turner had based only on accident reports, photographs of the tires, death certificates, and medical records. Part of the deal was that all future cases would fall within these ranges: there would be no going back. Firestone found this appealing because it wiped away a large block of lawsuits without the need for more litigation. Turner liked it because it cleared dozens of outstanding claims.

In the first round of negotiations Turner and Firestone came to terms on 25 cases in one night, totaling about $150 million, the amounts ranging between $3 million to $11 million—depending on the severity of the injuries. Then the attorneys celebrated by taking in the National Championship college football game on Jan. 3, 2001, at Miami's Pro Player stadium, where Oklahoma beat Florida State 13–2 in the Orange Bowl.

THE FOLLOWING AFTERNOON TURNER WAS ALONE, walking among the dead: 17 trampled Explorers in an abandoned Ford dealership, all of which once rode on Firestone tires and had badly crushed roofs. The Explorers came in a Seussian array of colors—red, blue, tan, white—set about 10 feet apart, laid out in a semicircle, with Bailey's in the middle, while damaged Firestone tires were scattered about. Turner had hired a trucking company to make five trips from Little Rock to Corpus Christi in an 18-wheeler, then had the place spiffed up until it was spotless.

Visiting his collection of battered Explorers in the days leading up to trial offered Turner a mental image in a way no photograph could. He viewed it as a vital step in preparing for trial. It enabled him in some cosmic way to almost relive the events. He would look at each Explorer in turn and try to imagine what it must have felt like for the passengers as their worlds came crashing down around them. He could almost hear the squeal of tires, the screams, the shattering glass and crunching steel.

He touched the hood of the Explorer that had once held José and Emma Pupo Fernandez and closed his eyes, visualizing their accident. They were involved in a violent crash on May 23, 1999, in Palm Beach County, Florida, when their left rear tire separated and they rolled over. José was killed while Emma Pupo, who was eight months pregnant, suffered severe injuries. Her baby Emma Teresa died three days later at a local hospital.

Turner moved on. He came to the Explorer that 28-year-old Scott Erickson was driving when he was killed, leaving behind his wife, Lori, who was expecting their first child. Then he arrived at Yogesh Jagasia's Explorer, which had killed three members of his family. Next was the one that belonged to Chris Houston, who had just gotten engaged when his life came to an abrupt end six months earlier after a tread separation.

He stopped at James Taintor's Explorer. Taintor, 26, and his 25-year-old wife Elizabeth, had been two of the lucky ones. His skull was fractured and he was in a coma for weeks after the rollover, while Elizabeth suffered serious cuts, abrasions, two herniated discs, and a mild concussion. Turner smiled when he remembered how he had been privileged to spend time with them during the congressional hearings, when he invited them to Washington. Although they would always suffer from their injuries, that hadn't dampened their spirit for life.

Mothers who'd lost children; wives who'd lost husbands; fathers who'd lost sons; young couples in the prime of their lives faced with staggering disfigurements and disabilities. The latest tally was that 148 people had died in Ford Explorer rollover accidents after Firestone tread separations, hundreds more seriously injured. There were ghosts in these machines. Turner promised he would exorcize them.

In the haunting silence, Turner tried to recall every single Explorer client he had ever had. There were more than 100, and the number was growing every day. Critics and cynics might claim the only sound Tab Turner ever heard was the ringing of the cash register. After all, his take on Bailey's settlement with Firestone alone would come to more than $3 million. But he would have accepted a lot less to battle Ford and Firestone, companies he believed had little regard for human life. He knew a major reason the issue had become so firmly etched in the public consciousness was because it affected people who were middle class on up—from congressmen to senators, teachers to doctors, lawyers and judges and small-business owners. Where Ford and Firestone saw consumers, Turner saw flesh and blood.

Although it was true he thrived on the heat of battle—the strategizing and brinkmanship—and loved performing on the big stage, what really drove Turner was the belief that he was doing good in a world often filled with bad. At the end of the day he could look into the mirror and like what he saw. He wondered if Ford and Firestone's attorneys could say the same.

Turner understood that the stakes were higher in Donna Bailey's case than in any other he'd undertaken. It would have a profound impact no matter what happened. If he lost, Donna might not survive. If he won, it would underscore what Turner had been saying all along about the Explorer—that it was inherently unstable—just as Ford was planning to unveil its 2002 edition, which had been expressly redesigned to eliminate rollovers. The pressure on NHTSA to expand the recall would also increase exponentially, even though Firestone had settled, because the tire had not been covered by August's take-back. It was life and death for all sides.

He looked forward to justifying to the court why Donna Bailey deserved every penny. He couldn't wait to tell jurors everything he had learned about the Ford Explorer over the last decade. He tried to imagine what their reaction would be when Donna Bailey was flown into court to testify accompanied by a team of doctors at her side. In court pleadings Ford said the driver overreacted by turning too sharply when the tread disintegrated, but Turner wanted to see jurors' faces when he showed them Mark Arndt's crash test video.

The last few days had been hectic. Ford and Firestone had made their experts available only a week before trial, and in some cases double- and triple-booked them, so Watts and Turner would have to have been in three different states at once to question them. But Turner and Watts revved up their jets to fly a half dozen of Watt's best and brightest attorneys to every deposition, taking on the most important ones themselves.

In 16 hours, Judge Hasette would entertain a series of key motions; "the paper war," Turner called it. She would rule on plaintiffs' requests to allow the jury to visit this warehouse to see these crumpled Ford Explor-

ers and compel CEO Jacques Nasser to testify. She would decide on Ford
motions to exclude Turner's experts and Arndt's crash test video, to leave
out accident data and limit the scope of evidence—anything that could
reflect poorly on Ford. And she would entertain yet another plea from
automaker attorneys for a continuance. But Turner hadn't lost one
motion this whole trial and didn't expect to now.

Turner took one last look at the wrecked Explorers and said a little
prayer for the victims. When he was finished he shut off the lights and
locked up.

31 Terms of Surrender

TURNER KNEW FORD WAS SERIOUS when he noticed the overnight bags. He and Watts were in court that morning to discuss the flurry of motions both sides filed when Doug Seitz, one of Ford's attorneys, informed them that some executives from Detroit were flying to Corpus and wanted to meet. This wasn't Ford's first attempt at discussing the Bailey case. A month earlier, Turner had been negotiating another case with Ford lead counsel Bob Grant, when Grant said, "I don't want to talk about that, I want to talk about the hurricane brewing in Corpus Christi." Turner told him he wasn't interested. Grant said, "You'll have to talk to us sometime" and Turner replied, "That's fine. We'll talk sometime."

In the interim, Ford, confronting more than 200 rollover lawsuits, had gone on a settlement spree, reaching agreements on a slew of Explorer cases around the country. Representing six of the plaintiffs was Bruce Kaster, who told *USA Today* three of the suits didn't have a trial date and three others hadn't even been filed yet. One of the lawsuits Kaster came to terms on involved Medhat Labib—the case Kaster had been working on when he began his long drive across the state to unseal Firestone records four months earlier. Ford also contacted Watts about settling 30 cases his firm had filed, but he told the automaker he planned to take Donna Bailey's case to trial before settling any others.

Turner told Seitz the Ford executives could meet him at Watts' office, and he and Watts quickly formulated a good cop/bad cop strategy. They figured Ford would lowball them, then get back on the plane and fly home. After their session in court they returned to Watts' office, when they realized the automaker had sent the one man at Ford who could sign off on a settlement without needing permission from above: John Mellon, head of the company's product liability section. Turner used to deal with him often when he was a mere legal foot soldier for the corporation—until he was promoted up the ladder and got too good to deal directly with the likes of Tab Turner. But here he was, ready to talk settlement. With him were Jonas Saunders and Peter Tassie, who had recently settled an Explorer case with Watts. All three Ford lawyers had brought overnight bags.

They gathered in a conference room, the Ford attorneys on one side of the table, Turner and Watts 20 feet away at the other end. Since Firestone hadn't filed any motions in a while, and its personnel in depositions had been getting pretty much a free ride, Ford knew something was up.

While Watts broke the ice, Turner sat sullenly. When Watts finished, Turner told the Ford lawyers there wasn't "enough money on God's green earth to settle this case." The only reason he was here at all was because Watts had asked him. As he stood to leave, he glared at them and said, "See you in court." Then he repaired to another room to continue work on the case. It was Friday afternoon and jury selection was set to begin Tuesday morning.

Negotiations spanned the rest of the day and ran into night. Every once in a while Watts would leave the Ford attorneys to consult with Turner, whose standard reply was, "Nope, not enough."

But a settlement was in the air. CBS reporter Sharyl Attkisson had a feeling the Bailey case might settle when she couldn't track Turner down. She had been reporting on Ford and Firestone so long, at times she imagined the companies sending henchmen to trail her after some of her more critical reports. She had "this paranoid fear" that on her long drive home she would end up "a mystery accident late at night" since it was "so easy for one of them to do something to your tires." The story had become such a part of her life that for Christmas she gave tire pressure gauges as stocking stuffers to family members. A few days earlier in a gut-swirling interview with Donna for CBS News, she filmed her undergoing painful rehabilitation.

"A year ago," Donna Bailey "was a poster child for adventure sports," Attkisson intoned. "Now, she's a symbol of the Ford/Firestone fiasco." The last thing Donna recalled before waking up in the hospital was that "the car rolled over and I broke my neck. And I can remember just watching my friend try to kick in the windshield to get me out and that I couldn't breathe or move." She confessed to Attkisson it had been hardest on her children, who in essence had lost their mother in the rollover.

Attkisson had another piece ready to run the night before jury selection and needed to know minute by minute whether or not the case would be going to trial. Between leaving Turner several phone messages, each more frantic than the last, she managed to buttonhole other attorneys who believed a settlement must be at hand. But Turner, with nothing new to tell her, continued to duck her calls.

Late in the evening, Watts came to Turner with an offer for about $12 million. It wasn't as much as Firestone had paid, but at this point in the litigation, with public opinion squarely against Firestone and their own surveys revealing the general jury pool believed the accident was Firestone's fault, they decided to accept it. But that didn't mean negotiations were over by a long shot. Turner had a number of "non-economic" terms he wanted added to the settlement.

Watts told the Ford attorneys it was important that Donna Bailey's case stand for something more than money. No matter how much Ford paid her, Donna would still be in a wheelchair the rest of her life. The plaintiffs demanded that Ford unseal documents involving the Bronco and Explorer, including early Explorer stability tests in which the vehicle tipped up on two wheels, memorandums from Ford to Firestone ordering the tire maker to take weight out of the tire to aid in fuel economy and cut cost, and directives from Ford setting tire pressure at 26 psi to lower the center of gravity to help prevent rollovers. They wanted it stipulated that whenever Ford submitted documents to NHTSA or Congress, that Turner and Watts would receive copies within 15 days. Finally they asked Ford to perform a "root cause" investigation.

In the stillness of early morning, Watts informed Turner that Ford had finally capitulated. Before Turner would accept Ford's surrender, however, he had one more demand. When Watts heard it he laughed out loud.

NEITHER TURNER NOR WATTS GOT MUCH SLEEP, but they were wired nevertheless. They dropped by Donna Bailey's room to tell her the news and explain the terms of the settlement and the impact it would have on other cases. Not only was it the biggest personal injury settlement in an auto crash case in history and would set the bar higher for the hundreds of lawsuits against Ford and Firestone to follow, it would also pull the lid off of important data that until then the companies had always been able to keep secret. Bailey's case would go down in textbooks as a watershed in litigation. There was one more thing. Ford attorneys were on their way over to apologize in person.

Bailey met her attorneys' gaze then stretched her lips in a smile. "Y'all are mean," she said.

Not long after, Mellon, Tassie, and Saunders made their way down TIRR's hallways, doing their best to ignore the video camera capturing their every step. Part of the deal was that Turner could tape them apologizing, as long as the sound was turned off. The camera caught them opening the door and entering her room, gathering at the foot of Donna's bed as Turner moved aside.

Mikal Watts introduced them and the Ford attorneys took turns expressing their sincere condolences. They told her they felt for her, and although they didn't come out and say they were sorry, to Donna they seemed humble and sincere.

After the Ford attorneys left, Turner had one more thing to take care of. He called Sharyl Attkisson, who had become downright abusive in some of her voice mails. When she picked up he said, "You won't believe this . . ."

That evening on the *CBS Evening News*, Attkisson reported, "On the eve of what was to be the first trial an eleventh hour deal: quadriplegic Donna Bailey settled. An extraordinary ending to the case Ford and Firestone feared the most. Bailey will now get undisclosed millions to pay for the care she needs for the rest of her life. But what's most remarkable are the other terms."

She broadcast part of the tape Turner provided after she dispatched a courier to bring it to the local CBS affiliate in Corpus Christi. While Mellon, Tassie, and Saunders stood by her bedside, Attkisson narrated: "Bailey wanted a personal apology from Ford. And last night, three top Ford attorneys quietly climbed on a plane, flew to her hospital bedside, and apologized face-to-face." She then cut to Donna who said, "The gist of the whole thing was that they were truly sorry for what . . . happened to me, and I felt like it was very sincere."

After the segment ran, a Ford spokesperson called Attkisson to ask why she was doing this to them. The spokesperson claimed visiting Donna Bailey at her bedside had been Ford's idea all along. Then Ford released a statement claiming the automaker had not apologized. It had merely been offering its sympathies.

Donna knew it hadn't been an out-and-out apology, but she took it as one. She had been through too much to let it bring her down and had a lifetime to worry about. At least now she wouldn't have to fret over how she would pay for her medical needs or care for her children.

She was rich woman. But she would give it all back and then some for the life she had been living the day before the accident, when no rock was too high to scale, no road too steep to run, no river too dangerous to traverse. Her son Jeremiah had grown almost a foot since she'd been in the hospital, and she'd missed her teenaged daughter Cassie flower into a young woman. Donna would never again experience the feeling of being with a man, the rush of rappelling down Enchanted Rock, the burn of a hard run, the hugs of friends and family, the simple joy of making her way through the world when the only limitations she faced had been from within. All that was now gone.

Ford and Firestone could never give her back what she'd lost. Still, this was the best she could have hoped for under the circumstances—and she was grateful.

32 SEVEN-PERCENT SOLUTION

RICK WAS AWAY ON A MUCH-NEEDED ski vacation in Vail, Colorado, when he caught Ford's apology on TV. Before he hopped a plane home, he called Donna to ask why she had accepted the company's first settlement offer. Hadn't he advised her to turn it down no matter what? That was basic deal making 101. But Donna hushed him. "Mind your business," she said. "It's my life and I can do what I want."

He realized she was right. Donna didn't need him anymore. The minute she had gotten her rights back, she was in charge of her life again. Rick had tried to fulfill Donna's wishes all along, no matter how he felt about her choices. But this wasn't his rodeo; it was God's rodeo. He knew he had to let go.

But nine days later, Donna called Rick in a panic. LaValle had dropped by Donna's room with the dispersal agreement for her signature. Because she and Rick had discussed the issues she knew how much to expect after more than $2 million was deducted for legal expenses and medical bills. The cost of her stay in San Antonio had been $500,000. TIRR was almost $300,000 and growing every day. The sip and puff wheelchair went for $60,000. Remodeling Donna's mother's house for wheelchair access, another $28,000. Tire and vehicle experts charged tens of thousands of dollars. Every time Turner or Watts cranked up their jets it cost $4,500. Hotel rooms, phone bills, fax charges, postage due, restaurant bills, per diems. She accepted all of it as part of the cost of bringing the lawsuits. But she when she got to the final tally she was shocked to learn she had been shortchanged by $1.7 million.

There must be a mistake, she said. The lawyers were only supposed to receive a contingency fee of 33 percent, not 40 percent. When she questioned LaValle about it, he whipped out the contingency fee contract he had gotten her to sign a month earlier and pointed to the "X" next to her name.

Blinking back tears she accused him of tricking her and LaValle turned cruel. He told her if he could fool her so easily, maybe she wasn't mentally competent to handle her own affairs. Perhaps she shouldn't have petitioned to get her rights back after all.

When Rick heard about this he flew into a rage. He immediately phoned LaValle, and between curses and insults said, "I can't believe you would do that to her."

LaValle tried to pacify Rick by saying there were things he didn't know about his sister. He claimed Donna had said she "wanted to be treated like everyone else." When LaValle told her what he usually charged she agreed to the 40 percent fee. Rick ordered LaValle to be at the hospital at 8 a.m. for a meeting—and to bring Turner.

Rick slept little and drank a lot that night, ending up at Donna's room at the crack of dawn. She told him she wanted to go home. Rick had lined up care managers and a caseworker. Their mom's house had been remodeled and Donna was ready to move in. But Rick explained the only way they would get the money to make this happen was to sign the dispersal form. Until then everything was on hold. Donna was inconsolable. The last thing she could afford was a protracted legal battle over lawyer fees. She had been so close to going home, and now she didn't know where she would be. Rick promised he would take care of it.

At 8 a.m. LaValle and Turner showed up and Rick pounced. They went to a hospital conference room and Rick pointed to the dispersal form. He told the lawyers they would receive $8.7 million for their efforts, not the $10.4 million they were charging. Rick produced the original employment contract that LaValle had signed in April 2000. In response LaValle produced three other contracts he had signed with the Bailey family, each of which stipulated a contingency fee of 40 percent.

Rick was stunned as he leafed through them. In the case of the first one that his brother Tim signed and Rick witnessed, he clearly remembered LaValle assuring them the initial employment agreement took precedence, and not to worry about the clause that awarded a 40 percent contingency. He just needed the new agreement to get the vehicle out of hock from the salvage yard. As for the other two, Rick hadn't even seen them before.

What about this one? LaValle asked. It was dated Aug. 11 and signed by Donna's ex-husband Michael Bailey.

"You can't do this!" Rick hollered. "Michael had no authority to sign anything." His blood pressure was approaching stroke level. He quickly set up a conference call with Michael Bailey, who said he signed the contract under the impression LaValle needed it to file legal paperwork. He hadn't been aware of the higher contingency fee and agreed he did not have the legal right to represent Donna's interests. Rick threatened to contact the ethics board and go to the state attorney general's office. "You will not fuck us!" he screamed.

Turner had heard enough. He hadn't even known this was an issue until this morning. He thought the meeting was to tie up loose ends and sign the dispersal sheet. LaValle had neglected to tell him about Rick calling to complain about the fees. Although public perception was that Turner acted as LaValle's boss, that was not how things worked. LaValle, as with all other referral lawyers, was in charge of all client communications. He met with family members, gave status reports, and dealt with the various issues that popped up. All Turner knew about the family was what LaValle told him. He had learned a long time ago that the bigger the settlement, the bigger the post-settlement disputes. Rarely had he negotiated a large settlement where some family member wasn't upset about something. Sometimes it was how much experts billed. Sometimes it was crash test costs. Sometimes it was the fee. That was just life.

Turner didn't handle the money in his office. That was why he had staff. When he saw the dispersal form for Bailey a few days before, it had been calculated at the 33 percent rate. He e-mailed it to LaValle and Watts to check over. Later that day his assistant talked with LaValle, who informed her that the fee was actually 40 percent. Turner assumed LaValle had gotten the family's permission to raise the fee. He didn't think much about it until he arrived at the hospital.

LaValle tried to justify the most recent contract he had in his hands, the one Donna X-ed in December when she got her rights back. After meeting Donna, Turner found it hard to believe that LaValle could have fooled her into signing anything. A week earlier, when Turner explained the terms of the settlements to her, she was powerful of mind and spirit. She seemed to understand everything he told her and her eyes burned with the recognition her legal battle was about to come to an end. LaValle's explanation that Donna wanted to be treated just like every other client had the ring of truth to it. But, as Rick pointed out, the Dec. 13 contract was not legally binding because it was signed after a trial date had been set. It was highly unusual for attorney-client contracts to change during the course of litigation. It was also rare that a vehicle defect case went for less than a 40 percent contingency.

   Turner interrupted LaValle in mid-sentence and told him to be quiet.
"Let me handle this," he said. LaValle was just getting Rick in a lather
anyway. If LaValle really had the conversation he claimed he did with
the family to raise the fees, why didn't he document it? Turner also found
it fishy that LaValle had not gotten Rick's signature on any of the contracts stipulating a 40 percent fee, since there was no question Rick had
been the one handling Donna's affairs. Given the facts, if he were Rick
he would have been angry, too.
   When faced with situations like this, Turner would ask himself what
his father would have done. Although Turner resented being drawn into
this tussle, he was pleased it would be relatively easy to resolve. Turner
voided the second agreement and told Rick they would abide by the first.
   What was sad to Turner was the case against Ford and Firestone had
resulted in a record-breaking settlement for the Bailey family. Instead of
focusing on how great it was, this dispute would stick with Rick like a
bad disease.
   Turner checked his watch. He had a deposition in Houston later that
day and then could return to Little Rock. It dawned on him he hadn't
been able to spend a lot of time with his three little girls in the last few
weeks, and missed them terribly. He called his pilot to set a flight plan so
he could leave right after the deposition.
   "We're going home," he said.

33 THE LETTER

FOUR MONTHS AFTER DONNA BAILEY SETTLED, Firestone chief executive John Lampe was in Cuernavaca, Mexico, attending a banquet in his honor, schmoozing in Spanish with Mexican dealers and their wives, when his cell phone rang. It was late, around 11 o'clock on a Thursday night in May 2001, which meant it must be important. While couples danced to mariachi music, Lampe strained to listen to the person on the other end. What he heard shook him to the core.

Executives convened an emergency meeting at company headquarters and were telling Lampe to get back to Nashville as soon as possible. They heard that in a few days Ford planned to announce a massive recall, which would pull almost every Firestone tire on every Ford vehicle off the road. Keith Bradsher of the *New York Times* phoned company publicists to get Firestone's response to an article he was running the following morning, reporting that Ford had concluded there were problems with millions of tires not covered by the August 2000 recall, and that the automaker was leaning toward forcing Firestone to take them back.

Lampe knew he shouldn't have been surprised. Relations between the two companies had remained tense even after the recall faded from the news. A month after Lampe had called on regulators to investigate the Explorer as well as the tires at Senate hearings, he traveled to Dearborn to meet with Nasser in the hopes they might begin to smooth things over. But Nasser was not in a forgiving mood, telling Lampe he was "very displeased, very unhappy," with Firestone and didn't appreciate its conduct as a supplier. Firestone had also gotten wind that Ford was talking to other tire companies about upping their production.

While the two companies worked feverishly to replace 6.5 million tires in the original recall, completing this Herculean task in four months instead of the year they thought it would take, both struggled. Firestone was fighting for its life, as growing numbers of consumers were opting for competitors' brands on new and old cars alike. Ford's well-being was threatened by two embarrassing recalls on its redesigned 2002 Explorer, a wider variety of snazzy SUV models marketed by competitors, and by a sluggish economy.

Meanwhile, the companies continued to press each other for additional information. Firestone wanted Ford to hand over safety data on its Ranger trucks, which also came with Firestone tires as standard equipment. The tire maker suspected that statistics would prove that even after tread separations, Ranger trucks didn't roll over as easily as Explorers did. At the same time, Ford was pressuring Firestone to share damage claims on its tires. On May 11, Firestone forked over its fourth-quarter warranty and damage claims for 2000 to Ford, and Ford reciprocated by releasing information on the Ranger to Firestone. Then the two companies got down to crunching the numbers.

Lampe told the executives in Nashville he would phone Nasser to get to the bottom of this. Early Friday morning Lampe drove to Mexico City and phoned Nasser from the airport, but Nasser's secretary told him the Ford CEO was not available. Lampe was boarding a plane in 30 minutes but said he would call back when he got to Dallas/Fort Worth, and if Nasser was still not available, he wanted to talk to someone else. After landing in Dallas, Lampe tried Nasser again, but he was still unavailable. Instead Lampe spoke with Carlos Mazzorin, Ford's vice president of global purchasing. When Lampe asked about the Times story Mazzorin claimed that Ford had not made any decision to recall the tires, it was all just media-driven speculation. "There's nothing I can tell you," Mazzorin said.

Lampe didn't believe him. Keith Bradsher was not one to go out and publish wild statements. In his story he had cited three unnamed sources "close to Ford's review" of Firestone's data. Bradsher reported that Ford's analysis found that certain lines of Firestone tires had twice the level of problems as tires historically had, but not nearly as many as the recalled Decatur tires, which had damage rates of up to 100 times normal. Most notably, claims for Wilderness AT tires made at the Wilson factory—where Alan Hogan once worked—were three times the industry norm.

Bradsher quoted a Ford official who said, "There is a general conclusion that there are some models that have problems with them beyond those recalled, and the question is whether the problems are bad enough to justify a recall." Another remarked, "We've got another problem that might be bigger than the last one." Lampe could read between the lines.

For Ford the issue wasn't whether it would recall more tires. It was how many tires it was going to recall.

"Carlos," Lampe said, "we need to sit down and talk. This thing is escalating to the point where we just don't have the respect and trust that we need to have." They agreed to meet at Firestone headquarters, since Ford had a corporate plane and Firestone didn't. Mazzorin wanted to come down Saturday, but this set off alarm bells. If Ford wanted a meeting Saturday, that indicated it planned to take action Monday or Tuesday. Lampe told him he had plans already, so they agreed to meet Monday, with Lampe promising to pick up Mazzorin and his colleagues at the airport personally.

Over the weekend Lampe joined his management team comprised of American and Japanese executives, lawyers, and public relations professionals for marathon meetings. Slowly a strategy took shape. Above all it was important that Firestone spoke to its audience: its dealers, who wouldn't sit idly by if Firestone rolled over. And if the company lost its dealers, it could go under. Firestone had to be seen as willing to fight. The automaker was about to drop a two-ton bomb on Firestone, and the tire maker knew it needed to do something dramatic. The consensus was that Firestone should sever the relationship with Ford before Ford did it to Firestone. To remain consistent with Firestone's contention it was more than just a tire issue, Lampe would ask Ford to participate in a joint study of the problem, looking at both the tire and vehicle. If Ford refused, Firestone would go on the offensive. Executives in Tokyo were at first reluctant to go along. In Japan a company doesn't fight with its customers. But realizing another recall was inevitable, they signed on to the decision Sunday morning.

Early Monday morning Lampe dictated a letter to Jacques Nasser: "Today, I am informing you that Bridgestone/Firestone Inc. is ending its tire supply relationship with the Ford Motor Company," he wrote. "Business relationships, like personal ones, are built upon trust and mutual respect. We have come to the conclusion that we can no longer supply tires to Ford since the basic foundation of our relationship has been seriously eroded." He went on to say that there were "significant safety issues with a substantial segment of Ford Explorers," and that he believed that Nasser had been "attempting to divert scrutiny" of the Explorer "by casting doubt on the quality of Firestone tires."

As he signed his name, Lampe became emotional. He thought back to the companies' shared 100-year history, and hated to be the one to bring it to a crashing close. He wished there was another way. Then he got in his Nissan SUV and drove to a private hangar at Nashville airport, where he picked up Mazzorin and his party of Ford officials. For the 10-minute ride to Firestone headquarters they made small talk. Lampe told them about his trip to Mexico. They took over a paneled conference room on the first floor where Ford presented its data and Lampe and Firestone presented theirs. Not surprisingly, their conclusions were antithetical. Ford laid out evidence that suggested that Firestone was responsible for 203 Explorer rollover deaths, while Firestone's interpretation of the data had led the tire maker to conclude the vehicle's instability was at the root of the problem.

Finally Lampe asked Mazzorin whether Ford had made a decision about recalling the tires.

"No," Mazzorin responded.

"Will you agree to a joint investigation?"

Again Mazzorin said, "No."

Lampe reached into his pocket for the letter, asking Mazzorin to hand deliver it to Nasser. "I'm very sorry to have to do this," Lampe said, trying not to choke on his words. "Firestone had always valued its relationship with Ford, it's been a good relationship, and I'm sorry it can't continue."

Then he had an assistant drive them to the airport.

EVEN BEFORE MAZZORIN AND COMPANY stepped out of the building, Firestone's publicity team had already issued a press release and were hitting the media with gale force speed. While they were en route to the airport, CNN broke in with a news flash and the wire services were battling each other over the story. By the time Mazzorin returned to Dearborn, it was all over the news.

But Ford did not sit idly by very long. The next day the automaker announced it would spend $3 billion to replace 13 million Firestone tires, including 1.5 million Wilderness tires mounted on Explorers as replacements during the August 2000 recall. "We simply do not have enough confidence in the future of these tires keeping our customers safe," Nasser said at a hastily called news conference.

Not surprisingly, Lampe took issue with Nasser's screed: "Our tires are safe," he asserted. "The real issue here is the safety of the Explorer."

The one thing both companies could agree on was that they would never agree.

EPILOGUE

SIX WEEKS AFTER HER SETTLEMENT, Donna Bailey was released from TIRR and driven to her mother's house, where family and friends tied bunches of yellow ribbons. After supervising the construction of a new home overlooking Neuces Bay—complete with ramps, specially designed pulleys and an elevator—she became active with the Big City Mountaineers, an outdoor counseling group for troubled youth. Donna has established several scholarships for teenagers and is considering going back to school for her master's to be the world's first wheelchair-bound kinesiologist. Twelve years after the accident that made her a quadriplegic, Donna is still alive.

Ford Motor Co. introduced a completely redesigned four-door Explorer in 2001 that was wider and employed an independent rear suspension, changes Tab Turner had been advocating for years, although continued to build two-door models—the kind Bailey was traveling in when she was paralyzed—the old way. For the first time the Explorer passed a *Consumer Reports* stability test, while the two-door Explorer Sport Trac fared the worst in the magazine's "Annual Reliability Survey," with 44 problems per 100 vehicles, double the industry average.

The automaker continued to flounder, its brand sullied by the Firestone affair, its stock price tanking, workforce demoralized, and dealers up in arms. In October 2001 the company board fired Jacques Nasser and replaced him with Bill Ford, Jr., who assumed the CEO role in addition to his chairmanship. When Ford addressed the company faithful on his first day on the job, he was given a standing ovation. Nevertheless, the company continued to struggle. It lost a combined $6.2 billion in 2001 and 2002, sales fell dramatically even with zero percent financing and generous rebates, and its stock lost two-thirds of its value. The rest of the decade was no kinder to the automaker, and it suffered along with the other American automakers when the recession hit in 2008. Its stock, which once had exceeded $35 a share, fell to about a buck a share. It has rebounded somewhat since, but Ford continues to struggle both in sales and in quality, according to JD Powers. The company also faced another safety crisis from a number of lawsuits over the safety of its Crown Victoria sedans. Several cases involved highway patrolmen whose cruisers, when struck from behind at high speeds, blew up when the gas tank exploded. Ford never admitted culpability.

Firestone's independent analysis conducted by Sanjay Govindjee found that several factors caused the rash of tread separations, including climate, tire design, usage, and manufacturing differences at Firestone's Decatur factory. In 2001, Bridgestone closed the plant, which employed 1,500 workers, and announced it would recall an additional 3.5 million tires at a cost of nearly $30 million. Later that year it also replaced Chairman Yoichiro Kaizaki. In May 2003 the company settled a nation-wide class-action lawsuit brought on behalf of owners of its recalled Wilderness AT and ATX tires. Under the proposal, lawyers received $19 million, while customers got a free tire rotation, discounts on an align-ment, or new tires. Firestone also agreed to pay $7.8 million for a con-sumer awareness program. Turner objected, pointing out, "It appears to give little to nothing of benefit to consumers." The company now con-tends its tires were never defective. Nevertheless, with the Firestone brand name permanently sullied, Bridgestone quietly phased it out, and the tire maker is a faint memory of what it once was.

Anna Werner and her KHOU colleagues were honored with a num-ber of prestigious awards, including Peabody, Scripps-Howard Founda-tion, and Werner's second National Edward R. Murrow award. Werner is currently a reporter for CBS News and based in Dallas, Texas.

Jason Vines left Ford to become president of SUV Owners of Ameri-ca, a trade group. He then left to head Chrysler's PR efforts, and when he got fired he left the auto industry altogether. For a while he worked for a software company, and then left that to start his own PR firm in metro Detroit.

David Bickerstaff 's career as an expert witness came to a crashing close. In March 2001 U.S. District Judge John Copenhaver, Jr. found "by a preponderance of the evidence" that "a conspiracy existed between Ford and its officers" and Bickerstaff from July 1990 until 1996. Bick-erstaff, who returned to England, declared he had no assets.

While covering the story for 13 weeks—unprecedented for CBS News on a consumer safety issue—Sharyl Attkisson had two run-ins with Firestone resulting in the company threatening legal action. She proudly posts the letters in her office. Attkisson was nominated for an Emmy award for her work on the Firestone safety scandal.

The Civil Justice Foundation honored Alan Hogan with the same "whistle-blower" award it gave Erin Brockovich and Jeffrey Wigand (of *The Insider* fame).

Joan Claybrook retired from Public Citizen in 2009.

Ralph Hoar, founder of Safetyforum.com, passed away in September 2001 due to complications from prostate cancer.

Sean Kane, through his work with Strategic Safety, has been working to make car child seats safer.

Bruce Kaster continues to torment tire companies.

Mikal Watts has won several roof crush and medical malpractice cases, and lost a high profile suit against Bayer for its cholesterol-lowering drug, Baycol.

Peter LaValle, Paul LaValle's father, sued him for a portion of his contingency fee in Bailey (*La Valle v. La Valle*), claiming his son stole the case from him. In May 2003, Paul LaValle ran for mayor of Kemah, Texas, and lost by 151 votes. Repeated attempts to contact him were unsuccessful.

Tara Cox received settlements from Ford for $10,000 and $15,000 from Firestone. After her lawyers got their percentages, she ended up with $6,000 from Ford and about $10,000 from Firestone.

The Trial Lawyers for Public Justice named Tab Turner Attorney of the Year in 2001. He continues to sue SUV makers and has been a major player in the battle against Ford over its Crown Victoria police cruisers, a number of which have exploded after high-impact rear collisions. In September 2010, Tab Turner won a $131 million verdict against Ford in a rural Mississippi courtroom. The case involved a highly prized New York Mets prospect named Brian Cole, who was killed in a March 2001 Explorer rollover while leaving spring training. Ford quickly settled for a confidential amount before the punitive phase could begin. Turner also represents Israelis who are suing Lebanese banks that they claim helped finance Hizbullah terrorists attacks.

Over the years, almost 300 people died in Ford Explorer rollovers after Firestone tire failures, and thousands more were killed or injured in Explorer rollovers of all kinds. There are still millions of Ford Explorers on the road today.

NOTES

PROLOGUE

3   Background on Sen. Philip Hart: "The Death of Conscience," by Charles Lewis, Newsletter of the Center for Public Integrity, October 1998.

3   Hart Building inscription: Senate.gov Web site.

3   *Mountains and Clouds*: Data regarding size and weight from Senate.gov and "The Architect of the Capitol" Web site.

4   "It's a bad tire on a bad car": Interview with Tab Turner.

4   trucks and back-up alarms: *Little v. Bunn Construction Co.*, which resulted in $25 million verdict in Alabama. Bennie Little, 28, was crushed to death during a road-paving project when a Ford F600 dump truck, used as a water truck, backed over him without warning.

4   farm machinery and safety guards: *Friederichs v. Huebner*, 1983.

4   cancer-causing asbestos: The first lawsuits against companies responsible for asbestos-related illness were filed in 1929. Two state supreme courts—New Jersey in 1982 and Louisiana in 1986—determined that asbestos maker Johns Manville was liable for asbestos-related illnesses even if the company had not been aware of the substance's danger. Over the past 25 years, Halliburton has settled more than 194,000 asbestos claims but faced an additional 146,000. A former subsidiary, Harbison-Walker, made Halliburton liable for 182,000 more. And in October 2001, a jury awarded $150 million to workers who didn't even exhibit symptoms of cancer from asbestos exposure.

4   fast-food restaurants and super-sized liability: *Fast Food Nation: The Dark Side of the All-American Meal*, by Eric Schlosser, Houghton Mifflin Co., 2001.

4–5   Details from Turner's document search and meeting with congressional researchers: Interview with Tab Turner.

5   Affidavit of James D. Avouris, Ford Motor Co. staff technical specialist, Tire Mechanics, attesting to having conducted high-speed durability tests on Firestone P235/75R15ATX tires at 26 psi in 1989, September 11, 2000.

6   John C. Garthwaite letter: Ford Saudi Arabian dealer correspondence with Firestone/Ford, February 25, 1999.

6   Firestone was "not telling us the whole story to protect them from a recall or lawsuit": UAE Ford manager Glenn R. Drake e-mail to other Ford executives, January 28, 1999.

6   "the U.S. [Department of Transportation] will have to be notified": Internal Ford memo from Chuck Seilnacht to Dave MacKinnon, March 12, 1999.

7   "a horrendous period": "A Ford Behind the Wheel: The chairman steps up his defense of the family firm," Newsweek, September 25, 2000.

7–8   Harvey Firestone-Henry Ford background: Various sources, including: *Firestone: A Legend. A Century. A Celebration*, by Paul Dickson and William Hickman, Forbes Custom Publishing, March 2000; "Ford, Firestone Tire Separation Problem Echoes Earlier Situation," *Knight Ridder Tribune Business News*, May 24, 2001; "Corporate Smashup May Sever Family Ties," *New York Post*, May 23, 2001; "Breakup of Ford, Bridgestone/Firestone Is a Messy Split," *Knight Ridder Tribune Business News*, May 22, 2001; "Ford, Firestone Marriage Sorely Tested," *Automotive News*, September 11, 2000; "Tire Recall Throws a Wrench in Decades-Old Ford-Firestone Relationship," *Knight-Ridder Tribune Business News*, August 16, 2000; "Ford-Firestone 'Marriage' on the Rocks," *Christian Science Monitor*, August 16, 2000.

8   "During all those years in business . . .". "Ford, Firestone Tire Separation Problem Echoes Earlier Situation," *Knight Ridder Tribune News Service*, May 24, 2001.

INTRODUCTION

9   Descriptions of lawyers as "conniving," "dishonest," "greedy" and so forth: Various sources, including " 'Greedy' Lawyers Are Often the Public's Allies," commentary by Steven Lubet, *Newsday*, October 4, 2000. Former U.S. Chief Justice Warren E. Burger, who said: "Seventy-five percent of all American lawyers are incompetent, dishonest or both," *Trial Lawyer's Guide*, 1971. Em-

ployment Law Forum of California, www.employlaw.com; http://overlawyered.com. "Lloyd's Chairman Blasts U.S. 'Litigious Culture,' " *Insurance Journal—The Property Casualty Magazine*, April 9, 2003.

10   Stella Awards e-mail: First appeared on the Internet in 2001, author unknown.

10   Stella Awards as a hoax: "Urban Legends Reference Pages," by Barbara and David P. Mikkelson, 1995–2003, www.snopes.com.

10–11   Details of Stella Liebeck's suit against McDonald's: Numerous newspaper reports, including "Blaming Victims for Insurance Costs," by Tom Feran, *Cleveland Plain Dealer*, August 2, 2002; "Taming Trouble Torts: Some wonder whether reports of litigation explosion were overblown," by Mark Sauer, *San Diego Union-Tribune*, April 21, 2002; and "Public Perceptions and Empirical Data," in syllabus of Prof. Ralph L. Brill, Chicago-Kent College of Law.

11   Civil Justice Reform Group (CJRG): a coalition of general counsels from more than 50 of the Fortune 100 firms and founded by former Ford Motor General Counsel John Martin, Jr. in 1994 (Public Citizen). Membership in Tort Reform Association and Americans for Lawsuit Reform is kept confidential but listed on various law firm Web sites (i.e., Jackson & Wilson, Laguna, California; McCrory & Assocs., Toledo, Ohio).

12   10,000 every year die in single-vehicle rollovers; one-third of all vehicle deaths in the U.S.: National Highway Traffic Safety Administration; and "G.M. Critical of Regulator Who Faulted S.U.V. Safety," by Danny Hakim, *New York Times*, January 15, 2003.

12   The rollover fatality rate in single-vehicle crashes among SUVs is two-and-a-half times greater: "Blowout: The way Bridgestone/Firestone and Ford handled tire recall may have made a bad situation worse," by Jennifer Bott, *Detroit Free Press*, October 5, 2000.

12   1,461 [Explorers] . . . rolling over: Fatal Accident Reporting System (FARS), a Federal database.

12–13   One in 2,700: statistics calculated by dividing total number of Explorers by number of fatal rollovers. One in every 500 Broncos statistics arrived at by taking total number of Bronco IIs (800,000) and dividing by the number of fatal rollovers (1,419 where at least 1 person died). Figures are approximations.

13   "one of those sharks out there who think they've found the keys to the ATM": Jason Vines quote in "What's Tab Turner Got Against Ford?" by Michael Winerip, *New York Times Sunday Magazine*, December 17, 2000.

CHAPTER 1

15   Descriptions of the trip to Enchanted Rock: Interviews with Donna Bailey and Tara Cox; depositions of Tara Cox and Kevin McCord (*Bailey v. Ford Motor Co., Bridgestone/Firestone, Inc. and Tradewind Ford Sales, Inc. D/B/A Crosstown Ford Sales*), both taken on December 11, 2000.

16   Kim Cox had purchased the 1997 Explorer: Interview with Kim Cox.

16   separation developed around the tire's shoulder and further details of tread separation: deposition of James Gardner, Firestone's tire expert, January 3, 2001. (*Bailey v. Ford Motor Co., Bridgestone/Firestone, Inc. and Tradewind Ford Sales, Inc. D/B/A Crosstown Ford Sales.*)

17–20   Description of the accident and aftermath: interviews with Donna Bailey and Tara Cox; depositions of Tara Cox and Kevin McCord; police report compiled by Richard Bernhardt, Texas Highway Patrol, March 10, 2000.

18   flipped on his siren and floored it, and other descriptions of Sgt. Ray Gutierrez: depositions of Sgt. Gutierrez and Trooper Richard Bernhardt, December 12, 2000. (*Bailey v. Ford Motor Co., Bridgestone/Firestone, Inc. and Tradewind Ford Sales, Inc. D/B/A Crosstown Ford Sales.*)

19   A simple blowout shouldn't cause a car to jackknife off the road, and so forth: deposition of Kevin McCord.

19–20   After Tara changed out of her bloody clothes and descriptions of the events in the hospital in Floresville: Interview with Tara Cox and depositions of Tara Cox and Kevin McCord.

CHAPTER 2

21–30   Turner and LaValle conversation, and all Tab Turner personal and professional background: Interview with Tab Turner.

23   dressed down Turner's secretary: Interview with Lee Jones, Turner's former secretary at Friday, Eldredge & Clark in Little Rock, Arkansas.

23   routinely read him the riot act: Interview with Sharyl Attkisson.

23   swear to never to talk to him again: Interviews with Tab Turner, Lee Jones, Russwin Francisco.

23   Dinner anecdote: Interview with Lee Jones.

23–24   Descriptions of Turner: Interviews with various sources, including Joan Claybrook, Lee Jones, Paul Byrd, Mikal Watts.

CHAPTER 3

31–32   in anticipation of litigation and details of Ford's document collection scheme: deposition of *Fred Parrill, Zisman, et al. v. Ford Motor Co.*, December 19, 1991; December 20, 1991 and February 6, 1992.

31   "obstruction of justice": Turner "Motion for Sanctions" in *Dickerson v. State Farm Mutual Automobile Insurance Co., Michael Leonard Hill and Ford Motor Co.*, Harris, Texas, this version filed in 1999. Motion first filed in 1994.

32   "outright fraud": "The Slow Lane in Vehicle Safety," by Myron Levin, *Los Angeles Times*, December 5, 1999.

32   On Aug. 13, 1982, a test driver put a Bronco II through its paces: "Legal Maneuvers: Ford Attorneys Played Unusually Large Role in Bronco II's Launch," by Milo Geyelin and Neal Templin, *Wall Street Journal*, January 5, 1993.

32   Jeep "knockoff": ibid.

32   Loopholes in the Clean Air Act of 1970: *High and Mighty: SUVs— The World's Most Dangerous Vehicles and How They Got That Way*, by Keith Bradsher, Public Affairs, 2002.

33   A 1986 Ford TV advertisement: From Ford's "Built fun tough" TV campaign.

33   "The irony is that people are buying SUVs": Interview with Brian O'Neill.

34–35   *60 Minutes* segment on the Jeep CJ-5: Broadcast on CBS in December 1980. Also interviews with Brian O'Neill and Benjamin Kelley, Insurance Institute for Highway Safety.

34   "pure theatrics": *60 Minutes*, December 1980.

34   "There wasn't anybody building a utility vehicle in 1980": "Legal Maneuvers: Ford Attorneys Played Unusually Large Role In Bronco II's Launch," by Milo Geyelin and Neal Templin, *Wall Street Journal*, January 5, 1993.

34   decree that Army jeeps were not to be sold to the public: "NHTSA Inaction on Rollover Issue Seen as Typical," by Myron Levin, *Los Angeles Times*, September 18, 2000.

34   The military had mandated special training: ibid, and "Accident
          Reports Involving M151 Ford Jeeps," Department of the Army,
          Director of Safety; Headquarters, United States Army, Europe,
          January 1969.

34   Ford executives decided to test the Bronco: Ford dynamic testing
          of prototype Bronco II and CJ for wheel lift tendencies, January
          23, 1981; also undated Bronco II "overturning" memo by James
          Avouris found in Bronco I materials.

34   [Bickerstaff] became concerned: "Ford CG [Center of Gravity]
          Reduction Study," by David J. Bickerstaff, January 22, 1981.

34   Engineers were shooting for an index of 2.25 but early designs
          Bickerstaff reviewed yielded a figure of only 1.85: "Light Truck
          Engineering (LTE) Program Report," by David J. Bickerstaff,
          February 5, 1981.

34–35   Bickerstaff submitted five proposals to make the Bronco II less
          tipsy: "Ford LTE Program Report," February 18, 1981; "LTE
          Program Report: Rear Suspension/Frame Redesign for Improved
          Stability," February 19, 1981; and memo from Bickerstaff to Da-
          vis/Parrill et al., about stability index improvement investigation,
          February 20, 1981.

35        $7 billion Ford squandered on the forgettable Contour: "Ford
          Direction Looks to the Futura," by David Versical, *Automotive
          News*, April 16, 2003.

35   reliance on the Twin I-Beam suspension was controversial at
          Ford: Interview with Tom Feaheny.

35   at Ford's Arizona Proving Grounds in April 1982 a Bronco II on
          15-inch wheels tipped over at 35 mph: "Legal Maneuvers: Ford
          Attorneys Played Unusually Large Role In Bronco II's Launch,"
          by Milo Geyelin and Neal Templin, *Wall Street Journal*, January
          5, 1993; also "LTE Program Report," April 28, 1982, which
          showed outrigger contact on numerous occasions during Bronco
          II testing.

36   Ford immediately halted all testing on the Bronco II: Memo from
          Bickerstaff to Kert/Ritz, August 14, 1982.

36   But he began to sing a different tune: "Lawyers Taking Aim at
          Ford on Veracity of Expert," by Danny Hakim, *New York Times*,
          April 23, 2003.

36   "Ford understood that irrespective of how the vehicle actually
          performed": "Legal Maneuvers: Ford Attorneys Played Unusual-
          ly Large Role In Bronco II's Launch," by Milo Geyelin and Neal
          Templin, *Wall Street Journal*, January 5, 1993.

36   "canning their defense to the Bronco II": Tab Turner, closing
            argument in *Cammack v. Ford Motor Co. and Max Mahaffey Ford,
            Inc.*, June 20, 1995, Harris, Texas.
37   There was an "understanding" there would be no written
            documentation, and "closing the loop," and so forth: deposition
            of *Fred Parrill, Zisman, et al. v. Ford Motor Co.*, December 19, 1991;
            December 20, 1991 and February 6, 1992; and Turner Motion for
            Sanctions in *Dickerson v. State Farm Mutual Automobile Insurance
            Co., Michael Leonard Hill and Ford Motor Co., Harris, Texas.*
37   From Ford personnel destroyed 50 documents to "carefully
            covered its tracks": Turner Motion for Sanctions in *Dickerson v.
            State Farm Mutual Automobile Insurance Co., Michael Leonard Hill
            and Ford Motor Co., Harris, Texas.*
37   A 1988 Ford internal analysis of federal accident statistics
            projected 141 "first event" rollover deaths a year: Ford graph us-
            ing 1981–1986 FARS data, June 17, 1988.
37   The Insurance Institute for Highway Safety concluded in a 1992
            report: IIHS news release on Bronco II rollover rates, April 13,
            1992.
38   "have a probable adverse effect upon the general public health
            and/or safety": "Ford Fighting to Smooth Bronco II Safety Ques-
            tions," Associated Press, June 15, 1992.
38   manufacturing more than 800,000 of them: U.S. and Canada
            sales figures, Ford Motor Co. From 1984 to 1990 Ford made
            814,979 Broncos (702,724 four-wheel drives and 112,255 two-
            wheel drives).

CHAPTER 4
39   Cammack accident details: Trial transcript, *Cammack v. Ford
            Motor Co. and Max Mahaffey Ford, Inc.*, June 1995, Harris, Texas.
39–40   Details of Robert Cammack's fight against Ford and relationship
            with family: Interview with Robert Cammack.
40   O'Quinn in turn brought in Tab Turner: Interview with Tab
            Turner.
41   A federal jury in Binghamton, New York, in November 1992
            awarded a woman $1.2 million for injuries, and details of case:
            "Ford Has Loss on Claims Tied to Bronco II," by Milo Geyelin,
            Wall Street Journal, November 20, 1992.
42   Turner's cross-examination of Bickerstaff and other trial details:
            Court transcript, *Cammack v. Ford Motor Co. and Max Mahaffey*

Ford, Inc., June 1995, Harris, Texas; also interviews with Tab
Turner and Robert Cammack.

42–43   Text of Bickerstaff letter in which he says he will testify in
"Ford's favor":

TO: Art Anderson
COMPANY: Snell & Wilmer
DATE: June 20, 1990
Dear Mr. Anderson:
           We have attached some copies of purchase or-
ders/invoices which reflect our fees.
           Our present rate for short-term contracts for new business
is $5,000/day. Long term contracts are $4,000/day.
I feel I should be reimbursed my current rate. I would suggest you
retain our services to assist you in preparing myself, in Ford's favor, as we discussed per our phone conversation of 6/18/90.
           I believe that fees of $2,000 per half diem and $4,000 per
diem plus reimbursement of reasonable expenses is appropriate
based on the evidence attached.
FROM: David J. Bickerstaff
DJB & A, Inc.

44   "get rid of it before the same tragedy happens to someone else":
        "Jury Says Crash Should Cost Ford $25 Million," by George
        Flynn, *Houston Chronicle*, June 23, 1995.

44   "Get rid of it!": Interview with Robert Cammack.

44   cut the award to $5.8 million: "Texas Judge Cuts Damage Award
        Against Ford to $5.8M from $25M," Dow Jones News Service,
        August 25, 1995.

44   carmaker filed an appeal based on a technicality and other details
        of appeals process: Interview with Robert Cammack.

45   jury heeded the advice of trial lawyer Randy Barnhart: "Jury
        Orders Ford to Pay $62.4 Million in Rollover Suit," Associated
        Press, October 30, 1995.

45   "Ford . . . should not be punished for the driver's reckless
        judgment": "Ford Hit by $62.4 Million Award," by Milo
        Geyelin, *Wall Street Journal*, November 1, 1995.

CHAPTER 5

47   "SUVs are simply the latest example of America's gear fetish":
        "Bad Sports Or: How We Learned to Stop Worrying and Love
        the SUV," by Paul Roberts, *Harper's*, April 1, 2001.

48   25 new Bronco II rollover cases: Interview with Tab Turner.

48   679 rollover claims: "Documents Show Ford's Concerns Over
        Explorer Autos," by Myron Levin, *Los Angeles Times*, August 24,
        2000.

49   an Explorer prototype exhibited a greater tendency to raise its
        wheels than a Bronco II: Ford memo concerning stability of the
        UN46 [Ford Explorer prototype] being worse than Bronco II, and
        that it could be improved by widening, lowering and using a
        smaller tire, May 1, 1987; also *Ford Test Report*, November 25,
        1988.

49   passing the Consumers Union test had become an implicit
        requirement for Explorer due to the potential for adverse publici-
        ty: Ford memo emphasizing the importance of how the Explorer
        performs in the Consumer's Union (avoidance maneuver) test
        and the need to return to Arizona for more testing, May 16, 1989.

49   computer simulations continued to underscore its tendency to lift
        two wheels: Ford ADAMS report, Fall 1988.

49   "the relatively high engine position of the Explorer": "Inside the
        Ford/Firestone Fight," by John Greenwald, *Time*, May 29, 2001.

49   The Explorer prototype lifted two wheels off the ground "with a
        number of tire, tire pressure, suspension configurations." Memo
        from D.S. Starr, research engineer at Ford, to James Avouris, et
        al., May 10, 1989.

49   "The Chevy T-Blazer passes J-turn requirements with an
        apparent large margin of reserve": Ford report, subject: "1990
        Explorer Handling Stability."

50   "management is aware of the potential risk": Memo from Roger
        Stornant, Subject: "UN46 Steering Linkage Issue—Index Bars,"
        September 11, 1989.

50   contributed $559 million to the company's coffers that year, with
        a profit margin of 38.8 percent: "Ford Passed Up Chance to
        Boost Explorer's Stability," by Myron Levin, *Los Angeles Times*,
        September 18, 2000.

50   Ford management began raising concerns: Ford-Firestone e-mail
        exchange concerning Ford's request that Firestone change tire de-
        sign to a low rolling resistance polymer and raise tire pressure to
        30/35 psi for a 1.6 mpg improvement on CAFE (corporate aver-

age fuel economy) standards; also memo from Dave Wotton at Ford to Reichenbach at Firestone with tire objectives for the 1995 model Explorer being same traction, better rolling resistance and better wear properties.

50   He had three options, etc.: Deposition of James Burdette, Fuel Efficiency Engineer, December 21, 2000.

51   *Ad Age* reported: *Ad Age*, May 1, 1995.

51   the change actually raised the Explorer's center of gravity: "Ford Passed Up Chance to Boost Explorer's Stability," by Myron Levin, *Los Angeles Times*, September 18, 2000.

51   reduced the strength of the metal reinforcing the roof: ibid.

CHAPTER 6

53–60   All details from interviews with Anna Werner, David Raziq, Chris Henao of KHOU-TV; Lance Olinde, attorney; Rowe Brogdon, attorney; Alan Hogan, former tire builder at Firestone's Wilson, North Carolina, plant; and Joan Claybrook of Public Citizen.

CHAPTER 7

62–65   Channel 11 (KHOU) transcript of February 7, 2000, Firestone broadcast.

65   Karbowiak of Firestone dispatched a threatening letter: Complete text as follows:

February 10, 2000
Mr. Robert W. Decherd
Chairman, President and CEO
A.H. Belo Corp.
400 South Record Street
Dallas, TX 75202
Mr. Peter Diaz
President and General Manager
KHOU-TV * Channel 11
1945 Allen Parkway
Houston, TX 77019-2596
Gentlemen:
    I am writing to you on behalf of Bridgestone/Firestone, Inc. to express our disappointment with the "Defender" series on KHOU-TV concerning Firestone Radial ATX tires mounted on Ford Explorers. This series, broadcast on various segments be-

ginning on Monday, February 7, contains falsehoods and misrepresentations that improperly disparage Firestone and its product, the Radial ATX model tire.

The program and related activities give the unfortunate appearance that KHOU is more concerned with sensationalism and ratings during the February sweeps period than its commitment to the presentation of truthful and objective reporting. As responsible executives and managers of a major media company and one of its leading TV outlets, you should be concerned with the obvious fact that your reporter, AnnaWerner, and/or her producers have been co-opted by plaintiffs' personal injury lawyers and their purported "expert" witnesses to present a one-sided view of Firestone's product.

This series has unmistakably delivered the false messages that Radial ATX tires are dangerous, that they threaten the safety of anyone using them, and that they should be removed from every vehicle on which they are installed. Each of these messages is simply untrue. The company has manufactured more than 12 million Radial ATX tires which have been used on many millions of vehicles, and have been driven hundreds of billions of miles. This is a good product and Firestone proudly stands behind it. Every automobile accident and particularly each one that involves death or serious injury is unfortunate and regrettable. Such accidents, however, are not explained merely by reference to tread separation. In the rare event of the failure of any steel-belted radial tire, the most likely way for all such tires to fail regardless of manufacturer is tread separation. That is a phenomena of the radial tire construction when something has occurred which will cause the tire to fail.

The critical issue totally ignored by your broadcasts is what caused the tread separations in the instances you report—the fact of a tire failure is not proof of a defect in a tire. It has long been recognized that tires operate in an external environment which affects them, much as illustrated in our statement to your station which answered the question asked by Anna Werner with respect to the three incidents cited by Houston Channel 2 some years ago. Each of those tire failures was clearly caused by external factors, such as punctures. Throughout the report, you failed to inform your audience of this type of balancing information regarding the kinds of factors which cause any tire to fail in the tread separation mode—information which we provided to you and which is also readily available in the public domain. Your reporter chose to ignore that portion and much of the substance of our statement when the responses did not meet her objectives. In fact, I am advised that the failure to report such balancing information when it is in your reporter's hands prior to the broadcast may be grounds for finding of actual malice. KHOU's failure to report Firestone's position on this issue is equally dismaying because it is a disservice to your viewers, who should be advised that tire care and service are significant factors that contribute to vehicle safety.

Your story wrongfully and knowingly implies that virtually ever Explorer rollover is precipitated by a tire failure. The plaintiffs' attorneys who are supporting Ms. Werner on this story know that only a small fraction of the vehicle rollovers are precipitated by a tire failure regardless of the cause of the tire disablement. Ms. Werner clearly had those statistics readily available to her or could have easily developed them on her two-day visit to Washington, D.C. last week or in her contacts with NHTSA.

Firestone is also disturbed by KHOU's failure to explain the motivations of persons quoted and interviewed in the program. The bias and interest of individuals presented as "experts" in tire failure cases in the broadcast is barely described by the program's phrase "an expert witness who testifies against tire companies." Prior to the broadcast, Ms. Werner indicated that she was consulting with various plaintiffs' lawyers and plaintiffs' tire experts, whose objectivity is compromised by their financial stake in creating negative publicity about Firestone's products. Yet Ms. Werner makes no attempt to explain the lack of objectivity of the sources; instead she creates an aura of reliability of referring to the one on-screen plaintiffs' tire expert as "the dean of tire failure analysis."

In the broadcast, Ms. Werner asks "But why are the tires coming apart?" That is a question to which one would expect a factual and technical answer. But the program answers this key question solely by citing the statements of a former Firestone employee, Alan Hogan, who, on screen, makes a number of grossly misleading claims that are presented as applicable to Radial ATX tires. KHOU's fact gathering process should have determined that Mr. Hogan never built an ATX tire when he worked for Firestone, nor did he ever build tires on the system used for the production of ATX tires at the plant where he worked. This fact was never disclosed. Nor was it ever disclosed that Mr. Hogan left Firestone, after a brief period of employment, disgruntled and unhappy.

We are also concerned that the trailers advertising your Thursday evening show suggest that your one-sided presentation will continue as plaintiffs' expert Grogan explains the "simple solution to tread separations." While it may sound simple to the lay public, which is Mr. Grogan's intention, the fact is there is no scientific basis for his opinion that cap plies or, as he refers to them, "overbelts," improve the durability of tires at normal highway speeds. Rather, the primary benefit of cap plies is in high speed rated tires. Modern tires and vehicles are complex engineering systems resulting from sophisticated and scientific development processes which do not lend themselves to simple "one-liner" type of answers to complicated engineering matters. Goodyear, Michelin, Uniroyal-Goodrich, General, and Firestone, the companies who have made tires for a hundred years and know far more about tires engineered for the U.S. market than Mr. Grogan, share this view on the high speed usage of cap plies.

The falsehoods have continued in the updates KHOU has run since the initial broadcast. Last night KHOU announced that the broadcasts have caused Firestone to "respond" and implied that Firestone changed its policies to welcome inspection and potential replacement of Radial ATX tires. This is blatantly untrue. As Firestone noted in its initial statement to KHOU on February 4, Firestone has had a long-standing policy of customer satisfaction, which includes inspecting its products for consumers free of charge. Further, that program also includes the potential of "adjustment" for credit or replacement of tires under appropriate circumstances, a component of the program that has been our policy for more than three decades.

In addition, rather than spreading the misinformation as you have done to date, you would better serve your viewers in the Houston area if you would point out to them proper tire maintenance procedures (all Ford Explorers with Firestone tires come with Firestone's Tire Maintenance and Safety Manual in the glovebox) as well as proper driving methods in the event of any tire disablement. The Texas Drivers Handbook published by the Texas Department of Safety is an excellent reference for such information.

Finally, as we stated previously, any persons who may have concerns or questions about any Firestone tires should be referred to their local Firestone store where their tires and any concerns can be evaluated and addressed.

Very truly yours,

Christine Karbowiak

Vice President, Public Affairs

CHAPTER 8

67   Texas state judge Sam Bournias directed Firestone: "Anatomy of a Recall: How a small-town lawsuit in Texas cascaded into the biggest consumer panic since the Tylenol scare, plaguing Firestone and Ford with allegations of factory flaws and design errors," by Daniel Eisenberg, *Time*, September 3, 2000.

67   1,100 similar accidents: ibid., and interview with Tab Turner.

68   Turner was lukewarm to the idea of sharing their findings with the NHTSA: Interview with Tab Turner.

68   "Big John," "I was sent [to Washington] to serve and protect" and "vintage Dingell": "Fearless Crusader or Self-Serving Kingpin?" by Paula Dwyer, Business Week, October 28, 1991.

68   "symbiotic relationship between John Dingell": "Automakers Pump Cash into Dingell Re-election Bid," by Jeff Plungis and Deb Price, *Detroit News*, August 1, 2002.

68–69   [Dingell's] campaign finance records: www.opensecrets.org. For the 1999–2000 and 2001–2002 election cycles, John D. Dingell was the top House recipient from Auto manufacturers. Ford was largest single contributor in 2002 ($57,400) and second largest in 2000 ($31,500) behind GM: ($31,850).

69   "little yellow people": "Fearless Crusader or Self-Serving Kingpin?" by Paula Dwyer, *Business Week*, October 28, 1991.

69   the auto industry donated some $77 million; $12.5 million; and about $37 million on lobbying in 2000: "Road Outrage: How Corporate Greed and Political Corruption Paved the Way for the SUV Explosion," Arianna Huffington, www.ariannaonline.com/columns/, January 6, 2003.

69   "you can bet that money wasn't spent trying to convince Congress to designate a 'Windshield Wiper Appreciation Week'": ibid.

70   NHTSA acting only after reports of 37 deaths: "Chrysler Minivan Latch Failure is a Safety Defect that Involves Children," commentary by Ralph J. Hoar, www.safetyforum.com, undated.

70   Roof-crush standards have not been strengthened since 1973: Department of Transportation, National Highway Traffic Safety Administration, Federal Motor Vehicle Safety Standards; Roof Crush Resistance, request for comments, 1999, Docket No. NHTSA-1999-5572.

70   Dental Research received more money than NHTSA: NHTSA research budget: $58 million (in 2001), or about $1,400 per crash death; National Institute of Dental and Craniofacial Research: $382 million.

70–71   "policy and strategy" memo from January 1986: "Ford Has Opposed Congressional Meddling in Auto Issues," by Paul Wenske, *Kansas City Star*, September 30, 2000.

71   In 1996 Turner faced Curry and details of sudden acceleration case: Interview with Tab Turner.

72   "If they do what the normal people": From "What's Tab Turner Got Against Ford?" by Michael Winerip, *New York Times Sunday Magazine*, December 17, 2000.

73   "Pinto got a very bad rap": ibid.

74–76   Lists of auto recalls: Available at www.safetyalerts.com.

77   "The drive for quality has to start": Memo from Norm Lewicki to James Padilla, Group Vice President, Ford Motor Company.

77   if you took an Explorer, lifted it off the ground, flipped it upside down, lowered the vehicle to the ground . . . it would collapse under its own weight: Interview with Donald Friedman.

77–78   Jana Fuqua, Evelyn Joyner, Gordan Sudduth accident synopses: Interview with Tab Turner.

CHAPTER 9

79–84   Events and descriptions: Interviews with Rick Burchfield, Tim Burchfield, and Donna Bailey.

84   LaValle pulled out a contract: Rick Burchfield deposition, *LaValle v. LaValle*.

CHAPTER 10

85–88   Events and descriptions: Interview with Donna Bailey; Donna Bailey medical records—doctors', nurses' and psychologists' notes—San Antonio University Hospital.

86   "Oh, Donna, Oh, Donna Oh, Donna, Oh, Donna I had a girl": Words and music by Ritchie Valens.

88   Rick tried to locate the resources: Interview with Rick Burchfield and Rick Burchfield deposition, *LaValle v. LaValle*.

CHAPTER 11

89   front page of the *Sunday Chicago Sun-Times*: "Faulty Tires Carry Fatal Consequences," by Mark Skertic, *Chicago Sun-Times*, April 30, 2000; also "Tire Defect Cases Kept Under Wraps," by Mark Skertic, *Chicago Sun- Times*, May 1, 2000.

90   Ford asked Firestone to issue a dealer bulletin: James Avouris letter to Firestone, May 1, 1990.

90   7 percent worse on fuel economy: Deposition of Roger Simpson, Explorer Program Manager, Ford Motor Company, November 14, 2000.

91   Almost 72 million fewer pounds: In total, Firestone made more than 47 million ATX, ATX II and Wilderness tires at a savings of 1.5 pounds of rubber and steel per tire. For example, from 1989 to 1994 Firestone AT 16-inch tires weighed 30.1 lbs. From 1994 to 2000 the new Wilderness16-inch tires weighed 28.5 lbs.

91   Two-ton truck: Ford Explorer 2000 weight: 3,875 pounds. Ford Ranger 2000: 3,599 pounds.

91   Firestone survey of 243 tires on 63 vehicles: Firestone survey of trade-ins or lease return vehicles showed that 31 percent of the 15-inch tires were under-inflated and 51 percent of 16-inch tires were under-inflated. Nine tires had less than 20 psi. March 22, 2000.

93   the numbers of customer complaints were so high: Deposition of David C. Laubie, MDL (multi-district litigation) in U.S. District Court, Southern District of Indiana, May 10, 2001.

93   State Farm: In response to a request from NHTSA, Samuel Boyden, State Farm Associate Research Administrator, e-mailed a breakdown by calendar year and tire type—Firestone ATX, ATX II and Wilderness tires—for the period covering 1996 to April 2000.

93   80 percent of the warranty claims were belt edge failure–related: Deposition of David C. Laubie, taken for MDL (multi-district litigation) in U.S. District Court, Southern District of Indiana, May 10, 2001.

94   22 percent of the American market in sales to carmakers and 9 percent of sales to consumers: "Firestone Wasn't Pushed Out of Tires—It Jumped," by Jonathan Peterson, *Los Angeles Times*, March 19, 1988.

94   In 1975, 60 percent of tires in the United States were bias ply while 40 percent were radials: *Firestone: A Legend. A Century. A*

Celebration, by Paul Dickson and William Hickman, Forbes Custom Publishing, March 2000.

94 slashing 50,000 jobs: Interview with Akira Yeiri in *Keizaikai*, January 2, 1990.

94 shut some inefficient plants (seven alone in 1980): "Firestone Wasn't Pushed Out of Tires—It Jumped," by Jonathan Peterson, *Los Angeles Times*, March 19, 1988.

95 Akira Yeiri rushed to Akron: Interview with Akira Yeiri in *Keizaikai*, January 2, 1990.

95 a controversial choice within the company: Interview with Roger Schreffler, Asian Correspondent, Ward's Auto World, November 11, 2001.

95 Bridgestone had gotten its start and other Bridgestone historical background: Firestone: A Legend. A Century. A Celebration, by Paul Dickson and William Hickman, Forbes Custom Publishing, March 2000.

96–96 Sony chairman Akio Morita brought their two companies together: Interview with Akira Yeiri in *Keizaikai*, January 2, 1990.

96 "Firestone is selling its factories": Zaikai Tenbo, March 3, 1992.

96 Nashville truck-radial plant for $52 million in 1983: *Zaikai Tenbo*, February 10, 1989.

96 a tentative deal to purchase 75 percent of Firestone's manufacturing operations for $750 million: *Zaikai Tenbo*, May 1988.

96 trigger anti-Japanese sentiment: *Zaikai Tenbo*, February 10, 1989.

96 $1.93 billion: *Zaikai Tenbo*, May 1988.

96 only learned of Pirelli's bid when it was reported in the media: *Keizaikai*, April 12, 1988.

96 documents Pirelli submitted under the Italian Securities and Exchange Law: Interview with Akira Yeiri in *Keizaikai*, January 2, 1990.

96 to Michelin for $650 million: *Keizaikai*, April 12, 1988, citing a letter from Pirelli's Chairman Leonardo Pirelli to Firestone's CEO John J. Nevin.

97 "like a medium-sized whale swallowed a huge whale": ibid.

97 unpaid taxes in Argentina, environmental pollution suits: *Zaikai Tenbo*, March 3, 1992.

97 appalled by the conditions: *Zaikai Tenbo*, March 3, 1992.

97 40 millionaires at Firestone: Interview with Dennis Allen.

97 weren't enough Japanese managers who could speak English: ibid.

98 "Buy American" policy: *Keizaikai*, May 31, 1988.

98   in 1991 Firestone lost $350 million: *Keizaikai*, May 28, 1991.
98   Bridgestone asked Yoichiro Kaizaki to take over for Yeiri at
          Firestone and background on Kaizaki: *Zaikai Tenbo*, January 19,
          1999; also "Pushing Back: Bridgestone Boss Has Toughness, but
          Is That What Crisis Demands?" by Todd Zaun, Phred Dvorak,
          Norihiko Shirouzu, and Peter Landers, *Wall Street Journal*, Sep-
          tember 12, 2000.
99        $2 billion in debt: Memo from Masaharu Ono, July 25, 1994,
          Subject: New Cost Reduction Program—"Project 95."
99   "most significant" part to the plan: ibid.
99   "work that should be done in five hours, they schedule for eight":
          Zaikai Tenbo, January 19, 1999; also "Pushing Back: Bridgestone
          Boss Has Toughness, but Is That What Crisis Demands?" by
          Todd Zaun, Phred Dvorak, Norihiko Shirouzu and Peter
          Landers, *Wall Street Journal*, September 12, 2000.
99   Picketers carried signs that said "Nuke 'Em" and "WW II Part II:
          Japan's Bridgestone Attack on American Economy," and "I'm
          not a politician": ibid.
100   pointed to Bridgestone's record profits, which were $799 million
          in 1998: ibid.

CHAPTER 12
101–104   Videotaped family meeting at University Hospital, San Antonio,
          June 22, 2000. In attendance: Mike Bailey, Harold Burchfield,
          Jeremiah Bailey, Cassie Bailey, Carolyn Tritten, Rick Burchfield,
          Sherry Rose, Paul LaValle, Dr. Douglas Barber, Dr. John
          Madlener, Bev McGray (physical therapist), Christopher New-
          man (physical therapist student), Melva Perez (occupational ther-
          apist), Carlton Belk, RN, Nicole Bell, LMSW (Licensed Master
          Social Worker).

CHAPTER 13
105–112   Events, descriptions and background: Interview with Sean Kane.
111   193 complaints and 21 deaths: "Feds Investigate More Deaths
          Linked to Tires," by Justin Hyde, Associated Press, August 7,
          2000.
112   "this case is a costly and tragic illustration: "Ford and Firestone
          Missed Signals Ahead of Huge Recall," by Jenny Heller, Karen
          Lundegaard and Norihiko Shirouzu, *Wall Street Journal*, August
          10, 2000.

CHAPTER 14

114   Vines created a list: Interview with Jason Vines, conducted by
       David Kiley.

114   began in 1998, when Hector Rodriguez: "Ford Says It Knew of
       Venezuelan Tire Failures in 1998," by Timothy Aeppel, Norihiko
       Shirouzu and Robert L. Simison, *Wall Street Journal*, August 30,
       2000.

114   "because . . . it would give the 'subliminal message' ": Summary
       of meeting between Bridgestone/Firestone, Venezuela, and Ford
       of Venezuela, May 9, 2000.

114   "virtually no traffic rules, no speed limits": Ford of Venezuela
       Assessment Evaluation, Craig Williams, October 11, 1996, from
       "Firestone: Recall of the Radial ATX Tire," by Prof. Arun K.
       Jain, Executive MBA Program, University of New York State
       University at Buffalo, February 16, 2001.

115   shock absorbers that were too soft for Venezuela's roads and
       other details from the report: "Plaintiffs Memorandum of Law in
       Opposition to Ford's Motion to Seal Deposition Transcript and
       Require Return of Inadvertently Disclosed Document," United
       States District Court, Southern District of Indiana, Chief Judge
       Sarah Evans Barker, MDL #1371.

115   switching 15- and 16-inch Firestone tires to Goodyears and
       installing a bar to hold the new shock absorbers in place—a ser-
       vice that normally cost 273,000 *bolivares*": Deposition of Jorge. A.
       Gonzalez in *Gustafson, Devening, Wehking, et al. v. Bridge-
       stone/Firestone, Inc.*, United States District Court for the Southern
       District of Illinois, October 20, 2000.

115   Ford Venezuela President Emmanuel Cassingena became "very
       aggressive" and "rude": Summary of meeting between Bridge-
       stone/Firestone Venezuela and Ford Venezuela, May 9, 2000.

115   "under no circumstance" would he accept a statement that the
       "Explorer has suspension problems": ibid.

115   "We cannot recall these tires" and "Listen, either you're going to
       do it with us or we're going to do it without you": Interview with
       Jason Vines.

116   avoid "flat spots": "Saudi Accident Presaged Tire Crisis," by
       Daniel Pearl, *Wall Street Journal*, September 12, 2000.

116   "If this was a single case": E-mail from Glenn Drake to Ford,
       January 28, 1999.

116   "It appears to be increasingly obvious": Letter from John
       Garhwaite to Keshav Das, February, 14, 1999.

116   Firestone balked at this idea because it didn't want the U.S. Department of Transportation to find out: letter from Chuck Seilnacht to Dave MacKinnon at Ford, about Seilnacht's meeting earlier that day with Firestone representative John Behr, March 12, 1999.

116   dealer staff were instructed to inquire about usage; recommend Euro "H"-rated tires, "temporary program": "Saudi Accident Presaged Tire Crisis," by Daniel Pearl, *Wall Street Journal*, September 12, 2000.

117   customers received Goodyears: ibid.

117   "We are at a position": ibid.

117   "It is very pathetic": Faxed complaint to Amir Al Oraibi, National Field Service Manager, Oman, from Service Manager, Automotive Center, June 23, 1999.

117   "so far been able to control this issue": E-mail from Grodent Baptiste to Mike Kolin, June 22, 1999.

117–118   Southwest survey: Deposition of Deepak Parekh, United States District Court, Southern District of Indiana, Chief Judge Sarah Evans Barker. MDL #1371, November 5–7, 2001; and "Ford Increasingly Frustrated with Firestone," by Ben Klayman, Reuters, August 14, 2000.

118   "shit their pants": Interview with Jason Vines, conducted by David Kiley.

118   2,500 complaints involving eight categories of tires, and so forth: "Safety Group, Attorneys Call on Ford, Firestone to Widen Tire Recall," by Justin Hyde, Associated Press, August 14, 2000.

118   "They basically . . . called a time out" and discussion of press conference with Christine Karbowiak: Interview with Jason Vines, conducted by David Kiley.

CHAPTER 15

121   70 of them affecting 7.3 million vehicles and quickly realized this time would be different: "Blowout: The Way Bridgestone/Firestone and Ford Handled Tire Recall May Have Made a Bad Situation Worse," by Jennifer Bott, *Detroit Free Press*, October 5, 2000.

121–122   Crigger statement: Firestone press release, August 9, 2000.

123   [Vines] was . . . livid: Interview with Jason Vines, conducted by David Kiley.

123   Firestone's Web site crashed: "Tire Recall Flattens Firestone's Web Site," by Suzanne Gaspar, *Network World*, June 4, 2001.

123   "When customers hear there's a recall or a death involved": "Analysts Say Company Should Have Addressed Problems Sooner," by Vicki Brown, Associated Press, August 9, 2000.

123   "The premise under Firestone's action is wrong": "Spitzer: Tire Recall Should Be National, Not Phased In," by Anny Kuo, Associated Press, August 9, 2000.

124   ordered a subordinate: Interview with Jason Vines, conducted by David Kiley.

124   Donna Bailey moving to TIRR and blaming San Antonio for bed sore: Interview with Donna Bailey and Rick Burchfield.

CHAPTER 16

127–131 Events and descriptions: Interviews with Tab Turner and Sharyl Attkisson.

128   *USA Today* ran a front-page feature: "Officials Have Known SUV Tire Suspicions for Decade," by James R. Healey and Sara Nathan, *USA Today*, August 2, 2000; and "More Deaths Linked to Tires: Crash reports say treads peeled off, sometimes at 20 mph," by James R. Healey and Sara Nathan, *USA Today*, August 2, 2000.

130   Ford decided against recommending a higher tire pressure after computer simulations indicated it increased the risk of rollover: Ford "ADAMS" computer simulations stated the Explorer demonstrated "performance issues" at 35 psi but engineers expected more favorable results at 26 psi, Fall 1988.

130   detailing a crash test driver who rolled over in an Explorer: Occupational Accident/Injury Report, August 2, 1995. At Ford's Dearborn Proving Grounds, engineer Wei-Zen Shih rolled over several times in a 1995 Explorer at 80 mph. It was Shih's second rollover accident in seven months.

130   The Associated Press: Tire Deaths Causes, Associated Press, August 23, 2000.

130   *Los Angeles Times*: "Documents Show Ford's Concerns over Explorer Autos," by Myron Levin, *Los Angeles Times*, August 24, 2000.

130   *USA Today*: "Ford's Idea of Tire Inflation Differs from Others'," by James Healey, *USA Today*, August 21, 2000.

130   *Wall Street Journal*: "Agency Probes of Auto Defects Are Hampered," *Wall Street Journal*, August 23, 2000.

131   "Every day Tab would take one of those documents": "What's Tab Turner Got Against Ford?" by Michael Winerip, *New York Times Sunday Magazine*, December 17, 2000.

CHAPTER 17

133–148 Details and events: Interviews with Alan Hogan, Rowe Brogdon, Sharyl Attkisson and Laura Keeter, reporter, *Wilson Daily Times.*

141   "I might have [an airline boarding pass] at" and other dialogue: Deposition of Alan Hogan, *Van Etten. v. Bridgestone/Firestone, Inc.*, March 31, 1999.

142   "Relax," Brogdon said. "Have a cigarette": Interviews with Rowe Brogdon and Alan Hogan.

142   "chronic problem with tire separations": Deposition of Alan Hogan, *Van Etten v. Bridgestone/Firestone*, Inc., March 31, 1999.

143   Sharyl Attkisson's report: *CBS Evening News*, August 14, 2000.

145   "I think I need to fire you" et al.: Interview with Alan Hogan.

145   "I got 'em": Interview with Rowe Brogdon.

146   "Firestone Whistle-blower Attacked": *CBS Evening News*, August 16, 2000.

CHAPTER 18

149–164 Events and descriptions: Interviews with Tab Turner, Lee Jones, Ben Kelley, Russwin Francisco, Joan Claybrook, Donald Friedman and Sean Kane; additional material: Safetyforum.com bio of Hoar: "Celebrating a Legacy: 30 Years of Public Service."

149   "Your life is a diamond": *Facets*, by Ralph J. Hoar, written for his son, 1985.

150   "had blown up in [its] face" and NHTSA stability factor anecdote: Interview with Ben Kelley.

151   "there is no Ralph Hoar FOIA exemption": Allen Kam at Ralph Hoar memorial celebration, September 2001.

152   "May he rest in peace with Satan": Interview with Jason Vines, conducted by David Kiley.

152   "We ought to have a press conference": Interview with Tab Turner.

152   "an aging version of the Junior Leaguer," "the Dragon Lady" and "an evil, small-minded woman": "The Tiger in the Consumers' Tank," by Judith Weinraub, *Washington Post*, May 5, 1992.

153   "It was an incredibly fast education": Interview with Joan Claybrook.

153   Nader anecdote: ibid.

154 "a bully": ibid.

154 "We have so many men working on safety now": "Henry Ford Criticizes Emphasis on Safety," *Automotive News*, October 10, 1966.

154 Only 1 in 10 people used [seatbelts]: Interview with Joan Claybrook.

155 Department of Justice anecdote: ibid.

156 "Gravestone": "Credibility Blowout Deflates Firestone," *Chicago Sun-Times* editorial, September 5, 2000.

156 "We are aware of only one other vehicle safety [flaw] exceeding 34": "The Safety of Firestone 500 Steel Belted Radial Tires," Report by the subcommittee on Oversight and Investigations of the Committee on Interstate and Foreign Commerce, July 16, 1978.

157 article in *Mother Jones* magazine: by Mark Dowie, *Mother Jones*, September/October 1977 issue.

157 Benefits and Costs Relating to Fuel Leakage Associated with the Static Rollover Test Portion of FMVSS208: Ford Motor Company internal memo. Source: Mother Jones, September/October 1977.

157 Lily Gray was incinerated, and Richard Grimshaw was scorched: *Grimshaw v. Ford Motor Co.*, 1981.

157 Dan Lampe's life almost ended: "Dan's Story," Center for Consumer Law, Washington State Trial Lawyers Association, 2000.

157 Judy Ulrich's 1973 Pinto was rear-ended: "Ford Is Indicted on Criminal Counts over Pinto Deaths," Associated Press, September 14, 1978.

158 "half-truths and distortions": "The First 25 Years," by Adam Hochschild, *Mother Jones*, May/June 2001.

158 "How do we deal with this?" and Bradford crash-test anecdote: Interview with Joan Claybrook.

158 "It was scary" and Ford re-test anecdote: Interview with Joan Claybrook.

159–162 Research Safety Vehicle details and events: Interviews with Joan Claybrook and Donald Friedman, RSV inventor.

161 "Two hundred and fifty thousand dollars": Interview with Joan Claybrook.

161 "for educational purposes": "Destruction of the Research Safety Vehicle (RSV)," The Center for Auto Safety Web site, www.autosafety.org/article. php?did=314&scid=37.

161   "barrels of oil for body bags": "Rollover: The Hidden History of
        the SUV," Q & A with Gen. Jerry Curry, Frontline, PBS docu-
        mentary, broadcast February 21, 2002.

161   "recommended that we dispose": "Destruction of the Research
        Safety Vehicle (RSV)," The Center for Auto Safety Web site,
        www.autosafety.org/article.php?did=314&scid=37.

162   "they were a thorn": Interview with Donald Friedman.

162   book burning by the Nazis: Interview with Claybrook.

162   "The public can afford no further delay": "Firestone Should
        Immediately Expand Tire Recall to Protect Public," Statement of
        Public Citizen President Joan Claybrook, August 14, 2000.

162   "more than a million hits": "Tire Owners, Safety Lawyer,
        Consumer and Safety Advocates Call on Ford and Firestone to
        Lift the Lid of Secrecy and Recall All Firestone Wilderness
        Tires," Safetyforum.com press release, August 14, 2000; and
        "Firestone Flap: Web in Eye of Storm," by Karen Lundegaard,
        Wall Street Journal Online, August 15, 2000.

162   "stop playing statistical games with peoples lives": "Tire Owners,
        Safety Lawyer, Consumer and Safety Advocates Call on Ford
        and Firestone to Lift the Lid of Secrecy and Recall All Firestone
        Wilderness Tires," Safetyforum.com press release, August 14,
        2000.

163   While on a business trip and details from Coffin's accident and
        recovery: Statement   of   Goeffrey   H.   Coffin,
        www.safetyforum.com, August 14, 2000.

163   *Wall Street Journal*: "Ford, Bridgestone Seek to Present United
        Public Front—Firms Focus on Speeding Replacement of Tires,
        But Differences Persist," *Wall Street Journal*, August 15, 2000.

163   *Chicago Tribune*: "Expand Tire Recall, Safety Groups Insist Ford
        Continues to Back Firestone," *Chicago Tribune*, August 15, 2000.

163   *Los Angeles Times*: "Key Group Joins Call for Wider Firestone
        Recall Safety: Public Citizen calls the current program inade-
        quate," *Los Angeles Times*, August 15, 2000.

163   Associated Press: "Safety Group, Lawyers Call on Firestone,
        Ford to Widen Tire Recall," Associated Press, August 14, 2000.

164   Kane had broken the news embargo: Interviews with Sean Kane,
        Joan Claybrook and Tab Turner.

164   "No one can touch [it] because [it's] evidence": Interviews with
        Joan Claybrook and Tab Turner.

CHAPTER 19

165   Descriptions of Jacques Nasser as brusque, hard-driving, impatient, and so forth: Various media sources, including "Ford's Heir Apparent Is a Man Driven by a 'Common' Goal," *Financial Times Service*, November 20, 1998; "Jac the Knife," by Phil Scott, *Sydney Morning Herald*, March 8, 1997; "Jac Nasser Is Car Crazy," by Sue Zesiger, *Business 2.0*, June 1998; "Ford Family Is Back; Company May Take on a Gentler Persona," *Knight-Ridder Tribune Business News*, October 31, 2001.

166   petrol head: "Ford's Global Gladiator," *Business Week*, December 11, 1995.

166   "hair stand up on the back of your neck": "Remaking Ford," *Business Week*, October 11, 1999.

166   "nice guy with a politician's keen instinct" and "Bargaining for families" and "bust me down to private": "Idealist On Board: This Ford is Different," *Fortune*, April 3, 2000.

167   70,000 replacement tires: "Behind the Wheel: For Ford CEO Nasser, Damage Control Is the New 'Job One,' " by Robert L. Simison, *Wall Street Journal*, September 11, 2000; and "Three Ford Truck Factories to Stay Closed Another Week," *Milwaukee Journal Sentinel*, September 9, 2000.

170–172 David Kiley–Jacques Nasser interview details and events: Interview with David Kiley; "Ford CEO Handles Tire Recall," by David Kiley and James R. Healey, *USA Today*, August 17, 2000; and "Nasser Says Design Not a Problem," Q & A between David Kiley and Jacques Nasser, *USA Today*, August 17, 2000.

173   "Jac Nasser says he will get me tires": Interview with David Kiley.

173   "set aside six weeks of behind-the-scenes damage control": "Ford CEO Handles Tire Recall," by David Kiley and James R. Healey, *USA Today*, August 17, 2000.

173   "passionate argument" and details of meetings between Rintamaki, Grissom, Vines, Zino and Vines: Interview with Jason Vines, conducted by David Kiley.

174   "Could it be the recall": "Ford CEO Too Busy For Hearings?" CBS News, August 30, 2000.

CHAPTER 20

177–187 Events and descriptions: Interviews with Bruce Kaster, Paul Byrd, and Tab Turner.

178   same for Mark Skertic of the *Chicago Sun-Times*: "Faulty Tires
         Carry Fatal Consequences," by Mark Skertic, *Chicago Sun-Times*,
         April 30, 2000.
178   "the poor man's Firestone": Interview with Bruce Kaster.
179   List of brand names manufactured by Cooper—Atlas, Futura,
         Patriot, and so forth: *Anthony Talalai, et. al. v. Cooper Tire & Rubber
         Co.*
179   might have a higher defect rate: Interview with Bruce Kaster.
179+   Scharlotte Hervey accident and tracking down potential
         witnesses: Interview with Paul Byrd; "Tire Failure Leads to Two
         Lawsuits," by Ed Galucki, *Cabot Star Herald*, January 2, 2002;
         "Cooper Tire Settles Arkansas Case Five Days Before Trial," *Au-
         tomotive Industry Litigation Reporter*, June 4, 2002; "Road Warriors:
         A Tire Maker Finds Itself in a Maelstrom, As Trial Lawyers Cir-
         cle—Arkansas Suit Could Provide a Blueprint for Others," by
         Michael Orey, *Wall Street Journal*, November 15, 2000.
183   "Have you been drinking?": Interviews with Paul Byrd and Bruce
         Kaster.
184   Details of Kreiner case: Interview with Bruce Kaster; "Tire Killed
         Dad In '96, Kin Say: Horror's relived as Firestone embroiled in
         recall," *New York Daily News*, September 18, 2000.
184–185 Details of Decatur investigation; "on an ongoing basis" and was
         "open and obvious": Interview with Bruce Kaster.
185   "You should have picked a client": Tire Killed Dad In '96, Kin
         Say: Horror's relived as Firestone embroiled in recall," *New York
         Daily News*, September 18, 2000.
186      $375,000: ibid.
187   "The Firestone plant in Illinois that manufactured many of the
         6.5 million tires": "Testimony Indicates Abuses at Firestone;
         Managers Didn't Fix Tire Flaws, Ex-Workers Claim," by James
         Grimaldi, *Washington Post*, August 13, 2000.
187   "eight former employees of Bridgestone/Firestone have testified
         or promise" and "not enough to protect consumers": "McCain
         Joins Firestone Fray: Wants Tire Recall Expanded, Questions
         Review Safety Data," www.abcnews.go.com, August 14, 2000.
187   "I know I don't want a tire on my vehicle made by any manufac-
         turer with workers": "Retired Tire Builders Testify Against Man-
         ufacturer," by John Kelly, Associated Press, August 23, 2000.
187   raised the death toll to 88: NHTSA and various media sources.

CHAPTER 21

189–205 Congressional hearings testimony from transcripts compiled by Federal News Service, Inc.

189 "nervous" because he had "never made a public appearance like this before": Senate Hearings, September 6, 2000, transcript by Federal News Service, Inc.

189 "like watching death by a thousand little stab wounds": "Lobbying: Damage Control," by Shawn Zeller, *National Journal*, April 27, 2001.

189 losing $1 million a day: "Bridgestone Boss Leaves Bitter Legacy," by Eiichiro Shimoda, *Nihon Keizai Shimbun*, January 15, 2001.

189 $5 million and netted 60 times that, $285 million in 1998 alone: "Lobbying: Damage Control," by Shawn Zeller, *National Journal*, April 27, 2001.

190 gunning for chairman of the far more influential Commerce Committee: ibid.

190 "What we are interested in is: What went wrong with this recall?": "Ford, Firestone Cook Together in Stew of Federal Recall Hearings," by Michelle Mittelstadt, *Knight-Ridder*, September 6, 2000.

190 "could have been conducted sooner": CBS *Early Show* appearance reported in "Tauzin Treading Roughly on Carmaker, Colleagues Say," by Bruce Alpert, *New Orleans Times-Picayune*, August 31, 2000.

190 "This whole thing stinks": "Anatomy of a Recall: How a small-town lawsuit in Texas cascaded into the biggest consumer panic since the Tylenol scare, plaguing Firestone and Ford with allegations of factory flaws and design errors," by Daniel Eisenberg, Michael Weisskopf, Joseph R. Szczesny, Mike Eskenazi and Carole Buia, *Time*, September 11, 2000.

191 "Hey, Anna. Guess what?" and Werner-Henao exchange: Interviews with Anna Werner and Chris Henao.

191 "the catalyst for the recall"; "for their investigative efforts"; and "They deserve a medal": Congressional Hearings, September 6, 2000, transcript by Federal News Service, Inc.

191–192 "I can't believe you haven't thought of that"; "surprised"; "significantly higher" and "Unfortunately, the records": ibid.

192 Ono testimony, "the oath of truthfulness" and questioning by House members: ibid.

192 sending ripples through the Nikkei: Bridgestone's stock fell 17 percent in the days immediately following the hearings, from 1338 yen to 1110.

197   "I wanted you to hear directly from me": "Greeting Big Wheel at Ford CEO: Jacques Nasser, the automaker's globe-hopping chief, is latest executive to tell the public 'I'm sorry,' " by Susan Reimer, *Baltimore Sun*, September 6, 2000.

197   "very miffed": "Ford, Firestone Cook Together in Stew of Federal Recall Hearings," by Michelle Mittelstadt, *Knight-Ridder*, September 6, 2000.

197   "Given the Republicans' tardiness in scheduling the hearing": "Ford Chief Will Skip Hearing On Recall; GOP Congressman Criticizes Nasser," by Frank Swoboda and James V. Grimaldi, *Washington Post*, August 30, 2000.

198   Ford also bedazzled congressional investigators: "Lobbying: Damage Control," by Shawn Zeller, *National Journal*, April 27, 2001.

198   cloistered himself for five hours at Ford's Washington headquarters with image-maker Michael Deaver: "CEO Nasser, Not Chairman Ford, in Front Seat for Crisis," by Frank Swoboda, *Washington Post*, September 10, 2000.

198–205   Nasser testimony and questioning by House members: Congressional Hearings, September 6, 2000, transcript by Federal News Service, Inc.

CHAPTER 22

207   "Bridgestone wanted to apologize and leave it at that": "Lobbying: Damage Control," by Shawn Zeller, *National Journal*, April 27, 2001.

208   "If the tires are subject to our Bridgestone/Firestone warranty program": Bridgestone/Firestone press release, "Regarding the NHTSA Consumer Advisory," Masatoshi Ono, Chairman and CEO, September 2, 2000.

208   "because it became evident that we could no longer be of service to Bridgestone/Firestone": "Image Problem: P.R. Agency Bows Out as Firestone Problems Grow," by Margaret Litvin, www.abcnews.go.com, September 6, 2000.

208   "irreparably damaged" and "I think there a good chance that the brand is history": "Is Firestone's Clock Ticking?" CNNfn, September 8, 2000.

209   "has become such an inferno" and "the best thing: "Recall May Mean End of the Road for Brand," by Michael McCarthy and David Kiley, *USA Today*, September 11, 2000.

209 "that was opposite the best interests of Bridgestone": "Lobbying: Damage Control," by Shawn Zeller, National Journal, April 27, 2001.

209 eating up $11.4 billion in market capitalization: In 2000 there were 861,252,000 Bridgestone shares outstanding and the stock lost 228 yen in the days after the hearings. 228 yen x ~ 861,252,000 shares = 196.365 billion yen, or approximately $1.636 billion.

209–210 Background on John Lampe: Interview with John Lampe.

211 a Harris poll commissioned by the Wall Street Journal: "Bridgestone Aims Probe At Design of 'Bad Tires,' " by Stephen Power and Clare Ansberry, *Wall Street Journal*, September 13, 2000.

211 Bridgestone/Ketchum announcement: Bridgestone/Firestone press release: "Joint Firestone/Ketchum Statement," September 11, 2000.

211 It quickly set up an information sharing system: Interview Julia Sutherland of Ketchum PR.

212 "Read any crisis publication": ibid.

212–213 Ono and Lampe congressional testimony and questioning by Senators: Senate Hearings, September 12, 2000, transcript by Federal News Service, Inc.

214 Afterward Lampe met with reporters: Interview with Julia Sutherland.

214 "anybody who gets in the way of this will end up getting steamrolled": "Ford Chairman Says New Explorer Customers Will Be Able to Choose Tire Brand," *Dow Jones Business News*, September 14, 2000.

214 Direct, often hostile questioning, and so forth: House Hearings, September 21, 2000, transcript by Federal News Service, Inc.

216 "You burden this bill with complex": "House Prepares Vote on Weaker Recall Bill," by Earle Eldridge and Sara Nathan, *USA Today*, October 6, 2000.

216 "deep disappointment that the fix" was in "by the special interests": " 'Fix Is In' on Auto Safety, McCain Says," by Lynn Sweet, *Chicago Sun-Times*, October 8, 2000.

217 Lampe reception at Century City: Interviews with John Lampe and Julia Sutherland.

CHAPTER 23
219–225 Events and descriptions: Interviews with Tab Turner and Mikal Watts.

219 "defective and unreasonably dangerous at the time it was designed, manufactured and distributed": *Bailey v. Ford Motor Co.,
Bridgestone/Firestone, Inc., and Tradewind Ford Sales, Inc. D/B/A
Crosstown Ford Sales, Inc., Nueces County, Texas*. The complaint also
asked for punitive damages based on the defendants' gross negligence and willful, wanton and reckless conduct. The Ford Explorer was designed to replace the Bronco II. . . . The Bronco II
has been judicially determined to be a defective and unreasonably
dangerous vehicle. The design and testing history behind the development of the Bronco II establishes the knowledge that Ford
had at the time it designed and distributed the Explorer. Ford's
knowledge included a knowledge that SUVs designed with the
combination of a narrow track width and high center of gravity
had a dangerous tendency to flip in ordinary turning maneuvers
when operated as a passenger-type vehicle. Ford knew this fact
when it sold the Explorer. Ford also knew that the Explorer was
not equipped to properly handle emergency maneuvers at interstate highway speeds as evidenced by rollover accidents involving
company owned vehicles. Ford likewise knew that the Explorer
was not equipped with reasonable safety features to protect occupants when a rollover did occur. Ford consciously chose to market the vehicle despite this knowledge and placed the consuming
public at risk of extreme danger. Likewise, both Ford and Firestone knew, prior to this crash, that the tire in question was defective, unreasonably dangerous, and was producing death and
injury due to catastrophic tread separations. The conduct justifying an award of punitive damages includes, but is not limited to,
the defendants' malicious, willful, wanton and reckless design,
manufacture, marketing, testing and distribution of a product
which it knew was unreasonably dangerous and defective. The
amount of punitive damages to be awarded is within the discretion of the jury. . . .

220 preferred state court over federal court: Interview with Tab
Turner.

220 It never ceased to amaze: ibid.

2221 several motions for discovery: "Interrogatories to Bridge-
stone/Firestone" and "Interrogatories to Ford Motor Co.," *Bailey
v. Ford Motor Co., Bridgestone/Firestone, Inc., and Tradewind Ford
Sales, Inc. D/B/A Crosstown Ford Sales, Inc., Nueces County, Texas*.

223   They agreed to meet at the airport, Turner and Watts' initial meeting and meeting with Turner, Watts, and Zummo: Interviews with Tab Turner and Mikal Watts.

CHAPTER 24

227–230 Events and descriptions: Interviews with Mark Arndt, Tab Turner, and Mikal Watts; and "Tread Separation Test Proposal," by Mark Arndt, Steve Arndt, and commissioned by Tab Turner, June 15, 2000.

228   "Why the hell is this so expensive?": Interviews with Mikal Watts and Mark Arndt.

229   Description of vehicle rollover: Video provided by Arndt & Associates, and interview with Mark Arndt.

229   "Call 911. Call 911. Mark? Mark?": Ibid.

230   "Mikal, I ruined your test," and so forth: Interviews with Mark Arndt and Mikal Watts.

CHAPTER 25

231–236 Events and descriptions: Interviews with Donna Bailey, Rick Burchfield, Tim Burchfield, Tab Turner, and Mikal Watts.

231   "Howdy, Steve": "What's Tab Turner Got Against Ford?" by Michael Winerip, *New York Times Sunday Magazine*, December 17, 2000.

236   "They pamper me": ibid.

CHAPTER 26

237–241 Events and descriptions: Interviews with Tab Turner, Mikal Watts, and e-mails between Turner and LaValle, courtesy of Donna Bailey and Rick Burchfield.

239   attached a copy of a contract he'd induced Michael Bailey into signing a couple months earlier: August 11th, 2000, agreement, and Rick Burchfield deposition, *LaValle v. LaValle.*

CHAPTER 27

243   submitted a motion: "Motion in Support of Motion to Accelerate Trial Setting," November 16, 2000, *Bailey v. Ford Motor Co., Bridgestone/Firestone, Inc. and Tradewind Ford Sales, Inc. D/B/A Crosstown Ford Sales, Inc., Nueces County, Texas.*

243   In a supporting brief: "Brief in Support of Motion to Accelerate Trial Setting," November 16, 2000, *Bailey v. Ford Motor Co.,*

Bridgestone/Firestone, Inc. and Tradewind Ford Sales, Inc. D/B/A Crosstown Ford Sales, Inc., Nueces County Texas.

244   Forbes pegged him: "50 Highest Paid Trial Lawyers in America," Associated Press, October 1, 1989, based on estimated 1988 income.

244   "shrimp dip case": "The Spoils of Tragedy," *Houston Chronicle,* August 3, 1992.

245   Donovan equated Donna's and "rather severe sunburn," and so forth: Deposition of Dr. William Donovan, November 27, 2000, *Bailey v. Ford Motor Co., Bridgestone/Firestone, Inc. and Tradewind Ford Sales, Inc. D/B/A Crosstown Ford Sales, Inc., Nueces County, Texas.*

246   Ford lawyers filed a motion: "Ford Motion for Reconsideration of Plaintiff Motion to Accelerate Trial Setting," December 1, 2000, *Bailey v. Ford Motor Co., Bridgestone/Firestone, Inc. and Tradewind Ford Sales, Inc. D/B/A Crosstown Ford Sales, Inc., Nueces County, Texas.*

246   "I represent Tara Cox": Interviews with Tab Turner and Mikal Watts.

246   "Lock and load": Interview with Tab Turner.

CHAPTER 28
247–255 Events and descriptions: Interviews with Tara Cox and Kim Cox and deposition of Tara Cox, December 11, 2000, *Bailey v. Ford Motor Co., Bridgestone/Firestone, Inc. and Tradewind Ford Sales, Inc. D/B/A Crosstown Ford Sales, Inc., Nueces County, Texas.*

253   produced the police report: Compiled by Richard Bernhardt, Texas Highway Patrol, March 10, 2000.

254   Ford was suing her: Papers served December 11, 2000, and filed December 13, 2000.

255   "I work with topless dancers": Interview with Tara Cox.

CHAPTER 29
257–259 Events and descriptions: Interviews with Donna Bailey and Rick Burchfield, and Rick Burchfield deposition, *LaValle v. LaValle.*

258   LaValle told Donna: Rick Burchfield deposition, *LaValle v. LaValle.*

258   new contingent fee contract: "Contingent Fee Contract" between Paul H. LaValle, P.C. and Donna Bailey, December 13, 2000.

CHAPTER 30

261   "We have the full attention of the Ford board of directors": "First Firestone Trial May Be Held Here: Portland woman's suit alleges tires to blame for crash that left her paralyzed," by Dan Parker, *Caller-Times*, December 22, 2000.

262   "You've got to stop this immediately": E-mail from Tab Turner to Paul LaValle, December 23, 2000, courtesy of Rick Burchfield/Donna Bailey.

263   "There is nothing any of us at Firestone": Letter from John Lampe to Donna Bailey.

263   Firestone agreed to settle every single ATX case: Interviews with Tab Turner and Mikal Watts.

263-266   Turner and SUVs in warehouse: Interview with Tab Turner.

CHAPTER 31

267   "hurricane brewing in Corpus Christi": Interview with Tab Turner.

267   who told *USA Today*: "Ford Wastes No Time Settling Tire Cases," *USA Today*, December 27, 2000.

267   good cop/bad cop strategy: Interviews with Tab Turner and Mikal Watts.

268   "this paranoid fear": Interview with Sharyl Attkisson.

268   "A year ago": *CBS Evening News*, January 5, 2001.

269   "Y'all are mean": Interviews with Tab Turner, Mikal Watts, and Donna Bailey.

270   "On the eve of what was to be the first trial an eleventh hour deal": *CBS Evening News*, January 8, 2001.

CHAPTER 32

273–276   Events and descriptions: Interviews with Tab Turner and Rick Burchfield, and Rick Burchfield deposition, *LaValle v. LaValle*.

CHAPTER 33

277–280   Events and descriptions: Interviews with John Lampe, Jeff Eller, consultant to Firestone, Jill Bratina, Firestone publicist. Also "Ford May Seek More Firestone Tire Recalls," by Keith Bradsher, *New York Times*, May 18, 2001; Ford To Replace 13 Million Firestone Tires on SUVs," by Keith Bradsher, *New York Times*, May 18, 2001; and "A Corporate Collision; Ford-Firestone Feud Accelerated After Effort to Head It off Failed," by Caroline E. Mayer and Frank Swoboda, *Washington Post*, June 6,

2001. John Lampe letter: Dated May 21, 2001. Full text as follows:

Dear Mr. Nasser:

Today, I am informing you that Bridgestone/Firestone Inc. is ending its tire supply relationship with the Ford Motor Company. While we will honor our existing contractual obligations to you, we will not enter into any new tire sales agreements in the Americas with Ford beginning today.

Business relationships, like personal ones, are built upon trust and mutual respect. We have come to the conclusion that we can no longer supply tires to Ford since the basic foundation of our relationship has been seriously eroded. This is not a decision we make lightly after almost 100 years of history. But we must look to the future and the best interests of our company, our employees and our other customers.

Our analysis suggests that there are significant safety issues with a substantial segment of Ford Explorers. We have made your staff aware of our concerns. They have steadfastly refused to acknowledge those issues.

We have always said that in order to insure the safety of the driving public, it is crucial that there be a true sharing of information concerning the vehicle as well as the tires. You simply are not willing to do that. We believe you are attempting to divert scrutiny of your vehicle by casting doubt on the quality of Firestone tires. These tires are safe, and as we have said before, when we have a problem, we will acknowledge that problem and fix it. We expect you to do the same.

I wish you and the Ford Motor Company continued success and regret that we cannot continue our relationship going forward.

Sincerely,

John T. Lampe

EPILOGUE
281–283 For the first time the Explorer passed a *Consumer Reports* stability test: "Mitsubishi Montero Fails 'Consumer Reports' Test," by David Kiley, *USA Today*, June 21, 2001.
281   Explorer Sport Trac fared the worst: "2001 Model Year Reliability Snapshot: Consumer Reports' Annual Reliability Survey

Finds Narrowest Gap Yet Between Domestic, European Makes," Consumers-Union press release, March 12, 2002.

281   It lost a combined $6.2 billion in 2001 and 2002 and so forth: "A Family's 100-Year Car Trip," by Danny Hakim, *New York Times*, June 15, 2003.

282   Govindjee report: "Firestone Announces the Completion of the Independent Expert's Analysis," Firestone press release, February 2, 2001.

ACKNOWLEDGMENTS

This book was a two-year journey that would not have been possible without the extensive cooperation I received from the people who appear in its pages, particularly Tab Turner, Donna Bailey, and her family. Tab Turner not only provided mountains of internal documents from Ford and Firestone (and helped me make sense of them) but also opened up his life to me. He let me tag along on a number of eye-twirling trips, held a seat for me in court, let me hang out during press conferences and in media interviews, and shared chips and soda pop on his plane while we hopped from one airport tarmac to the next. As busy as he was, he always made time to answer my (often) persnickety questions.

I am also deeply indebted to Donna Bailey for speaking with me about her traumatic experiences, and Rick and Tim Burchfield, who offered extensive interviews and sent me boxes of material—medical records, background material, correspondence, journals, accident scene photos. All they asked for in exchange was "GATA," Texan, they explained, for "Get After Their Asses."

The original concept for *Blood Highways* (first published as *Tragic Indifference* in 2003 by HarperCollins) came from Jon Furay and Manuel Wally, who worked with me every step of the way—from brainstorming ideas to preparing the book proposal to editing the manuscript. Without them there would be no book. This updated second edition was deftly handled by Dorothy E. Zemach for Wayzgoose Press.

Others proffering valuable assistance were: John Lampe and Jill Bratina, who organized interviews with a number of people associated with Firestone; Anna Werner, David Raziq and Chris Henao of KHOU; Sharyl Attkisson (*CBS Evening News*); reporters David Kiley (*USA Today*), Milo Geyelin (formerly of the *Wall Street Journal*), Julie Bisbee (*The Monitor*) and Jackie Northam (National Public Radio); safety advocates

Joan Claybrook of Public Citizen, Lee Jones and Russwin Francisco of Safety Forum, Sean Kane of Strategic Safety; and crash experts Mark Arndt, Donald Friedman and Tom Feaheny; Robert Cammack, Tara Cox and Alan Hogan; and attorneys Mikal Watts and Bruce Kaster.

I'd also like to thank my researchers: Ken Belson, who dug up invaluable information on Bridgestone in Japan; Elizabeth Gold, Sean Little and Rebecca Myers; and Lisa Smith, Amma Walcott, and Jill Steinberg for transcribing hours and hours of taped interviews.

Finally, I owe a debt of gratitude to my wife Charlotte, who rarely lost her patience and good cheer. One day shortly after I started this project we were walking in Manhattan and I pointed out (for the umpteenth time that day) a Ford Explorer with recalled tires. She noted my newfound obsession with SUVs and tires and said, "Just promise me one thing: that your next book won't be about breast implants."

I promise.

Adam L. Penenberg
June 2012
www.penenberg.com

Index

About the Author

Adam L. Penenberg is a journalism professor at New York University who has written for *Fast Company*, *Forbes*, the *New York Times*, the *Washington Post*, *Wired*, *Slate*, *Playboy*, and the *Economist*. A former senior editor at *Forbes* and a reporter for Forbes.com, Penenberg garnered national attention in 1998 for unmasking serial fabricator Stephen Glass of the *New Republic*. Penenberg's story was a watershed for online investigative journalism and portrayed in the film *Shattered Glass* (Steve Zahn plays Penenberg).

Penenberg has published several books that have been optioned for film and serialized in the *New York Times Magazine*, *Wired UK*, and the *Financial Times*, and won a Deadline Club Award for feature reporting for his *Fast Company* story "Revenge of the Nerds," which looked at the future of movie-making. He has appeared on NBC's *The Today Show* as well as on CNN and all the major news networks, and has been quoted about media and technology in the *Washington Post*, the *Christian Science Monitor*, *USA Today*, *Wired News*, *Ad Age*, *Marketwatch*, *Politico*, and many others. He released two novels in 2012, *Virtually True* and *Trial & Terror*, both published by Wayzgoose Press. His website is www.penenberg.com.

CPSIA information can be obtained at www.ICGtesting.com
Printed in the USA
LVOW10s0404300115

424942LV00023B/513/P